Understanding Cities

Understanding Cities is richly textured, complex and challenging. It creates the vital link between urban design theory and praxis and opens the required methodological gateway to a new and unified field of urban design. For too long, urban design has been viewed as a satellite of architecture and urban planning, occupying a 'no-man's-land', which has prevented its rightful independence. Cuthbert sets out to challenge this assumption.

He rejects the idea of yet another theory in urban design, and chooses instead to construct the necessary intellectual and conceptual scaffolding for what he terms 'The New Urban Design'. Using spatial political economy as his most important reference point, Cuthbert both interrogates and challenges mainstream urban design and provides an alternative and viable comprehensive framework for a new synthesis. By implication, this critique necessarily ranges across all the environmental disciplines that are undeniably involved in the intellectual debate that this process of reconstruction entails.

Building both on Michel de Certeau's concept of heterology – 'thinking about thinking' – and on the framework of his previous books *Designing Cities* and *The Form of Cities*, Cuthbert uses his earlier adopted framework – history, philosophy, politics, culture, gender, environment, aesthetics, typologies and pragmatics. Overall, the trilogy allows a new field of urban design to emerge. Pre-existing and new knowledge are integrated across all three volumes, of which *Understanding Cities* is the culminating text.

Alexander R. Cuthbert is Emeritus Professor of Planning and Urban Development at the University of New South Wales in Sydney. He has degrees in architecture, urban design and urban planning, with a doctoral degree from the London School of Economics. He has taught, practised and lived in Greece, Britain, America, Hong Kong and Australia. He has over 100 academic publications.

Cuthbert places urban design in the context of urban political economy: he does so in masterful fashion and as a result has provided a book that will be important to students of architecture, planning, and urban design but also to scholars in a broad spectrum of social science. For design professionals, Cuthbert offers a robust new intellectual framework. For social scientists, Cuthbert demonstrates the importance of theorizing urban design and development.

Paul Knox, Distinguished Professor, Virginia Tech

In this last instalment of his major trilogy, Alexander Cuthbert presents us with a framework of knowledge that is essential for urban designers. This is a major intellectual contribution to the urban design field, one that flatly and rightly rejects physical determinism and the notion that urban design is merely large scale architecture. Cuthbert deconstructs the old paradigm and skilfully reconstructs a much more robust one that draws from the social sciences and spatial political economy to enhance our understanding of cities and their design.

Anastasia Loukaitou-Sideris, Professor of Urban Design and Planning, UCLA

With his three book 'tour de force' Cuthbert makes a seminal contribution to outlining a unified field for Urban Design so that it can assert its place among the built environment disciplines. Understanding Cities invites scholars and reflexive practitioners to understand and build upon the knowledge shaping the discourse of new Urban Design. All Built Environment disciplines will be enriched by this contribution.

Taner Oc, Emeritus Professor of Urban Design and Planning, Editor – Journal of Urban Design

Understanding Cities
Method in urban design

Alexander R. Cuthbert

Routledge
Taylor & Francis Group

LONDON AND NEW YORK

First published 2011
by Routledge
2 Park Square, Milton Park, Abingdon, Oxon OX14 4RN

Simultaneously published in the USA and Canada
by Routledge
711 Third Avenue, New York, NY 10017

Routledge is an imprint of the Taylor & Francis Group, an informa business

British Library Cataloguing in Publication Data
A catalogue record for this book is available from the British Library

Library of Congress Cataloging-in-Publication Data
Cuthbert, Alexander R.
 Understanding cities: method in urban design/Alexander Cuthbert.
 p.cm.
 Includes bibliographical references and index.
 1. City Planning. 2. Urban design. 3. Cities and towns. I. Title.
 HT166.C8862011
 307.1'216–dc22   2010031272

ISBN13: 978–0–415–60823–7 (hbk)
ISBN13: 978–0–415–60824–4 (pbk)
ISBN13: 978–0–203–81793–3 (ebk)

Typeset in Sabon by
Florence Production Ltd, Stoodleigh, Devon

MIX
Paper from
responsible sources
FSC® C004839
www.fsc.org

Printed and bound in Great Britain by
TJ International Ltd, Padstow, Cornwall

For Ayu

Contents

Figures

AN URBAN DESIGN

	Designing Cities (Orientation/Sources)
INTRODUCTION	Critique of mainstream/proposed theoretical framework and definitions.
THEORY	Social and political change. Capitalist development. Postmodernism/form.
HISTORY	Space and society. The urban landscape. Urban form and design.
PHILOSOPHY	Social justice. The phenomenon of place. Semiotics and meaning.
POLITICS	Public space. The meaning of construction. Democracy/space.
CULTURE	Urban space/cultural setting. Consumption/the public realm.
GENDER	Gender symbols. Non-sexist cities. The urban landscape.
ENVIRONMENT	Sustainability, conservation, heritage. Zoopolis.
AESTHETICS	Aesthetic theory, and ideology. artefacts as art. 'Public art'.
TYPOLOGIES	Architecture, nature and rationalism. Urban form/s.
PRAGMATICS	Design professions. Prescribed knowledge. Research typologies.

TRILOGY – CONTENT MATRIX

The Form of Cities (Theory)	Understanding Cities (Method)
Theoretical issues and problems. Science and logic.	Propositions for a meta-methodology of urban design.
Detailed critique of mainstream. Benefits of Spatial political economy. Globalisation.	Theory: Method: Heterology. The natural sciences versus the social. 'Urban' design.
What is history. Materialist theory of history. Chronologies, typologies, utopias, fragments.	History and progress. Writing history. Mainstream prototypes. Future history.
Paradigms – Vienna, Frankfurt, Chicago, Paris. Semiotics, phenomenology, Marxian political economy.	Meta method – Vienna, Frankfurt, Chicago, Paris, Los Angeles.
Ideology and power, urban planning, the public realm.	Ideology and politics. Land rent. The state. Urban planning. The public realm.
Modernism. Postmodernism, authenticity, symbolism. The New Ruralism/Urbanism.	Capital, culture, sign. The urban symbolic. Monuments. The New Urbanism. Branding.
Gender and society. Patriarchy, capital. Gendered space. Gender and urban design.	The historical nexus. Feminist method. Flanerie. Gender and urban design.
Nature, development and the city. Sustainable cities. Sustainable urban design.	Pre-existing and natural capitalism. Urban density and form. The edible city.
Objects/experience. Urban form. Contextualism. Rationalism. Symbolic capital.	Aesthetic production/judgement. Freud, Saussure, Marx. Regulation and design.
Taxonomy, typology, morphology, system. Social and formal typologies.	Globalisation, mega-projects and the spectacle. Iconic space and neocorporatism.
Cultural capital. Professional intervention. Knowledge systems. Space. Education.	The power of polemic. Manifestos pre- and post-1945. Urbanism and manifestos.

Tables

Preface

This book is about deconstructing urban design in order to give it a new birth and in the process to suggest the structure of knowledge required by an educated urban designer at the onset of a new millennium. As a process, this takes place largely in the immanence of the imagination and only secondarily in the assembly of the material world. It is about hope, love, reflection, monument and myth, desire, death, space, sculpture, ideology, street names, columns and cobbles, memory, architecture and understanding. From these elements, among others, is generated the chemistry from which the ephemerality and transience of urban form comes about. Only then does the design of cities become an object of exchange, of despair or admiration, and of the social production of the urban imaginary. But the urban design of the past century has for too long been the purview of a limited club, and we now seek a common inheritance outside vested interest and professional encroachment.

Understanding Cities concludes a research project begun in 2001. The task was to complete three books or, more accurately, three volumes of the same book, and to explain in my own fashion the essential features of a creative process called urban design. I have been engaged with the discipline for most of my life, both in practice and the academy in Scotland, Greece, the United States, Hong Kong and Australia. The first volume, *Designing Cities* (2003), presented a philosophical position and a framework for urban design knowledge outside the mainstream. It constituted an edited volume of readings, but one with a difference. The intention was not merely to assemble as many readings on urban design as the publishers would allow, letting the readings speak for themselves. In *Designing Cities*, this process was reversed. The articles were chosen in support of a theoretical model whose basic orientation was towards spatial political economy. In so doing, the object was to present a critique of mainstream urban design and to express the need for change. With it came a plea for a deeper and more engaging role for urban design within the social sciences generally and spatial political economy in particular. The next two volumes attempt to work through the implications, first for theory, then for method.

The second volume, *The Form of Cities* (2006), is a text that covers most of the structural features of the system presented in the first volume and is concerned with the overarching theoretical issues within ten identified components, which represent an inclusive framework for new knowledge. The third volume, *Understanding Cities*, is a book on method or, more accurately, meta-methods. The purpose of all three volumes has been to enhance our understanding of urban design by suggesting an overall framework of knowledge that will permit the discipline a new identity. Hopefully, a new sense of respect will follow, along with greater depth in theory and praxis. In the process, this will automatically place it alongside architecture and urban planning, rather than being subsumed to their interests. It should also finally expunge from our collective memory the inescapable idea, in the former, that a city is merely a larger building and, in the latter, that all we need to do is generate yet another set of design guidelines to move forward. In the process of writing, it will be necessary, as in much of science, to falsify many of the assumptions that have traditionally mystified the subject – ideologies and manifestos that have rendered any legitimation impossible. I maintain that such mystification, deliberate or otherwise, has allowed urban design to be colonised by the associated built-environment disciplines to suit their own purposes. Removing such obfuscation clearly demands that these same disciplines go through a similar process of self-evaluation, having now lost part of their power/knowledge. The same is true of the professions that serve them, and for whom territory denotes existence. This overall process of change is one that is usually met with great resistance, as it signifies a climacteric in the way an entire field may be viewed. Orthodoxy is challenged in theory, practice and education; institutional frameworks are questioned in all three regions, and individual beliefs possibly held for decades are called to account.

Despite such clear resistance, as in science the falsification required by the development of new theory does not imply a lack of respect for the knowledge that has steered us into the present, any more than Einstein's theory of relativity denoted a disrespect for Newton's theory of gravitation. However, it is a simple fact that for any new theory to evolve, prior theory must be falsified and is usually torn down in the process. Nor does such deconstruction suggest that the entire edifice and assumptions of the old paradigm necessarily become redundant. New theory simply clarifies our way of seeing the world. But, unlike science, there is not much in urban design that needs to be demolished, as the existence of substantial theory is singularly absent. So, in tearing apart its history, much of the old theory must be reordered rather than eliminated – despite the idea that the end of history is already with us, or even 'the end of the end of history' (Fukuyama 2006, Kagan 2008). In other words, theory simply has its relations to the present redefined. The same is true in urban design, although, in *The Form of Cities*, I have tried to convey that a generalised incoherence pervades much urban design thinking, as there are several isolated theories *in* urban design with rather low levels of refutability, but none *of* it (Cuthbert 2006). There has been no logic binding the pieces together. Following this basic observation, all three books, including this one, have been focussed on certain guiding propositions:

1   The first proposition is that mainstream urban design is self-referential and is neither informed by, nor committed to, any external authority in intellectual terms.
2   The second proposition is that urban design must reorient itself to social science as its wellspring, specifically urban sociology, geography and economics.
3   The third proposition is that to be scientific, a discipline must have either a real or a theoretical object of enquiry.
4   The fourth proposition is that the theoretical object of urban design is civil society, and its real object is the public realm.
5   The fifth proposition is that our understanding of the production of design outcomes must change from a modernist, Beaux Arts obsession with form, the Eureka Principle and the cult of master/disciple to one where the organic production of urban forms and spaces are inseparable from economic and social processes.

(Cuthbert 2006)

In considering these propositions in some depth, I came to the conclusion that urban design practice was perilously close to a social technology, without the grounding in social theory that would allow critical self-reflection to flourish. Thus, it is also deprived of a conscience that permits an ethical and moral backbone to exist, and I hasten to add that this is not a reflection on the designers' own commitments. This situation, if accepted, effectively locates urban design as being several realms removed from any substantial theory at all.

In consequence, urban design is littered with a widespread anarchy in its theoretical base, with a false sense of authority left to prevail in practice. Anyone who wishes may call themselves an urban designer and remain unchallenged, if they have been in any way involved in building the city. Hence, architects, planners, engineers, landscape architects, lawyers, surveyors can all call themselves urban designers with impunity. I see this as unsatisfactory, and this situation was a major impetus in writing the above books. I was also aware of a proverbial Gordian knot that in criticising professions for their territorial imperatives and proposing an independent and liberated urban design knowledge, yet another would be created, thus adding to the problem rather than alleviating it. The answer to the conundrum is that, although a new profession may be expendable, new knowledge is not. Anyone claiming to belong to the discipline should be aware of the laws that govern it, the ideologies of control, the explicit content built up over millennia and, most importantly, their place within the overall schema of the subject in which they profess expertise. To allow every individual to decide this for his or herself is to promote the worst kind of anarchy.

This trilogy has been some nine years in the making and, in the process, I have learned a great deal that has modified certain of my opinions and introduced others. So I plead guilty to certain overall inconsistencies in the texts that owing to my own learning process, I have been unable to eliminate. In this volume, I will make every effort to correct some of these reflections, so that the work retains the capacity to be self-critical of its own content. In conclusion, two items are important. First, I would make no claim that my critique of mainstream urban design could not occur in many different ways, and therefore my work is presented as one possible set of ideas to be discussed and refuted so that we can all move forward on the basis of substantial theory. Indeed, I have been humbled by the writing, as its central accomplishment has been to demonstrate to me the limitations of my own knowledge. Second, to those who would claim that I have at last removed urban design entirely from design issues and design knowledge, I would plead guilty to overstating my case. But I have taught urban design studies for twenty-five years and consider that I am, first and foremost, a designer in the 'designer's' sense of the word. In all things, good design is at the top of my list – but I need to feel that there is more than my own individual talent at stake, that there is much to share in the realm of ideas, and that urban design as a discipline must stand on a bedrock of social and urban theory that must inform and enlighten our design decisions.

Acknowledgements

I wish to thank all of those who have contributed to my project. As all three volumes owe a great deal to the tradition of political economy, paramount among these is that great ark of an institution, the London School of Economics and Political Science, which took the substantial risk of allowing an architect to undertake a doctoral degree. Many individuals will also be wholly unaware of their influence on this text, for they are the very theorists from whom I have learned so much, and I hope that my contribution is some small testament to their leadership. I would include Allen Scott, Manuel Castells, Jean Baudrillard, Marc Gottdiener, Rob Krier, Tariq Ali, Franz Fanon, Roland Barthes, Pierre Bourdieu, Manfredo Tafuri, Aldo Rossi, Neil Smith, Charles Jencks, Mike Dear, Mark Poster, Michel Foucault and countless others. Most have set standards of excellence in critical thinking that I could only aspire to. The imagination of novelists has also carried me far, and I have found great solace and inspiration in the writing of George Sebald, Tim Winton, Salman Rushdie, Don Dellilo, Elfriede Jelinek, Pat Barker, Gabriel García Márquez, Mario Vargas Llosa, Ian Rankin and many more great friends whom I have never met. In completing the first two volumes of this trilogy, I also had professional support of the highest calibre from Blackwell's staff in Oxford, and I was saddened that such a great Oxford tradition of scholarly publication could so easily vanish.

I also wish to thank my colleagues at the University of New South Wales for many years of quality control over what remains, in my opinion, one of the exemplary programmes in post-graduate urban design – thanks to Professor Jon Lang, Professor James Weirick, Dr Bruce Judd and the late Professor Paul Reid. Closer to home, an enduring friendship with Professor Jeff Henderson, Professor Harry Dimitriou, Nick Miles, Jamie Simpson, Mike Cuthbert, Keith McKinnell, Michael Bounds, Chris Abel, John Zerby and Lance Green has carried me far. In addition, several people have played a crucial role in the production of the final text, and my great appreciation goes to Alex Hollingsworth, Louise Fox, Emma Brown and Siobhán Greaney of Routledge, and Rosie White and Louise

Smith of Florence Production Ltd. My appreciation also to Jules and Ange, Sophia and Sarah Kirby for their support and friendship over a difficult period, and to Jim and Sandra Bagnall for just being who you are. Finally, my heartfelt thanks to three very special people whose generosity of spirit I can never repay, Thanks to Dr Philip Van Zanden, without whom this book would never have been completed. His care and attention to my well-being are unsurpassed. Thanks also to my great Sufi friend, Dr Jean Cavendish, for an exemplary life, and to my beautiful wife Ayu, a Balinese blessing. The usual sanction for the text also stands – that all errors of omission are solely my responsibility.

Alexander Cuthbert, Gandapura, Bali, October 2010

Introduction

'Method' is not the name of some 'tool-kit', some series of procedures or protocols to be performed when confronted with a set of objects, it is rather the name that we should give to the way we apprehend and comprehend the objects we attend to ... How we make contact with the world, how we apprehend it and give it sense, I am going to argue, is not a matter of epistemological absolutes, but it is something that is, or should be, open to scrutiny in terms of ethics, as well as aesthetics and politics. Method falls on the side of form, rather than content. It is what underwrites intellectual production.

(Ben Highmore)

Understanding cities

Having sketched out a theoretical framework in *Designing Cities* and having worked through the detailed implications in *The Form of Cities*, Volume 3, *Understanding Cities*, is the logical extension into epistemology, from *'what should we think about?'* to *'how should we think about it?'*, or – critically – *'how should we think about thinking?'*. At the outset, I need to be clear that I am using the same basic principle applied to method as I did with theory in *The Form of Cities*. Here, I have no intention of addressing method *qua* the functional processes of funding, managing and building covered best by the real-estate and construction management disciplines (Klein 2007), techniques and standards in urban design (Gindroz 2003, Eran and Sold 2005), research methods in urban planning (Bracken 1981) or the urban design control mechanisms that implement planning policies in the regulation of projects (Goodchild 1997, Sendich 2006) or, specifically, urban design guidelines. The latter is a favourite topic of urban design theses, a subject almost mined to extinction for content.

Instead, I intend to outline those *meta* methods that organise our thinking, rather than the inherent strategies of getting the job done, processes that Michel de Certeau refers to as *heterology* – 'a metamethodology which is dedicated to encouraging heterogeneity and allowing alterity to proliferate' (Highmore 2006: 8). So, as method, this book is not concerned with *what to do* about urban design projects, but *how to think* about what to do. In order to distinguish metamethodologies from methodologies, I feel the need for a clean linguistic break, and will borrow de Certeau's use of the term *heterology* instead of metamethodology. For some purists, this use of the word will be unsatisfactory, as de Certeau defines it as *a discourse on the other*. In the sense that a metamethodology is a discourse on a discourse, my use may be justified, and my apologies go to the fundamentalists who may for some reason be unhappy with this interpretation. Wherever appropriate, I will retain the word *methods* to cover mainstream design approaches, and *practices* (or technologies) as well as the procedures used by the design professions to organise urban projects. At risk of confusing the issue further, I will, as appropriate, use the word *method* generically, to cover all variations of the term. These distinctions will become clear in use.

My trajectory therefore continues to use the differentiation introduced previously, i.e. to enunciate a theory and heterology *of* urban design rather than a new theory *in* urban design. In this effort, I will try and stick as closely as possible to the specific content of *The Form of Cities*, using the concepts and ideas deployed there as the points of departure for each chapter to follow. In the process, the reallocated weight of each subject might vary if there is a good reason to do so. In addition, as in the history of capital formation, so theorising urban design is also subject to uneven development. The same will be true in the application of spatial political economy to all aspects of heterology. In other words, a consistent and even surface to the idea of method is both unlikely and unwarranted. As became clear in writing *The Form of Cities*, some regions were saturated with ideas derived from this source, e.g. history, culture, conservation etc., while others, such as aesthetics, were either singularly more difficult to comprehend, or had a much greater resistance to the chosen theoretical framework. This was, of course, anticipated and will likely be no different in the following text. So for those urban designers who are looking for some formulaic typologies or processes that will make their projects better, stop reading now! For those who are prepared to accept a challenge, whereby critical self-reflection is the order of the day, read on.

Chapter summary

The overall guiding principle in the organisation of this book has been that each volume has been structured so it can be read three ways – independently to the others, in series, or in parallel. So this volume not only completes the trilogy, it also derives its structure and focus from the preceding two volumes. Articles presented in *Designing Cities* will be used as prototypical background data from which various heterologies may be discussed. As in *The Form of Cities*, each article referred to will be coded 'DC' for *Designing Cities*, with a section and page number, e.g. DC8: 275 means Chapter 8 (Aesthetics), page 275. Similarly, the wealth of theoretical issues and debates contained in *The Form of Cities* represents the guiding source from which the various heterologies to be discussed will emanate, although my own learning since the book was begun might, on occasion, modify this relationship. Referencing *The Form of Cities* will therefore adopt a similar notation, e.g. FOC8: 171 means *The Form of Cities*, Chapter 8 (Aesthetics), page 171.

Chapter 1 – Theory – deviates minimally from the overall adopted form, using the heading Theory/Method as several key theoretical issues, previously mentioned but not discussed, lie at the core of the chapter. The reason for this will be transparent to most readers. In this context, *the method of urban design* begins with a paradox – we cannot simply launch into questions of method without reconnecting to the methodological ramifications of particular theories. The most important distinctions are clearly those drawn between the natural and social sciences and the place of urban design in context, or perhaps creatively across boundaries. Here, the writings of Paul Feyerabend, philosopher of science, loom large. His anarchistic views on science appear singularly appropriate, given the current condition of urban design theory. Central to this discussion will be the debates that took place around 1985 as to whether an *urban sociology* is possible, and where knowledge has taken us since that time. We will then take a look at the implications for method and examine core mainstream theory in terms of its incapacity to deal with the larger considerations of heterologies *of* urban design.

Chapter 2 – History – begins with an overview of the concept of *progress*, which has had an overwhelming impact on the way modern civilisation is conceived and structured. Without it, life would probably be even more dislocated than it is at present. From national economies to family budgets, we are saturated with the idea that we are actually going somewhere, but are we? Second, the idea of *writing* history is addressed, as memory, artefacts and the text constitute our basic resources for heterologies of history. For the sake of simplicity, the concept of *text* will be used to include, for example, art and film as well as written evidence. Third, the method of writing mainstream urban design history will be analysed in order to reveal heterologies that have been deployed by certain of its major proponents in constructing what we currently perceive as urban design history, contrasting these with a seminal example derived from political economy, that of Manfredo Tafuri.

Chapter 3 – Philosophy – advances on the method of historical analysis, including all of the difficulties inherent in trying to separate the two disciplines. Here, heterologies of philosophy encompassed by the various approaches to urban design will be discussed, advancing the methodological orientation implicit to each. Schools of thought that have been particularly influential for both urban studies and urban form, namely Vienna, Frankfurt, Weimar and Chicago, will be referred to, concentrating on the Paris and Los Angeles Schools. Moving from particular philosophies of urban space rooted in specific geographies, we then investigate those based in semiotics, phenomenology and political economy, all of which are central to any philosophy of urban design. In order to ground these ideas, methodological approaches of the most influential scholars are examined.

In *Chapter 4 – Politics –* the places of political action, civil society and the public realm are considered in terms of their overall methodological implications for urban form. In this task, we begin with a general analysis of the methods through which capital is extracted from space, a process that is central to urban design in all of its forms. The central mechanism through which this is accomplished, that of rent, is then examined. Next, state legitimation, the key ideology that legitimises the extraction of profit from urban space, is reviewed, to demonstrate its impact on the design of cities. I then move to discuss the actual methods that are available to analyse what we call public space, a concept that is exceedingly difficult to isolate and define.

Chapter 5 – Culture – opens with a general review of the connection between cultural representation and commodity production, prior to analysing its relationship to the methods deployed in tying such concepts together – the promotion of taste and style in relation to signs, symbols and branding. As urban design is the dominant method by which cultural values are erected in space, two key methods are exemplified, namely the monument as *sign* and the New Urbanism as *brand*. The design implications of monumental construction are analysed in relation to a wide-ranging series of examples that reinforce their use as a key design mechanism useful in both the construction and deconstruction of sign systems, which monuments represent. The second method used to illustrate the method of cultural transmission through branding is the New Urbanist agenda, as the predominant design philosophy operating today, adopted by thousands of practices and agencies now on a global basis.

Chapter 6 – Gender – focusses on the general implications of gender for method in urban design. Exemplars in this respect were Henri de Saint Simon, Charles Fourier and Robert Owen. These and other projects had a small but significant impact on the necessary changes to space implied by gender equality, one that lasted well into the twentieth century. From this background context, more recent science has investigated the relationship between nature and nurture, asking whether or not there is such a thing as the female mind, and, hence, the vexed question as to whether or not there can be such a thing as a specifically feminist method of investigation and design. Either way, a ubiquitous heterology of illustrating the concept of gender differences in the urban context (and, hence, for design implications) is that of Baudelaire's *flâneur*. The concept in its various guises is investigated as a useful methodology to encapsulate the subjective experience of urban design and its social significance for gender differences.

In *Chapter 7 – Environment –* the methodological implications for the relationship between nature and urban design will be investigated. The promise of natural capitalism emerges as a highly questionable heterology, given the state of the (un)natural capitalism that currently prevails. I then discuss the approach of natural ecology and certain fundamentals of the relationship between density and urban form, prior to a detailed examination of the concept within three urban design heterologies, namely vertical architecture, the edible city and the New Urbanism. Several conclusions are drawn from the chapter, which side-steps debates on suburbification versus urban consolidation, and instead challenges our manner of thinking about skyscrapers, suburbs and typologies of urban form.

Chapter 8 – Aesthetics – discusses the overall implications of aesthetics for urban form and culture within the context of globalisation and transnational urban practices. The two major movements in urban design embodying the dominant aesthetic positions of the twentieth century, namely contextualism and rationalism, are mined in order to reveal what might be inferred for process, including the failure of both to generate an aesthetic vocabulary for application to the problems of urbanism in the twentieth century. The dominant emergent heterological implications of symbolic capital, regulation and theming continue the theoretical content of FOC8 as signifying the dominant discourse at the beginning of the twenty-first century.

Chapter 9 – Typologies – begins with the concept of globalisation as the prevailing form of capitalist enterprise and examines how capitalism as a system of practices affects space in ways different from prior modes of production. Next, the formal production of urban space as a commodified product is described, specifically incorporating professional firms as complicit in this process. Then an overall assessment of development types and spatial structures emerging from globalisation is undertaken, concluding with the spaces of the spectacle as an ikon of capitalist commodity production. The chapter concludes with the other half of the world, which is unable to even enter into the benefits of accumulated wealth manifested in the fixed capital of the built environment – slum, semi-slum and super slum, those whom Fanon refers to as *The Wretched of the Earth* (Fanon 1963) – the burgeoning mass of humanity where urban design adopts inconceivable forms and spaces that challenge all our concepts of urban space and its formation.

Chapter 10 – Pragmatics – concludes this study with a review of the heterologies that have guided design practice in environmental and urban design, concentrating on the twentieth century. Pursuing the idea of heterology as 'thinking about thinking', the manifesto represents a dominating concept across the built environmental disciplines. Polemical power is examined, along with the twin concepts of protest and resistance that the manifesto incorporates. The realm of urban development and social change follows, directly investigating and engaging the extensive use of manifestos in art and architecture. The influence of manifestos in the realm of urban design is then exposed, a field not known for its polemical qualities but nonetheless substantially affected by those manifestos that focus on the public realm, ideology and politics.

1 Theory/heterology

If at first a theory is not absurd, then there is no hope for it.

(Albert Einstein)

I do not feel obliged to believe that the same god who has endowed us with sense, reason and intellect has intended us to forgo their use.

(Galileo Galilei)

Introduction: intuition, experience and science

The idea of method imbues all disciplines and all regions of knowledge. In many cases, it surmounts even the idea of theory. Moving forward and getting things done is the way of the world, and this process more often than not has greater significance than contemplating why things happen as they do. This is true of the built environment disciplines, specifically architecture, landscape architecture, urban design and urban planning. All are carried out under the purview of professional organisations enshrined in their respective cocoons of practice, codes of ethics, ideologies and charters, royal or otherwise. Each has evolved in its own manner, over millennia, into the institutions we see today. With the possible exception of urban planning, they have grown out of craft-based practices, where the process of creation usually transcended its explanation. The method of production was largely inherent in the process of creating form from the raw material of nature, and contemplation over theory was largely irrelevant.

However, this does not imply that theoretical and methodological discourse was totally absent from human endeavour in these disciplines. We have inherited a whole series of texts from history, sourced from observation, imagination, intuition and experience. Beginning with Marcus Vitruvius Pollio and his treatise *De Architectura*, circa 27 BC, many others followed in his wake, including such luminaries as Sebastiano Serlio – *Regole Generali d'Architettura*, 1537;

Quatremère De Quincy – *Dictionaire d'Architecture*, 1825; Gilbert Laing Meason – *On The Landscape Architecture of the Great Painters of Italy*, 1828; and Camillo Sitte – *City Planning According to Artistic Principles*, 1899. More recently, Bannister Flight Fletcher's *A History of Architecture on the Comparative Method* (1897) also remains a classic. Their work still informs practice and scholarship in urban design. Despite this inheritance, these masterpieces were wholly eclectic works, brilliant but disconnected from any documented field of knowledge. Today, urban design still lacks an explanation of itself that allows any significant social identity to legitimise action and process. So far, and despite the enormous debates over scientific progress, there has been little or no attempt by mainstream urban design 'theorists' to locate the discipline within this overall schema, or even to offer a challenging debate as to why it *should not be* located in the realm of scientific advance, that is, within the natural or social sciences.

In its attempts to explain nature and the world in which we live, science has been at the forefront of human creativity for millennia. The logical as opposed to the intuitive search for knowledge had begun in the ancient cradles of civilisation: Sumeria, China, India and Africa. Here, the processes of reason and rationality had their origins, a constellation of discoveries that eventually allowed Nicolaus Copernicus to theorise the correct location of man within the universe, and his student Galileo Galilei to come up with the proof in his *Dialogue* of 1630. It was with these two men that the great scientific revolution of the Enlightenment began in Europe, a movement that has dominated the idea of *method* since that time. So it is with science that we must begin our investigation into how the form of cities has come about, and the usefulness of the scientific process to that event.

The method of science

> The time is overdue for adding the separation of state and science to the by now customary separation of state and church. Science is only one of the many instruments man has invented to cope with his surroundings. It is not the only one, it is not infallible, and has become too powerful, too pushy, and too dangerous to be left on its own.
>
> (Paul Feyerabend)

> The grand aim of all science is to cover the greatest number of empirical facts by logical deduction from the smallest number of hypotheses or axioms.
>
> (Albert Einstein)

In the minds of most professionals, science represents rationality, truth, logic, fact, deduction and proof (Kuhn 1962). It provides us with incontrovertible information about the world around us. It represents the current state of demonstrable knowledge, not to be refuted except by other scientists. Science is held to have special merit owing to its authority in, for example, discovering the genetic basis for life, moving civilisation forward through technological advances, and having the capacity to cure or ameliorate a multitude of diseases, among a great many other accomplishments. It is therefore unsurprising that we accord science special privilege, and at least since the enlightenment have looked to it as a saviour, using scientific knowledge from chemistry, biology, physics, astronomy and a variety of other spheres of consciousness to solve human problems. The use of the term *science* has then been extrapolated into other areas of knowledge, adding credibility by way of association. At its broadest compass, we therefore have a division into natural and social sciences, where the *social* then adopts a mantle that may not actually reflect the complexity and appropriateness of the methods of the natural sciences.

What then is the scientific method, or indeed is there such a thing, given the immense array of phenomena to be encompassed? What separates science from other forms of explanation (for example, religion in general and creationism in particular) is usually taken to be the difference between proof and belief, or rationality and faith. Science begins by observing some part of the universe and then generates a hypothesis that is consistent with the observations that have been made. The hypothesis may be formed on the basis of several key propositions that support it. Predictions can then be formulated, and the hypothesis can be tested and modified on the basis of its ability to explain what has been observed. The testing of theories on the basis of evidence and hypothesis formation came to be known as the hypothetico-deductive method, and this method was then taught as a universally valid tool for explaining the universe, applicable to the natural sciences and across all scales of endeavour (see Figure 1.1).

Such orthodox conceptions of science have been termed *positivist* or *empiricist*, with so many associations and practices that it is somewhat similar to using the term *capitalist* to describe the global economy since the cold war thawed. Despite more recent scepticism, the positivists maintained that there was such a unity represented in the scientific method that it was equally valid for the study of nature as it was for the study of man. As man was part of nature, and it was the job of science to study nature, ergo the same methods could be applied across the entire spectrum of human activity, with some variation depending on the subject matter. The universally adopted method could then be described as having six main stages, depending on how one decides to break down the process:

- statement of a problem;
- generation of proposition(s);
- formation of a hypothesis;
- testing of the hypothesis (prediction);
- consolidation of a theory;
- application to 'real-world' solutions.

The same series could also be reduced to observation, hypothesis formulation, prediction and experimentation, feeding back the results to modify initial

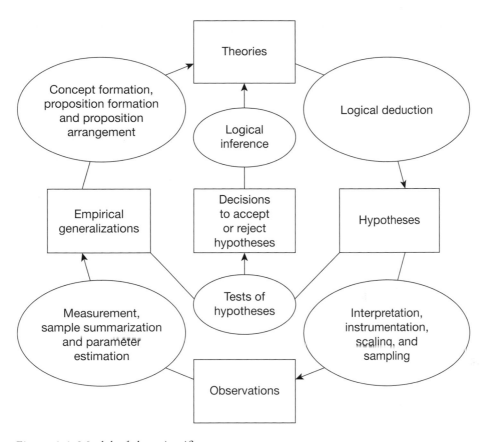

Figure 1.1 Model of the scientific process

Source: J.C. Moughtin, R. Cuesta and C.A. Sarris, *Urban Design, Method and Technique*. Oxford: The Architectural Press, 2003, p. 7, Fig. 1.3

assumptions and, thence, to perfect the theory. The outcomes then become accepted as the 'laws of nature' and are held to be universally valid.

Paradoxically, while a central quality of science for the positivists was that it spoke the truth, and that this truth was demonstrable, another was that it also had to be *falsifiable*. By the very nature of the process, this fact must be transparent to all. Without it, science would have already discovered everything about a fixed and unchanging universe. Several rules follow from this – that all theories are only temporary statements, that the best theories stand the test of time as they are the most difficult to refute, and that all 'truth' is relative. Given this relativity, the importance of metaphysics and the residual need for imagination to be exercised, all science is limited by the burden of proof. Without it, science cannot accept any other reality. Because it is factual that science has frequently been falsified, it is then clearly arguable that scientific truths constitute only partial representations of 'the real world'.

Even within this overall *Weltanschauung*, there is considerable variation as to the operation and validity of specific methodologies, where at least three appropriate methods from the natural sciences may be adopted:

1   Scientific research begins with pure observations, and generalisations or theories are produced from them.
2   Scientific research begins with a tentative theory that is expected to explain some observed phenomenon, and observations are made to test whether this theory can be accepted.
3   As observed irregularities are produced by hidden mechanisms, it is necessary to build models of mechanisms and then to look for evidence of their existence.

(Blaikie 1993: 3)

In the process of demonstrating the truth of statements, a conflict in the relationship between induction or deduction in respect to reasoning has been legion and suggests that, in fact, they are both part of the same research process. In addition, six classical positions can be identified, all of which dictate changes in the strategy of investigation, and/or methods used in analysis such as the above (Blaikie 1993: 9). These are:

Positivism	Critical rationalism
Negativism	Classical hermeneutics
Historicism	Interpretivism

Despite these variations, Blaikie states that, in effect, there remains only one central position, that of positivism, to which the others are reactions rather than new theories. In answer to the question as to whether the same methods of the natural sciences can be applied to the social sciences, only positivism answers 'yes'. Negativism answers 'no'. Both historicism and critical rationalism say 'yes' and 'no' in equal measure, and the last two say 'no'. Interpretivism not only says 'no', it maintains that natural science and social science are qualitatively different activities, and so their methods require entirely different forms of science. As if this was not sufficiently complex, Karl Popper has noted that *metaphysics* also has a significant role to play in theory building (Popper 1959, Simkin 1993).

So one outcome of recent theory is that many scholars today have serious reservations in using the word *science* as a meaningful descriptor of theory/ method in any useful sense – 'There is little agreement on what kinds of methods characterise science beyond the rather bland point that it is systematic, rigorous, and self-critical, and that physics and chemistry are exemplars of it' (Sayer 1984: 14). Added to this, and despite Popper's claim that scientific proof is impossible, and that theories can never be proven, only falsified, Chalmers suggests that this is also untrue: 'a strong case can be made for the claim that scientific knowledge can neither be conclusively *proved* nor conclusively *disproved* by reference to the facts, even if the availability of these facts is assumed (Chalmers 1999: 11; my italics). Hence, Feyerabend's famous claim in regard to a fixed theory of rationality (science) that, 'there is only one principle that can be defended under *all* circumstances and in all stages of human development. It is the principle that *"anything goes"*' (Feyerabend 1975: 5). But this statement is not a plea for the wholesale denial of responsibility, and Feyerabend's remark is made in the context of a lifetime's participation in the philosophy and history of scientific practice (Feyerabend 1987, 1995). Nor is it a call for wholesale ignorance to prevail; quite the opposite, as is demonstrated in his carefully argued thesis throughout *Against Method* that, 'humanitarian anarchism is more likely to encourage progress than its law-and-order alternatives' (Feyerabend 1975: 5). Other similar texts have adopted the same theme on a regular basis – *Abandoning Method* (Phillips 1973), *Beyond Method* (Morgan 1983) and *After Method* (Lay 2004). Feyerabend's postmodernity has also been explored, in 'science as supermarket' (Preson 1998).

Consequently, debates have raged at least over the last fifty years, and possibly since David Hume, over whether or not there was one science or many (Giddens 1974, Hacking 1983). Nonetheless, social science has had widespread acceptance and has become the common terminology. But the problem does not stop there. Nested inside this we have, for example, economic science and political science, and, within the latter, descriptions of historical materialism as a science. This line of reasoning goes even deeper, into Marxism, for example, as a branch of historical materialism, where Marx's thinking is not merely constrained to political philosophy, but by some (including himself) is also seen to be a science (Althusser 1965, Althusser and Balibar 1970). In this case, there is clearly an argument in favour of this idea, as *material*ism implicitly involves matter. What constitutes *matter* has been a focal point both of science and Marxism since their inception, and the historical dimension of science as a causal agent in social development is indisputable. So the development of science and society *qua* scientific materialism deals with how reality has been defined in accordance with scientific beliefs, including the social. Marxism focusses on science in two ways: first, in terms of a claim as to the actual process of analysis, particularly in the economic sphere, and, second, in terms of a topic of research and investigation: 'For Marx, social practice is a condition, but not the *object* of natural science; whereas it is *ontologically* as well as *epistemologically* constitutive of the social sphere' (Hacking 1983: 325). Although sharing the philosophical problems involving matter and the relationship between history and science, as well as the specific location of science as a part of the superstructure or of the economic base, it would appear that there is some general agreement that the methods of the natural and social sciences must take different paths. Given that urban design is the object of our enquiry, with its focus on civil society and urban space, we must now look at the somewhat recent extension of natural science into the science and epistemology of the social.

The method of social science

The above debates suggest that the best view of science we can adopt is one that is a continuum from 'pure science' and positivism on the one hand, through a whole spectrum of possibilities, to some of the more rarified research methods in the social sciences on the other. This divergence is well illustrated in Table 1.1, which shows the difference in approach between realist and constructivist methodologies. However, one apparent difference between the two is the extent to which quantitative research methods which characterise the natural sciences give way to more qualitative approaches in social science, despite the fact that many social scientists insist on extensive quantification of 'the data' to demonstrate their point. While it is clear that the study of society in all its richness and subjectivity can never be meaningfully reduced to ticking off boxes in survey forms, the reduction of the world to numbers still guarantees an air of legitimacy for many scholars. But once one starts to look at how society is constructed, the subjective nature of human relations demands altogether different consideration (Millet 2004, Hay 2005). For example the distinction as to what constitutes 'the economic' from 'the political' is the *raison d'être* of political economy, which

Table 1.1 Choices between methodological issues: realism and constructivism

Issue	Alternative positions	
Nature of reality	Realist Single	Constructivist Multiple
Starting point	Theory Technical language Outside	Observation Lay language Inside
Role of language	1:1 correspondence with reality	Constitution of social activity
Lay accounts	Irrelevant Corrigible Trans-situational	Fundamental Authentic Situational
Social science accounts	Generalisable across social contexts	Specific in time and space
Researcher	Subject-to-object Detached Outside expert	Subject-to-subject Involved Reflective partner
Objectivity	Absolutist Static	Relativist Dynamic
Theory of truth	Correspondence Political	Consensus Pragmatic
Aim of research	Explain Evaluate	Understand Change

Source: N. Blaikie, *Approaches to Social Enquiry*. Cambridge: Polity Press, 1993, p. 216

assumes that every economic decision is simultaneously political since there is no economic decision that does not affect the lives of real people politically at the same moment. These distinctions also apply to other concepts such as what constitutes social class, the urban etc.

Therefore, there is no hard and fast line between natural and social science as far as method goes. Whereas critical theory, realism and structuration theory all assert some methodological connection between the two, hermeneutics and feminism reject any meaningful influence. Of these five methodologies, Blaikie (1993) notes that the crossover from the natural to the social is facilitated in each case by classical hermeneutics, a field that has evolved into contemporary hermeneutics and one that currently has a special place in urban research. The basic difference is that, 'Technical human interest makes use of empirical–analytic methods of positivism to yield the instrumental knowledge of the natural sciences, while practical human interest makes use of hermeneutic method to yield practical knowledge' (Demeterio 2001: 56). As a theory of society and as a methodological approach to social science, hermeneutics is not the easiest of subjects, as evidenced in the writing of some of its more important figures (Heidegger 1952, Ricoeur 1981, Thompson 1981, Bubner 1988, Gadamer 1989, Kogler, 1996). In addition, hermeneutics encompasses both phenomenology and interpretivism, and all are concerned with the idea of *texts* and their interpretation within a particular cultural milieu and consciousness. The key theorist in the field of phenomenological hermeneutics is arguably Paul Ricoeur, who shared with Jürgen Habermas (and Feyerabend) the idea that science was only another self-legitimating narrative among many, and as such had to be properly positioned and deconstructed in order to reveal its truths (see also FOC3: 69–72).

'Hermeneutic' is defined in *The New Oxford Dictionary of English* as 'concerning interpretation, especially of scripture or literary texts'. Hermeneutics is therefore intimately connected with the analysis of texts, documents that explore the ideologies, experiences and events that constitute the residue of human history. Similarly, hermeneutic interpretations of texts are also closely related to analogous interpretations of urban form and structure. The built environment may be perceived as a 'text' that can be read and is accessible to deconstruction, interpretation and the revelation of meaning. While hermeneutics can be traced back to Hegel (loved by Marx as much as Adam Smith was despised) and later to Schleiermacher and Gadamer, the springboard into contemporary hermeneutics originated in Jürgen Habermas, who was one of the most significant forces in the Frankfurt School for Social Research (see next chapter and FOC3 56–8). Originating in the mid 1920s, just after Habermas was born, the institute was arguably the most important school of its kind in the twentieth century, as indeed the Bauhaus was for art and architecture. It contributed two important figures who have had significant influence on urban studies, namely Walter Benjamin and Theodor Adorno. Habermas's most influential works were arguably *Towards a Rational Society* (1971) and *Knowledge and Human Interests* (1972). The classical version of hermeneutics, based in the work of Schleiermacher, tried to establish objectivity and a common understanding of social processes, whereas contemporary hermeneutics emanating from Heidegger maintained that such objectivity was impossible, as all forms of interpretation were locked into history and culture. He considered that texts constituted discourses whose medium took a written form, and were linked to concepts of language, meaning, deconstruction and writing. As such, hermeneutic investigation had only a tenuous historical connection to natural science and rationality.

To a large extent, the same is true of feminism, but for different reasons, owing to the simple fact that in the first instance such difference does not originate in *rationality* but in *gender*. The four remaining approaches to methodology – critical theory (Habermas), realism (Bhaskar), structuration theory (Giddens) and contemporary hermeneutics (Gadamer), all emerge a priori from natural science. As such, feminist theory is a radical departure from the theoretical continuum of androcentric offerings, and I am conscious of the fact that, so far, I have been unable to mention a single female contributor to the development of social science whose views hold equal sway in a male-dominated scientific practice. Inevitably, the feminist position is that the androcentric view of the world has distorted all human experience by its historical rejection of the gender difference as in any way significant to the natural or social sciences. For example, in Andrew Sayer's otherwise outstanding realist text on *Method in Social Science*, feminism is only mentioned once and written off in a single line that says, 'Marxism is learning from feminist theory' (Sayer 1984: 72). That was some twenty-five years ago. More recently, it appears that not much has changed, as, for example in *Social Theory and Social Change* (Noble 2000), feminism does not appear at all.

The reason for such omission is at least partially due to the idea that feminism constitutes a perspective, not a *theory* of social science, and I have discussed the feminist position at length in terms of its relationship to theory in FOC6: 127. Although most methodologies fall under its critique and may require serious adaptation, feminism remains what has been termed 'a perspectival paradigm' rather than a paradigm proper (Fulbrook 2002: 40). In the context of feminist history, for example, she states:

> If we even look for a moment at 'feminist history', we find a multitude of different historical approaches: Marxist feminists, psychoanalytic feminists working in the post-structuralist Lacanian tradition, liberal feminists and so on, might all be focussing on what to a mundane outsider, might be the 'same' subject: women. But they construct this subject very differently in terms of their theoretical concepts of gender.
>
> (Fulbrook 2002: 4)

So feminism is defined more by the theories that feminists choose to adopt and the particular methods they use in analysis, although these may not differ radically from those used by men. Feminism is also caught in the gender trap, owing to the instability of the terms used, e.g. *men* and *women*, and the identification of individuals with these roles and how they are acted out in society.

Feminist theory is inextricably caught up with the problem of gender, and the problem of separating *women* out as a category independent to gender roles and definitions is inescapable. Key feminist icons have supported a variety of different methodological positions: Simone De Beauvoir (1972) promoted French Marxist feminism, where women's oppression was firmly seen as a consequence of patriarchal capitalism. In other words, women's subservience could best be analysed through their unpaid role in the domestic mode of production, an entire economic sector that is not recognised within the market economy as part of capital. Kate Millett views women as a separate social class, and, as such, sexual politics plays a central role in her analysis of women's subordination (Millett 1971). Laura Mulvey is interested in how patriarchy sexualises and stereotypes both men and women: 'Mulvey's objective is consciously political, seeking to deconstruct the fundamental patriarchal conditions of *phallocentrism* ... Mulvey's analysis attempts to demonstrate how the ubiquity and centralisation of the male gaze upon the female form is an outcome of significant psychological and therefore cultural processes' (Lewis 2002: 194, Mulvey 1996, 2006). Each of these positions constitutes a heterology with implications as to how women's liberation is to be accomplished and played out in social space, and even more arcane examples of the feminist project, such as adversarial and socialist feminism, post-colonial feminism, audience postmodern feminism and celebra tory postmodernism can be discerned (Lewis 2002: 212).

It is clear, therefore, that, when we move from the natural to the social sciences, the shift is not merely one of method based on the 'nature' of the problem; in the case of feminism and gender issues, it is also a profoundly political (ideological) shift as well. Taken together, both feminism and ecology provide excellent examples of the highly complex problems surrounding the volatile mix of ideology with protoscientific method in the social sciences. The implications of each for 'thinking about thinking' about the built environment are profound, and the spatial question at the centre of our concerns adds a whole other dimension to the problem of method: what space, a central object of urban design, is 'about'.

Science and the urban

As we have seen, science is still 'class divided' into the natural and the social, but social science can also be further split into two main sectors of interest to the environmental professions, namely aspatial and spatial social science. To a large extent, this divide constitutes a development in the history of sociology, as the great masters of the discipline such as Marx, Durkheim, Weber and Simmel were not concerned with space. In effect, they abstracted social content from its form, choosing to study social processes while neglecting any direct relation to the form of the city, let alone to the arrangement and form of its spaces. But, as Andrew Sayer has noted:

Social processes do not happen on the head of a pin, objects have spatial extension and two or more of them cannot occupy the same place simultaneously . . . So even though concrete studies may not be interested in spatial form *per se*, it must be taken into account if the contingencies of the concrete and the differences they make to outcomes are to be understood . . . Moreover, social science deals with systems whose form can be deliberately arranged so as to manipulate and take advantage of the constituent causal mechanisms, be they those of new towns or communication systems.

(Sayer 1984: 134–5)

The single concern that distinguishes the various built environment disciplines, whose central focus is on space, is the word *urban*. To most academics and practitioners it is a word with no meaning other than that it has something do with cities, and the term is variously deployed to delineate *urban* planning from planning, *urban* design from design and *urban* geography from geography. Most urban designers would be unfamiliar with Louis Wirth's classic essay *Urbanism as a Way of Life* (1938a, 1938b), where the use of the term *urban* was among the first attempts to distil the meaning of the word from human experience. Herbert Gans's later paper, *Urbanism and Suburbanism as Ways of Life*, is probably better known (Gans 2005 (orig. 1962)). Castells' text, *The Urban Question*, derives much of its inspiration and intellectual precedents from Louis Althusser. The work is subtitled *A Marxist Approach*, despite the fact that, in his introduction, Castells notes that,

this theoretical preference (or venture) poses particularly difficult problems for urban analysis. For here the Marxist tradition is practically non-existent and the development of theory must be linked to the historical recognition of the new problems posed by everyday experience.

(Castells 1977: vii)

Nonetheless, his adopted method from the start reflected an immersion in Marxist structuralism and its objects of class struggle, ideology, oppression, politics, the development of capital and other issues.

The method of applying the processes of historical materialism and political economy to the spatial problems of cities and society emerged slowly during the 1960s and was galvanised by the Paris riots of May 1968. This division between spatial and aspatial social science was further elaborated by the addition of the word *urban* to sociology. The distinction was first adopted by several theorists, including François Lamarche, Jean Lojkine, Manuel Castells and others. But, undeniably, it was Castells' seminal text *La Question Urbaine* (*The Urban Question*), first published in French in 1972, that compressed all of the issues into a single work; interrogated the term *urban* for the first time; and concretised urban sociology as a nascent branch of social science (Saunders 1976, Gottdiener 1995, Hashimoto 2002). At that time, the basic questions were: What kind of science is it? What is its claim to theory? What are its objects? What constitutes an appropriate *urban* analysis? What indeed does *urban* mean? Castells formulates the problem of scientific method as follows in Pickvance (1976):

Does Urban Sociology have a real object?

If so, is that theoretical object 'Urban?'

If not, does urban sociology nevertheless have a real object which could be described as urban?

Pickvance further notes that Castells' method is to examine the question of the relationship of science to urban sociology by asking:

Has urban sociology had a theoretical object in the past?

Could it have an urban theoretical object in the future?

Does urban sociology have an urban real object?

If it has neither urban theoretical objects nor real urban objects, can the (non-urban) theoretical and real objects it has sought to understand be retrieved and made the basis for scientific urban sociology?

(Pickvance 1976: 4)

In his paper 'Is there an urban sociology?', Castells states that urban sociology has no theoretical object (Castells 1976). The term *urbanism*, which constitutes the theoretical basis for the discipline, is not a theoretical definition; rather, it is a sociocultural type, and he notes that this is even true of Wirth's paper mentioned above. This leads him to the conclusion that urban sociology has no specific real object. He maintains that, on the one hand, this is partly owing to the umbrella status given by the term *urban*, and its vanishing relevance when contrasted to the term *rural* on the other. Urban and rural have been integrated within the productive relations of modern capitalism, and no meaningful distinctions can be applied that separate them from each other. Despite this, Castells notes that *urban* sociology has tended to tackle two types of problem, namely *relationships to space* and what he calls *the process of collective consumption* (Castells 1976: 74).

Castells' strategy was to reverse the usual stress on productive forces and instead reorient his method of economic analysis from production to consumption. Unlike planning practice, which deals with land as a two-dimensional matrix upon which the formal categories of land use may be placed (content-free), Castells' method was to integrate the economic, social and spatial functions within a single political economy of space (FOC9: 226–9). In so doing, he designated *the urban* as the locus of collective consumption, the space of everyday life where people lived, raised their children, relaxed, had celebrations and reproduced the species. This function was subdivided into simple reproduction, namely housing and its closely related activities, and extended reproduction –

such items as educational facilities, parks and gardens, hospitals etc. The critical point was that the activities of the urban were local, place-based, somewhat immobile and rooted in social reproduction and the family. What feminists now term the domestic mode of production is more or less homologous with Castells' definition of the urban. Given that Castells did not recognise the term *rural* as meaningful of anything in particular, by definition, all other economic functions became non-urban, market-based activities. As urban design is concerned first and foremost with the public realm, its central task in Castells' terminology would be to make the necessary connections between urban functions on the one hand, and non-urban on the other. Its other task, which I feel has similar significance, is the construction of symbolic forms, and at this point I refer to Castells' definition of social change, urban planning and urban design adopted in FOC1: 17. In the spirit of this work, it is clearly impossible to separate urban design from its social functions, which are interlinked with other processes, particularly urban planning. As I have argued elsewhere, virtually all definitions of urban design to date are tautological and get us nowhere. Castells' statement stands out as a singular attempt to integrate functions that I have chosen as a point of departure for Volumes 2 and 3 in the trilogy:

> We call urban social change the redefinition of urban meaning. We call urban planning the negotiated adaptation of urban functions to a shared urban meaning. We call *urban design* the symbolic attempt to express an accepted urban meaning in certain urban forms.
>
> (Castells 1983: 303–4; my italics)

Castells held that the spatial attributes of each were singularly important. The major distinction between urban and non-urban functions was critical. Whereas urban functions were place based, non-urban functions occurred over space and time. Industries had global mobility, and their activities could span dozens of countries, as for example in the automobile industry. This further eroded the concept of *rural*, as urban functions clearly took place there, and so 'rural' became a major locus of industry – mining, forestry, agriculture, power generation etc. Furthermore, such industries could be deconstructed and reassembled with shifts in economic conditions, labour markets etc. Hence, traditional definitions of urban and rural were exposed for their total absence of analytical rigour.

Added to this was another important methodological distinction as to the management of the urban system. Given the overall perspective that urban planning was the agent of the state in regulating land supply and providing items of collective consumption, and that this was done in the interests of capital, de facto the urban planning profession was biased to the interests of big capital. Therefore, it could never truly represent the people. Collective interests could only be constituted in what Castells termed *urban social movements*, the spontaneous assembly of populations to protest what they perceived to be unjust – airport noise, destruction of the natural environment, pollution etc. All of this required the environmental professions to rethink their societal role, what their labour actually constituted, and the role of social justice in building the city. Urban designers could not stand outside this onslaught and, like the planners in McLoughlin's time, pretend that their role was value-neutral in the overall scheme of things, which remains pretty much the position today. Castells then goes on to enunciate the method of sociological analysis of the production of space and the impetus towards a sociology of urban planning (which he defines as 'a form of class political practice' (Castells 1976: 277)). Of great importance here to the idea of urban design, and by association to urban planning, is the need to view forms and spaces *not* as an exercise in Euclidean geometry, perspective and aesthetics, as defined by the practitioner, but in consideration that:

> Transformations of space must thus be analysed as specifications of trans-formations in the social structure. In other words, one must see how, in relation to the spatial unit being considered, defined in terms of the requirements of the research, the fundamental social processes constitutive of social structures are articulated and specified spatially.
>
> (Castells 1976: 31)

Such articulation does not only generate functionally different spaces and places for the new, it simultaneously reorients the system of meanings that were inherent to the old and transforms them to new symbolic and material purposes. This transformation constitutes a weakness in Castells' method, despite the fact that he is very aware of the urban symbolic, structures of meaning, semiotics and values. What he later refers to as *the urban symbolic* is poorly worked through, a phrase that covers the entire symbolic framework of urban space and form. Nonetheless, his contribution has been immense, and it was for others to address this question, stimulated by his entire *oeuvre*.

The intensity of the debate began to weaken ten years later, from 1985, when a second emasculation critique of urban sociology began to form around a return to considerations of basic economic processes (production, consumption, administration and exchange) as well as concepts of power, the designation of social conflict and the need for interdisciplinary and comparative studies (McKeown 1987, Milicevic 2001, Perry and Harding 2002). Methodologically, the new urban sociology nonetheless continued, for example in Castells' pursuit of urban social movements in *The City and the Grassroots* (1983), while the trend to postmodern analysis and methodologies became more widespread. Milicevic suggests that the period post 1985 was also characterised by many of the leading actors in the movement having to define their radicalism, such as the extent of their sympathy for the left or actual membership of political groups such as Labour (Harloe, Pickvance and Paris) or communist (Lojkine and Preteceille). Milicevic also suggests that Harvey and Castells abandoned the Marxist approach. Although Castells' position definitely moved away from a strict Marxist paradigm, David Harvey has pursued his Marxian commitment right up till the present, and his materialist perspective remains palpable (Harvey 2003, 2007). Harvey is committed to historical materialism even in his most 'postmodern' work, *The Condition of Postmodernity* (Harvey 1989), one that has had a significant impact on members of the environmental professions who are more conscious of the depth of postmodernity than its whimsical contribution to architectural form. More recently, Castells has advanced a new theoretical perspective for urban sociology (Castells 2000).

Urban design heterologies

In this chapter, we have looked at three heterological sources that collectively account for a huge measure of human knowledge, namely natural science, social science and scientific observations and innuendos from urban sociology. But such knowledge is partial, simply because it does not encompass or even recognise more arcane forms of learning that are not based in proof, such as mysticism, religion, voodoo, myth and magic. It also shows a distinct bias in that the prior sources have been sympathetic to the idea of science as a standard for rationality, where the idea of hypothesis and method has validity. But we must also remind ourselves of the imprimatur 'that there is no knowledge outside science – *extra scientiam nulla salus* – that is nothing other than a convenient fairy tale' (Feyerabend 1975: 113).

As we know, urban design is a social practice that has been conducted for millennia, at least since the great pyramids were built at Gizeh in Egypt, 5,000 years ago. The ancient Egyptians believed that naming something brought it into existence, and urban design only came into being as a recognisable discipline through the process of naming during the twentieth century (Cuthbert 2007: 180–1). However, unlike architecture, planning, landscape architecture and engineering, and other fields such as medicine and law, it was not established as a profession. One reason may be that it was difficult to say exactly what it was, other than *big architecture*, and little attempt was made to do so. It seems that it was easier to live with the confusion rather than think through the problem, one that remains today. When we try and decompose the given name *urban design*, we find that the word *urban* has no meaning attached to it that is remotely useful, and this, in combination with *design*, results in a phrase that may be used for any purpose whatsoever, as long as it has some connection to urbanisation, and perhaps not even that.

Whether or not urban design is a recognised profession or a definable discipline or field has not prevented direct connections to science in the three aspects denoted above. Elaborating on these prior epistemologies, it is possible to suggest that natural science offered functionality in terms of process, quantitative methods and political neutrality. Social science offered legitimacy in terms of content and qualitative research methods, and urban sociology offered to bring these together into a defined region of study that had no prior existence. In addition, wrapping urban design in with architecture and planning, owing to its intimate and enduring overlap with these disciplines, will be unavoidable in this context. If we start with the rational scientific process, we can immediately identify significant connections. As early as 1953, even before this approach had reached the planning fraternity, Karl Popper, in *The Poverty of Historicism*, had already anticipated some of the problems that urban planners had yet to grapple with, well before a narrow and distorted functionalism came into being in 1969:

> But the difficulty of combining holistic planning with scientific methods is still more fundamental than has so far been indicated. The holistic planner over-looks the fact that it is easy to centralise power but impossible to centralise all that knowledge which is distributed over many individual minds, and whose centralisation would be necessary for the wise use of centralised power. But this fact has far-reaching consequences. Unable to ascertain what is in the minds of so many individuals, he must try to simplify his problems by eliminating individual differences; he must try to control and stereotype interests and beliefs by education and propaganda. But this attempt to exercise power over minds must destroy the last possibility of finding out what people really think, for it is clearly incompatible with the free expression of thought, especially critical thought.
>
> (Popper 1957: 89–90)

From Popper's statement, we can anticipate that far from being involved in a value-neutral activity governed by universal laws and practices, science is inextricably tangled with other unquantifiable social structures and ideologies such as politics, knowledge, freedom, beliefs, propaganda and critical thinking. Already it was possible to speculate that a scientific approach to methodologies in planning and the environmental disciplines had some problems attached to it. The environmental disciplines were, however, on a somewhat different tack, and the use of general systems theory became widespread in the 1970s and 1980s, specifically by the urban planning profession. As the whole epistemology of scientific endeavour and planning is bound up with the concept of prediction, it suited planning admirably to adapt the scientific method to its own use in projecting future states, anticipating developments and assessing their potential consequences. It was obvious that at some point, planning and science had to intersect. This occurred in 1970, when Brian McLoughlin wrote his classic, *Urban and Regional Planning: A Systems Approach*. Systems theory originating from the scientist Ludwig Von Bertalanffy rapidly became the holy grail of urban planning, as its relation to science now seemed assured:

> At once we see that the problem of prediction is intimately bound up with scientific method in general and theory building in particular. For it is hardly possible to predict in the absence of some general idea about the phenomena in question.
>
> (McLoughlin 1970: 167)

The foundation for this view of planning heterology was of course the building of databases, which he identifies as the most critical part of the planning process. The second was model building, or simulations of specific features of cities and regions. With these two tools, scientific insight into the process of cause and effect was thought to be guaranteed. Lacking these central features, the entire structure of planning would falter, as wrong prediction could spell disaster in any number of ways. Science also offered certainty as well as a politically neutral process, as science and politics were seen to be wholly separate regions of human action. The holy grail was in sight. Planners would be able to eliminate their own bias, as the rationality of the model would permit them to turn opinion (subjectivity) into quantification (objectivity). Rationality would prevail. Decisions could be made without prejudice or favour. At last, a democratic model of change could be introduced to the planning process that would get rid of the messy subjectivity of prior eras, one that McLoughlin referred to as 'error-controlled regulation' (see Figure 1.2). This was where the fatal error occurred, a point that McLoughlin tried to correct for the rest of his professional career. Six years later, in 1976, Andrew Sayer was to lay bare the fallibility of the systems approach in his 'Critique of urban modelling', followed closely by Scott and Roweis (1977), who delivered a withering critique of mainstream planning ideology in 'Urban planning in theory and practice – a reappraisal'. Shortly after that, a more realistic definition of urban planning was suggested, not as some quasi scientific process offering infallibility to planners on the abnegation of their own subjectivity, but as 'the professional mediation of territorial politics' – no modelling allowed (Roweis 1983: 139).

So, at least since 1970, the idea of rationality has driven the orientation of urban planning practice and, like functionalism in architecture, remains with us today, albeit in fragments, many years after its usefulness has expired (Baum 1996). Over this period, and in support of the systems approach, a rational comprehensive science also generated the *rational comprehensive model* for planning, one that has formed the basis for urban planning and design for the last fifty years (Chapin and Kaiser 1979). The model has been a major anchor in any criticism of planning theory right up until the present time, so that planners may learn from their mistakes (Saarikoski 2002, Stein and Harper 2003). By 1984, statements were still being made in support of the rational comprehensive model, which, 'though widely attacked in academic circles, still remains the only substantive problem solving methodology we can count on' (Blanco 1984: 91). To be fair, the model was already being subjected to significant criticism in the face of other emerging planning approaches (Dalton 1986). However, ten years after that, the modelling approach, which began with McLoughlin and was widely criticised in Sayer (1976), was still being promoted up to the new millennium (Knaap *et al.* 1998, Guhathakura 1999). Other commentary on the rational comprehensive model has a wide array of origins, demonstrating the extent to which the concept of scientific rationality has prevailed over a wide range of disciplines, e.g. political ecology (Harrill 1999), planning practice (Saarikoski 2002) and participatory planning (Alexander 2000, Huxley 2000).

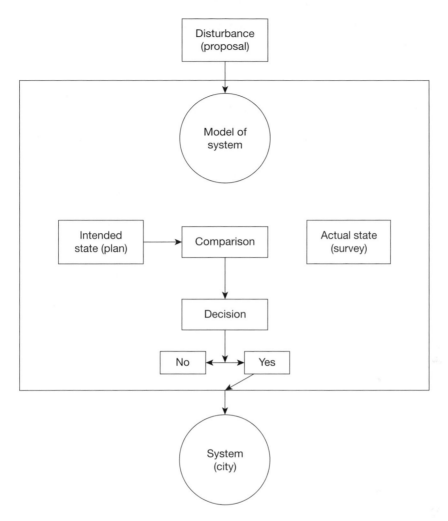

Figure 1.2 McLoughlin's error-controlled regulation

Source: Redrawn from J.B. McLoughlin, *Urban and Regional Planning: A Systems Approach*. London: Faber and Faber, 1970, p. 86, Fig. 4.2

Other forms of planning theory and methodology are expounded in Mandelbaum *et al.* (1996). In addition, Dalton (1986), Baum (1996) and Alexander (2000) have each provided significant overviews of the persistence of rationality, which impacted both by association and application in urban design. The direct application of rationality, modelling and systems thinking similarly prevailed in project design and management. Recently, two important edited books have appeared on the problem of method in urban design (Roberts and Greed 2001, Moughtin *et al.* 2003). It is also reinforcing that one of these has been executed by women, who need to claim a much larger stake in the urban design process. While both books represent an invaluable contribution to the field, in the sense that they cover a wide range of information valuable to students, nonetheless they suffer equally from two major defects.

The first is that both are firmly rooted in the mainstream, in urban design orthodoxy. No new avenues are revealed. In other words, practically all the material has already been published elsewhere in more comprehensive texts. The second is that despite the fact that both have been published since the year 2000, the most important idea of the new millennium, that of sustainability, is totally ignored in both. So, for the real story on sustainable urban design, we have to look to other published work, such as Jenks and Burgess (2000) and Thomas (2003). In Moughtin *et al.* (2003), the methodology of sustainable development is mentioned in the introduction, and again briefly in the conclusion, and forgotten in between. There is no chapter on 'Sustainable urban design'. The concept is even less visible in Roberts and Greed (2001). So, one of the most significant requirements of cities for our future survival, namely that of sustainable urban design, has been expunged from any connection to method whatsoever. However, there seems to be an even greater omission in both texts, which is the capacity to talk about method and technique, completely divorced from theory. Paradoxically, and given the position of planning within the state apparatus, this is probably the only realistic position to take. In Moughtin *et al.*, urban design is tied in to five forms of planning practice taken from Hudson (1979), namely:

- synoptic planning
- incremental planning
- transactive planning
- advocacy planning
- radical planning.

Logically, it would have made sense to then give the book some consistency by demonstrating the effect each planning strategy had on the production of urban form. The difficulty is outlined in Figure 1.3, which tries to capture the relationship between the scientific process discussed above and the scientific *design* process, as if these methods are seen as a direct reflection of each other. Therefore, it is instructive, given prior discussion, that the chapter framework is directly derived from natural science, missing out on any hypothesis as to how things actually happen – survey, analysis, generation of alternatives, project evaluation etc. – what the authors call *the integrated design process* for planning, which coincidentally includes everything from architecture to regional development. All go through the same sequence (Moughtin *et al.* 2003: 6, 8, 77; see Figure 1.4). From the introduction to the final chapter on project management, urban design is integrated directly into the rational scientific model, without which the text would collapse. The same is largely true for Roberts and Greed, and the only diagram on urban design method intersects with those of Moughtin *et al.* (Roberts and Greed 2001: 55; see Figure 1.5). In a more recent text (Lang 2005: 26, 31), a superior model of the rational design process is pursued, with

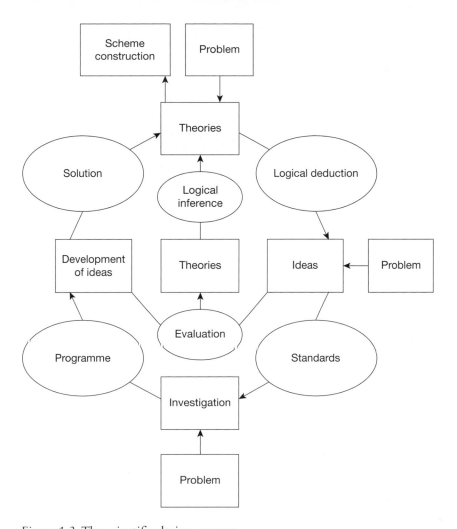

Figure 1.3 The scientific design process

Source: J.C. Moughtin, R. Cuesta and C.A. Sarris, *Urban Design, Method and Technique*. Oxford: The Architectural Press, 2003, p. 8, Fig. 1.4

application to one of the typologies, which he terms 'all-of-a-piece' urban design (see Figures 1.6 and 1.7).

So, from several recent texts (and many older ones), it would appear that method in mainstream urban design exhibits at least six key features:

1   There is an overarching dependency on the rational scientific model derived from the natural sciences.
2   Urban design methodologies also exhibit most of the structural features of natural science in the adoption of hierarchic thinking, modelling and system theory.

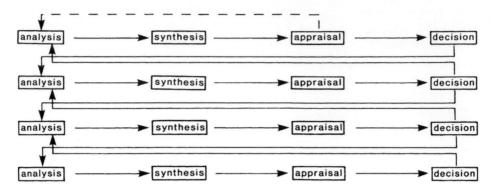

Figure 1.4 The integrated design process

Source: Redrawn from J.C. Moughtin, R. Cuesta and C.A. Sarris, *Urban Design, Method and Technique*. Oxford: The Architectural Press, 2003, p. 6, Fig. 1.2

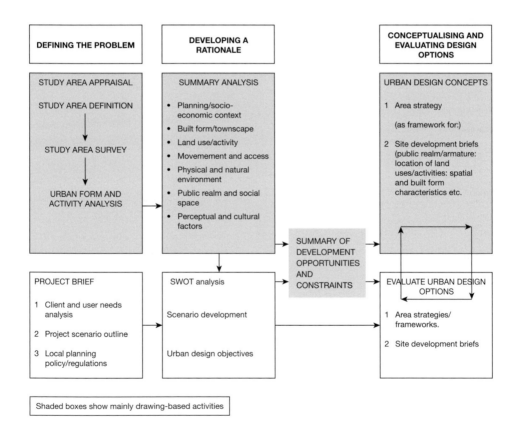

Figure 1.5 An urban design area rationale and strategy

Source: T. Lloyd-Jones, 'A framework for the urban design process'. In M. Roberts and C. Greed, *Approaching Urban Design: The Design Process*. Harlow: Longman, 2001, p. 55, Fig. 5.1

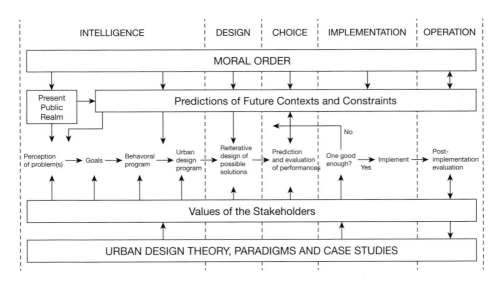

Figure 1.6 A model of the rational design process

Source: J. Lang, *Urban Design: A Typology of Procedures and Products*. New York: Elsevier, 2005, p. 26, Fig. 2.2

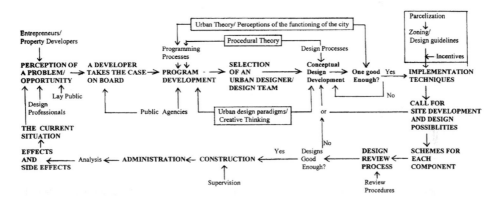

Figure 1.7 The major steps in an all-of-a-piece urban design

Source: J. Lang, *Urban Design: A Typology of Procedures and Products*. New York: Elsevier, 2005, p. 31, Fig. 2.6

3   The discipline is also substantially tied into an atheoretical vision of *planning*
    and adopts planning ideology as to the various typologies of practice.
4   Its self-conception is atheoretical, rendering critical self-reflection of any
    substance virtually impossible.
5   Expositions of design methodology are almost entirely constructed through
    recycling pre-existing knowledge of the subject in different forms.
6   Some of the most important descriptors of contemporary urban design
    impacts such as globalisation (economic), postmodernism (culture) and the
    New Urbanism (practice) are not mentioned in the index to either book
    (Roberts and Greed (2001) or Moughtin *et al.* (2003)).

However, if we look at developments in social science, we find that current
research is opening up new avenues for urban design theory and practice on a
daily basis. Much of this is through qualitative research methodologies derived
from significant and substantial theory (Silverman 2001, Weinberg 2002,
Neuman 2003). The continuation of the new urban studies into a variety of
different trajectories has similarly demonstrated a unique capacity to see the form
of the city differently derived and differently constructed.

Conclusion

The debate over whether the same methods used in the natural sciences are
transferable to the social sciences remains unresolved. Nonetheless, there is a
convincing argument that positivism rules, despite the fact that science itself is
suspect as a useful descriptor of derived method. None of this has prevented
social science from establishing its own territory, with a shift towards more
qualitative methodologies. This trajectory also recognises the importance of a
feminist genre, one that segues into all other forms of interpretation. For urban
design, the intractable problem remains, namely that we have some partial and
unsatisfactory theory *in* urban design, but we have none *of* it. So our vision of
the world has been wholly self-referential, i.e. urban design is what urban
designers do. In the same vein, what we do usually depends on where we originated as professionals, e.g. architecture, engineering, law etc. Whereas each of
these disciplines possesses its own integrity, urban design comes to be defined
as a satellite of each, with no possibility of any synthesis. As long as this
situation persists, the question as to whether urban design methodologies should
originate in the natural or social sciences is irrelevant – they will be derived from
whatever seems to be appropriate at the time.

We have also seen that urban design methodologies remain seriously connected
to rationalism as the favoured methodology, one where linearity, hierarchy and
modelling dominate (see Figure 1.8). Hence, the suggestion that urban design
should adopt a context derived from the social sciences, particularly spatial
political economy, stands in contradiction to the continuing rationalist position
in urban design methodologies. How then do we supplant a navel-worshipping

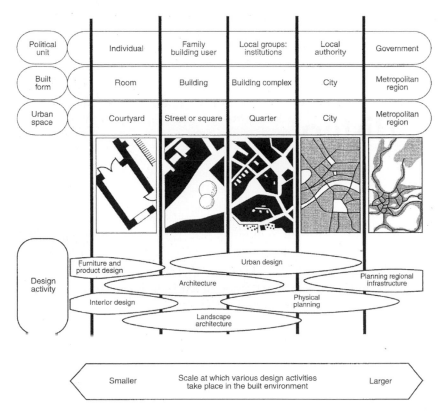

Figure 1.8 Perceived hierarchic nature of the built environment

Source: B. Ericson and T. Lloyd-Jones, 'Design problems'. In M. Roberts and C. Greed, *Approaching Urban Design: The Design Process*. Harlow: Longman, 2001, p. 5, Fig. 1.3

rationalist process with contextual and encompassing urban design methodologies that are qualitative, feminist and sustainable? To retain our design skills and meaningfully inform their use, we are therefore forced to look much deeper into the human condition if we wish to develop an urban design knowledge that is courageous, humane and relevant. I maintain that such understanding can only come from social science-based practices currently ignored by our multitude, beginning with some of the principles and ideas denoted above, and elaborated over the next nine chapters.

2 History

History, Stephen said, is a nightmare from which I am trying to awake.

(James Joyce)

History becomes the myth of language.

(Michel de Certeau)

The distinction between past, present and future is only an illusion, however persistent.

(Albert Einstein)

Introduction: history, truth and time

At the outset, I draw the reader's attention to the thirty historical texts that I set out in FOC2: 11, which are a fair representation of the mainstream urban designer's way of 'seeing' history. Each forms part of standard reference material in most university programmes, and they will be used as the focus for an examination and critique of heterologies in urban design. First, however, we must retreat much further back, to the nature of history itself – what is it, how do we interpret it, and how do we write it?

In examining the methods that are used to understand the past, we cannot get past the fundamentals of time, progress and writing. As we shall see, past, present and future are relatively recent concepts, at least in the values attached to them. The same applies to the idea of progress – what is our destination and why? Does the very idea hinder our development in the present? If history is moving forward, where is it going? In the same vein, what is history if in fact it goes nowhere? Can history *come to an end*, as some scholars have suggested? Nor are emergent epistemologies necessarily outcomes of any specific theory or theories. In other words, and depending on the subject matter, it may be possible to demonstrate a theory many different ways, all of which are valid. Epistemology may represent the beginning of the process, with theory as the destination rather than the origin. This is more likely to be true in the social sciences than in the natural sciences, but it is in the latter that urban design is more firmly rooted. If we take the history of urban form as an example, there are few common epistemologies, despite the fact that history is usually conceived chronologically. For most historians, seeking to escape from the concept of time as an absolutely linear process to one of relativity, the former appears to be the most difficult idea to relinquish.

Directly connected to this are the methods historians have used to analyse history in general, the heterologies used in diverse forms of interpretation. Clearly, what constitutes history is intimately bound up with the methods embedded in the analytical process. In many ways, they define what history is. History becomes the subject of epistemology rather than an enduring chronological sequence, and if we examine much recent material on historical research, the idea of theory does not appear to preoccupy most scholars. For example, in a recent text, *What is History Now?*, there is no mention of the word *theory* in the index, and there are no headings in the text (Cannadine 2002). Semiotic preference is given to perspectives, positions, ways of knowing, textual analysis etc., eschewing the term theory on the suspicion that it has been distorted by its relationship to the grand narratives of modernism. In consequence, the overwhelming orientation of current research is towards the methods through which history is revealed – narratives great or small, deconstruction, individual voices, disciplinary focus and other means.

The position that history may be conceived as an abstract idea possessing its own inherent logic and values was abandoned many years ago. Consequently, any commitment to the proposition that history is merely the sum of its own chronological events, driven by accurate records and perfect memory, is virtually extinct. Events did not happen as the logical outcome of some self-perpetuating and enduring truth. Having accepted this idea, it becomes clear that history cannot be understood, in the sense that there is never any single jumbo history waiting to be accommodated by those who attempt to explain or interpret time. Instead, we must ask how the past was experienced by a myriad of actors, interpreters and enforcers, where any absolute concept of *facts* and *truth* must first be abandoned in order for valid interpretations to emerge:

> For these reasons, the past we study as historians is not the past 'as it really was'. Rather it is what it felt like to be in it. The growing bibliography of the history of passions, sentiments, sensibilities, anxieties and the like, is a measurable recognition of this.
>
> (Fernandez-Armesto 2002: 155)

So today, history emerges from a veritable universe of particles, where any objective or verifiable 'truth' lies in whatever connectivity or similarity may be made among or between them.

As an outcome of such relativity, it is transparent that history can only be seen or experienced through a lens of some kind, as it has no absolute existence in geography, time, science or religion. The grand narratives of the past, while they are still plundered for 'facts', are no longer recognised as having any kind of common currency in interpretation. To name but three of the greatest historians, Darwin saw the evolution of the species in terms of his theory of natural selection. While it retains its extraordinary explanatory power for the theory of evolution, it has nothing to say about subjectivity. Marx analysed the production of society in terms of historical materialism. While his major concerns with exploitation, social class, imperialism, ideology and other concepts remain part of the toolkit of many scholars, his ideas did not encompass the realm of human experience upon which historical interpretation now depends so heavily. Freud saw the development of the species in terms of the structure of the human mind and its origins in the psychology of existential experiences and collective consciousness – its symbolic formations, archetypes, psychology and discontents. Nonetheless, the differences between these world-views pale into insignificance when compared with contemporary historical epistemologies encompassing an immense range of structure, function and subjectivity, from individuals and their world-views, to the complexity of a globalising world.

History and progress

Clearly, history and what we call progress are intimately tied together. While modernity was the cultural form of industrialism, postmodernity is the cultural form of post-industrial societies. Second, while these ideas are teleological, implying linear, necessary development to be measured in terms of gross development product (GDP), globalisation also demands that we retrack our ideas of history and progress, which may or may not coincide with certain contemporary visions of where history might lead. For example, Christianity views history as a linear, finite process that begins with a week of creative activity and ends with the second coming (Parousia) sometime in the future. The Enlightenment considered that history was open-ended, but with the logical outcome of a perfect society at some future time. Neither is too different from Marx's vision of a perfect socialist state in communism, but only after the ravages of capitalism had been tamed by popular revolt and a wholesale transformation of the relations of production. Significantly, modernity was the first period to conceive of itself, and therefore of other historical periods, as epochs, in a futile attempt to grapple with destiny. Modernity was both the first, and also the last, epoch.

With the rise of globalisation and postmodernity came a spate of books dealing with our own historical extinction – Gibson-Graham's *The End of Capitalism* (1996), Francis Fukuyama's *The End of History* (2006), Nigel Harris's *The End of the Third World* (1990), Jeremy Rifkind's *The End of Work* (1995) and others. Why was this case? Michel Foucault, who died in 1984, could be described as the first historian of discontinuity. He argued that, as our concept of 'the human' is historically conditioned within various epistemes, or historical discourses, the concept of a finite 'human being' did not exist (Schottler 1989). Neither did any history that presupposed it, which prophetically included all interpretations of history to date. This opened up the idea of *post-history* as the appropriate form of interpretation for a globalised world. Jean Baudrillard contends that the period of post-history we now inhabit is one where image and reality are so intertwined that we live in an age of hyperreality. Globalisation transforms us from being the consumers of media to being their products. 'Real life' therefore disappears, and a simulation ensues, as in the metaverse of Neal Stephenson's novel, *Snow Crash* (1992). Owing to the rate of historical change, Baudrillard argues that history simply vanishes, along with any necessary destiny or outcome, in effect denying history as having any epistemological value whatever as, in the vanishing, nothing is left to understand.

What this generates is one enormous (global) paradox. On the one hand, all national economies and institutions define history/progress as the ever-increasing production of commodities measured by GDP. On planet earth, only Bhutan has, as its stated object, gross national happiness (GNH). On the other hand, some philosophers and historians are telling us that we are not going anywhere. For example, in a challenging book, *Straw Dogs* (2002), John Gray states that 'Humans cannot live without illusion. For men and women of today, an irrational faith in progress may be the only antidote to nihilism. Without hope that the future will be better than the past, they could not go on' (Gray 2002: 29). We could also add that governments are similarly placed: without the concept of GDP, they simply could not govern, because their economic strategy in its entirety is founded in this single principle.

Gray argues that the very idea of progress is dependent on two basic ideas. The first is that Western thought teaches us that we are different from other animals that simply react to the circumstances within which they find themselves. In theory, we are supposed to be able to control our destiny, which of course is not possible, but we believe it anyway. Second, this position is due to what we call our 'consciousness', which allows us to speculate that where we are can be replaced by where we might be, or could be, at some other future time. Whether this has any value or not is debatable. He points to the idea that all interpretations of modernity have proved to be fantasies, and that 'death camps are as modern as laser surgery' (Gray 2002: 173). He claims that there is a direct relationship between death by violence, efficiently administered, and our ideas of progress. While knowledge has advanced, ethics have remained static. He suggests that little is valuable for what it *is* but what it *might become*. As a result, we live our lives as simulacra of some unattainable future state. This hypothetical position also coincides with terminal and enduring happiness once everything has been achieved, and the meaning of our lives has been realised. But, as he suggests, 'Searching for meaning in life may be useful therapy, but it has nothing to do with the life of the spirit. Spiritual life is not a search for meaning but a release from it' (Grey 2002: 197).

Writing history

Up until the beginning of the twentieth century, history tended to be defined as political history, where conquest, wars, states, the actions of dictators, generals and the whole gamut of demagogues dominated historical analysis, combining to create a simulacrum. In other words, the adopted form of interpretation was political, ideological and a twisted version of reality, with the field organised round linear concepts of time. As a reaction to this, Marc Bloch and Lucien Lefebvre founded the *Annales d'Histoire Economique et Sociale* in 1928, with its influence still echoing today. Today, the *Annales* School remains as important to the development of history as the Frankfurt School is to social science or the Bauhaus is for architecture and urban design. The *Annales* School began by rejecting positivism (empiricism) and with it the idea that had guided much prior discourse, namely the search for 'the truth'. As such, the school was radical and had wide-ranging objectives. Its focus was on a more comprehensive view of history. As we shall see below, studying history is largely an atheoretical pursuit, and it is enlightening that the dominant historical institution in the twentieth century is usually described in the context of new methodological approaches, in the absence of any encompassing or substantial theory. Until the Second World War, the *Annales* School was still defined in terms of its resistance to prevailing ideologies. Since then, it has emerged as a school of thought in its own right, whose main figures included Emile Durkheim, Ferdinand Braudel and Roland Barthes. After the student uprising in Paris in 1968, *Annales* once again shifted its focus away from the writing of total histories characterised by Braudel's structuralism and his ideas of *la longue durée*. This also included a rejection of quantitative methods for a more qualitative orientation with human subjectivity, psychology, consciousness and culture, as well as Marxian notions of ideology (Braudel's method is reflected in Giovanni Arrighi's *The Long Twentieth Century*, published in 1994). Nonetheless, with the last phase of the *Annales* School, the method/concept of historiography became the dominant method of the writing of history that remains with us today.

As a discipline, historiography shifts the focus from what is being recorded or interpreted to the method of its accomplishment. More accurately, it suggests that the *emballage* brought by the historian to the process of making history must be considered an integral part of the telling of history. Jordanova defines historiography as 'the writing of history and the study of historical writings: more broadly an awareness of different ways of doing history' (2000: 213). Michel de Certeau, on the other hand, observes that, while discourses speak of history, they too are historically situated. Production takes place in the relation established between the two. As he remarks,

> Discourses are not bodies floating 'within' an all encompassing whole that can simply be called history (or even context). They are historical because they are bound to operations that are defined by functions. Thus we cannot understand what they say independently of the practice from which they result.

Elsewhere, he says that, 'historiography uses death in order to articulate a law of the present' (de Certeau 1988: 20, 101).

Overall, history in general does not embrace theory well, and there are relatively few great theorists of history, in contrast to the multitude of disciplines that form it: 'Although (some) historians work closely with theoretical perspectives, this does not tend to take the form of producing theories of history, at least it has not done so in the twentieth century' (Jordanova 2000: 55). Conversely, we could also say, in a Mcluhanesque manner, that *the message is the method* – that the process of actually writing history, of historiography, displaces the need for theoretical intervention to the extent used in other disciplines. So, in principle, any encompassing theories of history become impossible and, arguably, stand in the way of significant comprehension, particularly given a dimension of 4.6 billion years of human evolution. Since there are always a virtually infinite number of interpretations and a similar variety in subject material, generalisation becomes impossible. Even Darwin's contribution, while enormous, only encompasses biology, creating a free-for-all for a myriad other disciplines to flourish with their own special histories. In accommodating difference, a retreat from structuralist forms of explanation was required, now fully recognised for their limitations and deficiencies.

So the rejection of structuralism and the abandonment of the concept of *la longue durée*, the search for authenticity and linear concepts of time, all opened up the floodgates to an infinite combination of disciplinary bases, ideologies, technologies and epistemologies. Their use in contemporary historical analysis is so vast that it can only be touched upon here. At the same time, recourse to the possibility of greater theoretical intervention emerged with the movement towards cross-disciplinary research. For example, papers delivered at the Institute of Historical Research in London, in 2001, were presented as chapters in *What is History Now?* – an updating of the great English historian E.H. Carr's famous 1961 paper, 'What is history?', delivered at Cambridge University in 1961. These papers were grouped by discipline, for example social history, political history, religious history, cultural history, or by dominant focus – gender history, class history, intellectual history and imperial history (e.g., Thompson 1963, Scott 1999). By definition, this excludes history as a discipline *in itself*, as it has no significant meaning unless it is tied into some other form of interpretation, in other words to derived method. Linked to the absence of significant theory, it then becomes an abstraction, defined only through the relation between writing and discourse, between the process of writing history and its object. Highmore deals with the impenetrable problem of the relation between history and historiography when he says, 'there is no direct contact with the past, of course, only commerce with its traces . . . – historiography (history-writing) – leaving the word "history" to signify the unreachable terrain of the past' (Highmore 2006: 23).

In an attempt to simplify some of these problems related to boundaries, various kinds of history have been identified, as well as a mass of criteria through which the discipline attains specific forms. These have been reduced to six main categories (Jordanova 2000). *Period* deals with notions of causality and time.

Under *Methods*, she uses the examples of oral history and demographic history. *Places* address urban history in the sense of geography and scale – regions, countries etc. *Theories* would encompass concepts such as historical materialism, Darwinism and psychology. *Types of human being* may be classified under gender, race, demographics (children, geriatrics etc.) and *institutions*, where she includes public policy, welfare states etc. This, however, is an extremely rough and ready set of groupings that might be better set out as a matrix, where important relations could be established, for example the relation between theories and methods (if any), the relationship between disciplines such as science and art etc., although she does single out sociology, anthropology, culture, philosophy and literature as important contributors to the overall project of writing history. Michel de Certeau deals with this confusion, not by imposing an arbitrary structure that might be compelling under the circumstances, but by pursuing the idea that some frame of reference is necessary that permits contradictions to remain suspended in their relations without the need being felt to resolve them. He states that, 'The mixed function of historiography can be specified by several features that deal first of all with its status in a typology of discourses, and second, with the organisation of its contents' (de Certeau 1988: 92). Later, he goes on to discuss what he calls 'concepts' or historical categories equivalent to the methods of the natural sciences:

> thus 'the period', 'the century' etc., but also 'the mentality,' the social class,' 'the economic conjuncture,' or 'the family,' 'the city,' 'the region,' 'the people,' 'the nation,' 'the civilisation,' or even 'the war,' 'the heresy,' 'the festival,' 'the plague,' 'the book,' etc., not to speak of notions such as 'the ancien régime,' the 'Enlightenment,' etc. These units often convey stereotypical combinations. A predictable montage offers familiar patterns: the life – the work – the doctrine; or its collective equivalent: economic life – social life – intellectual life. 'Levels' are piled up. Concepts are packaged. Every code has its logic.
>
> (de Certeau 1988: 97)

As if this complexity was insufficient, we also have to deal with the passage of time, at its most basic dealing with synchronic studies *in* time, and diachronic dealing with studies *over* time. It remains to be determined how 'thick' a synchronic study can be before it becomes diachronic, and how long a diachronic study may be in terms of periodisation (when something supposedly starts and finishes). For example, Jordanova (2000) spends twenty-five pages of her book discussing time purely in terms of periodisation, probably the most basic and functional method of dealing with the concept – taxonomies, calendars, institutional forms, cultural styles etc., even the potential in the idea of metaphor is reduced to purely functional ends, e.g.

> Another way of delineating periods, by themes, also warrants careful reflection. Examples include 'the age of anxiety'; 'the age of equipoise'; 'the

golden age'; or 'the aristocratic century'. The underlying principle is by now familiar: it is the desire to lend unity to a period, in this case by a combination of description and metaphor.

(Jordanova 2000: 134)

In contrast, instead of viewing history as discrete temporal collectivities (however these are described), de Certeau's *oeuvre* deploys the method of multiple time frames coexisting in the present, what is now referred to as *polychronic* time (Serres and Latour 1995). This is a much more sophisticated approach to time than the insistence by many historians that time only has one dimension, that of periodisation. Highmore uses modernity and post-colonialism as examples to explain de Certeau's approach to time, where he suggests that modernity is not 'past' or 'incomplete', explaining it as 'the dynamic suturing of the past and present' – the omnipresent nature of the past and the permanent accommodation of the present into history. Thus 'modernity is the name for contemporary life fashioned out of shards that are simultaneously striving for the future and looking back, over their shoulder to the past' (Highmore 2006: 82). De Certeau's approach to time is probably better explained in recourse to other media such as film, for example Alain Resnais's *Last Year at Marienbad* (1961), or in literature, W.G. Sebald's *The Rings of Saturn* (1995). But in order to see how far these ideas are grounded (or otherwise) in the history of urban form, we must now turn to a few exemplary discourses that inform it.

History and mainstream urban design

In order to situate the above discussion, I will discuss the taxonomy of thirty historical texts (Table 2.1) first mentioned in *The Form of Cities*, focussing on a few key examples. From this list, one thing is immediately apparent, that the majority use the same method of linear, chronological analysis using a similar periodisation (Ancient, Egyptian, Greek, Roman, and Medieval etc.). But even within the majority view there remains a wide range of possibilities for interpretation e.g. one could adopt a materialist or liberal perspective, choose to focus on domestic or institutional arrangements, or investigate the economic or social base of the civilisations studied. But in the spirit of this text, we are not primarily concerned here with *what* any historian is talking about so much as *how* they are talking about it – the heterologies that underwrite the basis of their thought.

So, as a general principle, this chapter does not ask, for example, 'what was Lewis Mumford talking about in *The City in History*?' or 'which periods did he cover?'. Or again, 'how did his method of investigating history contribute to our understanding?'. What we want to reveal are the answers to questions such as, 'how did he conceive of history, and what methods did he use in doing this?'; 'how did his life experience frame his method?'; 'who did he get his ideas from?'; 'to what extent did he consider chronology to be useful, and why did he use this approach?'; 'what were the building blocks of his methodology?'; or, reflecting

Table 2.1 Thirty classic urban design histories

Geddes, P.	(1915)	*Cities in Evolution*
Childe, G.	(1935)	*Man Makes Himself*
Gibberd, F.	(1953)	*Town Design*
Korn, A.	(1953)	*History Builds the Town*
Tunnard, T.G.	(1953)	*The City of Man*
Hilberseimer, L.	(1955)	*The Nature of Cities*
Mumford, L.	(1961)	*The City in History*
Gutkind, E.A.	(1964)	*The International History of City Development*
Sprieregen, P.	(1965)	*Urban Design*
Reps, J.W.	(1965)	*The Making of Urban America*
Bacon, E.	(1967)	*Design of Cities*
Benevolo, L.	(1967)	*The Origins of Modern Town Planning*
Moholy-Nagy, S.	(1968)	*The Matrix of Man*
Rykwert, J.	(1976)	*The Idea of a Town*
Rowe, C. and Koetter, F.	(1978)	*Collage City*
Morris, A.E.G.	(1979)	*The History of Urban Form*
Benevolo, L.	(1980)	*The History of the City*
Boyer, C.	(1983)	*Dreaming the Rational City*
Roseneau, H.	(1983)	*The Ideal City*
Fogelson, R.E.	(1986)	*Planning the Capitalist City*
Hall, P.	(1988)	*Cities of Tomorrow*
Kostoff, S.	(1991)	*The City Shaped*
Kostoff, S.	(1992)	*The City Assembled*
Benevolo, L.	(1993)	*The European City*
Boyer, M.C.	(1994)	*The City of Collective Memory*
Lang, J.	(1994)	*Urban Design: The American Experience*
Hall, P.	(1998)	*Cities in Civilisation*
Eaton, R.	(2001)	*Ideal Cities*
Gosling, D.	(2003)	*The Evolution of American Urban Design*
Robbins, E. and El Khoury, R.	(2004)	*Shaping the City: Studies in Theory, History and Urban Design*

Source: The author

our theme, 'what was he thinking about when he was thinking about Classical Greek urbanisation?'; or ultimately, 'what was it that guided his thinking in the first place?'. By answering such questions, the process of history presented by Mumford and others becomes contextualised by a multitude of factors that qualify what is being presented as a rational exposition of urban development over the last 10,000 years.

We can ground this idea in a single example. Most urban design students should know that, in 480 BC, in Asia Minor (Turkey) Hippodamus created a plan for Miletus that is universally hailed as a masterpiece in urban form, one of the most perfect urban design plans the world has seen. This plan is usually interpreted from purely formal perspectives – it is famous because of its mastery of urban space and form, its geometric and orthogonal perfection, its adaptation to site conditions, the use of the grid as an organising framework and the use of perspective, serial vision and other devices. But few traverse these technologies to appreciate what he was thinking about when he conceived it, e.g. heterologies derived from classical Greek thought such as mathematics (Fibonacci series), medicine (optics) and philosophy (harmony, balance etc.) that informed his art. Had a similar project been required elsewhere, merely copying the form would be superficial and inadequate, probably even disastrous. We would have had to accommodate the same principles used by the designer and apply them to differing geographies and typologies, possibly to different social and economic circumstances. The resultant design solution might look nothing like Miletus, as we have not copied and reapplied the form; we have copied and reapplied its content, but probably with singularly greater effort. In other words, as urban designers we tend to judge and reinvent products, not the patterns of thought used by the designer as the substance of their creative process. Until we can at least tackle some of the issues connected to this problem, we will not know how we know. We will be unable to connect our learning to practice, because we will only be addressing form and style, without understanding the substance of thought itself.

Beginning then with classic urban design histories, most follow a chronological sequence, for example Childe, Gutkind, Sprieregen, Bacon and Morris. The most influential of these was probably Mumford's *The City in History* (1961), his twenty-third book. The few clear exceptions to this rule are those of Moholy-Nagy, Rowe and Koetter, Fogelson, Boyer, and Tafuri. Peter Hall's book, *Cities of Tomorrow*, gives the impression of a different urban history, but its subject matter remains chronologically ordered, despite the fact that he uses chapter headings such as 'Cities of imagination', 'The city of the dreadful night' etc. So, in order to exploit differences, I will briefly discuss Mumford, Moholy-Nagy, Rowe and Koetter, and Tafuri. In addition, Hall's encyclopaedic works, as well as the focus on memory by Boyer are both essential reading. Childe, Fogelson and Tafuri, while producing very different work, use the method of political economy in analysis, and Tafuri will serve as an example of this method. The central limitation of such a process is obvious – that I will not be able to demonstrate how any particular theorist's views have changed over time (e.g. Tafuri, Mumford). Therefore, I will use each discourse as representative of an epistemology rather than a developmental process.

Prototypes

Lewis Mumford: The City in History *(1961)*

To urban designers, Lewis Mumford is probably the most revered of all historians, and his book, *The City in History*, is the most popular, despite the fact that Benevolo's *The Origins of Modern Town Planning* (1967) runs into seven volumes. Because of his primacy in mainstream theory, I will dwell more on Mumford's epistemology than the others, for the simple reason that it is by far the most complex and interesting. The fact that he himself was illegitimate, was raised by his mother, and never knew his father, might suggest why Mumford's zeal for social justice and democracy could have emerged, and these are enduring themes that run throughout his work. Similarly, even in some of his earliest writing, he also expressed his support for women's rights and the promotion of feminism. One can also speculate that the sheer extent of Mumford's interests in social science, politics, geography, regionalism, culture, ecology and architecture was also due to the fact that he never attained an academic degree, an accomplishment that imparts both constraints on, and opportunities in, intellectual life. So, while his importance to the built environment disciplines is undeniable, his focus and adopted methods do not emerge from an academic training in any of these associated disciplines. Instead, Mumford's methodology was profoundly affected by the Scottish philosopher Patrick Geddes, who influenced his aspiration to establish his own intellectual territory – a regional social science he called *sociography*. He politicised this interest by becoming a founding member of the Regional Planning Association of America (RPAA). Although Mumford is best known as a historian of the city, the term 'city' is only included as part of the title in five of his books. So it is clear that his dominant world-view came from a combination of social science and culture on the one hand, and the possibilities of technology as exemplified in his *Art and Technics* (1952) on the other.

Lucarelli notes that, despite Mumford's commitment to technology, his interests were always tempered by human purposes, reflecting Mumford's question, 'What [does it matter] if industrial society is run more efficiently, if it is run in the same blind alley in which humanity finds itself today?'. He goes on to say that, despite Mumford's commitment to politics,

> Mumford's critique is aesthetic and moral, not political. It is important because he keeps his attention on the self, and on the connection between the self and nature. And it helped him to reintroduce his concern with art and literature as necessary to the imaginative perception of life: an understanding needed for the revival of the inner life.
>
> (Lucarelli 1995: 39)

Aesthetic or otherwise, Mumford's writing is littered with political commentary. Although Mumford was not a Marxist, he definitely adopted his own brand of socialism and had many harsh things to say about the capitalist system. For example, his method of implementing his organicist ethic was to revolutionise capitalism. The power of the state was to be harnessed through a state monopoly over the means of production in the sphere of energy. Among other principles, he believed in:

1 the decentralisation of communities, along with the decentralisation of political power;
2 the use of state monopolies to counteract private-sector greed;
3 a rehumanisation of the labour process to combat the alienation of the working class;
4 defining limits to luxury consumption (limiting desire) and concentrating on satisfying basic human needs.

In studying civilisation over historical time, his epistemology was to interweave an archaeology of substance, based on the institutional frameworks of state power, capital, ideology and culture, and then to elaborate on the human condition that emerged for the mass of the people, along with a moral commentary knitting everything together. His socialism was no doubt promoted through friendships with intellectuals of the left such as Patrick Geddes, Thorsten Veblen, Clarence Stein, Frederic Osborne and others. He also expressed singular admiration for Thoreau (an anarchist) and Peter Kropotkin, whom Mumford tactfully describes as 'a geographer' (1961: 514). More significantly, Kropotkin was Bakunin's successor and was noted for framing the theory of anarchistic communism in Russia. Mumford's analysis in many ways conforms to a somewhat unorthodox form of historical materialism, which nonetheless exhibits an incredible command over the machinations of capitalist ideology and urban development. In *The City in History*, Mumford's method of approach was to a degree highly eclectic, in that it did not commence by assuming a frontal attack on capitalism; rather, it tore it up, piranha-like, over the whole book, through thousands of tiny cuts; for example, in regard to Amsterdam in the seventeenth century:

> At this point, commercial success showed itself for what it was and largely still is: civic destitution. From the standpoint of an expanding capitalist economy, indeed capitalism's prospects of profits which rested on continuous turnover, demanded the continued destruction of old urban structures, for the sake of their profitable replacement at even higher rents.
>
> (Mumford 1961: 444)

One may compare this statement, which preceded David Harvey's comments in *The Urbanisation of Capital*, twenty-five years later:

> Capitalist development therefore has to negotiate a knife-edge path between preserving the exchange values of past capital investments in the built environment, and destroying these investments in order to open up fresh room for accumulation.
>
> (Harvey 1985: 25)

To try and reduce Mumford's lifework to a predominant method is a pointless task, and one could even say this about a single work such as *The City in History*.

On the other hand, it is possible to suggest five component parts of his analysis, as well as three mechanisms that he uses to elaborate his ideas. The archaeology from which his epistemology was constructed (but not exclusively so) would include, first, his commitment to organicism, which Lucarelli defines as 'the restoration of nature's influence on culture through architecture, literature and the built environment' (1995: 22); second, a wholistic ecological approach to urban development; third, politics are omnipresent in his analysis and closely related to element four, namely the importance of institutional arrangements as the building blocks for social relations, and within this the dominance of the state and capital. Fifth, over all the odds, the significance of culture as a triumphal expression of the human spirit prevails across all of his work, despite serious resistance by the forces of darkness and despair.

The interaction of these major components is frequently qualified by three mechanisms that Mumford deploys in the manner that an artist uses colour to enhance his composition. First, we have his frequent use of metaphor, often combined with what I have previously called his 'gothic prose', as in his transference of the use of 'citadel' (ancient) into what he calls 'the underground city' (of the Victorians). Indeed, the whole of the following passage is metaphorical:

> The masters of the underground citadel are committed to a 'war' they cannot bring to an end, with weapons whose ultimate effects they cannot control, for purposes that they cannot accomplish. The underground city threatens in consequence to become the ultimate burial crypt of our incinerated civilisation.
>
> (1961: 481)

The second mechanism is the use of biological analogy and anthropomorphism, for example describing Rome as 'Parasitopolis', suffering from 'megalopolitan elephantiasis' (1961: 237). He also has a penchant for the use of biological terms such as predation, symbiosis, embryonic, miscarriage, protozoa etc., all used to describe urban phenomena or states. Similarly, moving from the body to the mind, Mesopotamia had a 'paranoid psychical structure' (1961: 39), and Rome declined in a catastrophic degradation from 'Patholopolis' to 'Psycho-patholopolis' (1961: 234). Concepts such as 'sublimation' and 'regression', derived from psychology, are also frequently used as descriptors. Third, and more significantly, he uses the terminology of humanistic socialism as his overarching philosophical and moral compass.

Sibyl Moholy-Nagy: The Matrix of Man (1968)

In *The Form of Cities* (FOC2: 30), I briefly outlined Moholy-Nagy's contribution in respect to mainstream theory and said, 'In the spirit of the age, like Mumford, her vision of urban growth is again organic, anthropomorphic and oriented to death and dissolution'. Although it is true that Mumford's writing frequently had an air of eldritch horror about it, it only constituted a small part of his output, whereas the phrase almost encompasses Moholy-Nagy's book *The Matrix of Man* in its entirety.

From the outset, Moholy-Nagy's method of analysis presupposes that the organisation of cities assumes certain archetypal forms based upon 'eternally recurrent constellations of matrix and content' (1968: 18), which she describes as:

Geomorphic	Machu Picchu (Figure 2.1)
Concentric	Vienna (Figure 2.2)
Orthogonal–connective	Teotihuacan (Figure 2.3)
Orthogonal–modular	The Japanese Royal City of Kyoto (Figure 2.4)
Clustered	Canberra, Australia (Figure 2.5)

Therefore, from the start, she is absolutely clear as to what her method will be: 'It is the purpose of this enquiry into urban origins to seek out examples and define these five settlement configurations which occur the world over, and to set spinning a kaleidoscope of their images' (1968: 18). This object is in fact achieved, and the book is replete with interesting figures and drawings. The real question, however, is whether there is anything substantial to learn from doing this over the subsequent three hundred pages. Moholy-Nagy applies her chosen method by assembling a diverse range of images illustrating the various typologies. Although the examples chosen are all fascinating, and the commentary enlightening in many cases, the differences between them in terms of time, location, climate, topography etc. are so enormous that any comparison between settlements becomes pointless. At best, we come out of each chapter knowing that, for example, in Chapter 1, many settlements, primarily ancient, adapted well to natural circumstances, and that many cities are round.

Most of the deficiencies in method result from basic beliefs first stated in the introduction, and four seriously flawed and governing ideas are significant. First, the above quotation assumes the outcome prior to the study even beginning. The geomorphic classification is not the result of a prolonged study, nor is it even a hypothesis to be tested. We are asked to believe that the chosen categories represent proven fact, and to suspend any judgement as to their validity. Second, she states that, 'rightly or wrongly it is assumed that in the building of communities, as in many other human endeavours, the strongest, most convincing solutions were achieved in the beginning' (1968: 18). This idea reflects a widespread flaw in most architectural urbanism, that cities somehow have 'solutions', reflecting an overarching physical determinism and misplaced belief in design. Even accepting the idea is tantamount to saying that the Roman plan for Londinium was superior to anything that came after – and how are we to judge that? But the principle that these solutions were even invented 'in the beginning' is preposterous, as is the proposition that any 'initial idea' was the

Figure 2.1 Example of a geomorphic settlement: Machu Picchu
Source: The author

best. Most cities, like the rest of life, evolved gradually on the basis of trial and
error, and what we have today, in every case, is the *best* solution to the problem,
for the simple reason that speculation on other solutions, while entertaining,
constitutes misguided Utopianism/essentialism and simply avoids the elementary
facts of urban development.

   The third example guiding a typological approach to urban 'solutions' is also
connected to the belief that, 'The current "urban crisis" and its pessimistic, self-
destructive diagnosis, differs from previous environmental revolutions in its
contextual misdirection. We have developed a stupendous ability for incongruous
comparisons' (1968: 12). Leaving aside the fact that this comparison is somewhat
incongruous itself, and that the so-called 'urban crisis' has been a permanent
feature of urban development within capitalism, the idea that cities are
contextually directed is also absurd. It assumes that contextualism might have
been more appropriate, ignoring both the reality of urban growth as well as the
impossibility of retrospective choice. Fourth, probably the most contested

statement in the entire book is that 'the history of urban origins is the history of design imagination'. Although it is possible to misinterpret this statement, as the use of 'design imagination' is a contestable concept, Moholy-Nagy leaves us in no doubt that she is referring to architects when she quotes Marx's statement about bees, hives, imagination and architects. Leaving aside issues previously raised as to what constitutes *urban*, *design*, *history* etc., surely no one could possibly believe that we have the architectural profession to thank (or to curse) for the origins of cities?

Finally, and in conclusion, Moholy-Nagy offers a series of options under each heading without any commentary as to why they are there. These include such examples as the Pedregulho linear housing by Alfonso Reidy on the outskirts of Rio, 'which was abandoned before it was occupied', pyramid housing clusters for Siberia (never built), Luis Baragan's sculpture outside Mexico City, and the subterranean master plan for underground shopping in Montreal. We are left to make of these what we will.

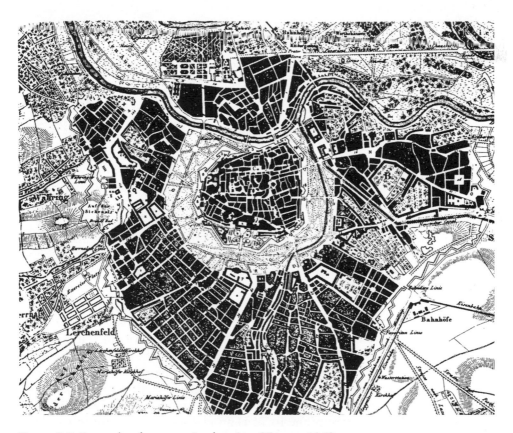

Figure 2.2 Example of concentric planning: Vienna, 1860
Source: S. Moholy-Nagy, *The Matrix of Man*. London: Pall Mall, 1968, p. 79, Fig. 79

Figure 2.3 Example of orthogonal–connective settlement: Teotihuacan
Source: © Markussevcik/Dreamstime.com

Rowe and Koetter: Collage City *(1978)*

> For all the avant-garde movements – and not only in the field of painting
> – the law of assemblage was fundamental. And since the assembled objects
> belonged to the real world, the picture became a neutral field on which to
> project *the experience of the shock* suffered in the city. The problem now
> was that of teaching that one is not to 'suffer' that shock, but to absorb it
> as an inevitable condition of existence.
>
> (Manfredo Tafuri 1980: 179)

Paradoxically, the short quotation given above from Manfredo Tafuri
summarises perfectly the approach of Rowe and Koetter's *Collage City*, a work
that has had cult status within the architectural community since it was first
published in 1978, although the authors' mention that the book was actually
written in 1973.We are left to guess why it remained unpublished for the next
five years. *Collage City* is notable in that it differs radically from most other
architectural histories, and it is possible that I am doing it a disservice by
including it as a text whose prime focus is an exposition of urban history. On
the other hand, our interest is in method, and the book definitely provides a foil
to the others under discussion, offering as it does a sustained critique of the

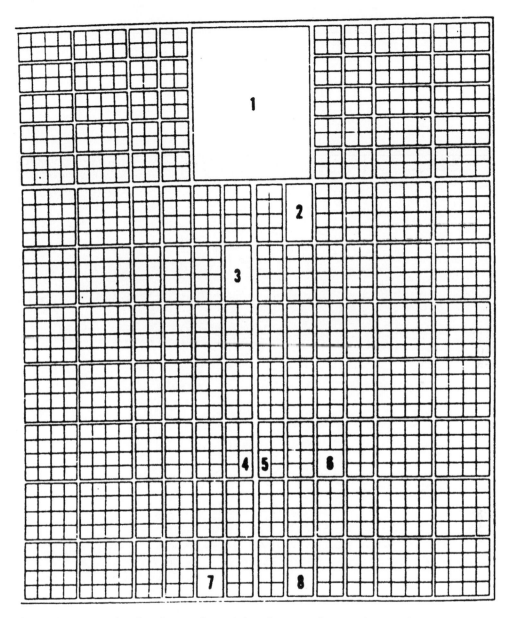

Figure 2.4 Example of orthogonal–modular planning: the Royal City of Kyoto, AD 792
Source: S. Moholy-Nagy, *The Matrix of Man*. London: Pall Mall, 1968, p. 162

modern movement in architecture in the twentieth century, with other significant historical referents. *Collage City* adopts the idea of Utopia as its guiding theme, and the reason that I include the above quotation from Tafuri is that I feel that it encapsulates the intentions of Rowe and Koetter better than the authors themselves have been able to accomplish. As method, they state their intention to produce:

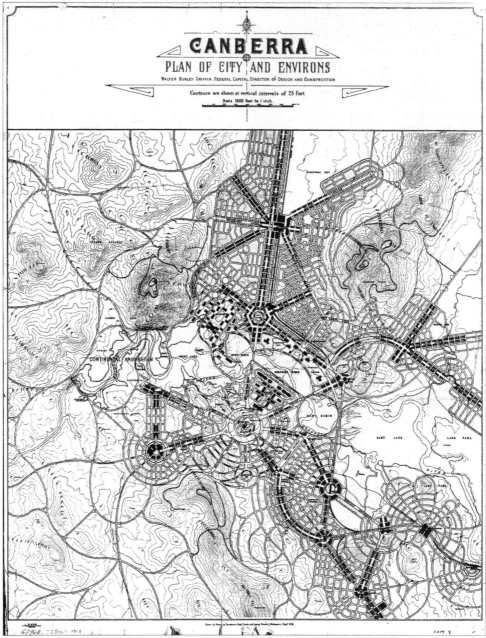

1918 Plan (of City and Environs) — the last official general plan of the city signed by Griffin as Federal Capital Director of Design and Construction.

Figure 2.5 Example of clustered planning: the original 1918 plan of Canberra, Australia

Source: National Library of Australia

A proposal for constructive dis-illusion, it is simultaneously an appeal for order and disorder, for the simple and the complex, for the joint existence of permanence and random happening, of the private and the public, of innovation and tradition, of both the retrospective and prophetic gesture.

(Rowe and Koetter 1978: 8)

Collage City is a demanding text, made even more difficult by the authors' use of *collage* as method, a French word that has two levels of meaning. First, at its simplest, it means 'collection', but more often a contrived collection of unrelated things. Second, the word denotes a technique used in modernist painting, e.g. Dada, Surrealism, Cubism, where various different materials are placed together on a canvas and organised to become a single work of art. Associated with this is the term *bricolage*, coming from the French verb *bricoler* (do it yourself), which is often used to describe a design approach relying on trial and error rather than a science-based methodology. Hence, the method used by Rowe and Koetter is to use a multiplicity of images to convey complexity and difference in meanings that may be associated with the concept of Utopia, in this case the Utopia (more accurately *dystopia*) of modern architecture and urbanism. In my own rereading of the book, I felt that the concept of collage dominated unreasonably. Not only do the graphic images make a *mélange* of history, the text does as well. In the spirit of collage, meanings are produced as much by the reader's own associations as they are by the erudition of the text. Frequently, the only guide we have is in the necessary semantic and syntactical structures of the English language. Ideas litter every page, and, although many are challenging and inspirational, in the spirit of collage, there is virtually no structure for the reader to grasp. Indeed, it might have been better to number each paragraph, as Debord did in *The Society of the Spectacle* (1983), or to have adopted Baudrillard's method in his *Cool Memories* series, where Volume 3 is entitled *Fragments* (Baudrillard 1990, 1996, 1997). In all three volumes, Baudrillard's ideas are set out randomly in paragraphs for readers to absorb however they wish. Using this device, Rowe and Koetter could then have remained true to the original idea.

So, the method is collage, the subject matter is history, and the content is the modern movement. Tafuri's comment on absorbing the shock of the city rather than suffering it does not sit comfortably with the authors, and there are signs of considerable angst within the text:

the city of modern architecture . . . has remained either a project or an abortion: and more and more, there no longer appears to be any convincing reason that things will ever be different . . . [and] . . . both as a psychological and physical model has been rendered tragically ridiculous

(Rowe and Koetter 1978: 3, 4)

Overall, the method of the text parallels the somewhat random nature of the design process, which all architects recognise as a fundamental part of their creativity. Such randomness characterises the difference between architecture and engineering. Problems occur, however, when the same method is applied to writing without some transformation of the subconscious nature of the design process to the text. Collage even deploys itself at the level of individual sentences, and one struggles to make sense out of, for example,

> The Parousia of modern architecture. A bundle of eschatological fantasies about imminent and apocalyptic catastrophe combined with others about instant millennium. Crisis: the threat of damnation, the hope of salvation. Irresistible change which still requires human cooperation. The new architecture and urbanism as emblems of the New Jerusalem. The corruptions of high culture. The bonfire of the vanities.
>
> (Rowe and Koetter 1978: 32)

Like in any creative work, Rowe and Koetter take singular licence with all of the rules, and it remains up to the reader to decide whether or not there is something more to be communicated through the chance processes of collage or the more logical histories of other writers. Even in the final section 'Excursus', in the place of what might normally be called 'conclusion', the authors state, 'We append an abridged list of stimulants, a-temporal and necessarily trans-cultural, as possible *objets trouvés* in the urbanistic collage' (1978: 151), which is as inconclusive and puzzling as the prior conclusion to *The Matrix of Man*. What follows is a random selection of images that are even more disconnected than the collage of the text, grouped into memorable streets, stabilisers, potentially interminable set pieces, splendid public terraces, ambiguous composite buildings, nostalgia-producing instruments and concluding with the garden. Although the images are fascinating, they are also incoherent and fail to inform us of anything significant about urban design. Clearly, mainstream history required at least some clarification of its charter, and this was to come in the political economy of Manfredo Tafuri, a few years later.

Manfredo Tafuri: Architecture and Utopia *(1976)*

> The fate of capitalist society is not at all extraneous to architectural design. The ideology of design is just as essential to the integration of modern capitalism in all the structures and suprastructures of human existence, as is the illusion of being able to oppose that design with instruments of a different type of designing, or of a radical 'antidesign'.
>
> (Tafuri 1976: 179)

First among the intellectual illusions to be done away with is that which, by means of the image alone, tries to anticipate the conditions of an architecture 'for a liberated society.' Who proposes such a slogan avoids asking himself if, its obvious utopianism aside, this object is perusable without a

revolution of architectural language, method, and structure which goes far
beyond simple subjective will or the simple updating of syntax.

(Tafuri 1976: 179–80)

Written as an enlarged version of a paper titled '*Per una critica dell'ideologia
architettonica*', Manfredo Tafuri's *Architecture and Utopia* (1976) is one of the
most penetrating summaries of architecture and urban design written in the
twentieth century. It is both polemical and, to a degree, messianic in tone and
was met with significant violence and resistance when it was first published, as
it denoted the end of architecture as it was then known. The book is also one
of the most challenging to comprehend, despite the fact that, at one level, its
message is brutally simple – architects as urban designers are themselves
functionally integrated into the ideological structure of capitalist enterprise
whose outcomes they wish to alter. As such, all of their utopian propositions
have been largely rejected or adapted to other purposes.

Tafuri pursues this idea from Laugier and the Enlightenment through the
utopian socialism of the nineteenth century, to the visionary plans of Le
Corbusier and the problems of urban agglomeration of the late twentieth century.
But Tafuri's method, while chronological, is tied not to the development of urban
forms but the ideas that modified and changed them. His method follows this
progression by integrating shifts in urban form with the ideological development
of capitalist enterprise as a whole. He states at the outset:

In order to discuss these principles however, it is necessary to enter into
the field of political theory as this has been developed in the most advanced
studies of Marxist thought from 1960 to the present. Ideological criticism
cannot be separated from this context, it is an integral part of it, and all
the more so when it is conscious of its own limits and sphere of action.

(Tafuri 1976: xi)

Tafuri adopts several major trajectories that weave together into a richly
textured methodology. First, his fundamental ideas are with a progressive
Marxist analysis based in political economy, utopianism and ideology. He begins
with the Enlightenment and Laugier's urban design ideas contained in his
Observations sur L'Architecture (1985 (orig. 1763)) and progresses from that
point. His overarching theme is that of Utopia. Utopianism is not merely taken
as a practical objective of production, as it was for Howard, Owen, Stein and
others, but as a major philosophical and intellectual challenge that stands
between capitalist development and something more humane. Being integrated
into this process, he is convinced that as a consequence of the architect's
ideological role, the tasks of architecture are primarily not concerned with form
as much as with the political process: 'what is of interest here is the precise
identification of those tasks which capitalist development has taken away from
architecture' (and it is also interesting to note that, around the same time, Manuel
Castells was referring to a similar process in urban planning, in *The City and*

the Grassroots). As such, Tafuri sees these tasks as supra-structural, as opposed to super-structural, although it seems that both would in fact be correct. Tafuri is therefore focussed on an analysis of the architect as ideologist, heavily involved in forming the very structures from which they seek liberation.

In addition to Marxism and utopianism, a second theme that informs Tafuri's method involves concepts developed from social science, including, but not limited to, Max Weber, George Simmel, Peter Marcuse, Karl Mannheim, Walter Benjamin and others, and theories of economics – Marx, Keynes, Pareto and Schumpeter – and phrases such as '[architecture] being directly related to the reality of production' (p. 48) are commonplace. He also deploys the basic terminology of a fundamentalist political economy throughout the book as part of his basic analytical vocabulary – production, consumption, exchange, ideology, alienation, working class, bourgeois thought etc. Third, his recourse to art in parallel with architecture as a method of understanding the inherent contradictions of capitalism is ubiquitous. Much of the modern movement in art is mined in order to illuminate critical thinking of the period – the creation and destruction of values, the opening up of new forms of resistance or oppression, the generation of political manifestos, or the possibility of liberation from exploitive labour and alienation etc. For example, he describes the specific goal of futurism and Dada as 'a desacralisation of values', using Walter Benjamin's description of these movements in art with a wonderful but appalling pun, 'the end of an aura' (p. 56). Despite this use of art as enlightenment, he is also conscious of the inevitability of art as an outcome of industrial production.

The history of the future

The history of the future has always been a dominating obsession with urbanists, and an extended coverage of Utopias is outlined in *The Form of Cities* (FOC2: 32–7). Overall, utopianists should heed the statement that 'you should never choose the ideal city or the ideal environment or the ideal woman since, if things fail the responsibility will be hellish' (Baudrillard 1997: 32). But the concern with a realistic future history (rather than an imagined one) probably started with Lewis Mumford's two books: first, *The Story of Utopias* (1962 (orig. 1922)), and second, *Utopia, the City and the Machine* (1965). This has continued right up to the present day with books such as Downey and McGuigan's *Technocities*, (1999) and Ruchelman's *Cities in the Third Wave* (2000). The last two are wholly concerned with the impact of modern technologies on a burgeoning placeless-ness and loss of identity in American cities and the role of architects in shaping the cultural landscape. A dominant issue in futurology is the impact of tele-communications on urban restructuring. Core cities may be threatened with extinction due to emergent new geographies generated by the very formlessness of digital and fibre-optic technologies, among many other impacts. Technological urbanism, however, is a conservative growth strategy preferring to go back to scientific rationalism rather than making more humane and risky choices. Kevin

Robbins echoes this sentiment when he states, 'The notion of a virtual community . . . is about escape from the real world of difference and disorder into a mythic realm of stability and order' (Downey and McGuigan 2000: 47).

An overarching commitment to technology, devoid of social content, with a blind acceptance of 'progress' driving development, is very likely to lead us into a world of two architectures, one of profusion and one of despair, as the economic differences of the 'Society of the spectacle' become magnified in a neocorporate global world of increasing competition and inequality. As image, we can speculate that the experience may not be far from what Umberto Eco calls 'the New Middle Ages' (Eco 1986). This could easily be accomplished through the erosion of medieval and modernist concepts of the city by destroying historically defined signifiers, reducing densities and eliminating central business districts, as the space of flows ultimately dominates. The new power structures of globalisation will be multivalent and hidden, notable by their very absence. Power will not be exerted crudely through the architectural expression of state or corporate power, but through the nature of the commodity itself, which stands for the material expression of specific social relations. Empire will project no visible symbols of the new political order, and will more likely make its presence felt within neo-Benthamite structures of surveillance and control (Hardt and Negri 2000, 2005).

Ownership of the image is likely to dominate consumption processes, as urban design becomes the agent of environmental theming in a world of commodity fetishism. Cities that attempt to project a unique image and opportunities, either real or symbolic, are likely to do so on the basis of their capacity to commodify history, simulate authenticity, provide sites for spectacles or conserve exotic natural settings. Reconstructed centres for spectacle and commodity fetishism, now forming a central objective in urban growth strategies, are already part of (urban) status anxiety in most major metropolitan centres (De Botton 2004). The Olympic site in Sydney, for example, has now been adapted to accommodate Formula One racing cars. Airports are already morphing into what might be termed *themeports* – destinations rather than points of transfer, where all the benefits of local culture can be artificially reproduced without traversing immigration. For those who do not wish to travel for 'original' experiences, the post-tourist simulacrum will negate travel and provide a satisfying surrogate as simulation transcends reality. Why should one go anywhere? Paraphrasing the character the Duc Des Essentes in Huysman's novel *A Rebours* (1833), Alain de Botton suggests that 'the imagination could provide a more than adequate substitute for the vulgar reality of actual experience' (De Botton 2002: 27). In a very real sense, we do not need to look to the future – it is already here.

Conclusion

The overarching feeling in contemporary historical analysis in general appears to be that theory is more of a hindrance than a help. As we can see from the above examples, there is no standard method of denoting urban history. Although there may be no overarching theory of history, frequently forgotten is that the objects of historical analysis (science, economy, culture etc.) all possess significant theory of their own, so that the dearth of theory is not a mandate to forget about it. On the contrary, it reinforces the idea that the connection between historical analysis and the adopted theoretical structures of the environmental disciplines becomes crucial. Overall, urban design histories reflect the denial of any significant theory and, with few exceptions such as Tafuri, remain fascinating in their mutual isolation. This, however, does not support a denial of responsibility on the part of designers and theorists to challenge this state and to move knowledge forward in new ways. An overarching theme exemplified by Rowe and Koetter, as well as Tafuri, is the ideological position of the architect/urban designer since the birth of modernism. We are all involved in the production of the very ideological system that we wish to change. Seeking a way out is like trying to follow the contours of a Möbius strip to some final destination. Tafuri's answer is to imbue a precise and incisive way of *seeing* the Möbius strip for what it is, the overall trajectory of capitalist development and the place of the designer within it. He offers us one of the few significant heterological approaches to urban design in the twentieth century, a meta-method that can be reapplied to other situations, unfortunately extended in an almost unreadable English translation of his *The Sphere and the Labyrinth*. In contrast, the more mainstream design approaches, although interesting, offer neither great insight nor any method beyond the superficial, furthering the need to shift our emphasis from historical method *in* urban design to a heterology *of* urban design that Tafuri clearly demonstrates.

3 Philosophy

We feel that when all possible scientific questions have been answered, the problems of life remain completely untouched. Of course there are then no questions left, and this itself is the answer.

(Wittgenstein, cited in Fann 1969)

Introduction: origins

The word *philosophy* comes from two Greek words: *philos*, meaning love of something, and *sophia*, meaning wisdom. So we can get a rough idea of what philosophy may be about by accepting that it has something to do with the love of wisdom (as opposed to knowledge). Happy certainties, however, stop there, and a world of speculation begins. Philosophy contains an essential paradox indicated by the above quotation from Wittgenstein, namely that it allows us to ask questions that have no answers (Wittgenstein 1967, 1974). Conceptual clarity is then dependent on what is revealed in the process of debating ideas and clarifying propositions. Wittgenstein's response to the idea that philosophy is useless was to state that although ideas cannot be *said*, i.e. spoken, they can be *shown*. This is a highly significant observation for understanding the subject matter of the following chapter. Although I may be unable to state what the philosophy of any particular individual *is*, their philosophy may be shown in their work and revealed by what they do – it is inherent to their method.

Since the ancient Greek philosophers, the definition of what constitutes philosophy has continually shifted its emphasis. Pythagoras, the Greek mathematician, named philosophy, and Aristotle defined the activity as *thinking about thinking*. But, since the time of the Hellenes, Descartes, Locke, Hegel, Marx, Heidegger, Russell, Spencer, Quine and countless others have progressively explored various regions of philosophy, probing the meaning of our existence (Lechte 1994). Philosophy therefore addresses every possible aspect of human thought, including science, religion, art, language, ethics, mysticism etc. Clearly, philosophy is not limited to the Western world. China, for example, has had its own philosophers, such as Confucius, Lao Tzu and Mencius, all of whom have had a profound impact on Chinese culture and also in India, with the Astika, Nastika, Carvaka, Jain and Buddhist Schools.

Philosophy begins with curiosity and imagination. What is the meaning of life? What is beauty? What comes after death? What is time? If I exercise my free will, what exactly am I exercising? Is the negation of god the same as not believing in her? Philosophy is an arbiter of responses to such questions. It is also an activity of speculation – one cannot indulge in philosophy if the answer is already fixed in one's mind. To a certain degree, philosophy parallels science in that it formulates questions, produces hypotheses, enunciates solutions and arrives at certain answers. The fundamental difference, if we accept Wittgenstein's position, is that philosophy has no proofs. Whereas science advances on the basis of disproving hypotheses, it still depends on proofs for its advancement. Philosophy relies on the comparison between different positions or viewpoints. Comte-Sponville says that, 'Philosophy is not a science, nor is it wisdom, nor even knowledge: it is a meditation on what knowledge is available' (2005: xii). We can also say that all philosophy is a critique of language, in the sense that whatever the object of our attention, we must resort to language to express it. Hence, Wittgenstein articulated many of his ideas in what he called language games, developing what he termed *the picture theory of the proposition* in order to explain what was impossible using words. In other words,

> Why doesn't one teach a child the language game 'it looks red to me' from the first? Because it is not yet able to understand the rather fine distinction between seeming and being? . . . The red visual impression is a new concept.
>
> (Wittgenstein 1970: 422–3)

Philosophy is the heterology from which all others arise, as, without it, meanings could not be attached to nature and explored in context. In Chapter 1, I indicated the importance of logical empiricism for the development of a contemporary philosophy of science and to social theory in general (see also FOC3: 53). Also mentioned was the significance of philosophy to six influential schools of urbanism, despite the fact that the more one searches within them for a generally accepted philosophy, the more it disintegrates to a question of individual method or the kinds of topic that are to be investigated.

Influences

The main schools of thought that have influenced our considerations of urban form and content were noted in *The Form of Cities* (3: 55–65). These schools were centred in specific places, although in certain instances individuals could associate with a particular school without actually living at the epicentre (the current Los Angeles School is today's best example). I denoted the six schools as Vienna, Frankfurt, Chicago, Weimar and Dessau, Paris and Los Angeles.

Vienna

The period known as *fin-de-siècle* (turn of the century) witnessed an explosion of creative activity in Vienna and the birth of the two heterologies of urban design that remain with us today, namely functionalism, whose main proponent was the Viennese engineer Otto Wagner, and contextualism, whose central figure was a Viennese architect called Camillo Sitte (1945 (orig. 1889)). Although these paradigms remain alive and well, their original significance has been lost. The material production of urban form emerges from the political economy of the time, and the rationale that demanded these two styles around 1900 has since vanished. They now exist as a disembodied aesthetic deployed by architects and urbanists, where the original economic, political and cultural wellsprings that legitimised them no longer operate. So the extent to which the debate between contextualism and modernist functionalism appears anachronistic in the face of postmodernity and a new global economy remains an open question. Today's neocorporate state and business enterprise are generating new relationships in the formal structuring of cities. Therefore, the use either of functionalism or of contextualism to solve spatial problems represents an undeniable attempt to graft old historical patterns onto an economy that presumably demands its own spatial and architectonic logic. Hence, the dominant heterology is that of globalised production and its implications for an outmoded functionalism/modernism. It is always easier to design for the past than the present. Nonetheless, traditions die hard, and a chronic dose of modernism still continues to inform much architectural production.

Although functionalism and contextualism may now be considered super-structural aesthetic forms and the product of an outmoded historicism, at the end of the nineteenth century they represented serious choices between different forms of society. The explosion of intellectual activity taking place in Vienna was leading the whole of Europe into uncharted territory, and the form of the city for this new age was not merely a matter of aesthetic choice. It constituted no less than the symbolic manifestation of a new era. At an even deeper level, the adopted method of restructuring Vienna represented a new form of consciousness. Along with the economy, the human mind was also being reformed – Freud was revealing hidden psychological structures, Gustave Klimt and Egon Schiele were portraying the disintegration of the Hapsburg Empire, and Arnold Schoenberg was even reinventing the way we create music, with a twelve-tone musical scale that resulted in altogether novel compositions. In the words of Mies van der Rohe, if architecture really was 'frozen music', then it too was also being entirely reconceptualised.

For his part, Sitte's method of approach to contextualism evolved from interests in archaeology, the physiology of vision and space perception, Darwinism and, most importantly, to an intensely experienced sense of nationalism:

he was intensely Germanic or Teutonic in outlook and felt that any true art must have a basis in the national impulse of a people ... every serious subjective feeling, every higher spiritual aspiration must be and could only be *national* ... Sitte in turn patterned himself on Wagner's Germanic heroes, giving battle, like the Siegfried for whom he named his eldest son.

(Collins and Collins 1986: 32)

Such commitments, combined with an intensely experienced nationalism and romanticism, clearly led to a heterology where historical forms were worshipped. This was reflected in his love for the medieval city and the historical traditions of German urbanism and public space. His masterwork, *Der Stadtebau nach Seinen Kunstlerischen Grundsatzen*, or *City Planning According to Artistic Principles*, contains dozens of examples of German streets, squares and other civic spaces – Freiburg, Munich, Ulm, Stettin, Frankfurt, Wurzburg, Regensburg, Cologne, Lübeck and many others. Sitte's method emerged from these influences as the most powerful example of contextualist thinking in the history of urban form, not as a mere aesthetic choice, but one that, for him, expressed his own deeply held convictions about the redemption of national ideals through cultural regeneration and urban design.

The competition over the design of the Ringstrasse in Vienna in 1893 was won by the engineer/architect Otto Wagner, and with it came the demise of Sitte's nationalist aspirations, at least in the contextualist forms he envisaged. The differences in methodology for the redevelopment of the central city have seldom been so pronounced in any architectural competition. As if to rub salt into the wound, Wagner anointed his own submission with the Latin phrase *Artis sola domina necessitas* (meaning 'necessity is art's only mistress'; Schorske 1981: 73). Wagner's method was the totally functional approach of the engineer and the slide rule, and indeed Sitte's overt concern with artistic principles and beautification played no part in the brief for the competition.

Where Sitte had tried to expand historicism to redeem man from modern technology and utility, Wagner worked in the opposite direction. He wished to roll back historicism in the interests of the values of a consistently rational, urban civilisation.

(Schorske 1981: 74)

Wagner's attitude was, therefore, to embrace function as the only possible foundation for art and architecture, and to execute his plan for the Ringstrasse and greater Vienna on this base. Art, if it happened, was a by-product of other more elementary requirements, and his approach reflected this. Capitalist economics likewise introduced the idea that the city was to be managed as a productive enterprise; its function was purely utilitarian. Efficient transport for the production and circulation of commodities reified the need for monumentality in street design and, with it, the secondary place of the citizen. Baroque interventions in the form of squares and plazas became the answer to the anomie induced by linear facades along major thoroughfares. History was something to be designed, not evoked; city planning was to be based on modular spatial forms; urban space was designed to magnify the power of the state and its institutions; and all planting of street trees and vegetation was purely decorative, like icing on a cake. Thus, Vienna set the scene for urban design in the twentieth century.

Frankfurt

The *Institut für Sozialforschung* in Frankfurt (1923–44) was probably the greatest of all the schools of thought in the last century, despite the fact that it was limited to five significant scholars, namely Horkheimer, Theodor Adorno, Herbert Marcuse, Leo Lowenthal and Friedrich Pollock. But other famous men were also associated with the school, such as Walter Benjamin, Wilhelm Reich, Jürgen Habermas and Erich Fromm. For those wishing to study the school in greater depth, works by Slater (1977), Held (1980) and Arato and Gebhart (1982) are indispensable. Each individual scholar also has many published works, and those of Walter Benjamin and Theodor Adorno have particular relevance to our project. It is also germane that many of these scholars were Jewish and had to flee Germany prior to the Holocaust, with Benjamin being forced to commit suicide rather than be caught on the wrong side of the Spanish border by the Germans.

The Frankfurt School centred around the philosophy and epistemologies of what they termed *critical theory*, the heterology for most of their work, and it is tempting to describe it as a simple marriage between the methods of Marxism and those of Freudianism, in an attempt to bring together the whole individual who possessed both a psychological as well as a material existence (Marcuse 1962). Psychoanalysis built a foundation for a new form of communicative action (Habermas) and sublimated aggression (Marcuse). It also embraced the Marxian idea of the dialectic, or the continuing symbiosis between theory and praxis. However, the overarching paradox that in many ways drove the Frankfurt School was how the promise of the Enlightenment, with all its civilising tendencies, emancipation and learning, could have resulted in such a hellish descent into the Holocaust. The answer that the members gave was that the Enlightenment was itself responsible:

> It was the domination of modern society and culture by what they called technical reason, the spread of bureaucratic and instrumental rationality to every sphere of life, producing what they called the totally administered society – the society of totalitarianism – which had crippled and distorted the promise of the enlightenment.
>
> (Hall and Gieben 1992: 266)

The central problem was that rationality had morphed into technical rationality, thus excluding other forms of reasoning that were not scientific. The reasoned debates of morality, politics and culture were subsumed to one that was technical and therefore somewhat ruthless. Using Marxism as their intellectual alter ego, the Frankfurt School theorists added themes from Weber and Freud – for example, the internal divisions of the modern state; the emerging omnipotence of bureaucracies; the relationship between the individual and value pluralism; the alienation caused by a new class division of labour; meaningful engagement with the public sphere; and the relationship between the subconscious and social life. To this extent, they were involved in exploring new forms of political action that could result in the realisation of the whole person operating within an unselfconscious political economy – one at least partially free from its own internal dissonance and inconsistencies.

Although many consider the Frankfurt School of Social Theory to be the origin of critical theory, Turner is of the opinion that the Frankfurt theorists neither invented critical theory nor retain any property rights in the venture. They did, however, play a crucial role in bringing together its key intellectual traditions and also in developing a vision of how serious social theory could promote discourse in the public sphere (Turner 2000: 462). This tradition has been carried on predominantly in the work of Jürgen Habermas and his associates, but also by others working within the poststructuralist tradition, in gender and media studies, art history and other areas.

Of the six schools described here, the Frankfurt School can easily be dismissed as the least relevant to any understanding of urban design, for the simple reason that its discussion of urban form (with perhaps the single exception of Walter Benjamin) was virtually non-existent. Nonetheless, its growth encompassed the entire period of the Bauhaus and its orientation to the social function of architectural and urban production, over which it had a singular influence. The interaction between both schools of thought cannot easily be separated, particularly as members of the Frankfurt School were serious critics of art and society, a relationship central to the operation of the Bauhaus and its philosophy. For this reason, we could say that the Frankfurt School was heterological to the Bauhaus' entire existence – it represented much of what the members were thinking about when they considered their manifestos, art and social relations. Whereas the latter dealt with critical theory in the guise of art and architecture, the former dealt with critical theory in the form of texts and other literary works. Both provided searing social commentaries of the Weimar Republic, until they were silenced by fascism.

Weimar and Dessau – the Bauhaus

The State Bauhaus at Weimar was established in 1919. For all its sophistication, its founding heterology promoted a return to the medieval relationship between master and apprentice, rather than advancing new disciplinary directions driven by theory. Thankfully, new learning did not stop there, and, in addition to the Bauhaus and Frankfurt Schools, two other influential institutes were founded in

Germany around the same time. In 1920, the Psychoanalytic Institute in Berlin and the Deutsche Hochschule für Politik were also established. Within four years, four institutions were set up to investigate society, politics, psychoanalysis, art and architecture, all of which interacted in diverse ways, but particularly in the Bauhaus, where interdisciplinarity was a core activity of all learning.

Despite the fact that it originated in craft, the Bauhaus had to adapt quickly to new forms of industrialisation and embrace the technologies of mass production, whose tendencies it was supposed to counteract. Although its directors were all architects, the Bauhaus had an enormous impact on the development of the built-environment disciplines and fine arts, including, but not limited to, architecture, urban design and planning, painting, sculpture, photography, theatre and other art forms. It was one of the greatest sources of artistic inspiration throughout the twentieth century and was truly visionary in its outlook (FOC3: 60–3). Associated with the Bauhaus were many twentieth-century masters, including Mies van der Rohe, Walter Gropius, George Grosz, Ludwig Hilberseimer, Paul Klee, László Moholy-Nagy, Joseph Albers and Wassily Kandinsky. Although the Bauhaus could be called an 'art school', like many others across the planet, what made it so different? Why, across the whole of the twentieth century, does the Bauhaus stand out as completely unique, an institution head and shoulders above all the others?

The answer to this lies in our quest for heterologies. Despite the fact that the Bauhaus still represents the holy grail for many architects and urban designers, as the wellspring of modernism in design, the paradox is that few would embrace its shifting orientation to communism, Marxism, socialism and Soviet ideology in general, political perspectives that cannot easily be dismissed as formative in its success. In addition, a significant stimulus for the establishment of the Bauhaus lay in the work of the Englishman William Morris, also a socialist. The first Bauhaus director, Walter Gropius, actually supported Bolshevism, although he later had to temper his politics. The second director, Hannes Meyer, was a declared communist, and Mies van der Rohe, the third director, did his best to appear apolitical. Prior to his appointment as the founding director of the Bauhaus, Gropius had also belonged to an expressionist revolutionary alliance called the *Novembergruppe*, all of whom were on the far left of the political spectrum, an alliance that included the playwright Bertold Brecht, the composer Alban Berg and others.

It is therefore not surprising that Soviet ideology also dominated, one where constructivism in particular permeated all of the arts indiscriminately. Constructivism was the socially sanctioned art form of the Soviets at that time, and its philosophical orientation of integrating art and society had a huge influence on the collectivist ideology of the Bauhaus by artists such as Malevitch, El Lissitsky and Tatlin. After 1925, the focus on craft-based learning shifted radically to embrace the technologies of industrialism. After Oskar Schlemmer's manifesto for the first Bauhaus exhibition stated that the Bauhaus mandate was to build the 'Cathedral of Socialism', the work was pulped before it could be released, and, as Conrads wryly remarks, 'Several complete copies reached the public and brought the Bauhaus *under suspicion* of being an institution that dabbled in politics' (Conrads 1970: 69; my italics).

The Bauhaus was caught up in a pivotal period in history, where the movement from craft (based primarily in wood and stone) to mass production (using new, manufactured materials) was both unexpected and imminent. The confusion is clearly demonstrated in the various manifestos written by its members and directors. In 1919, Gropius was saying, 'Architects, sculptors, painters, we all must return to crafts! For art is not a profession ... let us then create a new guild of craftsmen without the class distinctions that raise an arrogant barrier between craftsman and artist!' (Conrads 1964: 49). Only five years later, in 1924, Mies van der Rohe stated, in a manifesto on industrialised building in regard to new trends in architecture, that:

> This will lead to the total destruction of the building trade in the form in which it has existed up till now; but whoever regrets that the house of the future can no longer be constructed by building craftsmen should bear in mind that the motor car is no longer built by the wheelwright.
>
> (Conrads 1970: 82)

Although there was no single Bauhaus method or philosophy, it is clear that, in the generation of commodities, paintings, sculpture, tapestry, architecture, urban design and planning projects etc., many of which remain masterpieces today, heterologies dominated. Its original focus on a medieval approach to teaching rapidly adjusted to the realities of socialised mass production. In order to grapple with this and other phenomena, thinking about thinking was central to its entire existence, and since that time the Bauhaus *Weltanschauung* has never been seriously challenged by any other school of art or architecture in terms of its accomplishments. The Bauhaus ethos was one saturated with political ideologies, with concepts and methods drawn from psychoanalysis, literature and social theory. Combined with openness to all forms of new knowledge, revolutionary activity and social change, its creative brilliance was guaranteed. This overall ethos is one that urban design programmes across academe could well resurrect today.

Chicago

In strictly urban theory, the Chicago School of Sociology was arguably the most significant institution of its kind in the twentieth century (FOC3: 58–60). It was also important as it developed a variety of models of urban growth propagated in the concentric theory (Burgess 1925; Figures 3.1 and 3.2), the sector theory (Hoyt 1933, 1939; Figures 3.3 and 3.4) and the multiple-nuclei theory of Harris and Ullman (1945). Most important to urban design was the biotic concept of community, retranslated in physical terms as neighbourhood, *quartier*, *barrio* and other terms. Later urban theory was to demonstrate the wholesale deficiency of using models such as these, Los Angeles being a serious case in point. Founded by Park and his student Louis Wirth, the school produced many significant practitioners and dominated urban theory for over thirty years. Park's original influences were those of philosophers John Dewey and George Simmel, whom he met during the course of his doctoral studies at the University of Berlin. His method of studying urban life at that time was 'using the same ethnographic models used by anthropologists to study the native Americans' (Lin and Mele 2005: 65). Recently, Michael Dear (2002) denoted Chicago and Los Angeles as the archetypes of the American city in the twentieth century. Both have national universities, internationally significant scholars and, in the urban realm, serious intellectual debate around the problems of urban growth and development. Dear's comparison is enlightening and will be referred to both here and below in the context of the Los Angeles School.

The Chicago and Los Angeles Schools represent methods of explaining urban growth and form and were based in cities that are wholly divergent in their development. It is not unsurprising, therefore, that the physical development of these cities was paralleled by the intellectual engagement that was necessary to comprehend them. The driving force behind the Chicago School was Robert Park, whose method was rooted in the systematic classification and examination of social phenomena and their interaction. His original stimulus, derived at least in part from the evolutionary naturalist John Dewey, was the concept of social

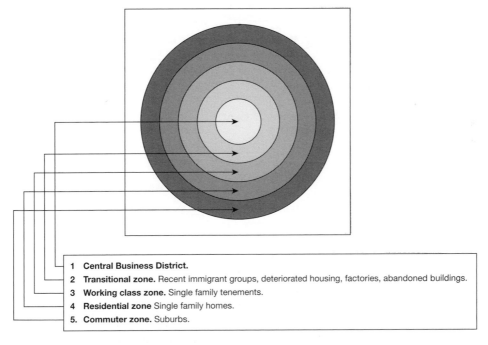

Figure 3.1 Burgess's concentric zone model of urban growth, 1925
Source: Redrawn from Burgess's original drawing by the author

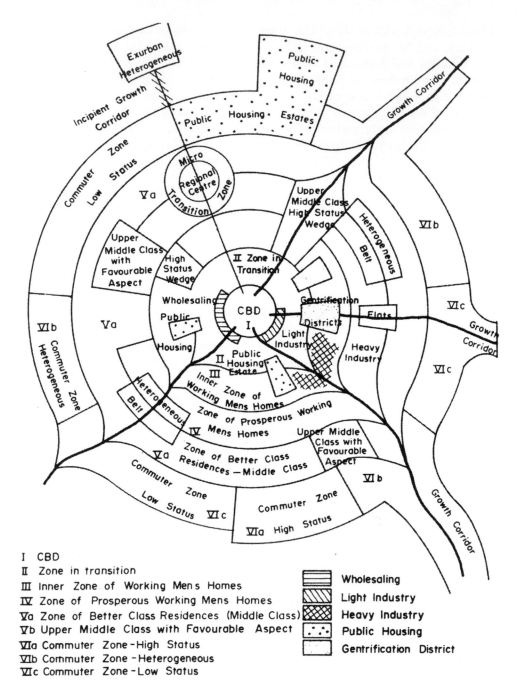

I   CBD
II   Zone in transition
III Inner Zone of Working Mens Homes
IV   Zone of Prosperous Working Mens Homes
Va   Zone of Better Class Residences (Middle Class)
Vb   Upper Middle Class with Favourable Aspect
VIa Commuter Zone – High Status
VIb Commuter Zone – Heterogeneous
VIc Commuter Zone – Low Status

Wholesaling
Light Industry
Heavy Industry
Public Housing
Gentrification District

Figure 3.2 Burgess's concentric theory of urban growth applied to Sydney and Melbourne

Source: I. Burnley, *The Australian Urban System*. Longman: Melbourne, 1980, p. 169, Fig. 1.2

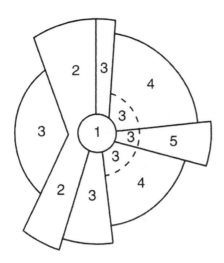

1   CBD

2   Wholesale, light manufacturing

3   Low-class residential

4   Medium-class residential

5   High-class residential

Figure 3.3 Hoyt's sector theory of urban growth

Source: M. Pacione, *Urban Geography: A Global Perspective.* London: Routledge, 2009, p. 142, Fig. 7.3

Darwinism, which then drove the Chicago School for decades, where the biotic order and evolutionary principles noted by Darwin were applied indiscriminately to human populations.

The characteristic properties of biotic organisation represented the basic model for Park and his followers to study urban life – habitat, territoriality, competition, conflict, symbiosis, accommodation and assimilation, and a basic model of community derived from the resultant complexity among and between their various associated forms. In addition, types of relation could be similarly characterised as predatory (harmful to the other), commensalitic (preying without harm) or symbiotic (mutual support). Park also used two other fundamental principles of dominance and succession to denote the development of the biotic process, on which basis he justified such phenomena as urban inequalities and the free operation of market principles. Having borrowed its key methodological framework from Darwin, the Chicago School has been criticised for its role as a life-support system for methodologies without any significant theory of its own. Research for its own sake dominated, and the development of any emergent social theory beyond its Darwinian origins was little to non-existent, dependent as it was on spatial models whose influence extended far beyond their expiry date.

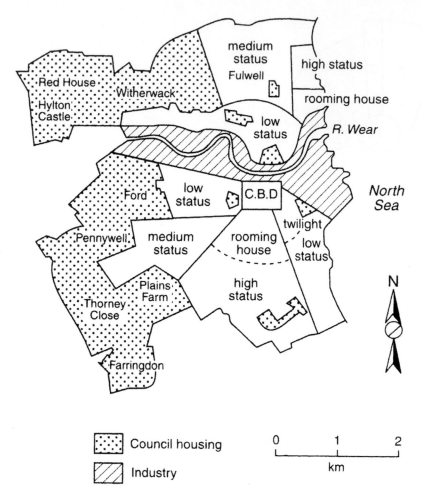

Figure 3.4 Hoyt's sector theory of urban growth and its application to Sunderland

Source: M. Pacione, *Urban Geography: A Global Perspective*. London: Routledge, 2009, p. 142, Fig. 7.3

In addition to Darwin, Park was informed by other evolutionists, such as Ernst Haeckel and Julian Huxley. He therefore drew heavily on the idea that the processes existing in biotic communities generated spatial systems that were analogous to those of humans and could therefore be similarly researched. The concept of the community therefore became a centrepiece of Park's effort to give form to human action, despite the fact that he recognised the part played in human social life of a moral and political order that did not exist in nature. This created a host of problems that were never resolved, resulting in the demise of the Chicago School:

The tension between human ecology as an approach within urban sociology and human ecology as a distinct and basic discipline within the social sciences runs throughout the work of the Chicago School. It is basically a tension between defining the perspective in terms of a concrete, physical, visible object of study, – the community – and defining it in terms of a theoretically specific problem – the adaptation of human populations to their environment. Whenever Park addressed himself to such methodological questions (which was not very often) he adopted as Wirth suggests, the latter position, arguing that a science was defined by the theoretical object it posed rather than the concrete object it studied.

(Saunders 1986: 53)

The same tension has existed until today, with concepts of 'community' emanating from the Chicago School deployed within urban design and planning projects as the fundamental socio-spatial unit, but devoid of the credibility that Darwin instilled. The concept of community, while pervasive, has never resolved the relationship between social and spatial forms, despite the massive amount of research that has been undertaken – for example, in the idea of *The Human Community* of C.A. Doxiadis – for well nigh thirty or so years from the late 1960s, with traces echoing into the present (FOC9: 208–11).

Paris

In 1968, not only was Paris a vortex for social change, it was also a locus of intellectual activity in urban studies and regional development, producing major scholars such as Henri Lefebvre, Alain Touraine, Manuel Castells, Alain Lipietz, Michel Crozier and Fernando Cardozo, most of whom worked together at the University of Nanterre in the late 1960s and early 1970s. But, without doubt, it was Lefebvre and his student Manuel Castells who between them revolutionised urban studies from the 1970s onwards, using methods radically informed and therefore radically different from the emasculated methodologies of human ecology. Lefebvre was 90 years old when he died in 1991. He lived through two world wars, had a Jesuit Catholic upbringing and had fought in the French resistance against the Germans and the Vichy government. Politically, he was both a Marxist and a Communist Party member, until he was expelled in 1958 (probably owing to his critique of Stalinism). Lefebvre was heavily influenced by Hegel's philosophy and wrote more than three hundred articles and sixty books, although few of these have been translated into English (Merrifield 2002: 62). As a Hegelian, he came into direct contact with phenomenology in Hegel's *Phenomenology of Spirit* (1977), although phenomenology does not appear to have substantially affected his own major works. He studied at the Sorbonne in 1920 and mixed with intellectuals and painters of Dada, surrealism and the situationist movement.

Lefebvre was pivotal in transporting the theoretical study of capitalist development into the realm of space, the landmarks being his books *The Survival of Capitalism* (1976) and *The Production of Space* (1991 (orig. 1974)). The latter work is arguably the most popular with urbanists, architects, designers etc., despite the fact that his basic focus is on the social production of space within capitalism. He admits himself that, although this may appear tautological,

> Many people will find it hard to endorse the notion that space has taken on, within the present mode of production, within society as it actually is, a sort of reality of its own, a reality distinct from, yet much like those assumed in the same global process by commodities, money and capital.
>
> (Lefebvre 1991 (orig. 1974): 26)

Halfway through *The Production of Space*, Lefebvre switches from social production to spatial architectonics. Here, his method of examining space shifted in concert with the idea of space as a concrete reality. The difference between space and power is then contained within the concept of 'a disjointed unity'. While recognising the difference between grids of spatial practices from the micro level of architecture to the macro level of urban and regional planning, he nonetheless cautions that, 'grids of this kind are still confined to the classification of fragments in space, whereas authentic knowledge of space must address the question of its production' (1991 (orig. 1974): 388).

While there would seem to be no disagreement on this point from his former student, Manuel Castells, in his own seminal work, *The Urban Question* (1977), he attacked Lefebvre's work during the 1960s and, despite Lefebvre being his thesis supervisor, has stated publicly that:

> Touraine, a historian by training, was aiming to found a new school of sociological theory, and has taught me everything I know, in a fundamental sense. Touraine became, and he remains, my intellectual father. My entire intellectual life, my career and my life were shaped and protected by Touraine. Without him I could never have survived the repression of French academia.
>
> (Ince 2003: 12)

From Lefebvre, Touraine, Nicos Poulantzas and the French philosopher Louis Althusser, Castells' brilliance surfaced in *The Urban Question*, published in France in 1972, which set the intellectual bedrock of the New Urban sociology. A few years later, he acknowledged the intellectual debt he owed to Touraine by publishing *The City and the Grassroots* (1983), an extensive study of urban social movements that advanced Touraine's work into a new threshold for urban studies.

Los Angeles

From the demise of the Chicago School between 1950 and 1980, urban theory in the United States did not coalesce in any major centre of population, and the Chicago School remained the most successful influence in the twentieth century.

Prior to 1980, Los Angeles had been seen largely as a deviant, a city that had somehow avoided the normal growth of cities such as those proposed in the Chicago School models (Conzen and Greene 2008). But, during the 1980s, a group of scholars began to cluster round the problematic of a new kind of city that would come to be seen as paradigmatic of urbanisation at the outset of the twenty-first century (Scott and Soja 1986). That city was Los Angeles, where an entirely new form of urbanisation was evolving (Garreau 1991, Dear and Flusty 1998, Soja 2000). This took the form of a multi-nucleated metropolitan region, altogether different from the model proposed by Harris and Ullman, one where the historical process of the city centre dictating the centrifugal nature of urban growth was reversed (Gottdiener and Klephardt 1991).

Los Angeles, however, was entirely different to Chicago, mostly ignored as a decentralised, sprawling and chaotic no-place that was so physically and politically disorganised it was largely viewed as a black hole held together by freeways. The neat little models of the Chicago School, with their discernible and unified growth rings, or predictably neat zones of activity aligned in sectors along major transport routes, clearly had little relevance here. Over the last thirty years, Los Angeles has grown into a vast metropolis of some eighteen million persons. If we include adjacent communities, it is now the largest port in the United States, adding some 4,000 persons per week to its population:

> By 2020, according to estimates, the region will add six million more people – as some scholars put it, another two or three Chicagos. The great question is: how will the region accommodate those new multitudes in an area that is environmentally delicate, socially unstable, economically unpredictable, and politically fragmented? In a sense, Mr. Dear and his colleagues are trying to exorcise a social-science phantom: the Chicago School of urban scholarship, which dominated urban studies for most of the 20th century still influences thinking about the nature of cities.
>
> (Miller 2000: 15)

The demise of the Chicago School, a burgeoning awareness that something traumatic was happening in Los Angeles, and the congregation of serious intellectual scholarship all contributed to the concept of the Los Angeles School (Cenzatti 1993, Dear 2002, Molotch 2002). What exactly constitutes a school, as we have seen, is a difficult phenomenon to define – whether it is based upon shared physical or mental space, for example, can result in completely different concepts as to what a school is, the methods that distinguish it, and how it is supposed to operate.

Dear (2003) suggests that the first three criteria below are necessary aspects of a school, and that 4–7 are secondary, but nonetheless significant:

1   members are engaged on a common project (however defined);
2   members are geographically proximate (however defined);
3   members are self-consciously collaborative (to whatever extent);
4   it is externally recognised (at whatever threshold);

5   there exists broad agreement on the programme of research;
6   adherents voluntarily self-identify with the school and its research
     programme; and
7   there exist organisational foci for the school's endeavours (such as a learned
     journal, meetings or a book series).

Dear maintains that Los Angeles exhibits these traits and traces the origins of the Los Angeles School to a special issue of the journal *Society and Space* in 1986. It was devoted solely to commentary on Los Angeles and referred to it as the capital of the twentieth century and paradigmatic of development in other American cities, such as Houston, Miami and Phoenix, as well as trends at a global level (Soja 1986, Dear 2002, Portes and Stepick 1993). Other major works followed in quick succession, such as *Technopolis: High Technology Industry and Regional Development in Southern California* (Scott 1993); *City of Quartz* (Davis 1990); *Thirdspace: Journeys to Los Angeles and Other Real-and-Imagined Places* (Soja 1996); *Los Angeles: Globalisation, Urbanisation and Social Struggles* (Keil 1998); *The Postmodern Urban Condition* (Dear 2000); and *From Chicago to L.A.* (Dear and Dishman 2002). A great many more titles could be added to these, but the implication is that the same kind of phenomena that happened in Chicago in 1930, namely the coincidence of paradigmatic urban growth with significant research into its origins, had shifted to California by 1980, and had become seriously entrenched by the commencement of the third millennium. The Los Angeles School discussed here is primarily constituted in the field of urban geography, with a few wayward characters such as Mike Davis added on. But, in addition, and supported by it, there is also the Los Angeles School of Architecture, where historian Charles Jencks played a major role, with his book about Los Angeles, *Heteropolis: Los Angeles, the Riots, and the Strange Beauty of Heteroarchitecture* (Jencks 1993). Overall, the text reinforces the position of the Los Angeles School, deploying postmodern discourse in relation to urban development and its consequences for urban form.

    While it is impossible to sum up the diverse contributions of a school under a single research method or other umbrella, Dear notes that one of the most important features of the Los Angeles School hinges round the idea of restructuring [space] at all levels, from the neighbourhood level to the global. This is also complemented by, and to a certain extent is the outgrowth of, a left-of-centre political agenda. He quotes Mike Davis, who describes the participants as 'a new wave of Marxist geographers or, as one of my friends put it, political economists with their space suits on' and asks 'Are we the LA School as the Chicago School was the Chicago School, or as the Frankfurt School was the Frankfurt School?' (Dear 2003: 19). We can also fairly say that the guiding epistemologies deal with spatial restructuring in three major regions of scale, agglomeration and identity, and the methods used to study problems reflected these foci. Dear notes that the phenomena observed by the Chicago School were of an entirely different order to those of Los Angeles in the twenty-first century and suggests that the key differences are as follows:

- Traditional concepts of urban form imagine the city organized around a central core; in a revised theory, the urban peripheries are organising what remains of the centre.
- A global, corporate-dominated connectivity is balancing, even offsetting, individual-centred agency in urban processes.
- A linear, evolutionist urban paradigm has been usurped by a nonlinear, chaotic process that includes pathological forms such as common-interest developments (CIDs) and life-threatening environmental degradation (e.g. global warming).

(Dear 2003: 23)

While the Los Angeles School is united under the concept of restructuring, which Dear describes as a *proto-postmodern process*, characteristic of the Los Angeles School's approach, as method, it also has a penchant for inventing new terms to describe new phenomena, which vary from one discourse to another, depending on the viewpoint. Although this might be interpreted as an eccentricity of its members, it seems perfectly reasonable, given that the old vocabularies do not adequately address emergent urban forms. Hence, Dear's *ethnoburbs*, Garreau's *edge cities*, Scott's *technopoles*, Davis's *city of quartz*, Jencks's *heteropolis*, with its population of *heterophiliacs*, and Wolch's *zoopolis*; but Soja gets the prize with his *prototopos*, *mesocosm*, *exopolis*, *flexcities*, *carceral cities* and *simcities*, all tied together within the *splintered labyrinths* of Los Angeles and Orange County. As Miller states in the introduction to his article, 'Los Angeles scholars use their region and their ideas to end the dominance of the Chicago School' (Miller 2000). Although the invention of these terms might appear as sheer exhibitionism, on a closer examination, all have singular relevance in context, with major implications for designing cities. To date, the Los Angeles School has been a remarkably successful project.

Despite its bland exterior compared with the sumptuous exhibitionism of Vienna in 1900, Los Angeles exhibits a similarly massive range of activity in art and culture, along with the craft skills and technologies that support them. Added to this is the enormous diversity in ethnicity and difference, leading Jencks to describe Los Angelinos as heterophiliacs – a population addicted to the differences that their city offers them. After considering the methodological implications of different schools of urban thought evolving from the history of the twentieth century, we now look at those predominant philosophies that are heterological to the overall comprehension of urban form and design.

Phenomenology

The message of Norberg-Schulz not only represents a synthesis of these opposed aims [the contrast between internationalism and rootedness] but also a prototype for a methodological approach as opposed to a systematic one.

(Paolo Portoghesi)

The above statement in the foreword to Christian Norberg-Schulz's *Architecture meaning and place* refers to the heterology that informed Norberg-Schulz in most of his work, namely phenomenology. Norberg-Schulz constructs his method from three major intellectual strands, also noted by Portoghesi, namely the psychological, the existential and the traditional (Norberg-Schulz 1965, 1971, 1979, 1985, 1988). Along with the likes of Joseph Rykwert and Siegfred Gideon, Norberg-Schulz was one of the most noted architectural historians of the twentieth century. During his life he wrote a dozen books, many having landmark status. Norberg-Schulz was a Norwegian architect and the first to introduce the phenomenology of Martin Heidegger and Maurice Merleau-Ponty to the world of architecture, particularly the writing of the former on space and dwelling (see Norberg-Schulz's own text, *The Concept of Dwelling*, 1985). In his earlier work, he was sympathetic to a semiotic approach (preferring the Pierceian terminology, *semiology*) – which he quickly abandoned for phenomenology and existentialism. He was also an admirer of Kevin Lynch, in particular his analysis of urban phenomena in his *Image of the City* (1960). Norberg-Schulz pays homage to phenomenology in the introduction to most of his books, with references throughout each work. Which of these has primacy is a matter for debate, but his opus magnum is arguably *Genius loci*, which he subtitles *Towards a Phenomenology of Architecture* (1979). As I have already covered the theoretical base of phenomenology (FOC3: 69–72, DC: 8), I will dwell only briefly on the problem of definition and concentrate on how heterology turns into methodology in Norberg-Schulz's *oeuvre*.

The world of phenomenology begins with Descartes' famous phrase 'I think therefore I am'. But beyond that, the word *phenomenology* is agonisingly elusive in definition, and one must traverse offerings that range from the disarmingly simple to the utterly incomprehensible. It contrasts phenomenon meaning *appearance*, which in the philosophy of Immanuel Kant (1724–1894) referred to how something appears in the subject's consciousness, in contradistinction to *noumenon*, the thing-in-itself (Husserl 1969, Lyotard 1991). Added to this are two major divisions of hermeneutic phenomenology (Heidegger) and existential phenomenology (Sartre 1992, Merleau-Ponty 1962), which together help to reinforce the incomprehensible end of the spectrum, and at least one scholar has had the existential experience of being 'hopelessly lost in a sea of unfamiliar discourse, in a vast and deep ocean of knowledge' (Latham 2001: 43). More simple is the idea that, 'the central theme of Heidegger's work is that in coming to understand the nature of phenomena we must attend to the relation *between* things and ourselves' (Barnacle 2001: 10). In other words, the relational aspect of phenomena is all-important. I will revisit this idea later in the case of Norberg-Schulz's epistemology. In the case of existential phenomenology, we have the methodological objective that:

> the existentialist aim is to characterise the ordinary experience of human
> beings living in the world . . . In order to reveal the character of the subject
> and the meaning of the world, phenomenology should begin by describing

ordinary human activities in the world, and not thoughts, cognitions, or perceptions of that world, nor reflections upon ordinary activities.

(Hammond *et al.* 1991: 97)

Overall, the best way to comprehend phenomenology is through discourse and the working through of ideas in practice. In the case of existentialism, the novel is by far the best method of entering the world of the existentialist, for example in Sartre's novel *Nausea* (1949), or Albert Camus' *The Rebel* (2000), *The Plague* (1965), or *The Fall* (2006). Norberg-Schulz's offerings are unique in the design disciplines, and *Genius Loci*, meaning 'the spirit of the place', provides a unique opportunity to see how the theory of phenomenology is applied in practice. One feature that characterises his writing method is his need to configure individual words on every page, as if to suggest that their meanings are either confused, hidden or in some manner arcane. This style traverses the entire book, reinforcing the idea that words are wholly inadequate in themselves to describe the nature of architecture and space, but also to suggest that meanings are fundamentally inaccessible to us, except in the realm of the senses. On one page, taken at random, thirty-two words are bracketed in this manner, including 'thing', 'things', 'nature', 'uses', 'cosmic order', 'mentalities', 'time', 'character', 'data', 'light', 'climate', 'tends', 'disposes', 'friendship' and 'force', and these in only one column out of three, a habit that makes the process meaningless (Norberg-Schulz 1979: 168).

His position on architecture reveals quite clearly his phenomenological bent: 'That there are not different kinds of architecture, but only different situations which require different solutions in order to satisfy mans physical and psychic needs' (Norberg-Schulz 1979: 5). This position basically turns the architect's traditional obsession with style and appearance on its head, abandoning these in favour of the individual's experiences in the environments he/she inhabits. He comments himself that, in his prior works, he had attempted to analyse art and architecture using the scientific method, in accordance with the rules of natural science, but considers the concept of existential space more suited to person–environment relationships (DC8: 116).

Norberg-Schulz uses several sets of concepts whereby he defines his use of phenomenology as praxis and as a return to 'things' as opposed to 'abstractions and mental constructions' (Norberg-Schulz 1979: 7). In *Genius Loci*, he first introduces his application of phenomenology in terms of four components – place, structure, spirit and identity, where it is not architecture itself that is the focus, but how we experience it and how we may both construct and analyse this experience. Architecture is secondary to existence. He defines each carefully; for example, 'a place is a qualitative total phenomenon that we cannot reduce to any of its properties such as spatial relationships without losing its concrete nature out of sight' (Norberg-Schulz 1979: 12). Structure, on the other hand, is defined as landscape and settlement, to be analysed through the use of his definition of space as well as character or atmosphere. Landscape has four typologies – romantic, cosmic, classical and complex. By spirit, he refers to the title of the book and the Roman concept of *Genius loci*, using Louis Khan's idea that it is not what a place *is* that is important, but *what it wants to be*. He then uses the same method to analyse and distinguish between natural places and man-made places, moving into three urban settings – Prague, Khartoum and Rome – as concrete examples that inform his two concluding chapters on 'place as meaning' and 'place as contemporary urbanism'.

Having introduced the subject briefly in *Genius Loci* (Norberg-Schulz 1979: 22–3), a few years later, in *The Concept of Dwelling* (1985), his method of scrutinising and elaborating on meanings is applied to the word *dwell*. The term has become central to his work – where his definition of 'dwell' constitutes an existential foothold synonymous with the word dwelling, which he denotes to be the purpose of architecture. Such insistence on the definition of terms (as far as this is possible) and the search for deeper meanings in language is therefore a central pillar of his methodology. For Norberg-Schulz,

> to dwell implies the establishment of a meaningful relationship between man and a given environment . . . and that this relationship consists in an act of identification, that is in a sense of belonging to a certain place. Man, thus, finds himself when he *settles* and his being-in-the-world is therefore determined.
>
> (1985: 80)

He enunciates four modes of architecture, namely dwelling (as existence), the settlement or natural dwelling, urban space or collective dwelling, and institution or public dwelling. These main chords of his adopted methodology then become the first four chapters of the book. Dwelling has two aspects, identification and orientation. Modes of dwelling are then studied in 'what we may call the three interdependent constituents of the language of architecture, morphology, topology and typology' (Norberg-Schulz 1985: 26). Chapters 5 and 6 are called 'House' and 'Language', respectively. The simplicity of these structures, however, belies the intensity of the text, but there is no doubt that to read Norberg-Schulz is a much easier process of understanding the phenomenological method than to read those masters whose philosophy he follows – and he concludes in *Genius Loci* that, 'Today man is educated in pseudo-analytic thinking and his knowledge consists of so-called "facts". His life however is becoming meaningless, and ever more he understands that his "merits" do not count if he is not able to "dwell poetically"' (Norberg-Schulz 1985: 202).

Semiotics

The structures and vocabulary of language are enduringly deployed in analogy with architectural and urban space, and the term 'syntax' is a favourite form of expression used with regard to the relationship between parts of the built environment. Hence, the term 'the language of architecture' is commonplace.

Although the idea of syntax to denote physical spatial configurations and arrangements is useful, as a methodology, it goes no further than the material relationships between objects. It simply means that, in architecture and urban design, certain generic relationships between spatial elements can be identified, and even these are developmentally and culturally specific. Hillier and Leaman's *Space Syntax* (1976), Alexander's *Pattern Language* (1977) and his classic, 'A city is not a tree' (1973), are examples of this kind of thinking. If we want to discover meanings as opposed to relationships, we must use a different branch of language, namely semiotics.

Mark Gottdiener's work is emblematic of the use of semiotics in analysing urban form. His first major book was called *Planned Sprawl: Public and Private Interests in Suburbia* (1977), followed by *The Social Production of Urban Space* (1985). The first focussed on regional development, with the second summarising the main movements in urban theory. In neither of these books was semiotics mentioned, but the following year he produced an edited collection with Lagopoulos called *The City and the Sign: An Introduction to Urban Semiotics* (1986). One of his chapters in that book, *Recapturing the Centre: A Semiotic Analysis of the Shopping Mall*, is reproduced in DC8: 128. At that point, postmodernism was a relatively new phenomenon, arguably only fourteen years old if we accept Jencks's point of origin as 3.32 p.m. on 15 July 1972. Since that time, and largely as a result of post-structuralist thinking, semiotics and investigation into the construction and deconstruction of urban meaning have played a huge role in the attempt to escape from the sterility of modernist architecture. Twenty years ago, reference to semiotics in urban studies was extremely sparse, and his text added a new dimension to the development of progressive theory, particularly in urban design. In 1994, Gottdiener contributed to the debate on *The New Urban Sociology* with another definitive text, which summed up the developmental history of a new discipline originating with Lefebvre. In 1995, his *Postmodern Semiotics* was a text that was to set a benchmark in the field, followed a few years later with one that applied the theory to the urban landscape – *The Theming of America: Dreams, Visions and Commercial Spaces* (1997). Two years later, he published a book called *Las Vegas: The Social Production of the All-American City* (Gottdiener *et al.* 1999). As I have covered the theory in FOC3: 65–9, below I will refer to Gottdiener (1986, 1995) to illustrate the method of semiotics as heterological for the practice of urban design.

Semiotics allows us to understand the concept of meaning, how it arises, how it undergoes change and how it is enhanced or eradicated. In addition, one does not have to consciously deploy semiotic theory in order to use it, in the same manner that one does not have to understand ideology to act ideologically, given that we all behave in accordance with our lived experience and social indoctrination. For example, we can see from the discussion of Norberg-Schulz (above) that much of the time he is acting in accordance with a semiotic methodology, using, for example, the relations between signifiers and signifieds to get at the root of meanings in architecture. Nonetheless, we can argue fairly convincingly that much of his search for meanings is *semantic* rather than semiotic – his bracketing of hundreds of words denotes this.

In FOC5: 118–22, I gave an example of my own experience in Beirut and how the meanings attached to Martyr's Square had evolved over time. This process involved not only a physical modification of the built environment, but also how people now see the square based upon their own experience, particularly of civil war – Islamic or Christian, perpetrator or victim, child or grandparent, banker or investor. To each and every one, the experience of human memory and engagement with the past creates boundless associations that in some way remain locked into physical space and its renewal. Semiotics allows us to enter this process so that we can more effectively accommodate the transformation of physical space through design.

Fauque indicates one approach to urban semiotic methodology when he asks:

> If one assumes that the city as a vehicle for significations is a text that speaks to us . . . what are the signifiers which constitute the urban tissue on the level of expression (i.e. in the Hjelmslev model)? What is their nature? Are there any supports for signification, as in the case of consumer objects? From a methodological point of view, how can we hope to locate these signifiers? What is the order of the relations between elements, first on the paradigmatic level, and then on the syntagmatic level?
>
> (Fauque 1986: 139)

He then goes on to enunciate, in some detail, hypotheses and methods for the practice of a semiotic analysis, and Lagopoulos suggests a methodological approach to generate several semiotic urban models that use a Marxian modes of production approach (Lagopoulos 1986: 176–201). This is clearly demonstrated in *The City and the Sign* (Gottdiener 1986). There is no single semiotic method, as there is no single phenomenological approach, which is indeed frustrating for anyone who wishes to extract some formulaic responses from the process. However, in his article on shopping malls, and in reference to the built environment overall, Gottdiener suggests a generic method of semiotic decomposition based on the ubiquitous signs of capitalism and their signification in a world ruled by commodity production (Figure 3.5).

$$\frac{Sd}{Sr} = \frac{\substack{\text{substance} \\ \text{form}}}{\substack{\text{form} \\ \text{substance}}} = \frac{\substack{\text{underlying ideological purpose} \\ \text{design as concept/syntagm}}}{\substack{\text{architectural design/paradigm} \\ \text{material form/object}}} = \frac{\text{content}}{\text{expression}}$$

Figure 3.5 A semiotic decomposition of the built environment

Source: M. Gottdiener and A. Lagopoulos (eds), *The City and the Sign: An Introduction to Urban Semiotics*. New York: Columbia University Press, 1986, p. 294

In *The Theming of America* (1997), Gottdiener analyses a device that is now central to the entire strategy of urban design and urban form within capitalism, one that is enduringly impacted on an annual basis with the deepening of commodity relations and practices. For example, the concept of the theme park used to be a novel idea, but it was dissociated from the overall thrust of merchandising. Today, the theming and branding of buildings, spaces, events and cities are now commonplace. They are variously tied into urban planning policy from the neighbourhood to the nation, and frequently linked to conservation and community strategies. In today's neocorporate supermarket, a barcode, a brand or a theme is vital, preferably all of them at the same time. Gottdiener uses specific themed environments, casinos, restaurants, malls and airports, to demonstrate the methodology of the theming process. These include everything from standardised corporate architecture to the deployment of the decorated shed adorned with symbols as the precursor of the modern restaurant, from Burger King, Wendy's, KFC, MacDonald's, to the Hard Rock Café and countless others (Yakhlef 2004, Sklair 2005, McNeill 2005).

None of this is value-neutral, and the controlled signification of the urban realm as the method of commodity culture is clear to see, whereby the urban mall and other themed environments reduce the citizen to the endgame of capitalist enterprise. Ultimately, the endgame is for everything to become commodified, the perfect expression of a totalising market economy. The traditional role of the city as a place for debate, discourse, politics, free expression and social interaction in the public realm, unburdened by commercial programming, is usurped by the mall. It turns the social space of the traditional city into a totally commodifed space, along with the social relations that go with it. Despite this fact, Gottdiener does not consider that the method of commodity circulation and the semiotics involved need necessarily turn the citizen into a life-support system for processing commodities:

> Each individual user of themed, commercial space has the opportunity to pursue a form of self fulfilment through the creative act of consumption. If these places can be viewed as modes of domination because of their singular emphasis on the realisation of capital, they can also be considered spaces for the exercise of consumer resistance.
>
> (Gottdiener *et al.* 1999: 158)

Let's hope it works.

Political economy

The theoretical foundation for Marxian political economy was extensively covered in FOC3: 72–8, and in this concluding section I will concentrate on its implications for praxis. To do this, we must first recognise that the heterological framework has five major regions of engagement and terminology. First, historical materialism had its roots in three locations, German philosophy (Hegel, Feuerbach and Marx), British political economy (Locke, Hume and

Smith) and French socialism (Voltaire, Rousseau). Second, we have political economy (radical, politics of the left) in opposition to neoclassical economics (bourgeois, politics of the right), although this distinction requires significant refinement. Third, *Marxian* political economy equitably includes the English mill-owner Frederick Engels, who supported Marx both financially and intellectually. Fourth, we have the more recent development of what is generally termed spatial political economy (Castells, Harvey, Scott, Urry, Sayer, Massey and others), which developed specifically to counteract the aspatial concentration on political and economic processes. Fifth and finally, we also have the closely related disciplines of urban sociology and urban geography, which frequently appear homologous with each other. Given this basic set of relationships, any attempt to synthesise generic methods involves a *reductio ad absurdum*. To make this even more apparent, Walton notes that political economy alone has six areas of contribution to urban sociology, namely historical explanation, comparative studies, socio-economic processes, spatial relations, ethnicity and community and political movements (Walton 1993: 301). Given our focus on urban design and planning, I will focus on spatial relations, specifically the general methodological approach to planning as a state apparatus, concentrating on Castells's *The Urban Question*, but including examples from Allen Scott, Michael Dear and others.

Method has to operate within some system of referents, and, in spatial political economy, the basic components of analysis most commonly used include the various forms of capital (industrial, commercial, finance etc.), the chosen political form of the state, the position of labour power and its social reproduction, and the agency known as urban planning (Stillwell 2002). Interactions between these elements at various levels of physical scale and political engagement are circumscribed by methodologies appropriate to the topics under observation (social housing, redevelopment, infrastructure, conservation etc.). One reason why urban planning has been a particular target of spatial political economy is because of its function as mediator between the state and capital in the production and reproduction of labour and space. The state, however, is a chameleon that changes its form and colour, depending on historical circumstance and political intervention in its practices. Omitting liberal perspectives, at least six categories underwrite any methodological analysis of the state and urban planning within it – the state as a parasitic institution, as epiphenomenon, as a factor of cohesion, as an instrument of class rule, as a set of institutions or as a system of political domination (Clark and Dear 1984; Figure 3.6). So any methods used in analysis are first determined by a particular ideological approach to the state apparatus and proceed from there.

The production and reproduction of space are profoundly ideological/political events. Space is not merely an inert substance deployed by designers. Overall, urban planning adjudicates the process as the agent of state interventionism, on behalf of social reproduction, capital accumulation and the circulation of commodities. Therefore, it is centrally involved in the management of a key factor of production, namely land (and, as such, in the generation of land rent, profit and surplus value). It mediates capitalist property relations in regard to land

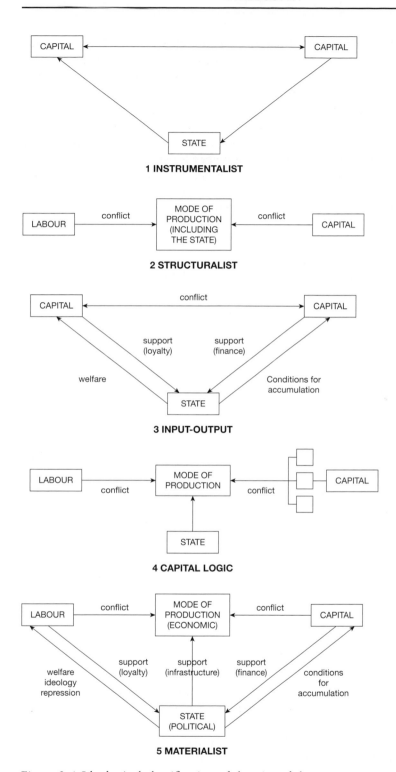

Figure 3.6 Ideological classification of theories of the state

Source: Redrawn by author from M. Dear and A. Scott, *Urbanisation and Urban Planning in Capitalist Societies*. New York: Methuen, 1981, p. 15

development on the basis of the differential locational advantages that lie at the core of speculation and profit. However, we must also recognise the position of the designer in our methodology. Although the concept of architectonic space may be a useful device that allows the creative imagination to flourish, the fact is that all forms of space, designed or otherwise, are socially reproduced within specific forms of capitalist enterprise, at a given historical moment, and within the exacting physical geography of pre-existing built environments. So the ideology of mainstream urban designers, that urban form is the material product of the design imagination, may be reversed. In actuality, the material relations are those of capitalist enterprise, and the built environment is an ephemeral and transient projection of those values. David Harvey puts this perfectly:

> In order to overcome spatial barriers and to annihilate space with time, spatial structures are created that themselves act as barriers to further accumulation . . . The effects of the internal contradictions of capitalism, when projected into the specific context of fixed and immobile investment in the built environment, are thus writ large in the historical geography of the landscape that results.
>
> (Harvey 1985: 25)

Harvey's methodology is therefore to analyse the formation and trans-formation of urban form on the basis that it is a form of capital whose uniqueness comes from its very immobility. Unlike shares, money or goods, it cannot be moved about at will and, while it is temporarily in place, needs a manager in the form of urban planning. In pursuing the latter function, our methodology should then examine the role it plays in regard to crisis management ensuing from the erratic performances of the big casino – the stock market, the associated capitals and their effect on land development. We should also look at how planning intervenes to stabilise the resultant inconsistencies, and analyse how planning mediates civil unrest by adequately providing for the extended reproduction of labour power (Harvey 1985).

One of the key critics of urban planning who has researched and theorised these interventions, particularly in his earlier writings, has been Manuel Castells, and his methodology has been enunciated in great detail in *The Urban Question* (1977) and the *The City and the Grassroots* (1983). Here, the assumption is that in executing its mandate as a state institution, it has become incapacitated as an instrument in the democratic and equitable management of social change. As part of the instrumentality of the state, planning cannot serve the public interest and represent big capital at the same time. As the actions of urban planning are compromised by its connections to the various capitals, i.e. it is a form of class political practice, Castells follows Alain Touraine's dictum that the only true representative of the masses against the requirements of capital are what he calls *urban social movements*. These may be broadly defined as any spontaneous, organised social uprising against what is perceived to be unjust.

A fundamental difference between urban planning and urban social movements is that so-called 'planning problems' tend to be class based. In contrast, urban social movements by their very nature tend to cut across class boundaries.

Hence, urban social movements coalesce around issues such as airport noise, freeway construction, land grabs, ethnic division and countless other problems. On one issue they may unite different social classes and ethnic groups, and they may divide the same groups on another. Touraine suggested three principles for the analysis of urban social movements: the movement's identity, its adversary and its societal goal. In *The Urban Question*, Castells offers in-depth research on urban social movements in Chapter 14, where his methodology is deployed in the analysis, for example, of the challenge to the urban reconquest of Paris – the struggle for rehousing in the *Cité du Peuple*; the urban claims of the Montreal citizens' committees; and the urban struggle and the revolutionary struggle in the Pobladores movement in Chile. Twenty years later, in *The Power of Identity* (1997), he gives more recent examples of how urban social movements have spawned new forms of resistance against the new global order, not all of them particularly constructive, namely Mexico's Zapatistas, the first informational guerrilla movement; the American Militia and the patriot movement in the 1990s; and Aum Shinrikyo what Castells calls 'The Lamas of the Apocalypse' (1997: 97). Inevitably, what this leads us to conclude is that the creation of urban form through the function of urban planning is a profoundly political act, and it is to the political dimension that we will turn in Chapter 4.

Conclusion

In philosophy lies the origin of all explanation. It is as important to urban design as it is to any other discipline. Mainstream urban design denotes only two major influences in the twentieth century: that of contextualism, derived from Sitte, and rationalism, derived from Wagner (see FOC: 179–84). However, as we have seen, the influence of philosophy can be divided, for discussion, into schools that have had a collective influence as well as the singularities of powerful individuals. Hence, I have chosen to expand this somewhat abbreviated influence on urban design to include five other major schools of thought – those of Frankfurt, Weimar and Dessau, Chicago, Paris and Los Angeles, and, in addition, three singularities in the form of semiotics (Saussure), phenomenology (Norberg-Schulz) and Marxian political economy. Although none of these approaches deals directly with urban design as *object*, something that may upset the mainstream, as *philosophies and heterologies* their influence over the field of environmental and urban design has been profound, and it is arguable that the dominating influence has been political economy, clearly demonstrable in the Frankfurt School, the Bauhaus, in Paris and Los Angeles. But, if the mainstream is to remain as the dominant modus operandi in urban design, then a concept of urban design as building design writ large will suffice, along with the heterological implications of rationalism and contextualism. Otherwise, five other heterologies of urban development and three singularities may need to be accommodated into the designer's vocabulary. Hopefully, the consequences will be a more informed urban design praxis, where resistance to the more oppressive functions of capitalist urbanisation remains possible.

4 Politics

Political language . . . is designed to make lies sound truthful and murder respectable, and to give an appearance of solidity to pure wind.

(George Orwell)

Introduction: ideology and capital

In this chapter, I will extend the theoretical dimension explored in *The Form of Cities* by asking 'what is the *method* of politics in regard to urban design?'. As urban designers, 'how do we recognise the political dimension of what we do, and how does it affect us even if we never ask the question?' Part of the answer lies in Gramsci's definition of ideology as a *lived system of values*. In Hitler's Germany, for example, it was easy to be a good fascist without actually 'knowing' what fascism was. Ideologies do not have to be understood to be lived. When it comes to urban politics, few urban designers would see themselves as part of an ideological conflict over ownership of, and access to, space. Henri Lefebvre notes the homology between ideology and politics in the production of space when he says that:

> Social space shows itself to be *politically instrumental* in that it facilitates the control of society . . . [and] underpins the reproduction of production relations and property relations (i.e. ownership of land, of space; hierarchical ordering of locations; organisation of networks as a function of capitalism; class structures, practical requirements); is equivalent practically speaking to a set of institutional and ideological superstructures that are not presumed for what they are (and in this capacity, social space comes complete with symbolisms and systems of meaning – sometimes an overload of meaning); alternatively, it assumes an outward appearance of neutrality, of insignificance, of semiological destitution and emptiness (or absence).
>
> (Lefebvre 1991: 349)

David Harvey states this more succinctly when he states that, 'Cities are built forms created out of the mobilisation, extraction and geographic concentration of the socially designated surplus product' (1973: 238). At the epicentre of this system lies the fundamental principle whereby capital, in its diversity, appropriates the collectively produced surplus and other forms of profit, thereby guaranteeing its rule in perpetuity. Erected on this foundation are two classes, those who own capital and those who own their own labour. Within this system, space is one form of capital and, like other resources, it is commodified and sold like any other good. Space is therefore deeply ideological, as it allows all forms of capital to function and to control the conditions for social reproduction and accumulation. Taken together, the statements of Lefebvre and Harvey get to the heart of the political dimension – it is ideological, it is concerned with space and it is therefore simultaneously deeply symbolic at one level, yet semiologically void at another. So the invisible becomes heterological for the visible. If we want to understand, as designers, the material world in whose creation we participate, we must first understand the reality of the invisible upon whose foundation we erect historically evanescent environments. The ideological system of capitalism has outlasted by far all but a handful of its physical creations.

However, as urban designers, we are also entitled to ask, 'why do we need to know this?'. And, of course, the answer is, 'we don't'. As I have shown, we can operate perfectly as vehicles for ideological practices without understanding what they are. As urban designers, we can continue as servo mechanisms for the invisible hand of the market, yet be blind to its indiscretions. But, in the process, we then choose to perceive space as a semiological vacuum, with all that it entails. Alternatively, we can embrace the dimension of politics/ideology and accept that it envelopes and penetrates everything we do, from the social production of the knowledge that we use to solve problems, to the methods of injecting semiotic content into space and its elements – monuments, buildings, public art, spatial forms, street names and other sedimentations that layer the urban realm. As we have seen from the historical process suggested in *Collage City*, underlying political and ideological frameworks cannot be understood merely by examining these fragments, but only by way of a clear and unambiguous examination of the methods deployed by capitalism (or otherwise socialism, in China and Russia) in regard to the use of social space (Low 2000). Of course, the infusion of politics into the urban fabric is designed, but not by architects. The design methods deployed address the underlying mandates of the system as a whole – ideology and politics, the institutional matrix that legitimates political action and the system of urban planning that underwrites the legitimation process, not least the urban design of its spaces and places.

Below, I will begin with a brief look at *the method of urban politics* within capitalist economies, focussing on the undercurrents that inform our seemingly neutral design concepts and ideas. By this I refer to those ideologies that inform capitalist urbanisation *as a whole*, and the methods used to extract value and surplus value from urban space. I do not take this to mean how political parties are formed, councils elected etc., but the manner in which capital establishes the conditions for its own expansion using the medium of the built environment. In this, we are still dealing with the interactions between the basic building blocks and processes of the capitalist system, namely:

- the operation of various forms of capital (financial, industrial etc.);
- the methods used to exploit the three factors of production in the material formation and transformation of cities (land, labour and capital);
- the basic economic processes required to accomplish this exploitation – production, consumption, circulation, exchange, and the urban symbolic, along with an effective system of urban administration;
- the institutional and ideological system that legitimises and reinforces private appropriation of the means of production (resources, factories, warehousing etc.), as well as the extraction of value from the built environment;
- the semiotic system that informs urban meaning in specific urban forms.

In order to explain these in context, I have chosen to limit my comments here to the hidden workings of capital, leaving concrete manifestations of its operation to the following chapter. Given space constraints, certain subtleties will necessarily be lost. So, for those who wish to pursue the topics further, I would make reference to a few master works in this region (Cohen 1978, Berman 1982, Therborn 1980, Althusser 1984, Balaben 1995).

The urban political agenda

Within the market economies of the capitalist system, land and its improvements, like labour, represent commodities to be bought and sold like any other good. Taken together, they aggregate a large proportion of the gross national product that accrues from land ownership. It is therefore necessary to the extended life of capital that both land and land development should not only be produced, but should also be continually reproduced within the urban system. This process necessitates the ceaseless destruction and modification of the built environment in the interests of capital accumulation from land and its improvements. Also, it refers, not merely to 'adding bits on the edges', but to a continual restructuring of the entire system of land development (for instance, through extension; redevelopment; reclamation; slum clearance; the renegotiation of political and administrative boundaries; the institutionalisation of squatting; the establishment of new towns; and the construction and deconstruction of urban infrastructure; not to mention the reinvention of history through urban conservation). As a general principle, I accept Lefebvre's dictum that space is both a material and ideological construct that emanates from the dynamic relationship between civil society, the state and capital (Poulantzas 1973, Miliband 1973, Frankel 1983). The contradictions that are subsequently generated reflect the collision of human interests emerging from the market allocation of land on the one hand and its political allocation on the other. Planning *qua* state intervention attempts to mediate in the ensuing conflicts, where the structural logic of the system of capitals does not permit an equitable distribution of the surplus product, nor the just resolution of class conflicts. As a result, 'the hardest crusts always fall to the toothless'.

Social capital may be divided into three types, each with a particular function within the overall system of capitals (Lamarche 1976). First, industrial capital controls the process of production and the creation of surplus value. Then, commercial capital controls the circulation of commodity capital. Finally, financial capital controls the circulation of money capital. Lamarche argues for the existence of an additional, specialised capital – *property capital* – the primary purpose of which is to plan space with the purpose of reducing the indirect costs of capitalist production. One may also argue that the reduction of the number of capitals involved to four oversimplifies reality. In effect, there are as many capitals as there are enterprises, each with its own particular dynamic and mode of operation. In the breakdown of social capital into a number of specialised capitals, property capital is charged both with the planning of land and the improvements that take place upon it and is therefore central to the urban design process. The function of the various actors within public and private enterprise has been clearly stated in Harloe *et al.* (1974) and Short (1982). Although it is tempting to assume that property capital accrues from profits derived from surplus value extracted through the construction process, the main source of profit actually emerges from the letting of floor space over the life of the building. Therefore, the real revenue to the developer is represented, not by the difference between construction cost and the buying price of a particular building complex (or indeed between purchase price and resale price), so much as the difference between the buying price and rent on floor space.

The urban morphology that results reflects the way in which fixed capital is signified in physical structures and the delineation of urban space. Spatial advantage and amenity reflect land prices and building density and to a large extent, the functional appearance of most buildings, as well as their physical condition. We are all familiar with what 'upmarket' and 'downmarket' mean. So, at its most basic, capital is reflected semiotically in the physical manifestation of wealth and poverty in built form, and its methods are reflected in what Marx called *the transmuted forms of surplus value* – monopoly and differential rent from floor space, interest on loans and profit from capital investment. Then, there are the two fundamentals – ground rent from land and surplus value from the labour process. If we divide the working day into two parts, *necessary* labour refers to that part of the working day during which the worker covers the cost of his/her own wage, i.e. what is consumed. The rest of the day, the worker is involved in surplus labour purely for the benefit of capital, i.e. when the value produced by labour exceeds what he/she consumes. The value of this *surplus* labour (surplus value) is privately appropriated as one of the most fundamental processes of the capitalist system.

Given these considerations, if we consider the basic factors of production, namely land, labour and capital, it is axiomatic that the built environment is collectively reproduced, but, in the main, it is privately appropriated. Also, the benefits of the environment so manufactured are extracted in various forms from the occupation of land and property. Much of this is based upon the differential locational advantages produced by the geographic distribution of built forms and structures. The only exception to this rule is in the concept of the public domain, and even then the use values of this environment that accrue to labour are not sacrosanct, and are increasingly open to privatisation. Hence, in building the city, a vast amount of surplus value is created through the labour process within the building industry, and the reproduction of surplus value from this activity is a product of the continual transformation of physical space. In the environment so generated, differential rent from floor space is obviously a major form of income, but this must be understood via the concept of ground rent. The 'transmuted' forms of surplus value are exactly that, and so it is the latter upon which I wish to elaborate as the point of origin of the entire system of speculation, as 'Rent is the economic form of class relations to the land. As a result, rent is a property not of the land, although it may be affected by its varying qualities and availability, but of social relations' (Bottomore 1983: 273).

Land rent

The concept of 'rent' occupies a critical position in relation to land use, and high-rise development in particular, as it provides the connection between political economy, spatial location and urban form. Rent may be defined as a payment made to landowners for the privilege of occupying and using land. It represents interest paid either on the consumption fund (money spent on social reproduction) or on fixed capital investment. Whereas neoclassical theory simply considers land, labour and capital as the basic factors of production, making no qualitative judgements about them, Marx was careful to distinguish between them and between each element and its effects. 'Capital-profit (profit of enterprise, plus interest), land – ground rent, labour-wages. This is the trinity formula which contains all of the secrets of the production process' (Marx 1959: 814). These mandates underwrite the class system – that a worker will always produce more than he/she consumes, and this excess is privately expropriated and reinvested in order to reproduce more capital.

Marx distinguishes between three forms of rent, which represent the main pathways or methods through which profit may be expropriated from land development, namely monopoly rent, absolute rent and differential rent. All of these take place within the secondary cycle of capital and are responsible for creating particular types of urban form, one of the most important being high-density development, as it maximises the owner's interest and reflects land prices at central locations. *Monopoly* rent accrues to landowners insofar as they can charge a monopoly price for some unique or special feature that the land may possess. Harvey is of the opinion that monopoly rents in Marx's sense arise only through 'substantial imperfections in spatial competition' (1973: 179). *Absolute* rent is more difficult to define, and indeed Harvey's definition is somewhat opaque (Harvey 1982: 349–53). Absolute rent considers the question of scarcity (a socially produced condition) and a landowner's ability to extract capital purely on this basis, by withholding land from exploitation and capitalising on speculated future profits. Discussing the formation of absolute rent, Lamarche has this to say:

> The developer's right of ownership enables him to extract a rent for the *real* advantages which his tenants actually benefit from, whereas that of the land-owner enables him to obtain a rent for the *potential* advantages which the property developer will actualise.
>
> (1976: 85)

Differential rent may be divided into two categories. Differential rent type 1 relates to the site-specific advantages of a property, although the owner–developer does not create these benefits. This form of rent is a function of differentially produced spatial advantages that accumulate in favour of the owner but that are external to his property. These may emerge from other private-sector investors in adjacent locations, or in improvements from government expenditures vis-à-vis: infrastructure, rapid-transit systems, public open space etc. Housing, insofar as it represents the concentration of wages as a potential market in the purchase of commodities, therefore serves the primary function of increasing differential rent type 1 by maximising opportunities for commercial and related uses. Differential rent type 2 is charged on the basis of the proximal capacity of different enterprises located within a particular development to generate excess profits. It is quite obvious from this that differential rent type 1 may be transformed into differential rent type 2 on the basis of an owner extending his powers through the purchase of adjacent properties. It is also obvious that the main nexus of differential rent type 1 originates from public investment in transportation facilities. The extension of business catchment areas and greater accessibility within the urban system may permit increasingly higher densities, land prices and profits to developers, at no personal cost. All spatially differentiated improvements created out of public revenues are ultimately capitalised in land prices and then appropriated in the form of rent. Differential taxes levied by the state on profits, wages and rents effectively diminish each of these quantities. Similarly, reduced rents charged to labour for the consumption of public housing effectively subsidise commodity production by reducing wage prices.

Therefore, public housing rental does not necessarily constitute a huge benefit to labour; it constitutes a subsidy to capital by reducing the wage necessary for survival. However, it is apparent that such rent does not fit within any of the four categories discussed above. The central reason is that, as public housing is a politically manufactured context and does not emerge directly from market forces (covering cost of capital, labour and profit), money paid to occupy such housing must be considered an *administered price* rather than a true rent. As such, it represents interest paid on the consumption fund itself (money allocated for the provision of social housing and facilities and other items of collective consumption). This is the principle that has underwritten the development, for example, of Singapore and Hong Kong and has been central to the phenomenal economic growth of these two economies, as well as their somewhat unique urban form and design. High-rise public housing, at the most phenomenal densities ever seen, is a testament to how much profit and surplus value have been extracted over the last half a century by industrialists and developers, by banks, insurance and financial institutions.

In order to maximise the extraction of profits from the urban system for capital, public housing should not be seen to intrude on this process, and it therefore becomes imperative that it should possess certain required qualities. For example:

- Public housing should not occupy land that interferes with the expropriation of the various forms of rent as defined above.
- With respect to absolute rent, the proviso can be added that the existence of squatter settlements throughout the world, substandard housing and redevelopment areas may be used as a justification for withholding land from the market, thus increasing its potential for absolute rent. In Hong Kong, for example, squatter settlements have been used in support of the government's high land price policy, where potential political unrest has been used as an excuse for withholding land from development. Planning authorities in developing countries can contribute to this situation via planning 'blight', where land adjacent to an area that is subject to planning action becomes affected by the 'uncertainty' factor in planning action itself, e.g. proposed major road system developments that, because of political, economic or other factors, acquire an indeterminate status, thus affecting all adjacent land prices.
- High-rise, high-density public housing development tends to take place where the three basic forms of rent are likely to be reduced below the margin of profitability, and where urban locational *disadvantages* are reproduced.
- The provision of public housing in this particular manner effectively maximises the potential of the urban system to generate rent in its various forms. Infrastructural and other costs are reduced, and the benefits of public investment into the urban system may be capitalised within the private sector through differential rents. Labour power is efficiently managed, and the increased costs of transportation are inevitably passed on to the consumer in terms of escalating travel costs.

Most importantly, high-rise housing represents (at least ideologically) a quick technological 'fix' for a profound and endemic constellation of social problems. From the available evidence, this particular political approach appears to fail catastrophically, at every significant level of consideration, in solving the so-called housing 'problem'. It succeeds neither in terms of technical efficiency, in improving health standards, in solving land-use problems in the inner city, nor in providing greater amenity and psychological security for the residents of such projects, a failure symbolised by the dynamiting of the prize-winning Pruitt-Igoe Housing Estate in St Louis in 1972 (Baum and Epstein 1978, Dunleavy 1981). Despite the undesirability of such housing forms as seen by future tenants, accessibility to public housing is itself heavily politicised in the process of selecting tenants, acting against particularly disenfranchised members of society and favouring others. In order to investigate exactly how this situation is located within a system of institutions that legitimise the total politicisation of social space, I must now turn to the relationship between capital, state legitimation and urban planning law.

The state and urban planning

Within the system we call capitalism, society is class divided. This division is reinforced by the actions of the state and the ideological apparatuses that support the overall system (Figure 4.1). Consequently, the judicial system and its legal mandate and, by extension, urban planning law may be viewed as ideological constructs. In their very conception, they legitimise the social and property relations of capitalism, the resulting class division and the inequalities that accompany it, the unequal allocation of rewards and benefits and the artificial manufacture of scarcity round which the system flourishes. In reference to the ideological commitment of planning and design to the idea of social harmony, David Harvey says, in his chapter on 'Planning the ideology of planning':

> The limits of this progressive stance are clearly set, however, by the fact that the definitions of the public interest, of imbalance, and of inequity are set according to the requirements of the reproduction of the social order, which is, whether we like it or not, a distinctly capitalistic social order.
>
> (Harvey 1985: 177)

Hence, a fundamental hiatus affecting the planning apparatus as a whole is the conflict *between* the various capitals for urban space, with the capacity of planning to mediate the conflict. As we have seen in Chapter 3, the existence of urban social movements is a response for some honesty in this overall equation, a claim reinforced by the increasing penetration of neocorporatist agendas into the fabric of the state and the increasing privatisation of planning policy and practices.

Hence, the state invents and reinvents the servo mechanism of urban planning in accordance with its own agendas (this has been selectively covered in FOC4: 83–9). All this means is that in, for example, Hong Kong, the state will have a different structure from that of Singapore, and planning will necessarily operate differently (Castells 1990). As the dominant function of planning is regulation, the institution of planning will be configured differently in each place, depending

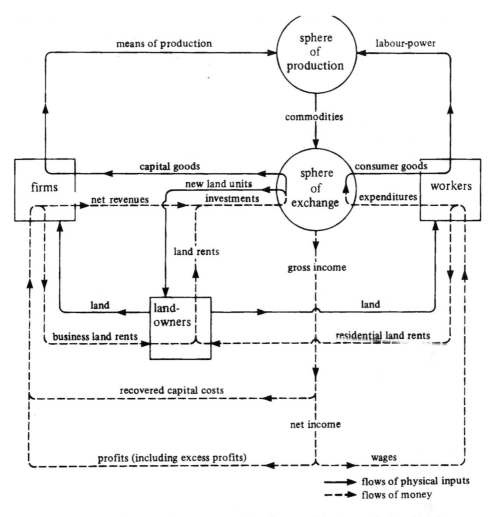

Figure 4.1 Commodity production: a simple schema of the interrelationships between capital, labour and land

Source: A. Scott, *The Urban Land Nexus and the State*. London: Pion, 1980, p. 29, Fig. 3.1

on the specificity of the ideological system. For example, in Singapore, tenancy of public housing is tied to superannuation benefits as a method of marginalising political controversy and social unrest affecting 80 per cent of the population. In Hong Kong, where so-called laissez-faire ideology held sway, a maximum of 50 per cent of the population has lived in social housing, hence reducing the price of wages to industrialists and developers. Political economy views planning as an intervention in the overall processes of the production and circulation of commodities and in the efficient reproduction of labour power. Planning is also called upon to manage conflicts emerging from the unequal distribution of the socially generated surplus. At the core of planning practice lies the management

of a big casino called the urban land market, where land and buildings are
commodified and sold like any other good (Figure 4.2). But land in its natural
state has little or no value within capitalism, which is forced to 'improve' it by
conversion to other functions contained in the fact of urbanisation:

> Urban land consists only in part of raw land. More importantly it is land
> whose use value has been dramatically improved by building it over, and
> by servicing it with infrastructure (namely collective means of production
> and consumption). In this way, urban land takes its quintessential quality
> as a system of collectively produced differential locational advantages ...
> in their unshrinking quest for economically advantageous locations, these
> users force a set of land use outcomes such that (in principle at least) any
> specific location is released only to the user who has the highest rent-paying
> ability at that location, and such that excess profits arising from differential
> locational benefits are bid away in the form of land rent.
>
> (Scott 1980: 29)

Rent is the chosen method of capitalism in the extraction of profit from land.
As the principle of 'rent' is uniform across the entire system of land management,
it is affected by (and affects) all forms of planning action, which are intimately

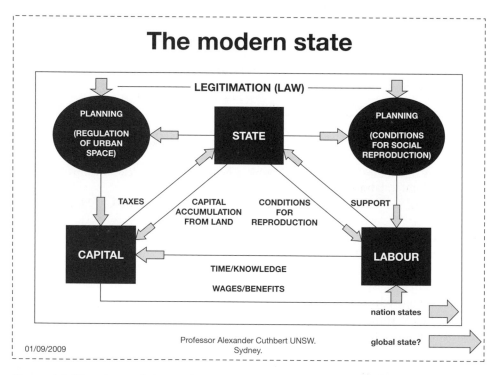

Figure 4.2 Planning and the modern state
Source: The author

bound up in its administration. Within cities, the highest rents exist at the most central location, which invariably corresponds to the highest building densities. In order to continually recreate and improve the circumstances for the extraction of rent in its various forms, planning is constrained by two mechanisms – increasing available floor space via increased density, and simultaneously increasing accessibility in order to make such an increase profitable. The phenomenon of high-density development and its geographic distribution in urban areas appears to go through ever-increasing and intensifying processes in relation to floor space, accessibility, transportation systems, planning action, escalating density of development and capital investment. As has been noted above, differential rents are extracted in proportion to the amount of floor space that a developer has available. This commodity is affected in its saleability by both internal and external factors (location, amenity, efficiency, configuration, price etc.) and in relation to the transportation system as the key parameter in the equation. Intervention by planning to 'improve' accessibility via public investment in infrastructure increases the potential for the expropriation of differential and absolute rents. As the government and the private sector derive mutual benefit in their respective ways from land development, planning comes under pressure from both sides to allow increased densities (hence, more floor space) via the relaxation of planning controls and constraints (plot ratios, height limitations, space and technical standards, conservation etc.). The paradox implied by the continual expansion of infrastructure to fulfil demand is that all new fixed capital in the form of the built environment represents a barrier to the reproduction of capital. Paradoxically, the very means to satisfy further accumulation in the form of transport and built form also constitute a physical framework of resistance to profits and speculation. To quote a by now historic statement by David Harvey:

> Capital represents itself in the form of a physical landscape created in its own image, created as use values to enhance the progressive accumulation of capital. The geographical landscape which results is the crowning glory of past capitalist development. But at the same time it expresses the power of dead labour over living labour and as such it imprisons and inhibits the accumulation process within a set of specific physical constraints. And these can be removed only slowly unless there is a substantial devaluation of the exchange value locked up in these physical assets.
>
> (Harvey 1985: 25)

The need to intensify development within the urban area and for planning guidelines to reinforce this process assist in making accessibility even more problematic. New demands are placed on planning to intervene and deploy even greater amounts of public funds, with increasingly sophisticated technical solutions to the movement of materials, goods and individuals (rapid transit, pedestrian moving sidewalks etc.), thus increasing accessibility, demands for floor space, the potential for further capital accumulation and higher, even more dense developments and so on. Such a scenario is played out *ad absurdum* in metropolitan areas throughout the world. Planning action, rather than being seen as the facilitator of solutions in the urban planning system, can be seen in this context as the means by which this overall process is deployed in the interests of speculation, and where all action for 'improvement' coincides with opportunities for new rounds of profit taking. In the face of incredible demands for floor space, this series of events also explains the paradox whereby many central areas of cities are left vacant, derelict or occupied by substandard or badly maintained facilities. In most instances, landlords can still extract some form of payment for the use of the site, while awaiting the appropriate moment to maximise the absolute rent that will accrue from the withholding of urban land from development.

Planning, consciously or otherwise, encourages this process in two ways: first, as indicated above, by allowing ever-increasing densities in the centre of urban areas, which encourage the withholding of urban land; second, by devoting vast reserves of manpower and resources to 'solving' the ensuing urban transportation problem, which so far has never been solved. As can be seen from countless examples worldwide, the transport 'problem' is insoluble, owing to its direct connection to population growth, commodity production and unsustainable urban planning practices. In the process, planning administration becomes so depleted of reserve funds that, inevitably, it cannot afford to compulsorily purchase land or supply the capital for urban redevelopment projects. The ensuing fiscal crisis, by now a permanent condition, forces planning to accommodate development needs on an unequal basis. It then falls victim to the neocorporatist agenda and is coerced into the voluntary euthanasia of the public interest.

Whether we choose to view planning as the representative of capital, as the promoter of the public interest or as some kind of coalition between them, we may discern four realms of space that planning administers. The first of these is the space of *production*, where private-sector interests exploit nature and labour to manufacture commodities. In this space, labour is sold for a wage that represents only a fraction of the surplus value so produced in the production process. The second is the space of *circulation*, which allows commodities and populations to circulate by means of transportation systems. The third is the sphere of *exchange* or personal consumption, which allows a spatial congruence to occur between the commodity and the purchaser. The significance of the commodity as a symbol of class differentiation is thus acted out in the material world. At the same time, the excess wage of labour is reinvested in the commodities that have been created, thus allowing the system continuous evolution. The fourth is the space of *collective consumption*, where labour is reproduced and educated by means of some form of housing tenure, the provision of health, education and welfare facilities, entertainment and other functions. Ideological beliefs in the form of organised religion, political affiliation and even sport etc. are also embedded as homeostatic elements in the overall matrix. In addition, however, we need a fifth space to permit human movement in what is termed *the public realm*. What we should consider when we are thinking about this *fifth space* is the subject of the next section, and I will use this term and *the public realm* synonymously.

The public and counter-public realms

The public sphere is the site where struggles are decided by means other than war.

(Negt and Kluge 1993: ix)

In the spirit of connecting mainstream urban design to something larger than itself, we need to enlarge our obsession with designing urban space, to include the forces that bring it about in the first place. To do this, we need to investigate the word *public*, before we can comprehend its method of implementation. Here, we have to distinguish between urban processes and the spaces in which they materialise. *The New Oxford Dictionary of English* defines a *sphere* as a *field of action, influence or existence* and a *realm* as a *kingdom or domain*. I will retain the former term for the social delineation of publics, and the latter for the spatial impacts and associations such publics entail (public realm, fifth space). Problematically, the universal yet questionable assumption that this fifth space has a concrete existence is paralleled by the intractable problem of definition. It is, without doubt, inordinately difficult to define the public realm, owing to complexities of ownership, form, management, transformation and substance (FOC4: 89–100). I will use the term *public space* in the currently accepted use of the term in social science, to include, not only streets, plazas, parks, shopping malls, pedestrianised 'precincts', neighbourhoods etc., but also the virtual space of the Internet.

As I have indicated in the previous chapter, for those in the environmental professions, the term *urban* is seldom explored in any depth and, at best, means 'something to do with cities'. Given that the word lies at the root of *urban* design involvement, this lack of exploration represents a serious omission from design education and practice. Unfortunately, the same is true of the *public realm*, where the term *public* and the congruent *public space* are assumed rather than analysed. For example, in *Architecture Theory since 1968* (an eight-hundred-page tome), reference to public space occupies only a single page, in an article by Kenneth Frampton (2000: 364). So the architectural design of the public realm can clearly proceed without any knowledge of what it is. While the fifth space is urban, its heterology is the public sphere, the arena of political engagement and conflict.

In the development of settlements at all scales, from the village green to the grand boulevards of Paris, the public realm is a concept typically used to describe a space where all individuals should be allowed to communicate freely with all others, within the law. In democratic societies, it is also supposed to be the locus where the entire range of opinions, from politics to religion, can be freely expressed, and where people can behave without censorship or fear, provided that the law is upheld. This hypothetical fifth space, however, is rarely defined or made explicit. Individuals are so used to the idea of some form of public realm, they seldom go beyond the assumption that such a space actually exists, or, more importantly, what influence, if any, they have over its access, ownership, use or disposal. This is particularly true of the design professions, and the term 'public realm' is used in everyday parlance with the tacit agreement that everyone understands what it means, and this is rarely the case.

As in the term *urban* discussed above, *the public realm* has an even less determinate reality. There has been little effort made to trace the social forms adopted by the public sphere to its contingent spatial structures and design implications, although there is no necessary or direct homology between the two. From the Greek *polis* to the virtual space of the Internet, it is clear that there is no concept of the public realm that is useful beyond a specific political economy of place and culture. In every era, the free movement of individuals in social space has taken place within a transient rule system imposed by multiple authorities that have seldom enacted the right of free movement into legislation. Today, we live in an age of neo-liberal politics and corporate governance, one where terror has been deployed as a system of control over subject populations, supposedly in the interests of their own protection, such that:

> A creeping encroachment in previous years has in the last two decades become an *epoch-making* shift culminating in multiple closures, erasures, inundations and transfigurations of public space at the behest of state and corporate strategies . . . From city parks to public streets, cable and network news shows to Internet blog sites, the clampdown on public space, in the name of enforcing public safety and homeland security, has been dramatic. Public behaviour once seen simply as eccentric, or even protected by First Amendment rights, is now routinely treated as a potential terrorist threat.
> (Low and Smith 2006: 1–2)

The authors also note that New York's zero tolerance policy, which has been extended globally to other cities, was subtitled 'Reclaiming the public spaces of New York', an example of the connection between political action and acceptable social behaviour (see also Katz 2006). State sanctions over public space are continually in a state of flux, and, with them, any idea we might have of an inalienable and consistent public realm. Given state protection to private space through legislation and urban planning practices, oriented to protect investments through infrastructure support, density and height controls, rights of light, compensation procedures etc., the public realm takes on the mantle of opportunity. In terms of political economy, it represents a major obstacle to capital accumulation, specifically property capital. Throughout the developed world, we may witness a continuing and relentless effort to absorb the public realm into its embrace, with an increasing degree of success. As part of capitalist enterprise, all property must be commodified, and the universal erosion of public space in cities is a signifier of this process (Kayden 2000).

At its most basic, fifth space performs the task of connecting the four forms of space indicated above, as well as the ideological function of cementing particular forms of representation – history, power, art, science, religion etc. – in the built environment. Hence, the difficulty in asking 'where is it?' constitutes a question of significant complexity and definition. If we then add the question 'who owns and controls it?' – the state, the private sector or 'the people' – we get into even deeper water. And if we then compound this by asking 'what is it for?', we can quickly grind to a halt with the sheer impossibility of the problem. Other concepts also come into play, such as those of right, freedom and social justice. Added to this, even ownership becomes problematic, as, in theory, the 'public' realm would belong to everyone and, hence, no one. In the realm of design, the spatial question is most significant, beginning with the idea that the other four forms of space are merely descriptive categories, and no homogeneity should be assumed in terms of spatial units. The spaces of production, consumption, circulation and exchange intersect with each other and the public realm in a myriad of land uses in the second dimension, in forms of building in the third dimension, and in the rate of dissolution and replacement in the fourth. The most basic analogy we can use here is that of a game of three-dimensional chess. But, in contrast to chess, where the units in play have only a single spatial function, the urban chess game contains, in addition, meanings, values, authority, power, difference etc. associated with the elements in the game.

The classic writing on the subject of publics in the last fifty years is arguably Habermas's *The Structural Transformation of the Public Sphere* (1989), which first appeared in German in 1962. Ten years later, Oskar Negt and Alexander Kluge wrote another seminal work on the subject, *Public Sphere and Experience: Toward an Analysis of the Bourgeois and Proletarian Public Spheres*. Habermas's text is a discourse on the evolution of the concept of the public sphere, and it deploys the method of political economy to analyse shifts in the development of publics using a chronological approach to modes of production up to the present time. Negt was a student of Habermas, and Kluge was a student of Theodor Adorno, and it is telling that their approach incorporates developments from Habermas's original position with Adorno's concerns for culture and the impacts of the mass media, which they refer to as *the consciousness industry*. Habermas's text is now showing signs of age, owing to the extraordinary developments both in theory and in social life since his book was written. Therefore, in contrast to Habermas's somewhat ordered presentation of the public sphere, Michael Warner introduces the concept of the counter-public sphere in *Publics and Counterpublics* (2002). This offers a more heterogeneous and inclusive approach to the huge diversity of publics not included in a traditional analysis of the public sphere. In addition to these texts, other offerings are significant, particularly Arendt (1958), Sennett (1986), Fraser (1990) and Calhoun (1992).

Habermas's method is to approach the problem of multiple publics as one of semantics and the use of particular terminologies relevant at specific historical moments. He frequently borrows terms from French and German to reflect developments in these countries that somehow redefine the term *publics*, noting that similar terms in each language (publicité, *Öffentlichkeit* and publicity) gave rise to the idea of publics at the beginning of the eighteenth century. Marx was of the opinion that the deconstruction of medieval social relations and the evolution of feudal into bourgeois society, where modern property relations were established, allowed civil society to come into existence. He defined the public sphere as a fourth dimension in concert with the state, the market and what he called the intimate sphere of the family. Possibly the best example of the distinction between *public sphere* and *public realm* is that of the classic Greek *polis* and *agora* of 500 BC, despite the fact that space had not yet been commodified and, hence, had a much greater relevance as public. Nonetheless, the relationship between the *polis* and the *agora* demonstrates the relationship between rights in the public sphere and spatial access or conferred use in the public realm:

> Rights in the polis were highly restricted to a very narrow and privileged social class recognised as free citizens, and many others were excluded – women, slaves, and the throng of common people. Likewise, the publicness of the agora was also circumscribed (albeit in a different fashion) and stratified as an expression of prevailing social relations and inequalities . . . Public space, in fact, comes into its own with the differentiation of a nominally representative state on the one side and civil society and the market on the other.
>
> (Low and Smith 2006: 4)

Negt and Kluge state in their introduction to *Public Sphere and Experience* that the classic bourgeois public sphere of property ownership needs to include a counter-public sphere that is not exclusively limited to bourgeois interests and includes other publics. They also observe the enduring hiatus of labour that, in resisting the public sphere, it also remains in conflict with itself, as the public sphere is also constituted by it. In addition, the traditional (bourgeois) public sphere was denoted in the enduring relation between public and private spheres, and that the bourgeois public sphere of property ownership has been overlaid by a host of industrialised public spheres of production, '. . . which tend to incorporate private realms, in particular the production process and the context of living . . . hence, the public sphere has no homogeneous substance whatsoever' (Negt and Kluge 1993: 13). They elaborate on this new public sphere as follows:

> The classical public sphere of newspapers, chancelleries, parliaments, clubs, parties, associations rests on a quasi artisanal mode of production. By comparison, the industrialised sphere of computers, the mass media, the media cartel, the combined public relations and legal departments of conglomerates and interest groups, and, finally, reality itself as a public sphere transformed by production, represent a superior and more highly organised level of production.
>
> (Negt and Kluge 1993: 14)

One thing we can remain certain of is the continually evolving relationship between the public and counter-public spheres and the public realm. In spatial terms, this now takes a multiplicity of forms, from the privacy of domestic life, to the private appropriation of land and the means of production, to the purchase and sale of property in virtual space. The public realm in many cities represents the last remaining undeveloped open space and, hence, is continually and unremittingly under development pressure, to the extent that the end of public space does not seem such an absurd idea. This penetration of corporate interests occurs in at least five dimensions: first, in areas such as such as beaches and lakes, parks, gardens, sports facilities, waterways, disused airports and docklands, reserve areas of horticultural or zoological interest, conservation areas etc., previously considered part of the public domain. Nor is this process limited to developed countries, and the rape of the developing world continues. An article in *The Guardian Weekly* recently demonstrated the unbelievable progression of this process, e.g. in Cambodia, where a repeat of Pol Pot's policies of social displacement is occurring without the associated genocide. Almost half of the country had been sold to private interests in eighteen months, 'causing the country's social fabric to unwind like thread from a bobbin'. This began through liquid assets accruing from the United States' sub-prime mortgage crisis in late 2008 sending venture capital looking for other opportunities These included massive swathes of the Cambodian coastline, which would normally be considered as constituting public space, despite the fact that it had previously been designated as 'state public land', which could not be bartered or developed.

Second, urban space donated by corporate interests to 'the public', in exchange for a variety of development rights, bonuses or exchanges, falls increasingly under the control of the same corporate interests after such benefits have been received (Cuthbert and McKinnell 1997). This principle also applies to air rights, underpasses, overpasses and other connections between buildings using public space. Third, public spaces in all centres of commodity production, such as shopping centres, malls and pedestrianised areas, are frequently controlled or otherwise colonised by investment interests. Fourth, linkage areas between and within so-called 'public buildings' are enduringly overrun by private-sector exhibitions, displays, sales outlets and other non-public functions. Finally, the entire process of surveillance and control of public space by private interests, in the form of electronic media and physical policing, is a burgeoning industry, and there is an entirely new architectural vocabulary for security brought on by the events of 9/11. Michael Warner notes that the frequently contrasting meanings given to the terms public and private can adopt many forms and, with these distinctions, comes the opportunity for a plethora of publics to evolve (Table 4.1).

In prior publications on Hong Kong, I investigated these distinctions in regard to the public realm and commented that, at its very centre, the problematic of the public realm concerned the principle of *right*, which goes back to the question of which fundamental rights people should expect from society, as opposed to those they actually possess (Cuthbert 1995, Cuthbert and Mackinnell 1997). In

Table 4.1 The relation of public to private

	Public	Private
1	Open to everyone	Restricted to some
2	Accessible for money	Closed even to those who could pay
3	State related; now often called public sector	Non-state, belonging to civil society, now often called private sector
4	Political	Non-political
5	Official	Non-official
6	Common	Special
7	Impersonal	Personal
8	National or popular	Group, class or locale
9	International or universal	Particular or finite
10	In physical view of others	Concealed
11	Outside the home	Domestic
12	Circulated in print or electronic media	Circulated orally or in manuscript
13	Known widely	Known to intitiates
14	Acknowledged and explicit	Tacit and implicit
15	'The world itself, insofar as it is common to all of us and distinguished from our privately owned place in it' (as Arendt puts it in *The Human Condition*)	

Source: M. Warner, *Publics and Counterpublics*. London: Zone, 2002, p. 29

turn, this tied into other related concepts, such as freedom, equality, justice, responsibility etc. Although we would expect freedom of movement and assembly, with space provided for those activities, to be a basic human right, it is immediately obvious that this is not the case. Magna Carta (1215) was the seminal example of a Bill of Rights, followed by France (1789) and the United States (1791). Since then, only Finland (1919), China (1949), India (1950), Canada (1960), New Zealand (1990) and South Africa (1996) have introduced a Bill of Rights, nine countries in all. So neither the actuality nor the form of the public realm can be assumed as a matter of right or inheritance.

Conclusion

Given the above context, it is clear that, when urban designers, landscape architects, architects, planners and others are involved in designing public space, the exercise of design skills should be the last of our considerations. First, we need to grapple with the heterologies that structure our concept of space and form, so that we can make more educated guesses as to design propositions. We need to understand that many counter-public spheres exist in fifth space, and that their representation is a matter of equity and of social justice. Although there may be correspondence between a public and an urban space, this reflection of one in the other is not necessarily homologous. Therefore, there is a contingent relationship between various types of public and counter-public and the types of space and form of representation that structure the public realm. Nonetheless, broad generalisations have some validity, such as the five types of space indicated above – production, consumption, exchange, administration and fifth space *qua* the public realm – although even these are collectively fractured and integrated in a diversity of ways. Importantly for designers, although fifth space is reputedly the public realm of private individuals, it also represents a major ideological canvas for the bourgeois public sphere, capital and the state. Unlike the other four forms, it has one unique property – it is the space where politics, ideology and culture are physically and symbolically condensed in the realm of monuments, to which we now progress.

5 Culture

Cultural studies may be defined as an interdisciplinary, critical, historical investigation of aspects of everyday life, with a particular emphasis on the problem of resistance, that is, the way that individuals and groups practice a strategy of appropriation in response to structures of domination.

(Ben Highmore)

Introduction: capital, culture and the sign

The period since 1975 has seen cataclysmic shifts in the previously cosy separation between culture and production, and some would argue that the Marxian distinction between the economic base and the superstructure has completely collapsed. Culture is now being rapidly absorbed into the realm of production, along with new significance accorded to *the culture industry* (Scott 2000). Problematically, 'one of the most perplexing features organically built into the logic of contemporary cultural production is that it is agnostic – anyway up to a point – about cultural values and predilections as such, just so long as profitability is assured' (Scott 2000: 212). Such activity provides the bedrock whereby the commodification of all aspects of human life becomes impacted. In consequence, a concept of culture is generated that, in the sphere of the personality, 'scarcely signifies anything more than shining white teeth and freedom from body odours and emotions' (Adorno and Horkheimer 1979: 167).

The spectre of culture integrated with production, requisite shifts in social class and the replacement of needs with desire heralds Debord's idea that 'Everything that was directly lived has moved away into a representation' (Debord 1983: 2). The processes of commodification are gradually supplanting those of traditional culture, where the social becomes a system of signs displacing the needs of normal human emotions to those of commodified attitudes, values, objects and symbols. Signs therefore become the central method of communication, the living medium of social relations. As I have mentioned previously, the commodity is not a material thing but a social relation. The use value of the object is clearly material, but the commodity itself is symbolic, constituting a code that mediates several relationships, between buyer and seller, between use values and exchange values, between brand and image, and between sign, signifier and signified.

I have covered these concepts at some length in FOC3: 65–9, but, briefly stated, culture and its components, such as language, architecture, food, dress etc., can be interpreted as forms of communication whose materiality stands as a sign for other things (emotions, ideas, desires, philosophies etc.). As signs are systemic, they can be decoded, i.e. they are enveloped by culture (During 1993). The sign constitutes the union of a form (signifier) with an idea (signified). If I can transpose an example of Roland Barthes, the Parthenon in Athens can be used to signify democracy. When it does this, the Parthenon is the sign that mediates the relationship between the actual building (object) and democracy (the signified). This relationship is locked into the Parthenon as a sign that encompasses both medium (building) and message (democracy). As culture may be defined as 'an assemblage of imaginings and meanings', where 'capitalism shifts more toward the exchange of meanings, products become more intensely symbolised through advertising and the social discourse of "taste"'. Value is placed on products according to their social status, as well as on their cost and scarcity. Products and services begin to attract symbolic value which can then be attached to the owner. With increasing frequency it is the symbolic value that is being purchased over use value (Lewis 2002: 6, Jensen 2007). This process can become self-consuming, as *branding*, and, in the realm of the urban, it starts to define urban policy and strategy (Greenberg 2003, Kumic 2008).

Without these relationships incarcerated in the commodity, capitalism as we know it would collapse. For this reason, Baudrillard ultimately came to the conclusion that nowhere do signs organise reality more than culture, and for this reason everything can now be understood as *cultural*. In fact, he noted that 'culture is the production and consumption of signs to the point where signs have begun to produce cultures' (Kumic 2008: 122). He goes on to argue that, in consequence, a role reversal takes place between the object and the sign or brand. Where one normally assumes that brand and sign are set in place to sell objects, in fact it is the brand that is actually being consumed. The extent to which the object vanishes is epitomised by a recent description of 'one of the world's hottest models'. She was described by the swimwear company Seafolly as 'the most significant *brand ambassador signing* in Seafolly's thirty three year history, and is *an international brand coup*' (Hoyer 2008: 9; my italics). As such, the individual had disappeared, to be replaced as a mere signifier of commodities and the simulacrum of a brand. Applied in an urban design context, the spatial logic of late capitalism is such that spaces and places are also established to support the brand and the overall production of a commodity-inspired culture.

Bourdieu argues that the material consumption of commodities is liberated from objects into symbolic exchange, whereby a vast array of signs are enclosed within material products and services. Hence, the tasteful selection and consumption of products is used as a social insignia for the privileging of particular individuals and groups. The selection of a product and the display of its value necessarily implicate consumption in the symbolic positioning of people and their everyday lifestyle and practices.

(Lewis 2002: 268; Tolba *et al.* 2006)

Reduced to basics, this means that one's community is also a symbolic construct where taste, branding and image are all-enveloping and constitute simulacra – the imitation of an imitation, where sign value competes with, or even overrides, use value. This is particularly true of New Urbanist communities, where the brand authenticates the sign. Baudrillard suggests that the mediation of signs then becomes the dominant reality.

The urban symbolic

In the preceding chapter, the ideological dimension of urban politics was addressed. But ideology is not only represented by extension into the three-dimensional formal properties of the built environment, into buildings, spaces and monuments as elements, but also into a binding synthesis of much greater complexity. Although politically sanctioned interpretations of national accomplishments abound, the dark side of patriarchal, racist, xenophobic and manipulative aspects of societies is usually marked by its absence.

All states tend to present sanitised and ideological representations of their own history, some going as far, like the Incas, as having history recounted as an idealised version of events. History is usually written as the dominant authority would like to see it, rather than as how it was experienced by those collectively involved in its creation. As a general rule, men and male values also dominate. When women appear, it is frequently in support of their reinforcement of male values, for example the monument to women's contribution to the Second World War next to Downing Street in London (Figure 5.1). Women and children are seldom seen, and monuments recognising resistance to state oppression as well as violence against individuals and groups are conveniently expunged. The same is true of external acts of war, the horrors of colonialism or massacres carried out against minorities whose religion, philosophy or merely the colour of their skin somehow displeased ruling elites. Massacres of one's own people in war are referred to as heroism. Therefore, the transcendent imaginary of social, political and gender equality is seldom seen, or, to quote Jean Paul Sartre's famous dictum, '*L'enfer, c'est les autres*' ('hell is other people'). We can take this further, in another quotation that closely ties culture to the concept of death and transfiguration:

For Marx, then, for revolution to succeed a relationship has to be established with death – with the dead. Looking around our cities we are

Figure 5.1 Monument to the women of the Second World War. Sculpture adjacent to
        Downing Street, London

Source: The author

continually faced with the figures of the dead: the officially mourned and
celebrated figures of politicians, inventors, heroes, fighters and suchlike.
There are also memorials to the dead who have died in wars. And yet the
un-mourned, the un-acknowledged dead, the dead who might spoil the
image of civic pride are absent.

(Highmore 2006: 170)

The same is true of society's unacknowledged anti-heroes – evil dictators,
corporate fraudsters, corrupt politicians, contentious authors, gangsters, serial
killers and other reprobates. Hence, our fifth space is inhabited only by the good,
the successful, the justifiable, the brilliant, the saintly and the moral. It is a space
largely sanitised of blame and critical self-reflection and, therefore, to a great
extent, of responsibility and correct moral judgement. What monuments portray

does not necessarily convey what we know and experience. This is, of course, quite understandable, but at the same time it is a profoundly ideological and dishonest portrayal of society. For this reason, and in order to understand all the representations contained in fifth space, they must be deconstructed at a variety of levels in order to reveal their semiotic content – from historical development, prevailing values and power, to the political subterfuge of the state and its enemies, and to the network of associated representations across urban space. Therefore, the overarching rule in the design of fifth space as a totality is that it constitutes a veritable minefield of stated and unstated discourse, on societies in particular and civilisation in general.

The cornucopia of monumental forms encompasses a vast diversity, from immense buildings to small sculptural elements, where the physical size of the monument bears no necessary relation to its significance. Examples would include palaces, churches, war memorials, triumphal arches, crescents, boulevards, obelisks, towers, sculpture, monumental artworks and fountains, as well as specific elements in grand architectural compositions. Closely related is the concept of public art, which I view as largely apolitical and therefore not monumental in my adopted sense of the term. If public art is funded by the private sector, it is usually for its own aggrandisement or to present a distorted version of reality. If it is funded by the state, it is usually for its entertainment value, serving as a soporific for the masses. I view public art as differing from monumental art in two significant dimensions, although clearly there is a blurring of boundaries. First, public art differs from the monumental in having its meanings largely eviscerated, as in any other form of mass media. For example, public art is either donated by, or demanded from, the private sector as compensation for development privileges, as in California's 'one percent for art' policy, where 1 per cent of the cost of major buildings in downtown areas had to be contributed for the purposes of art as decoration and entertainment. Second, monumental art has primarily an ideological function in building nationhood, sustaining religious commitments, promoting ethical and moral values, respecting the advances of science and technology etc. A good example of boundary conditions, where the difference between monumental art and public art is difficult to define is Richard Serra's sculpture *Tilted Arc* (FOC4: 98). As a case in point, as public art the sculpture generated so much public discussion that it was eventually removed from its site in Manhattan.

For this reason, I will adopt a definition of the concept *monument* as any object that is used in structuring the material world of fifth space but whose prime function is *ideological*. One immediately calls to mind examples such as the Eiffel Tower in Paris, Nelson's Column in London, *The Little Mermaid* in Copenhagen (Figure 5.2), *The Walter Scott Monument* in Edinburgh (Figure 5.3), Ossip Zadkine's statue in Rotterdam (Figure 5.4), the monument to Vittorio Emanuele II in Rome (Figure 5.5) and countless others. However, methods of classifying monuments have the same problems as any other taxonomy, whether by form, substance, historical location, design, content or other qualities. The sheer variety of monuments defies any simple categorisation that would be

Figure 5.2
The Little Mermaid sculpture, entrance to
Copenhagen harbour, Denmark
Source: © Lucjan Podstawka/iStockphoto

Figure 5.3
The *Sir Walter Scott Monument*,
Princes Street, Edinburgh
Source: © John Pavel/iStockphoto

meaningful in itself, and this has seldom been attempted to any useful degree. Most relate to the realm of archaeology or ancient monuments and are purely functional in reach.

Probably the most noted attempt at a more general taxonomy is that of the Vienna Classification of Monuments, based upon the Vienna Agreement of 1973 and contained within what is headed 'The figurative classification manual of the Office for Harmonisation in the internal market' (2002). Section 7.5.1 denotes ten categories of monument, a tiny fragment of the overall agreement. This overall classification system runs to sixty-six pages and deals with intellectual property rights and trade marks. Hence, its entire focus is economic, and there is no attempt to build in any qualitative system of values, judgement etc. Rather than classifying objects for aesthetic or cultural preservation, it actually charts the potential boundaries of commodified wealth with the mental and physical worlds. Virtually all the sources of capital accumulation from the material world have been classified under a single umbrella. Similarly, UNESCO includes monuments in its categorisation of specific sites for the award of World Heritage

Figure 5.4 Ossip Zadkine's sculpture, *The Destroyed City*, Rotterdam
Source: AKG Images/Bildarchiv Monheim

Site, to be protected under its agreement of 1972. This includes such icons as Venice, Mohenjo Daro, Borobodur, Persepolis, Delphi, Abu Simbel (Figure 5.6) and others. The overall categories are forest, monument, mountain, lake, desert, building, complex or city. Prior to 2005, separate criteria were established for culture and nature, under the overarching umbrella of having outstanding universal value, a separation no longer recognised. As of that date, ten criteria have been established, no doubt to dispel the artificial separation between the two qualities, and moreover:

Figure 5.5 Monument to Vittorio Emanuele II, Rome
Source: © Luis Pedrosa/iStockphoto

- to exhibit an important interchange of human values, over a span of time or within a cultural area of the world, on developments in architecture or technology, monumental arts, town planning or landscape design;
- to bear a unique or at least exceptional testimony to a cultural tradition or to a civilisation that is living or that has disappeared;
- to be an outstanding example of a type of building, architectural or technological ensemble or landscape that illustrates (a) significant stage(s) in human history;
- to be an outstanding example of a traditional human settlement, land-use or sea-use that is representative of a culture (or cultures), or human interaction with the environment, especially when it has become vulnerable under the impact of irreversible change;
- to be directly or tangibly associated with events or living traditions, with ideas, or with beliefs, with artistic and literary works of outstanding universal significance (the Committee considers that this criterion should preferably be used in conjunction with other criteria);
- to contain superlative natural phenomena or areas of exceptional natural beauty and aesthetic importance;
- to be outstanding examples representing major stages of earth's history, including the record of life, significant ongoing geological processes in the development of landforms, or significant geomorphic or physiographic features;
- to be outstanding examples representing significant ongoing ecological and biological processes in the evolution and development of terrestrial,

Figure 5.6 The Great Temple at Abu Simbel, Egypt
Source: © Vincenzo Vergelli/iStockphoto

fresh water, coastal and marine ecosystems and communities of plants
and animals;
•   to contain the most important and significant natural habitats for in-
    site conservation of biological diversity, including those containing
    threatened species of outstanding universal value from the point of view
    of science or conservation.

(www.answers.com/topic/world-heritage-site)

Conservation apart, the central motivation is again economic, as the accolade
of being denoted a World Heritage Site is thought to boost tourism and
development. Paradoxically, however, this is an extremely dubious proposition,
as benefits are by no means guaranteed and, in several cases, sites have been
known to suffer losses (Tisdell 2010, Tisdell and Wilson 2011). Many other
forms of classification exist, but these are usually highly specialised, dealing with,
for example, archaeological sites, medieval fortifications, geological formations,
places of ecclesiastical significance etc.

Arguably the most notable method of classifying monuments, one that has
survived the test of time, was that of Alois Riegl in his seminal study of
monuments in 1903 (Riegl 1982). He distinguished between *intentional* and
unintentional monuments, where the difference is between that of prospective

or retrospective cultural memory. Intentional monuments were those concerned with historical memory or recall, commemorating some historical event. These contain what he called commemorative value. Riegl considered that this type of monument was the only kind known until the Renaissance period. Unintentional monuments were those whose meanings were determined by the perceptions of the observer rather than the sculptor, architect or other person who created them. Such monuments contained age value, art-historical value and use value. Although, on the surface, they would seem to be the same, age value refers to the concepts of aura and authenticity, whereas art-historical value merged aesthetic qualities with its representation of human development. Use value refers to any functional attributes the object may have. Riegl considered that the distinction between art value and historical value was rejected during the nineteenth century, when it became obvious that monuments possessed both qualities simultaneously. Only by grappling with some of these associations can the psychological, cultural and political impact of monuments be understood, as they encompass every aspect of human history and consciousness.

So we may consider that the semantic content of monuments constitutes a form of apprehended memory, whose recall is continually retranslated in human experience and changing historical circumstances. By this, I mean not only that the object has a political function, but also that it forms part of an interlinked semiotic system throughout the urban areas of towns and cities. Seldom are monuments dissociated from the space and culture within which they are embedded (although the Statue of Liberty in New York is clearly an exception). A dominant trait, however, within this overall system is that monuments traditionally underwrite bourgeois values and present them as a false representation of majority aspirations. Paradoxically, this does not necessarily imply any conspiracy, as it is in the nature of any symbolic form that a multiplicity of interpretations can be given as well as received, and that the principle of distorted communication rules (Canovan 1983). Needless to say, such distortion can also be used to a variety of effects. In addition, it is in the nature of individuals to support the very system that holds them captive. The definition of ideology as a lived system of values has very blurred outlines. This situation is compounded by the fact that buildings frequently lie to us, and that the accepted norms apparent in architectural form may often present a false reality, as in the example of Greek architecture given above. Such is the nature of all monuments in the public realm of cities.

Both monuments and the processes of conservation are closely related, as the same value systems and ideological practices frequently inform both. This is certainly true in core economies, but it attains even greater significance for colonised people. In researching an article on conservation in Hong Kong, the political substance of what I was involved in was emphasised in an article in the *South China Morning Post*. A guilt-ridden expatriate suggested,

> that the best examples of colonial architecture are relics of a barbarian
> culture, and that conservationists would best be advised to concentrate their

efforts on Euston station or the Roman Forum, and leave the Chinese people
to decide what is or what is not part or their culture.

One local Chinese guru took up the challenge a few weeks later, deciding that
'all buildings that remind people of their colonial past should be torn down'
(Cuthbert 1984: 102–12). The same seems to be true of monuments, and the
sentiment was also echoed in Hungary after the Russians departed:

> In Budapest the city council has removed in excess of twenty monuments
> including those of Marx and Engels. Veterans of the 1956 uprising were
> among those seeking their removal. The Red Army Monument, however,
> has been retained in one of the City's main squares, but it is constantly
> under police protection.

(Johnson 1994: 51)

Figure 5.7
Soviet Army Memorial,
Main Square, Budapest,
Hungary

Source: Peter Erik Forsberg/
Age Photostock/Photolibrary

Although fifth space is the place where people communicate with each other and experience the city in all of its complexity, it is also the epicentre of urban conflict and the main locus for its expression. It is the space where ideology adopts a concrete and material form. There is no part of the urban fabric that is incapable of serving ideological purposes, no matter how poor or fragmented it may become. Urban forms constitute the vehicles whereby dominant values are stored and transmitted, where stories are told, individuals are exalted, nationhood is established and where the institutional power of the state, the military and organised religion is reified. The site of the monument, and its extension to other monuments and spaces, is as critical as the monument itself. Monuments can signify events that took place anywhere in the world or at the same location. As they also convey historical memory, they may be reproduced in countless forms across towns, cities and nations, commemorating, for example, the Second World War of 1939–45. Urban streets and squares can also mark the locus of countless internal political struggles, where governments have been overthrown, resistance has been crushed, individuals have been massacred and buildings have been destroyed. The public realm is therefore the site of collective consciousness, tradition, association and conflict, a symbolic universe of society's aspirations and historical development.

Monuments and design

Although the monument forms a critical part of the urban designer's portfolio, the significance and meaning of monuments are seldom explored. They tend to exist as reference points in a Euclidean exercise of two-dimensional geometry. The idea of the axis, which usually begins and ends with a monument as its focal point, is central to the methodology of urban design. It originated in antiquity and has been implemented as such for centuries. Axis, gridiron, street, square and monument are the dominant components of urban design in the Western world. Christopher Wren's 1667 plan for rebuilding London after the Great Fire of 1666 (Figure 5.8), Thomas Holme's plan for Philadelphia of 1683 and James Craig's plan for Edinburgh New Town of 1766 (won in a competition when he was 22 years old) are all historical amalgamations of these principles. More recent examples might include Walter Burley Griffin's plan for Canberra (1913) and Leon Krier's Luxembourg project of 1979. However, Baron Haussmann's plan for Paris is probably the consummate example of this principle, where monuments form the basis of his axial plan of 1853, the impetus for which had begun with Napoleon I sixty years previously, in 1793. Within this plan, the most outstanding example is the 5-kilometre axis originating at the Place de l'Étoile. This was only recently completed, in 1990, with the construction of La Grande Arche of La Défense, rising 110 metres into the air on a 100 metres square site designed by Johann Otto Von Spreckelsen. It is also notable that the triumphal arch that sits at the centre of the Place de l'Étoile derives from the monuments to war named after the victories of Roman emperors over their adversaries.

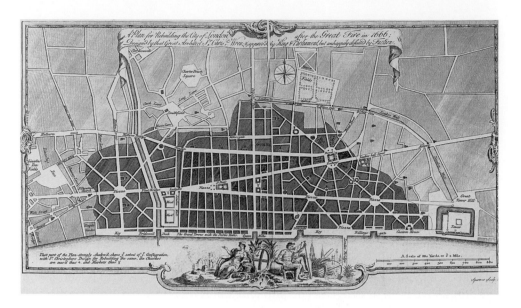

Figure 5.8 Christopher Wren's plan for rebuilding London after the Great Fire of 1666
Source: © Corbis

   The expressive function of physical scale is also important in the designer's
vocabulary. Embedded in the term monumental is an association with the
grandiose, but the term has no necessary connotation with scale, and many
monuments, although small, contain meanings and associations inversely
proportional to their size. Hence, in English, there is a semantic confusion
inherent in the use of the term. Some monuments are indeed monumental, such
as the Statue of Liberty in New York; others, such as the *Manneken Pis* in
Brussels, are less than 1 metre tall (Figure 5.9). Monumental architecture, however, frequently conveys the message that the citizen is inferior to the dominant
authority (the king, dictator, government or god). This strategy has not only been
put to great effect by many totalitarian states, fascist and communist alike, but
also by orthodox religion, for example Gothic cathedrals, St Peter's Basilica in
Rome etc., although the Basilica of the Sacré Coeur in Paris (Figure 5.10) is an
exception to this rule, standing as a symbol of conflict and struggle in French
society between the Communards and the Royalist forces (Harvey 1989). By its
very nature and its tendency to an oppressive use of scale, monumental
architecture conveys the message of individual subservience to institutional
authority in the form of religion, state, monarchy and politics. In reference to
Tatlin's monument to the Third (communist) International, Negt and Kluge state:

   What Tatlin's monument signifies becomes apparent only when it is
   contrasted with the design of bourgeois monumental architecture. The
   architecture of the French Revolutionary era too is by and large extant only
   in the shape of plans. These comprise huge static monstrosities, which aspire

Figure 5.9
The *Manneken Pis*, Brussels:
symbolic of various Belgian
legends
Source: © Ziutograf/iStockphoto

to the cosmos, the landscape, or to vast ideas such as justice; never
monuments to which human beings can relate.

(Negt and Kluge 1993: 279)

The smallest scalar elements involved in scripting monuments are probably
plaques on buildings and street names, which have enduring significance in the
commemoration of historical figures and events (Johnson 1994). For example,
the Boulevard des Champs Élysées, begun by Marie de Medici in 1616 and
opened in Paris by Louis XIV in 1667, is internationally famous and is frequently
described as the most beautiful street in the world. For the French, the name
translates literally as 'The Elysian Fields' and derives from the place in Greek
mythology where the blessed went after death. Street names are political simply
owing to the fact that their naming is seldom democratically executed, and they
usually support an edited version of history (Azarayahu 1986, 1996). Naming
streets and other urban spaces can be a profoundly political gesture that
enduringly masks the truth. Tiananmen Square, for example, means 'The Gate
of Heavenly Peace', a somewhat odd name for the site where university students
and workers were massacred. This event symbolised the cataclysmic death of
Chinese socialism, where a fundamental tenet was breached when the People's

Figure 5.10 The Basilica of the Sacré Coeur, Paris. Monument built on the site
        traditionally associated with the martyrdom of St. Denis, patron saint of
        Paris
Source: © Christian Musat/iStockphoto

Army was used against the very people it was supposed to protect. Needless to
say, the square was not renamed to commemorate and signify these events, as
exemplified in Beirut in the Martyr's Square (FOC5: 120–2). Street names are
frequently handed down by the state, for example '. . . after the unification of
Germany under Prussian hegemony in 1871, street names in Berlin commemorated not only members of the ruling Hohenzollern dynasty, but also mythical
heroes structured in the fabric of German nationhood' (Azarayahu 1996: 314).
This included Bismarck, who unified Germany and, for his efforts, has some 400
monuments erected in his honour (Figure 5.11). In contrast, since the takeover
of Hong Kong by China in 1997, street names such as 'Queen's Road West',
places such as 'Victoria Harbour' and monuments to colonial authority such as
that of King George VI all remain.

   Not only naming but also renaming can take place for political reasons.
Azarayahu quotes Milan Kundera's novel *The Unbearable Lightness of Being*
(1985), regarding the Soviet invasion of Czechoslovakia in 1968, where the signs
denoting streets and cities disappeared overnight, leaving the country nameless.
Under colonialism, destroying prior signs is usually the first strategy of invaders,
and readers will be aware that the first act accompanying the United States'
invasion of Iraq was to broadcast internationally the fall of a huge sculptural
monument of Saddam Hussein, an act that, at the time, appeared to have more
significance than the actual invasion. As a general rule, this process underwrites

Figure 5.11 Bismarck statue, Berlin
Source: Jonathan Carlile/imagebroker.net/Photolibrary

colonisation, and the symbolic destruction of memory is the first method of
eroding nationality and imposing a new regime (Fanon 1965, 1967, Said 1978,
Ashcroft and Ahluwalia 1999). For post-colonial societies, the reconstitution of
memory in symbolic forms is frequently agonising, and the regeneration of a
new identity for a new society is fraught with angst, as the history of colonisation
is now embedded as part of the history of the colonised people. Elsewhere, I
have discussed this problem in the context of societies that now have fascist
architecture as part of their own history and the problems this entails for urban
and architectural form (FOC 3: 67).

In the panoply of monumental imagery, war takes front stage. Few countries
do not, in some manner, eulogise war as a method of representing nationalist
supremacy. Defeats are seldom recognised. For example, there is no monument
in the German Republic to the countless thousands of men who died in the
catastrophic siege of Stalingrad and the fateful retreat back to Germany:

> Publics have been trained to view monuments and historical markers,
> whether massive obelisks, towering representational statues or modest
> plaques, as carrying a unity of universality and timelessness. Yet the
> decisions about what sites to mark and the formal aspects of the monuments
> are often highly contentious and politicised.
>
> (Walkowitz and Knauer 2004: 5)

This statement is clearly demonstrated by contrasting monuments in Washington DC, in the United States, where, on the one hand, controversy is marked by the insignificance granted to events of monumental import, whereas, on the other, controversy raged over a single war memorial. On a small street corner marker off Massachusetts Avenue in Washington, the vast scale of Chinese, Soviet and Cambodian annihilation of their own people by Mao, Stalin and Pol Pot is commemorated. It is the only monument to approximately *100 million* victims of communism (Kennicott 2007). Overall, Maya Lin's Vietnam Veterans Memorial is probably the most contested of all war memorials in the twentieth century (Figure 5.12). Completed in 1982, it is a testament to the fallen, both men and women. The design is a simple wall of polished black stone in a V shape that changes in elevation along its length. Its very blackness was criticised for looking like a gravestone rather than a eulogy. Virtually every element of the wall came under a barrage of vitriolic abuse, from the use of materials, to the abstract nature of the monument, and to Lin's Chinese ancestry. Racism, prejudice, bigotry and ignorance were all brought to bear, primarily, but not exclusively, by the remaining veterans. Lin had won the competition when she was a 21-year-old student, over another fifteen hundred entrants. In order to quell the tide of criticism, another monument was built close by in the somewhat universal heroic style, depicting three Americans of different race staring into space (MacCannell 1992). Despite the criticism, Lin's design is now one of the most visited and respected sites in the United States. There is also a half-scale touring simulacrum that visits other American cities, for those who cannot get to the original. This significance of war monuments in cities is underscored in *Memory and the Impact of Political Transformation in Urban Space* (Walkowitz and Knauer 2004). It is telling that, with a single exception, that of Lithuania, all other examples from the book deal with conflict, torture, death and nationalism (Table 5.1).

As wars between countries have resulted in countless possible forms of representation, so the recognition of gender is seldom noted (Nash 1993). Monuments reflect the political and ideological foundation of society in patriarchy, and the

Figure 5.12 The Vietnam Memorial, Washington DC, designed by Maya Lin
Source: © Rob Meeske/iStockphoto

Table 5.1 Examples of monuments, their location and representation

Monument	Location	Date	Memory
1 Marian Column (now empty space)	Prague, Czech Republic	1650	End of Thirty Years War
2 Wallace's Monument	Stirling, Scotland	1860s	Wars of Independence
3 Paradise Temple	Harbin	1923	Consolidation of Chinese sovereignty
4 Peace Memorial Park	Hiroshima	1950/ 1992	Civilian deaths of atomic war
5 Veterans Memorial	Washington DC	1982	Vietnam War
6 Parliamentary complex (unbuilt)	Sri Lanka	1985	National unity
7 Lake Xolotlan	Nicaragua	1985	Sandanista victory over Somoza dictatorship
8 Villa Grimaldi	Santiago	1990	Military use of torture against patriots
9 Unbuilt spaces of solidarity and remembrance	El Salvador	post-1992	8000 persons tortured or killed
10 War memorial	Poklonnaia Gora, Moscow	1995	Victory over the Germans
11 Masada	Israel	1995	Zionist struggle for survival
12 Holocaust memorial	Berlin	1998	Genocide
13 Memorial for the disappeared	Santiago	1999	Victims of Pinochet's death squads
14 Bali remembrance sculpture	Sydney	2003	Assassinations by Islamic extremists
15 Museum of Memory	Buenos Aires	2003	Interrogation and torture
16 Palace reconstruction	Vilnius, Lithuania	2010	Genealogy of place and culture

Source: D.J. Walkowitz and L.M. Knauer (eds), *Memory and the Impact of Political Transformation in Public Space*. London: Duke University, 2004, p. 68

erection of monuments exists almost exclusively to honour the activities of men in war, government, sport, the arts, science and other regions of human endeavour. This process attains enormous dimensions, as in the monument to Vittorio Emanuele II in Rome, built in marble to commemorate the first King of a united Italy (1885–1911). The incorporation of women into the fabric of buildings has a long history in the symbolic portrayal of human aspirations, states of consciousness etc., for example, Athena – wisdom, Venus – love, Kali – death, as in the Statue of Liberty in New York, representing the pursuit of freedom for all Americans, but nonetheless originating in France. Women seldom appear as leaders, but as 'other', not of themselves but as a symbolic representation of love, motherhood, truth etc., or otherwise objectified for the beauty of the female body

Figure 5.13 The Erechtheum building of the Acropolis in Athens, showing the caryatids
used as pillars (from the Greek *Karyatides* meaning 'maidens of Karyai')

Source: © oversnap/iStockphoto

(Warner 1985). Whereas men are represented in monuments as conquerors and heroes, with the focus on individual or collective accomplishment (as in the alternative Vietnam memorial), the method of representing women has been dominated by allegorical representation and passive compliance. Possibly the most classical method of representing women is in the depiction of the caryatids in the porch of the Erechtheum building on the Athenian Acropolis, first recorded by Vitruvius in *De Architectura*, his famous architectural treatise of the first century BC. The women's bodies substituted for columns on the basis that they could dance while carrying baskets on their heads (Figure 5.13). The extent of national passion evoked by such images was recently demonstrated in regard to the bronze 1.2-metre statue of a mermaid that has guarded Copenhagen Harbour since 1913. A national outcry ensued when the Danish government agreed to loan the statue to the Chinese as part of the World Expo to be held in Shanghai in 2010.

The symbolic representation of culture in the public realm is clearly a highly charged political activity. In representing only the positive aspects of culture, distorted communication occurs, and society is presented with a false image of itself. Much of this has the overarching intention of generating political acquiescence to a commonly shared ideology, with heroic images of society's most famous sons dying in battle or standing erect, staring into the cosmos. Luckily, there are also significant failures in this process, sufficient to maintain intellectual freedom and resistance to a monolithic portrayal of culture. Even abstract art, perhaps not the most obvious method of stimulating human passions, frequently generates unholy dialogue over the meaning of object, site, convention and value, and we have seen how Maya Lin's Veterans Memorial, or Richard Serra's *Tilted Arc* in Federal Plaza, New York, possessed the ability to generate meanings far beyond that of their immediate presence (FOC4: 397, 398).

Monuments are ubiquitous in Western urbanisation and, to a degree are part of its uniqueness, the concrete manifestation of culture as politics. They infuse the public realm of cities with ideologies that are simultaneously exposed and hidden, true and false, fantasy and reality, and where individual experience is subsumed, distorted and sacrificed to national and civic identity. However, culture is not only condensed in the public realm of fifth space. It has its domestic counterpart in the private realm of home and community, as exemplified in the globally emergent architectural movement called New Urbanism.

Heterology and the New Urbanism

There are two types of New Urbanism, not one as we are usually led to believe. The first is reified by Neil Smith in his paper, 'New globalism, new urbanism: gentrification as global strategy' (Smith 2002). Smith argues that, owing to the neo-liberalism of the third millennium, the relationship between capital and the state has been restructured:

This transformation, the outlines of which we are only beginning to see, is being expressed more vividly through an altered geography of social relations – more correctly, through a rescaling of social processes and relations that creates new amalgams of scale, replacing the old amalgams broadly associated with 'community' 'urban' 'regional' 'national' and 'global' . . . in effect a new urbanism.

(Smith 2002: 430)

As such, the first form of the New Urbanism reflects a sea change in the international division of labour, the shift from industrial economies to informational economies and the development of electronic communication and an informational economy among other phenomena. This situation allows traditional ideas of 'scale' to be scrambled and, with them, concepts of community that were previously based on shared employment and physical association of some kind. The burgeoning cost of commuting, due to diminishing oil reserves, has also been exacerbated, despite the expectation that electronic communication would supplant the physical transport of individuals. In addition, the demise of the welfare state and the shift from *social reproduction* to *socialised production* have devolved from the conflation of private-sector interests and the public good to state neocorporatism. Smith remarks that a serious escalation of social control has also occurred in the face of terrorism, mass migrations and crises in social reproduction.

Smith's (economic) New Urbanism also marks a monumental development in the accumulation of capital, where the shift to consumption referred to above has permanently altered social life (see also Sassen 2000, Smith 1996, Castells 1996, 1997, 1998). Whereas the old industrial order was marked by social provision in the realm of collective consumption in order to create efficiencies in production and hence capital accumulation, the new order depends on individual and luxury consumption to extend and deepen the process. The other New Urbanism (capitalised to retain continuity) – that of the architects and urban designers – is situated within this reconstruction of social space and social relations, a context from which it derives both its cues and its methods. In contradiction to the idea that the (architectural and urban) New Urbanism was invented by a specific architectural practice (Duany, Plater-Zyberk and Co.), like other social forms, it arose as a consequence of prevailing economic and social conditions during the 1970s, with its roots planted firmly in the nineteenth century, albeit at the *fin de siècle* (Rutheiser 1997). It already existed in England in the form of neo-traditionalism, and came into being in the United States on the basis of a pre-existing imported architectural practice, a necessary shift in ideology, its own historically derived typologies and vernacular, and a brilliant marketing exercise (Slater and Morris 1990, Franklin and Tait 2002). Indeed, its claimed originators, Patrick Geddes, Ian McHarg and Christopher Alexander were all British citizens. Whatever the sources, the New Urbanism attempted to counteract the wastelands of American suburbia with community-based developments that were human scaled, crime-free, racially integrated and oriented to public transport – laudatory objectives without doubt. What has been questioned in the literature on several fronts, however, is that both forms of the New Urbanism are caught up in a pre-existing built environment, where the formal architecture of New Urbanism can have little impact on global suburbification. Additionally, serious questions have been raised as to the New Urbanism's sociocultural prescription, and the claims that it has made in regard to fulfilling specific social objectives (Audirac and Shermyn 1994). Hence, questions have also been expressed about its capacity to improve on other forms of suburban and urban development (Hall and Porterfield 2000):

> To date however, the New Urbanist literature has not involved social scientific theory building and empirical testing, but rather marketing and manifestos instead . . . Unless New Urbanism is part of an overall strategy for revitalising inner-city neighbourhoods, it remains simply a shell, to be filled by what the marketplace wills. As an isolated approach, New Urbanism is open to criticism that it represents a quick real estate fix that relies on the discredited notion of physical determinism.
>
> (Bohl 2000: 777, 795)

While these material considerations are all welcome and undeniable, the transition to the new economy has been paralleled, as it has been in the past, with new forms of consciousness, perception and awareness. Unlike past eras, however, these qualities have been linked to capital formation in ways that dissolve many of the boundaries between object, product, profit and identity. We observe what we need and become what we desire. Promoting this process, the method of postmodern design lies in the creation of simulacra, the design of deceptive substitutes that replace so-called 'objective reality' as the foundation for life, while designing with images that are representational fictions, but nonetheless 'real' for the designer and client. The New Urbanism fits perfectly into this concept, where belonging to a New Urbanist community reflects one's good taste in selecting an appropriate brand, despite the fact that hyperreality prevails – a construct that conveys an appropriate language of signs and discrimination. Whether one wishes to place a value on this is a somewhat fruitless question, as it is a fact of global capitalism and postmodern culture – the era in which we live.

Hence, it is important to focus on the symbolic value that attaches to notions of cultural distinction where a new style of architecture and urbanism has come into existence. The concept of heterology assists in examining the substructures that underlie the principle assumptions of the New Urbanist epistemology in regard to the physical construction of culture and community – the important discourses and methodologies that allow the New Urbanism influence in the realm of cultural and symbolic capital. So what do we need to be thinking about when we think about urban design in the form of the New Urbanism?

Like most designers, architects are obsessed by style and taste (symbolic capital). Their concept of architecture is usually defined by it. Hence, we have

Egyptian, Persian, Greek and Roman, and, later, Victorian, art deco, art nouveau, modernist and postmodernist, and many others. Modernism had its own form of ethnic cleansing in its attempt to expunge all historically derived details and decorative features. God was in the details, as long as they were functionally expressed (a phrase originating from Flaubert, not Mies van der Rohe, as is commonly believed). As a reaction to such sterility, postmodernism decided that 'anything goes', feeling free to borrow or juxtapose any referents it decided were appropriate in context. Consequently, the latter tends to make architects uneasy, because there is no identifiable style to postmodernism. It is quite possible, therefore, that the rise of New Urbanism over the last fifteen years has, to a degree, offered the security lacking in a world struggling under the weight of a nebulous postmodernism (Marshall 2003). It offers both salvation and happy certainties in a time of confusion, taking the form of derived theory, land use, building typologies, design codes and the psychological security of an organised identity and community of like-minded people.

Although the iconic town of Seaside, Florida, was begun in 1981, Peter Katz's book *The New Urbanism* was the first to assemble a portfolio of projects sufficient to rationalise, with some authority, that a new movement in architecture and urban design was well established, at least in the United States (Katz 1994). So we can date the New Urbanism as originating from fifteen to twenty-five years ago. Since that time, a plethora of books and articles have emerged that debate many of the assumptions of this new philosophy (Duany and Talen 2002, Talen 2002a, Bell and Jayne 2004, Talen 2006). The historical origins have also been well documented in Al Hindi and Staddon (1997), and the neotraditionalism that has followed (Audirac and Shermyn 1994, McCann 1995, Tiesdell 2002). Beyond that, there is a fair measure of utopianism in the New Urbanist agenda, as well as a major cultural shift away from the traditions of mainstream American urbanisation (Saab 2007). Associated theoretical and methodological problems have been discussed in Banai (1996), Ford (1999), Ellis (2002) and Grant (2008), and an evaluation of land use and central commercial areas is given in Banai (1998). The movement also has its relationships to natural disasters (Talen 2008), its adaptation to ethnic minorities (e.g. Latino New Urbanism, Mendez 2005), social schisms (Bohl 2000, Smith 2002) and globalisation in articles about Moscow (Makarova 2006), the Middle East (Stanley 2005) or Malaysia (Sulaiman 2002). The methods of incorporating sustainable principles into New Urbanist projects have also been raised (Fulton 1996).

Following Antonio Gaudí's famous dictum, in order to be original, we need to return to the origin of things, in this case to Patrick Geddes or even Frederick Le Play (see FOC9: 206–8). Geddes was a polymath and arguably the originator of modern town planning (Boardman 1944, Mairet 1957, Kitchen 1975, Meller 1990). From these references, it is clear that interest in Geddes has not waned over the last century, the most recent major commentary being that of Welter (2006). Geddes's knowledge was immense, and he influenced a whole series of protégés, from Lewis Mumford to Ian McHarg (1969) and beyond, into the contemporary world of the New Urbanism. The central heterology used by

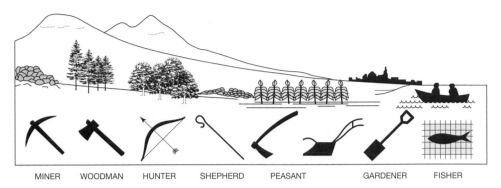

The Valley section with basic occupations

Figure 5.14 Patrick Geddes' original valley section with associated occupations
Source: Town and Country Planning Association

Geddes, stemming from around 1915, was what he called 'the valley section' (Geddes 1997 (orig. 1915): 15). However, the use of the term *section*, which instantly conjures up the fixed geometry of architecture, conveys a vastly oversimplified version of Geddes's philosophy. Geddes's valley section was, in fact, a constellation of the geography of place, including its inhabitants, the landscape, terroir and bedrock (Figure 5.14).

This idea informed the core of New Urbanist theory (Duany 2000, Duany *et al.* 2000, Brower 2002, Talen 2002b). Duany recognises Geddes's valley section as a point of origin, forming the theoretical and intellectual base for the New Urbanism (Grant 2005). Despite this, Geddes's idea of the valley section was not a *design* concept, as it has been used in the New Urbanism, but a commitment to natural process. Using the transect as such constitutes a fundamental misreading of Geddes's work, however well intended (Table 5.2). It is claimed that the transect is a new approach and an alternative to traditional methods of land use zoning practices:

> the transect approach is an analytical method and a planning strategy. It can be formally described as a system that seeks to organise the elements of urbanism – building, lot, land use, street and all of the other physical elements of the human habitat – in ways that preserve the integrity of different types of urban and rural environments.
>
> (Talen 2002b: 294)

In one major sense, this is quite revolutionary, simply because it assumes that all existing codes of practice for planning, building, construction, development and design can be suspended, akin to Alexander's pattern language (see Cuthbert 2007: 202). In so doing, the general thrust of capitalist urbanisation, based on profit and speculation, will have to be renegotiated to promote authenticity, a

Table 5.2 Description of transect zones

Zone	Main characteristics
Rural preserve	• Open space that is legally protected from development in perpetuity • Includes: surface water bodies; protected wetlands and habitats; public open space; and conservation easements
Rural reserve	• Open space that is not yet protected from development, but should be added to the Rural Preserve zone • Includes open space identified by public acquisition and areas identified as TDR (transfer of development rights) sending areas • May include flood plains; steep slopes; and aquifer recharge areas.
Sub-urban	• The most naturalistic, least dense, most residential habitat of a community • Buildings consist of single-family detached houses • Office and retail, on a restricted basis, are permitted • Buildings are a maximum of two storeys • Open space is rural in character • Highways and rural roads are prohibited
General urban	• The generalised, but primarily residential, habitat of a community • Buildings consist of single-family detached houses and rowhouses on small- and medium-sized lots • Limited office and lodging are permitted • Retail is confined to designated lots, typically at corners • Buildings are a maximum of three storeys • Open space consists of greens and squares
Urban centre	• The denser, fully mixed-use habitat of a community • Buildings include rowhouses; flexhouses; apartment houses; and offices above shops • Office, retail and lodging are permitted • Buildings are a maximum of five storeys • Open space consists of squares and plazas
Urban core	• The densest residential, business, cultural and entertainment concentration of a region • Buildings include rowhouses; apartment houses; office buildings; and department stores • Buildings are disposed on a wide range of lot sizes • Surface parking lots are not permitted on frontages • Open space consists of squares and plazas

Source: Adapted from *The Lexicon of the New Urbanism* (Duany, Plater-Zyberk and Co. 2000). Taken from an article by Emily Talen (2002) 'Help for urban planning: the transect strategy'. *The Journal of Urban Design*, 7(3): 293–312.

sense of civic republicanism and virtue, and a formulaic approach to aesthetics. This would seem a singularly unlikely possibility.

It is also clear that there is nothing new about *the New Urbanism*, and its concepts of what constitutes *urban* are barely skin-deep. Not only this, but there is a remarkable naivety with regard to how cities actually grow and change, a vast urban complexity that cannot be ordered by the simple application of physical models. Despite claims to promote racial integration, socio-economic mix, collective security and other societal objectives, the evidence to back up these claims is singularly lacking, and we are left with the symbolic capital locked into the brand. The transect assumes a standard progression of six zones, from rural preserve, rural reserve, suburban, general urban, to urban centre and urban core. These six zones each correspond to a pattern of density, building type, natural elements etc., which is seen as prototypical of each zone. The central problem here is that the valley section (one dimension) is then translated directly into a zone (two dimensions), and the resulting neighbourhood typology is determined as much by appearance as by any other factor. However, problematically, 'Residents, however, value appearance less for its intrinsic qualities than for its social implications. Duany's transect facilitates the creation of distinctly different compositions. Residents on the other hand look for distinctively different residential experience' (Brower 2002: 313, Volk and Zimmerman 2002). So the method of applying the New Urbanism seems to focus on the purchase of symbolic capital, which the brand guarantees.

However, Geddes's ideas do not provide the only heterologies for the New Urbanism, and American urbanists have been criticised for selective amnesia when it comes to their own history (Saab 2007). They forget that 'many earlier American utopian urban plans not only closely resemble the New Urbanist vision, in many ways in their attempted application, they are responsible for many of the conditions that the New Urbanists are trying to rectify' (Stephenson 2002: 196). Therefore, the New Urbanism has been informed by at least a century of experimentation with all kinds of model – theoretical, ethical, physical and economic – few of which are ever recognised. We can trace all of these to a point of origin in the City Beautiful movement in the United States, which began with the Chicago World's Fair of 1893, sponsoring a whole new vision of civic dignity and aesthetics. In addition, Ebeneezer Howard's classic text *Tomorrow* was published in England in 1898, containing his idealised model of country living in satellite towns. The construction of the archetypal Letchworth (1903) and Welwyn (1920) as the foundation for the Garden City movement followed soon after (Figure 5.15). Mumford notes that even then, Howard was reintroducing Greek concepts of natural limits to organic growth as alternatives to 'the purposeless mass of congestion of the big metropolis' (Mumford 1961: 515).

The New Communities movement during the 1920s and 1930s, established by people such as Clarence Stein, Henry Wright, Lewis Mumford and Alexander Bing, generated a host of experiments to integrate physical form with concepts of community. Many such community models were built, and the icons of the time were places such as Forest Hills Gardens on Long Island, Baldwin Hills Village in Los Angeles and Radburn in New Jersey. Howard's design model for what we might call 'Victorian New Urbanism' was of course paralleled by physical models of cities and residential locations in the Chicago School of Urban Ecology (FOC3: 58–60). Frank Lloyd Wright's Broadacre City of 1934 continued the experimentation with new forms of community, and the 1939 New York Fair and the New Deal provided a much-needed planning impetus for improved planning practice through the Second World War. Hence, the New Urbanism

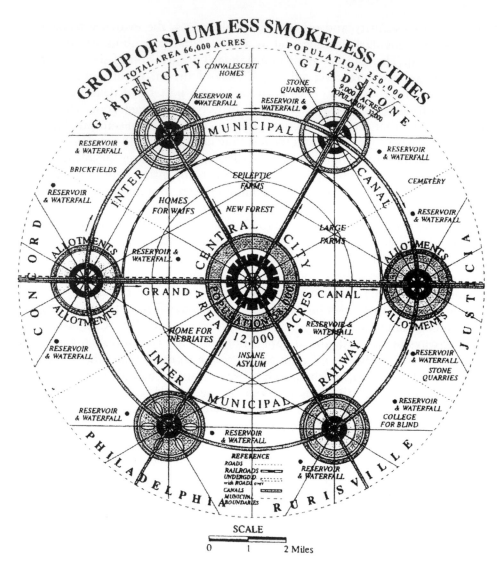

Figure 5.15 Ebeneezer Howard's prototype for the garden city

Source: M. Pacione, *Urban Geography: A Global Perspective*. London: Routledge, 2009, p. 169, Fig. 8.2

owes much to its origins in the Garden City, City Beautiful and New Communities movements, and to the many architects and planners involved in promoting new methods of furthering community development. The New Urbanism also perpetuates the enduring myth that physical determinism can automatically craft communities on the basis of specific demographic limits and building codes.

The importance of this historical legacy has meaning for the New Urbanism for several fundamental reasons. In searching for the *authentic* community, it relies on the past, rather than imagining the future, for justification in a diversity of manifestations – style, civics, social relations, community, imagery, institutional frameworks and demographics. Closely linked to concepts of authenticity and symbolic representation is the idea of style. Symbolic values *qua culture* require a medium (architecture, sculpture), a message (justice, democracy) and a form (art deco, abstract) synonymous with the style. The reason for this distinction is that these three methods of communication sit uneasily together. If you ask an architect what form his/her building takes, he/she has a variety of possible responses – it is a house (architectural form), it is an apartment (typological form), it is high rise (building form), it is New Urbanist (stylistic form/brand). The concept of form and style pervades all social transmission, from speech to architecture. In this context, I use the term *form* to denote the style/ manner of accomplishment of a work, rather than its typology or construction.

The archetypal image/style of a New Urbanist community would seem to depend heavily on the idealised lifestyle of small-town America in the 1950s, without any of the problems, despite the fact that many New Urbanist projects have distinctly urban locations. This is truly the urban imaginary, the simulacrum of a perfect place that never existed, one that can seemingly be reproduced in the present, and it is no accident that this has been referred to as 'Planning the American Dream' (Bressi 1994: xxv). Here, history, reality, authenticity and nostalgia are intertwined (Boyle 2003). Historical referents abound in a neo-conservative image of urban life. The New Urbanism places great stress on the idea of the authentic community, 'But how do they determine what makes a community authentic? Is this merely a marketing device, a means of differen-tiating their product from the competition? (Saab 2007: 195). While Ellis (2002) notes that nostalgia is used as a term of derision, it has been defined as 'a product of shared historical consciousness of general displacement that is able to make parochial misfortunes and individual losses socially meaningful. It provides to lonesome strangers a common refuge in history, even while it says their losses are irreversible' (Fritzsches 2004: 64–5). The idea of authenticity is one that can never be 'real', in the sense that reality is not one-dimensional, and so what is defined as real has a multiplicity of possible sources and representations. The word *authentic* is also used in opposition to fake, and, as Baudrillard and others have indicated, this distinction has no meaning in a world where we now live in hyperreality. The New Urbanism adopts (or copies) pre-existing imagery from 1950s small-town America, Cape Cod fishing villages, Victoriana such as Savanna, Charleston etc. and a myriad of other referents. Hence, the New Urbanism is a copy of a copy, the originals themselves being derivative from other forms of architecture. As Audirac and Shermyen point out, even fakes of 'genuine' New Urbanist projects are being built: projects that have the image but not the content of actual New Urbanist projects, based on their manifesto and design guidelines:

As the TND [traditional neighbourhood development] prototype bearing Krier's imprint, Seaside remains utopian in its isolated evolution. Yet

Seaside look-alike houses have sprouted in the neighboring resort developments, and traditional low-density beach-front sub-divisions catering to the
demand for turn of the century architecture are mixing in Caribbean
vernacular for inspiration. While Florida's 'Redneck Riviera' is adopting
postmodern architecture, one wonders if it or the rest of the U.S. will give
up suburban space and privacy and the automobile habit to adopt lifestyles
promoted by postmodern urban design.

(Audirac and Shermyn 1994: 171)

Therefore, while the New Urbanism is frequently criticised for its utopian
reconstruction of past cultural icons, like fake watches, copies at various levels
of authenticity to the original fake are being reproduced across the United States.
So much postmodern suburbia is becoming a fake of a fake of a fake. That
paradox, as Baudrillard has pointed out, is now the order of social life, and he
claims that there is nothing fake about any of it. Trying to separate out the
real/authentic from the fake/simulacrum has become a meaningless task. In a
recent trip to Indonesia, I was offered a choice of a fake watch or a better-quality
fake of the same thing. The difference between a watch and a home, however,
is that we live inside rather than outside the brand and therefore associate with
it much more powerfully. It is the brand value of the New Urbanism that is
significant, rather than the social context or images of the architecture. In the
context of small-town America and other self-contained New Urbanist projects,
the brand 'Seaside' would be lost without the New Urbanism to support it, in
much the same manner that the city brand *Bilbao* would be diminished without
Frank Gehry's Guggenheim museum, but, significantly:

In this sense a building is often said to have signature value that carries the
auratic signature of its author. However, where the iconic properties of a
building could generally be said to be important in revealing the architecture
as brand, the specific signature of an architect refers specifically to the aura
or brand of the architect. In marketing parlance, this runs the risk of
confusing 'brand architecture or structure' required to induce the master
brand, which is this case is the city.

(Kumic 2008: 227)

Conclusion

Overall, the public realm constitutes an enormous stage, where memory,
historical consciousness, space and form collide. But this is also the realm of
urban politics, where power is represented in forms that frequently deny any
objective truth. It is the place where history becomes sanitised and censored prior
to approval by state and publics, one where regions of conflict do not necessarily
coalesce round traditional definitions of social class. The construction of the
nation-state in urban form is a universally adopted practice, and, for anyone

involved in the design of spaces and places, this is the alpha point of monumental architecture. It is the locus of a culturally established collective memory. Monuments as signs and typologies as brands have a significant impact on cities that only seems set to deepen. However, we can hazard a guess that most of the aura surrounding monuments belongs to a pattern of ideological practices firmly fixed to past forms of accumulation. Currently, the concept 'brand' and its potential impact on the form of cities emerge as a reflection, not only of a new way of *seeing*, but also of a new way of *being* (consciousness). This is not the place to debate whether the phenomenon is good or bad, whether forms of consciousness take second place to materiality, or whether new horizons in the accumulation of capital are implicit at all scales of brand identity. Nonetheless, the New Urbanism as *brand* is yet another reflection of deepening commodity relations manifest in the built environment. Without doubt, practitioners of the New Urbanism are genuine in their belief that a vast improvement to the built environment will ensue from their methodologies, and indeed this may be true. But the overtones of a born-again architecture and urban design do not sit well with the actual ravages of capitalism and its practices. The bottom line is that the New Urbanism is contained within the capitalist economy and is subject to its rules. As long as the brand does not threaten any fundamentals within the urban land nexus, it will succeed, as indeed would any good architecture not incorporated into the New Urbanist ideology.

6 Gender

I came to see that most of my interlocutors felt uneasy because my reasoning interfered with their dreams: with the feminist dream of a genderless economy without compulsory sex roles; with the leftist dream of a political economy whose subjects would be equally human; with the futurist dream of a modern society where people are plastic, their choices of being a dentist, a male, a protestant, or a gene manipulator deserving the same respect.

(Ivan Illich 1983: 9)

Introduction: the missing component

In *The Form of Cities*, I referred to the chapter on Gender as 'the missing component'. Whereas many of the other elements in the book had at least some discussion in the context of urban design theory and practice, the element of gender appeared to be almost wholly absent. The same has been true of the academy, where most urban design programmes (and one could include all of the environmental disciplines in this) are void of teaching on the importance of gender to design. Chapter 6 in *The Form of Cities* tried to compensate for this omission by placing issues of gender on a par with other concerns. This, of course, was a mistake, as it is not simply another dimension of the designer's vocabulary, but a general principle, as in the case of sustainability, that should infuse every part of the design process. Neither can be considered an add-on to the designer's brief – 'ok, let's think about nature/women now' – but should be consciously welded into our perceptions of the world and how we live in it. The underlying reference point of all three books in this series is spatial political economy, and in the previous text I have illustrated the uneasy truce between a feminist perspective and one deriving from historical materialism. For the moment, I will assume that one cannot live without the other, recognising the partial yet interlinked nature of each as a fundamental form of explanation (FOC6: 127).

Significantly, however, the choice of spatial political economy is reinforced
when one comes to the idea of method, as one simply cannot look to the literature on urban design for any methodology or any consideration of issues
surrounding the question of gender (Kimmel 2008). Here, we must embrace
human geography, art history, cultural studies and other disciplines for insight.
I have always urged my students to read 'outside the box' if they wish to mature
as responsible designers, a task that will never be accomplished by trawling
through illustrations of the latest urban design projects or most of the current
literature, and I hope that this chapter will vindicate my advice. Of one thing
we can be certain, that, in discussing issues of gender, particularly gender and
patriarchy, we face the task of righting the whole of human history, something
that will not be accomplished overnight (Browne 2007). As to origins, although
we can go back centuries for isolated examples of the struggle for women's rights,
1980 has some significance as a starting point for feminist geography, when the
spatial dimension to women's conditions of existence came to the fore:

> It was less than ten years ago [prior to 1989] that the issue of the invisibility
> of women, both as the subjects of geographical study and as practitioners
> of the discipline started to emerge. In the intervening years we have seen a
> remarkable burst of energy by geographers interested in feminist theory,
> and in the documenting of women's inequality and oppression in all areas
> of social and economic life, and in all parts of the globe.
>
> (Bowlby *et al.* 1989: 157)

In the intervening period, there has also been a move to correct this situation
with reference to architecture and urban planning. In architecture, we may
witness a small but marked interest in gender studies, for example *Sexuality and
Space* (Colomina 1992), *The Sex of Architecture* (Agrest *et al.* 1996), *Designing
Women* (Adams and Tancred 2000) and *Decoding Home and Houses* (Hanson
2003). In planning, there is a similar dearth of references (depending on how
one defines 'planning') – but *Change of Plans* (Eichler 1995), *Women and
Planning* (Greed 1994) and *Gender and Planning* (Fainstein and Servon 2005)
are essential touchstones. Urban design is in a similar position to urban planning,
but, importantly, *Discrimination by Design* (Weisman 1992), *Approaching
Urban Design* (Roberts and Greed 2001), *Design and Feminism* (Rothschid
1999) and *Constructing Difference in Public Spaces* (Ruddock 1996) stand out.
Understandably, by far the greatest number of texts issue from urban studies
(particularly urban geography), notably *Women and Space* (Ardener 1981),
Women in Cities (Little *et al.* 1988), *Gendered Spaces* (Spain 1992), *Space, Place
and Gender* (Massey 1994), 'Gender and urban space in the tropical world'
(Huang and Yeoh 1996) and *Women in the Metropolis* (Von Ankum 1997).
These texts are emblematic of work in each area and are not meant to
devalue the many other groundbreaking works that do not fall so easily into
such limited categories, for example, Dolores Hayden's three masterful works –
Seven American Utopias (1976), *The Grand Domestic Revolution* (1981) and

Redesigning the American Dream (1984), which are essential reading, forming a genre unto themselves.

The historical nexus

In *The Way to Paradise* (2003), Mario Vargas Llosa charts two journeys: the first, that of Paul Gauguin, the visionary painter, and the second, his grandmother Flora Tristan. Their stories are interwoven, contrasting two visions of paradise on earth. Gauguin's journey takes him to the absolute periphery of French colonial power in Tahiti. Flora's quest also took her overseas, to Peru, her lifetime search for paradise being fought over the politics of utopian socialism in France in the middle of the nineteenth century. Whereas Gauguin's search for paradise focussed entirely on Gauguin, a journey mediated by sex, alcohol and the French penchant for eulogising *la pensée sauvage*, Flora sought maximum benefit for all. Her commitment paralleled several social movements of the time, whereby the principles of *liberté*, *égalité* and *fraternité* (liberty, equality and brotherhood) could be implemented as the central intention of the French Revolution. Flora was also interested in adding sisterhood to the equation. Arguably for the first time in human history, the organisation of labour went hand in hand with struggles over the emancipation of women. Significant to our discussion is the fact that there was also a small but important attempt to spatialise these relationships, with a move to revolutionise women's emancipation beyond production and patriarchy into domestic life, childrearing, sexuality and space.

Paradoxically, it was almost exclusively through the actions of men that the principles of utopian socialism emerged as radical experiments in community, via the three founders of the movement, namely Henri de Saint Simon (1760–1825), Charles Fourier (1772–1837) and Robert Owen (1771–1858). All were firmly committed to social change, using direct action as their method, unlike prior utopians such as Sir Thomas More, Etienne Cabet and others, whose visions remained in the realm of the imagination. The writings of these three individuals, specifically St Simon's *Letters from an Inhabitant of Genève* (1802), Fourier's *Theory of the Four Movements* (1808) and Owen's *A New View of Society* (1812) underwrote the philosophy of utopian socialism. Although revolutionary, the texts had not yet advanced to a stage where a surgical analysis of capitalism could take place. That had to wait until the publication of Marx's *Capital* (in German) in 1867. Within the Marxist paradigm, women's role was not tied to sexual freedom in its widest sense, but to their position within a proletarian revolution, the outcome of which would, in theory, automatically generate equality between the sexes. Hence, as Flora perceptibly notes,

> there was no hope for the Fourierists . . . Their original sin was the same as that of the Saint Simonians: not believing in a revolution waged by the victims of the system. Both distrusted the ignorant, poverty-stricken masses, and maintained with beatific *naiveté*, that society would be reformed

thanks to the goodwill and money of bourgeois citizens enlightened by
their theories.

(Llosa 2003: 71)

The seeming naivety of all three individuals, St Simon, Fourier and Owen,
stemmed from methods rooted in concepts of morality, ethics and ideology as
the basis of social harmony, not the relationship between the *economic* structure
and the social wage. To them, a specifically economic sphere was not a cause of
social unrest. Collectively, they also disagreed with prevailing concepts of religion
and politics as being fundamentally resistant to harmonious social development,

> since there is an axiomatic assumption of natural harmony between nature
> and human nature, the problem of antagonism and evil is displaced from
> the sphere of production . . . [at that time] the socialist critique of political
> economy precisely concentrated upon emphasising the impossibility of
> isolating a distinct economic sphere.
>
> (Steadman-Jones 1981: 86)

Hence, while the instigators of utopian socialism had a significant region of
agreement vis-à-vis social change, their methods were fundamentally different.
Saint Simon promoted an as yet unformulated social psychology, Fourier's focus
was on the *amatory* relations as opposed to *economic* relations of production,
and Robert Owen emerged from a new scientism that conflated the methods of
physical sciences with those of the social (see Chapter 1). As Saint Simon did
not attempt to give physical form to his ideas, the experiments of Fourier and
Owen in matching ideology to physical form remain seminal in the annals of
urban design.

Despite many of the nonsensical ramblings in his written work, and the
total irrationality of certain of his beliefs (e.g. that, when perfect harmony
was achieved, six moons would orbit the earth; that the world would contain
37 million each of mathematicians, poets and dramatists of genius), Fourier's
central concern was admirable – to reverse the degradation of the industrial
revolution by humanising all work, emancipating the lives of women, recon-
structing concepts of family life heretofore incarcerated by religious orthodoxy,
and promoting gender equality in all things. In this context, sexuality became
disconnected from work and reproduction. Fourier was a radical feminist who
rejected patriarchy (while remaining patriarchal) and advocated sexual liberation (while simultaneously rejecting equality of the sexes). He also condoned all
forms of sexual activity except those that involved pain or coercion. However,
his vision of human emancipation clearly did not involve democracy, as he
himself constituted the alpha and omega points of Fourierist philosophy. Despite
the fact that this philosophy was riddled with contradiction, his great accomplishment was to build many experimental communities and so to complete the first
significant attempt to match an ideology based on human emancipation with a
physical environment within which his philosophy could thrive. To date, this

has never been repeated, except perhaps in the kibbutz system established by Israelis in the (re)settlement of Palestine.

Fourier's method of stimulating social reform was to build what he called phalansteries, analogous with the Greek concept of *phalanx* or a military cohort. Each phalanstery had both industrial and agricultural functions, to provide an economic base for a self-contained housing community of exactly 1620 persons, within which many sub-groupings existed. He built thirty such communities in the United States between 1843 and 1858, which collectively represented *Harmony*, or the social context of the phalanstery. His concept had a global reach, which he envisioned would replace urbanisation based on the anarchistic relations of the market mechanism. Fourier gave detailed instructions as to the physical organisation of each phalanstery, in terms of the zoning of specific activities, as well as the detailed design of buildings, streets, courtyards, galleries and other urban functions. Most importantly, domestic labour was collectivised: food preparation, washing, child rearing and other activities that had previously been the sole domain of women became part of the social organisation of the community. For the first time, the domestic mode of production was restructured, and women's place in the kitchen was transformed into social labour on the same basis as men. The individual kitchen, the most powerful symbol of women's domestication, was abandoned. Victor Considerant, who became Fourier's architect, determined the main elevation of the phalanstery at around 700 metres, and Dolores Hayden notes that, 'Considerant's overbearing view of the architect as a designer and human activities as passive material to be shaped by design, had been shared by many other utopian architects' (Hayden 1976: 150).

Unlike Fourier, Robert Owen was an entrepreneur, whose fortune was based in the cotton industry, using new technologies to advance industrial production. However, like other socialists, Owen was committed to feminism, although there is some doubt as to whether or not his vision was utopian or merely an advance in socialised production through superior industrial practices. Nonetheless, the Owenites accepted gender equality as a foundation for their social project, promoting the liberation of women as equals within the law. Such adopted shifts in gender roles had major spatial implications, as the fundamental relationship between the sexes enforced through organised religion had been rejected and reformulated. Society and space required some reconstruction of the domestic realm and its integration into an entirely new matrix of gender relations:

> The nuclear family (which was held to be responsible not only for the direct subordination of women to men, but also for the inculcation of 'competitive' ideology) would be abolished and replaced by communal homes and collective child rearing. This transformation in living conditions would allow a new sexual division of labour to be produced: housework ('domestic drudgery') would be performed on a rotational basis (either by women or by children of both sexes) with 'the most scientific of methods available', leaving women to participate in all other aspects of community

life, from manufacturing and agricultural labour to government, office, educational and cultural activities. With childcare collectivised, and all economic pressures removed, marriage would become a matter of 'romantic affection' only, to be entered on mutual agreement and dissolved by mutual choice.

(Taylor 1981: 64)

Owen was one of the first to realise that the emancipation of the workforce actually resulted in profits rather than losses, owing to the increased prosperity, health, education and wellbeing of labour and children, and the subsequent efficiencies that emerged from increased social welfare. The village of New Lanark in central Scotland (Figure 6.1), linked to his cotton factory, became a pioneering example of utopian socialism, visited then and now by thousands of people annually, although it is arguable that the actual achievements of Titus Salt at Saltaire in Leeds were at least as marked (see Figures 6.2 and 6.3). Like Fourier, Owen also rejected Christianity along with the factory system of the industrial revolution based in greed, selfishness, exploitation and human misery. He became disenchanted with the guarded reception his ideas received in Britain, and emigrated to the United States, where he established another sixteen Owenite communities, the most famous of these being New Harmony in Indiana.

In her book *Seven American Utopias* (1976), Dolores Hayden analyses, in great detail, the attempt to establish paradise on the American continent by way of building ideal communities. Of these there were many, and from a huge variety of ideologies and religions, as well as the charismatic claims of many powerful leaders. However, the term *utopian socialists*, applied accurately by Marx and Engels to Saint Simon, Fourier and Owen, is misleading and does not apply to all types of utopian project. A more useful term is the French word *commune*, whose members were referred to as 'communards'. The word refers to the smallest unit of French government administration (*communard*). More generally, it means a communal settlement where ideologies, property, material wealth, labour and other factors are held in common, to varying degrees. The word also possesses the overtones of the French Revolution and the overthrow of the Bourbon monarchy in 1789. While Hayden chooses seven groups (Shakers, Mormons, Fourierists, Perfectionists, Inspirationists, Union Colonists and Llano Colonists), many other communes, sectarian or otherwise, established settlements in America during the second half of the nineteenth century.

However, many died out as rapidly as they arose. Some grew into major religious organisations, such as the Mormons, and the Oneida and Amana communities now represent major corporations in the United States. Both the utopian socialists and the many communes established in America offered a vast array of physical alternatives to traditional family life, from a redesigning of the nuclear family home to grand plans for towns and cities, such as New Harmony in Indiana, Nauvoo in Illinois, Topolobambo in Mexico, Hancock in Massachusetts, Llano del Rio in California or the Amana community in Iowa.

Figure 6.1 Artist's impression of New Lanark, a model industrial community built by the utopian Robert Owen in Scotland, 1785

Source: The Art Archive/Eileen Tweedy

Figure 6.2 View of rear entrances to houses in Saltaire village, West Yorkshire, 1833

Source: © Washington Imaging/Alamy

Figure 6.3 View over the Mill, Saltaire village, West Yorkshire, 1833
Source: Duncan Walker/iStockphoto

In between, designs for homes, industrial and agricultural buildings, temples, collective workshops, crèches, town centres, garden cities, communal apartment buildings and other structures were conceived and built. The collective result was an entirely new and experimental taxonomy of architectural forms, as well as of the relationships among and between these forms in space. Despite the enduring divisions of social class, most, if not all, of this restructuring took place through a redefinition of gender. The repressed anger of women's oppression is well expressed by Alice Constance Austin (architect and planner of Llano del Rio in California) that the traditional home functioned as a Procrustean bed on which, 'each feminine personality must be made to conform by whatever maiming or fatal, spiritual or intellectual oppression . . . and of the thankless and unending drudgery of an inconceivably stupid and inefficient system by which her labours are confiscated' (Hayden 1981: 242).

It is safe to say that, in virtually every commune, issues of gender and space inevitably involved sexuality, across all age barriers and from birth to the grave. As certain communes saw the traditional nuclear family as the source of women's enslavement, its deconstruction and spatial reorganisation also undermined women's position as property within patriarchy. In some cases, this allowed women complete sexual freedom, and, in others, the concept of patriarchy was significantly enhanced. For example, Mormon society was polygamous. In the Oneida community, group marriage was promoted, and couples were discouraged. The Amana, on the other hand, insisted on celibacy or monogamous relationships. What became clear overall was that a new sexual division of labour and sex roles resulted in new spatial structures. The concept of gender and gendered space challenged the concept of social class in the breadth of its implications for social reconstruction, and still does so today.

The transition to the twentieth century also saw some cataclysmic shifts in gender relations with the communist revolutions in Russia and China. Unfortunately, equality between the sexes did not occur quite as planned, and the revolution of the proletariat did not produce the effects Marx expected. Women's position in both of these countries in terms of emancipation remains significantly below that of its capitalist counterparts in the Western world. Defying one of its most cherished principles – equality for all – patriarchal socialism was a disaster for women's emancipation in all respects. Nor did cataclysmic social change generate even minimal shifts in the relationship between gender and space, as communes in both countries remained firmly rooted in the nuclear family system, albeit with a weakening of ties between parents and children. In the *Grand Domestic Revolution* (1981) and *Redesigning the American Dream* (1984), Dolores Hayden provides penetrating analyses of the domestic mode of production – the labour of half the world's workers, which goes unpaid and is therefore discounted as forming part of any national economy (without doubt contributing the *free* component within the free market system). By the end of the First World War, most experiments in utopian socialism of whatever genre had fallen apart.

Nonetheless, traces of communal living carried on. Ebeneezer Howard, a Fabian, continued experimenting with the idea of cooperative housing and shared domestic work as the foundation of his ideal *garden city*, a concept that today still reverberates in planning thought. He incorporated these ideas in his design for cooperative housing in Letchworth at Homesgarth (1909) and moved into one of his own kitchenless apartments with his wife (Hayden 1981: 231). Residents of the thirty-two apartments had the choice of communal dining or service in their own flat. The concept of the kitchenless house was pursued in several countries, including the United States, and the Great Depression of 1930–9 saw the establishment of many communes as a necessary part of survival, one that also had its European counterpart (Figure 6.4). The same was true in Russia after the revolution (Figure 6.5). In Australia, where land was available, many communes were established by emigrants escaping poverty and homelessness. After the Second World War, however, urbanisation in the West saw the nuclear family firmly entrenched as the fundamental social unit, reinforced by the physical isolation of one family from another in the creation of vast suburban sprawl. Somewhat later, around 1960, what remained of gender equality dictated by shared responsibility in labour became reoriented to political equality within the market economy, on the basis of an intrinsically feminist ideology, influenced by new developments in biology, neurology, philosophy and psychology.

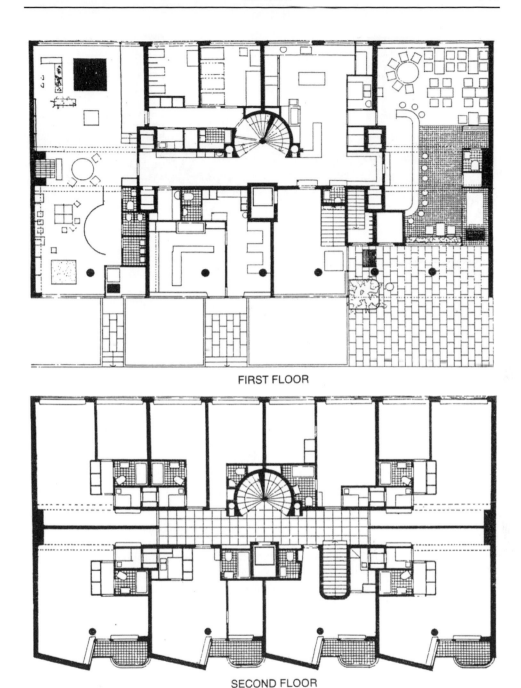

FIRST FLOOR

SECOND FLOOR

Figure 6.4 S. Markelius and A. Myrdal's collective house, Stockholm, 1935

Source: D. Hayden, *The Grand Domestic Revolution: A History of Feminist Designs for American Homes, Neighbourhoods and Cities*. Cambridge, MA: MIT Press, 1981, p. 165, Fig. 6.2

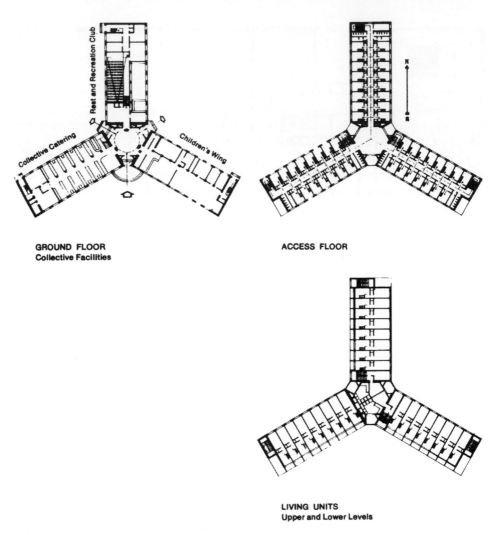

GROUND FLOOR
Collective Facilities

ACCESS FLOOR

LIVING UNITS
Upper and Lower Levels

Figure 6.5 K. Ivanov, F. Terekhtin and P. Smolin. Plans for communal housing with collective catering, 1924

Source: D. Hayden, *The Grand Domestic Revolution: A History of Feminist Designs for American Homes, Neighbourhoods and Cities*. Cambridge, MA: MIT Press, 1981, p. 259, Fig. 11.23

Sex, gender and the female mind

> There is no female mind. The brain is not an organ of sex. Might as well talk about a female liver.
>
> (Charlotte Perkins Gilman (1860–1930))

While it may seem unnecessary to a discussion over the integration of gender with design issues in cities, we cannot proceed without taking into account a brief consideration of scientific enquiry into the human brain and its relation to sex and gender (Harding 1991). Claimed biological differences between the sexes have been abused in a variety of ways to undermine women's freedom and reinforce patriarchy. Along with this, there is the associated and problematic concept of 'mind' (Kimura 1993, 1999, Blum 1997, Geary 1998, Hines 2004). Fundamental biological divisions between the sexes need some brief consideration to fully inform our understanding of women's needs in the built environment. For example, if Charlotte Gilman could have accessed the research that has occurred in the last century, she might have had some doubts about her statement. For example, she conflates *brain* and *mind*; argues that the brain has nothing to do with sex and is not an *organ*; and conveys the idea that somehow sex can exist independent of its functioning. Initial attempts to erase any biological difference between the sexes as part of the political agenda of radical feminism, as well as the gay cosmos, have given way to the fact that significant differences do exist, outside environmental influences. Current research is now exposing a broadening array of diversity in structure, function and biochemistry between the sexes. This leads to important differences in perception, behaviour, emotion and cognition, discoveries that have only recently been possible through sophisticated technological advances, such as functional magnetic resonance imaging (FMRI). Although these differences do not necessarily result in behavioural change, they remain significant. Although biology does not rule, it has its moments.

While most investigation has focussed on the male brain, more recent research has tried to bring some balance into the picture. Simon Baron-Cohen, the director of the Autism Research Centre at Cambridge University, has affirmed the specific biological differences between average male and female minds in a recent book, *The Essential Difference* (Baron-Cohen 2004). Similarly, *The Female Brain* by Loann Brizendine (2006), a pioneering neuropsychiatrist at Harvard University, is the result of extensive research into how women think and act as they do. Importantly, the differences between brain types go well beyond reproduction. She established the first clinic in the United States to study and treat the brain function of women. Her book begins to compensate for the fact that the male domain has been the focus of most existing clinical data on neurology, psychiatry and neurobiology, and her work represents a major contribution to the place of women in society. Most of the differences that have appeared are significant, but an important consideration (before politics intrudes) is that the female brain (biology) does not necessarily correlate with the female mind (gender). The BBC, for example, has a test assembled by a team of psychologists to indicate whether or not one has a *male* or *female* brain, independent of sexuality. The test offers a brain-sex profile, to discover whether one *thinks* like a man or a woman, and can be accessed at (www.bbc.co.uk/science/humanbody/).

The bottom line is that every brain is female at conception. Only after eight weeks *in utero* does a massive surge in levels of testosterone determine maleness or femaleness. Overall, men's brains are roughly 10 per cent larger, with approximately 4 per cent more brain cells (and about 100 grams more tissue), figures that may seem irrelevant as we only use something like 10 per cent of our mental capacity in any event. Whereas males will access the left brain more than the right, the dendritic connections in a woman's brain are more numerous and complex (Lippa 2002). The frontal cortex, where higher cognitive functions are located, is also larger. Hence, women have the capacity to transfer information more rapidly between the hemispheres, a fact that has an important bearing on language capacity and language learning. It influences, for example, recovery from stroke, where the speech capacity of men is more likely to be impaired (Blum 1997). These structural differences and the larger size of the hippocampus (location of emotion and memory) also enhance women's capacity for nurturing, making their recall superior to that of the opposite sex. As a result, men and women orient themselves in space differently, the former having a capacity to solve problems through the mental rotation of images, whereas the latter rely on superior memory function. Crudely stated, men tend to calculate where they are in space, whereas women proceed by feeling and remembering.

Not only is current research leading to a greater capacity to understand and treat certain forms of illness, it is also opening doors to a more encompassing understanding of gender and difference. Although this information may not translate directly into design concepts and strategies, in no way does it deny the significance of gender to design, and few (hopefully few men) – would say that it is unimportant. Hence, anyone looking for a straight-line graph connecting gender heterologies to design outcomes will be disappointed. However, the fact that we are more informed about this relationship will inexorably modify our consciousness and, hence, our capacity to deal with problems differently (Hines 2004, Geary 1998). The relationships between gender, equality, urban politics and social change are also influenced by the question of a specifically feminist awareness and, therefore, a specifically feminist method.

A feminist method?

The concept of a distinctly feminist method opens up the question of a specifically feminist science, scientific investigation being the dominant paradigm of all enquiry. So, does a specifically feminist science exist? Can a scientific counter-culture be established, one that promotes a uniquely feminist epistemology, yet one that is inclusive of men? The answer appears to be a resounding *yes* on both counts. It must also be pointed out that we cannot really talk of feminism, but feminisms, given the ideological range of feminist activity (see FOC: Chapter 6). The arguments are complex and challenging, and here I can only abbreviate some of the more important debates (see Bleier 1986, Harding 1991, Hesse-Biber *et al.* 1999, Lather 2007). In contradiction to the classic absolutist, androcentric tradition, the bottom line is that science is not a rational, abstract process, populated by billions of self-contained facts waiting to be discovered, with an independent existence outside values, subjectivities, meanings and gendered realities. Like everything else, science is a socially produced cultural institution. However, unlike other social processes, science feigns a special mantle, as it denies its ideological foundation within the social formation to claim objectivity in all things, an objectivity that transcends race, class, sex and gender. But it goes without saying that patriarchy has dominated science, as it has the economy and family life. Therefore, it is reasonable to assume that the traditions of science have as much bias as any other region of knowledge, with the systematic exclusion of women at all levels of the scientific process, from laboratory assistants to research of global significance: 'Since ideas are not generated in cultural vacuums, the exclusion of women from the practice of science and the consequent male, patriarchal structuring of science is reflected in [its] concepts, metaphors, assumptions and language' (Bleier 1986: 6).

Hence, feminism calls into question every aspect of the scientific process, on the basis that it has been biased and therefore distorted in its objectives, structure, epistemology and methods of investigation. Donna Haraway (1985), coming from a perspective rooted in primatology, suggests that feminism will not succeed in its quest by simply replacing one paradigm by another, but through modifying a region of research – *a field* – and thus reformatting it with new stories and explanations that describe its operation within a set of new narratives. As she remarks,

> Altering the structure of a field is quite different from replacing false versions with true ones. To construct a different set of boundaries and possibilities for what can count as knowledge for everyone within specific historical circumstances is a radical project.
>
> (Haraway 1985: 81)

However, Haraway's use of the term *field* is not so different from that of Bourdieu, who, in observing that 'science is an armed struggle among adversaries', also notes that,

> The objective reality to which everyone explicitly or tacitly refers is ultimately no more than what the researchers engaged in the field at a given moment, agree to consider as such, and it only ever manifests itself in the field through the representations given of it by those who invoke its arbitration.
>
> (Bourdieu 2000: 113)

It is this nuanced, relational quality that characterises much feminist research, in opposition to finding direct pathways to the truth, which is the dominant, androcentric focus.

When we address the idea of feminist method, we also enter an imaginary arena, which nonetheless is a politically charged and sensitive theatre of debate. Paradoxically, as postmodernism and many feminist writers have made clear, logic dictates that a single feminist method cannot exist, owing to the sheer complexity of the ideologies involved (FOC6: 128–30). It is more relevant to ask what kinds of problem women choose to address, rather than search for proto-feminist methods. Of course, this does not deny the value of each position, nor the positions' synergy, which stand collectively against millennia of patriarchal rule, sexual oppression and personal abuse. The targets are quite clear. All it says is that the innate problems of sexual inequality cannot be reduced to a single method of observation. In one way or another, this focus on gender primes all methodologies, underwriting issues that begin with the sex of god, and conclude with the vexed issue of which public toilets are open to which kinds of person. On the way, questions of biology, neurology, politics, philosophy, psychology, religion and innumerable other issues are encountered, with positions cogently presented by all sides. One thing that can be agreed on, however, is that, while sexuality is biologically determined, gender is a social construct, where even the commonly accepted terms *male* and *female* are extremely fuzzy concepts. This is enhanced by recent approaches that 'draw on definitions of gender that imagine it as a process by which subjectivities are produced and shift over time' (Nightingale 2006: 165). This position had already been stated in Ivan Illich's classic, *Gender* (1983), where he notes that, over historical time, very few societies have classified individuals by the erotic nature of their attraction to a particular gender. Such fuzziness is not only further impacted by race and class, but also by sexual orientation against the mainstream of human behaviour. Hence, there is now a significant literature termed 'queer studies' (Berlant and Warner 1993, Browne *et al.* 2007, Clarke and Peel 2007, Haggerty and McGarry 2007). Such studies carve out the territory of those whose sexuality is heterotopic, in Foucault's terms, or perverse, in Oscar Wilde's – who was of the opinion that 'sin is the only colour left in modern life'.

Therefore, it is reasonable to assume that feminist method may best be understood by making assumptions after enquiring what feminists actually do, which concerns dominate, and what strategies are proposed. For example, from our brief account of gender equality during the nineteenth century, patriarchy, the domestic mode of production, women's unpaid labour, the male gendering of domestic and urban space, and political and legal equality are clearly writ large in the female consciousness as territories in serious need of overhaul. By the same token, neo-Marxist political economy, embedded in questions of equality and space, remains, warts and all, one of the dominant modes of enquiry. Habermas, for example, considers the life-world to be composed of two public and two private spheres. These can be defined as the private sphere of everyday life and the private sphere of the capitalist economy; public spheres are represented in the individual realm of political participation and the collective public sphere of the state. However, this overarching model needs to be quali-fied, 'by observing how each of these four roles is different for men and women; we need in other words, to read the "gender sub-text" in order to see how questions of gender run through every aspect of modern society and its evolution' (Saraswati 2000).

Collections of essays on feminism and methodology regarding development reveal the complexity of the problem and its extension over the last twenty years

(Harding 1987, 2004, Hartsock 1991, Hesse-Biber *et al.* 1999). For example, Doreen Massey's work within the framework of political economy illustrates one major approach to feminist methodology (Massey 1984, 1994), as Donna Haraway's use of near science-fiction dystopia represents another (Haraway 1991). There are also a growing number of texts specifically oriented to feminism and methodology (Harding, 1991, 1998, Lather 2007). Whichever gender one belongs to, the roles that people play in society are fundamental to any epistemological investigation. Even science fiction has its role. In her *Cyborg Manifesto*, Donna Haraway goes one step further than most feminist writers to target nature fetishism, organicism, sexualism and the idea of identity. Her essay constitutes 'an ironic political myth faithful to feminism, socialism and materialism, based upon the idea of a cyborg, a cybernetic post-human hybrid of machine and organism, a creature of high-tech social reality as well as a creature of fiction' (Haraway 1993: 272; see also Haraway 1991, Hayles 1999). In the utopian tradition, the cyborg is envisioned as an artificially constructed phenomenon that inhabits a post-gender world. Sensationalism apart, its overall function is to liberate our minds from the normal strictures of gender politics, racism, patriarchy and oppression, so that future socially constructed boundaries and collective resistance to them may become more apparent. This is not so strange, as it is, in effect, the foundation of all planning (urban or other) – the dubious principle that, if we can predict the future, we may be able to avoid its worst excesses: 'Cyborg feminists have to argue that "we" do not want any more natural matrix of unity and that no construction is whole. Innocence and the corollary insistence on victimhood as the only ground for insight have done enough damage' (Haraway 1993: 278). In this context, Haraway's method is to correlate the evolution of the cyborg with the development of existing social institutions and the processes that flow from them, in a manner that recalls George Orwell's *Nineteen Eighty-Four* (1992 (orig. 1933)) or Aldous Huxley's *Brave New World* (1960). Hence, she redefines and reconceptualises existing spatial structures, such as home, market, paid workplace, state, school, clinic-hospital, church etc., so that the task of surviving the future has a greater probability of success. Nonetheless, her vision is unredeemably bleak, which is not to say that it is unlikely. The future of *Church*, for example, is predicted to evolve into a situation wherein:

> Electronic fundamentalist 'super-saver' preachers solemnising the union of electronic capital and automated fetish gods; intensified importance of churches in resisting the militarised state; central struggle over women's meanings and authority in religion; continued relevance of spirituality, intertwined with sex and health.
>
> (Haraway 1993: 291)

School is reformatted to contain a

> deepening coupling of high-tech capital needs and public education at all levels, differentiated by race, class, and gender; managerial classes involved

in educational reform and refunding at the cost of remaining progressive educational democratic structures for children and teachers. Education for mass ignorance and repression in technocratic and militarised culture; growing anti-science mystery cults in dissenting and radical political movements; continued relative scientific illiteracy among white women and people of colour; growing industrial direction of education (especially higher education) by science-based multinationals (particularly in electronics-dependent and biologically dependent companies); highly educated numerous elites in a progressively bi-modal society.

Whether women's place in such a society will be any better than it is currently is a moot point, with global warming potentially holding the casting vote. Leaving dystopia behind, what we can deduce from all of this is that science is in trouble. The development of feminist epistemology over the last thirty years has not only generated significant challenges to androcentric scientific orthodoxies, it has also proposed and executed its own gendered alternatives. However, while the literature on feminist politics, ideology, science and culture is now extensive, considerations of space and place remain limited. In order to accommodate this need, a brief account of the impact of gender on design is required, prior to that of the *flâneur* – a mythical character that has symbolised women's oppression in urban space for nearly 100 years.

Flânerie as heterology

> The ordinary practitioners of the city live 'down below', below the threshold at which visibility begins. They walk – an elementary form of this experience of the city; they are walkers, Wandersmänner, whose bodies follow the thicks and thins of an urban 'text' they write without being able to read it. These practitioners make use of spaces that cannot be seen, their knowledge of them is as blind as that of lovers in each other's arms. The paths that correspond in these intertwining, unrecognised poems, in which each body is an element signed by many others, elude legibility. It is as though the practices organising a bustling city were characterised by their blindness.
>
> (Michel de Certeau)

> The flâneur is the observer of the marketplace. His knowledge is akin to the occult science of industrial fluctuations. He is a spy for capitalists, on assignment in the realm of consumers.
>
> (Walter Benjamin)

For anybody involved in the urban design process, the actual experience of the city is paramount in the designer's consideration. The idea of the *flâneur*, written about for 140 years, is the embodiment of that experience, of walking in the city, taking in its sound, smells, secrets and vistas (de Certeau 1933, 1984, Parkhurst 1994, Wilson 1995, Huang 1996, White 2001). The *flâneur* is also a historically contingent, mythical character who has evolved with changing consciousness and development from historic boulevards to postmodernist urbanisation.

The term *flâneur* comes from a French verb *flâner*, meaning to wander about, hence, *flânerie* – to walk aimlessly for the sheer pleasure of walking in the city. The term has close relations, in English, to the rambler,

> who visits sites of leisure, pleasure, consumption, exchange and display in early nineteenth-century London: the theatre, opera house, pleasure garden, club, sporting venue and bazaar. By looking in its open and its interior spaces for adventure and entertainment, the rambler creates a conceptual and physical map of the city.
>
> (Rendell *et al.* 2000: 136)

While the rambler's orientation is towards sexual pleasure, the *flâneur* is embedded (after the sixth sense of intuition), in what we may call 'the seventh sense' of kinaesthesia, the sensation of bodily movement through urban space. He comports himself with the qualities of casual observer, voyeur and analyst of the city. He is a collector of filmic texts, impressions and transitions, as well as urban and architectural forms and spaces. He is the ultimate cognitive map. The concept of the *flâneur* was first initiated by Charles Baudelaire, in his *Paris Spleen* collection of poetry, from 1869. Baudelaire claimed that traditional forms of art were inadequate to express modernity, and that it was a mandate that the artists should immerse themselves in the metropolis in all its complexity. The *flâneur* was Baudelaire's embodiment of the urban experience.

More recently, the Marxist Walter Benjamin advanced the idea in his *Arcades Project* of 1935 into a critique of capitalism (Benjamin 1997, 1999). In this task, Benjamin was influenced by the sociologist George Simmel, whose essay 'The metropolis and mental life' (1903) remains a classic for all urbanists. So, the original *flâneur* is male, French, and the setting is Paris, amid the rebuilding of the city by Baron Haussmann, from 1851 to 1870 (although the process had commenced well before this point and continued well after his sacking in 1870). Therefore, Baudelaire's *flâneur* was probably trying to walk around in one of Europe's largest construction sites, a reason why Benjamin felt that the arcades of Paris offered unlimited opportunities to the *flâneur*, compared with those of the normal city streets. Since then, a significant body of literature has grown up around the overall theme of the *flâneur* (Mazlish 1994, Tester 1994, Gleber 1999, Parsons 2000, O'Neill 2002, D'Souza and McDonnough 2006, Wilson 1995). As O'Neill remarks:

> He is 'the reader' and writer of 'the spectacle' that is the modern city. He is the mobile observer of the public life of the modern world . . . he emerges as 'a historian, a reflective critic of the city, a close analyst of its architecture,

a collector of scenes and images, and an interpreter who translates his impressions and experiences into a way of being/existing in the world and often into texts that represent these experiences'.

(O'Neill 2002: 3–4)

The constellation of events and circumstances contained in *flâneur* vastly transcend its own simple definition, the central reason being that it condenses an array of factors significant to the study of urban form and experience. It provides a simple method – the idea walking in the city – that can be expanded to include a general critique of capitalism, particularly consumerism, to encompass gender, social class, utopianism, the urban–rural divide, film, the kinaesthetic experience and other important dimensions of urbanism. Many writers have addressed *flâneur*, both in theory and practice, including Michel de Certeau, Walter Benjamin, Georg Simmel, James Joyce and Edgar Allen Poe. Overall, James Joyce's revolutionary *Ulysses* of 1922 must, however, constitute the finest example of the genre. His account of a single day in the life of its *flâneur* anti-hero, Leopold Bloom, wandering through the streets of Dublin and sampling its offerings on 16 June 1904, remains a masterpiece of twentieth-century literature. Interestingly, Joyce finished writing *Ulysses* (1960 (orig. 1922)) and commenced his second great work, *Finnegan's Wake* (1992 (orig. 1939)), in Paris, in 1922:

The question then arises as to whether the flâneur is a historical concept with no relevance today, being overtaken by the wholly commodified flâneur of the late twentieth century – the tourist. O'Neill points out that the difference between them is fundamental – while the tourist goes from site to site, and the destinations are the essential experience, the flâneur is exploring the 'in-between' spaces where aimlessness is the aim. He is doing nothing other than 'the act of doing' itself.

(O'Neill 2002: 2)

In revealing issues of androcentric urban space (not to mention patriarchy, oppression, hegemony, inequality, social class and domesticity), the *flâneur* is obviously a man, and the role of women is implied, either by their annihilation from the scene, or their unwilling participation as an object of the male gaze. Virtually all of the writings about perceptions of space in cities and its associated *emballage* are once again a reinforcement of the concept that urban space, however many women it contains, still remains a male domain, both conceptually and actually. The only women who could carve out a space of their own in the time of Baudelaire and Benjamin were prostitutes. Colette, Anaïs Nin, Simone de Beauvoir and other radical feminists were possible exceptions to such rules. More recently, the concept of *flâneur* has been challenged by the term *flâneuse*, in order to lay claim to women's rights in the domain of public space and, hence, locate it fairly and squarely within the purview of feminist politics and criticism (Wolff 1985, Von Ankum 1997, Gleber 1999, Olofsson 2008). The *flâneuse* highlights the subordinate role of women in the domestic realm to the dominant male role in the public realm of social life. While the flâneur denoted an incipient modernity, women remained cloistered and suffocated within the domestic realm (Thompson 2000, D'Souza and MacDonough 2006).

The emergence of the *flâneuse*, a female who could freely roam the streets, as did her male counterpart, remained problematic, as challenges over territory inevitably end in bloodshed (Figure 6.6). Hence, the space of the department store and luxury consumption at the end of the twentieth century represented the first spaces where women could roam freely and without peril. The male domain was not threatened. Shopping, a distinctly bourgeois activity, clearly excluded working-class women, who remained entombed in domesticity. Nonetheless, the freedom of the bourgeois woman did not approach synchronicity with her male counterpart, as her own movement had been tied into new forms of capitalist consumption, later evolving into the supermarkets and hypermarkets of contemporary life. Production remained a male domain. The clear distinction is that the woman's freedom was inexorably tied to interior public spaces, where her security was/is guaranteed. Invariably, the street so colonised by the *flâneur* can be symbolised for many women in their own transition from one interior space to another, a journey that was not characterised by the inherent freedoms assumed by men in urban space. The conventions that apply to men do not apply to the woman, with the effect that her gaze is restricted, her presence as

Figure 6.6 The *flâneuse*: public space and the male double standard

Source: D. Hayden, *The Grand Domestic Revolution: A History of Feminist Designs for American Homes, Neighbourhoods and Cities*. Cambridge, MA: MIT Press, 1981, p. 29

a public is minimised and turned into a stylised display or an object of the voyeur's pleasure.

In order to assert the increasing role of the *flâneuse*, Jennie Oloffson has used a linguistic device, preferring to use the term fl@neur for the female. This is an intelligent gambit, because, in merging terms linguistically, we are forced to denote difference and therefore to recognise and reveal our own prejudices. Similarly, by merging the terminology, she creates a more radical methodology – not by adopting the more obvious and divisive tactic of a radical *other*, but by absorbing the opposition into the same *Weltanschauung*. It is an effective method to deny dualism and useless conflict. Hence, the move is at once defiant and insightful, as well as offering politically subtle yet undeniable resistance to male dominance across the entire spectrum of issues, from the material and the social, into the virtual world (Olofsson 2008). Interestingly, and in reference to the Norwegian theorist Dag Osterberg, she chooses to focus on the concept of *förtäntningar*, or densities, and states, 'not only is the study of densities paving the way for blurred boundaries between city and countryside; using the term also allows for alternative views of embodied relationships between humans and spatiality', and, hence, 'I see the fl@neur as occupying densities rather than boulevards' (Olofsson 2008: 8).

Therefore, concepts of *flâneuse* and densities challenge several components of *flânerie*: the urban–rural divide, the public and domestic realms, interior and exterior space in both, as well as the possibility of adapted forms of spatial restructuring. For example, we can now consider the idea of the fl@neur in the suburbs, and adaptations into the realm of the automobile, not forgetting that the *flâneur* is not an *individual* but an *analytical device*, offering greater understanding of cities. In Paul O'Neill's article, 'Taking the *flâneur* for a spin to the suburbs', he argues that the gradual progression from street to department store modified the *flâneur*'s relationship to the city: 'the demarcations between observer and observed, and more significantly between the individual and the commodity were now abolished, and the flâneur was now taken "into" the space of consumption' (Hulser 1997, O'Neill 2002: 4). Similarly, the movement from department store – still largely an urban phenomenon – was itself gradually swallowed by supermarkets and the suburban shopping centre, an event made possible by Taylorised Fordist production techniques that permitted mass access to the automobile. Hypermarkets extended the idea even further. This permitted the method of *flânerie* to be extended to the auto-*flâneur*, and an altogether different method of accommodating urban life, yet another extension of Baudelaire's original idea.

Although this process did not directly destroy *flânerie*, hopefully still alive and well in many great cities, it removed it, in whole or in part, from vast urban areas in the United States. Shopping centres annihilated the conventional literacy of cities, which Kevin Lynch (1960) denoted as paths, edges, districts, nodes and landmarks, in favour of a new vocabulary of brands, escalators, lifts, parking lots, hypermarkets etc. Similarly, our perceptual field now became extended into movement through space at vastly increased speeds. Whereas the *flâneur*'s body/movement was an indivisible process, a new 'auto-centaur' was born, a creature paralysed by its own body, unable to move without being welded to an automobile (J.G. Ballard's novels such *Crash* and *Kingdom Come* (1973, 2006) convey the flavour of this idea). As the *flâneur* and the *flâneuse* offered differing methods of analysing urban space, so the auto-centaur added a new dimension to the other two. In each case, however, progressive methods of analysis come into play, methods that allow us to plot the shifting relationship between capitalist processes of consumption and the changing matrix of urban space and design:

> The ability to define people to object relations and the knowledge and control of this economic exchange within capitalist space, allows for the possibility to create purpose made new spaces within which this exchange can be both monitored and controlled. Major examples can be found in the construction of completely new cities that were based on capitalist ideology, like Las Vegas, or [the] edge cities of Detroit or Chicago, or suburban developments like Celebration or Seaside in the United States, as well as British examples like Welwyn Garden City or Milton Keynes.
>
> (O'Neill 2002: 8)

Perhaps the real evolution of the *flâneur* is best exhibited by 'low riders' everywhere, but personified by Chicanos and Blacks in the United States, who use the automobile to wander slowly and aimlessly through the streets, like the Dandy, absorbing the sounds and lights of the city, albeit at a speed not much beyond the *flâneur*'s perambulations.

Heterology, gender and design

As the *flâneur* symbolises the male domination of space *qua* experience, so androcentric control is also exercised over its physical organisation and structuring. While the *flâneur* personifies the authority of the male *gaze*, control over the design and organisation of the city is similarly overwhelmed through decisions made by men. This fact is so self-evident it needs little reinforcement. Decisions about the organisation, structuring and design of social space are executed in both state and private sectors and in financial, administrative, planning, cultural and corporate institutions, where committees, boards of directors, shareholders and all forms of decision-making remain overwhelmingly dominated by men, even today. So the question of the emancipation of women at all levels of the urban design process begins with the education and employment of women and ends in the boardrooms in the highest echelons of government and business (Adams and Tancred 2000). At the level of the male consciousness, it involves nothing less than a revolution in the way we perceive the world (Akkerman 2006). The crisis of sustainable development emanating from cities is matched equally by the crisis of women's empowerment, and it is also self-evident that the crisis of global warming has occurred within the context of patriarchy.

In equal measure, the spatial division of labour deployed by patriarchal capitalism is not gender neutral (Andrew and Milroy 1988, Spain 1992, Massey 1994). It is the heterology through which women's subservience and control have been encapsulated in space (Drucker and Gumpert 1997). The methodology of urban transformations – from the planning and provision of central business districts to suburbs, sporting venues, entertainment districts, industrial zones and the whole panoply of urban functions – constitutes gendered realities. In most cases, they envelop the material context and the processes they encompass. These same realities constitute historically designated constraints in the form of a physically variegated matrix of oppression, supported and generated by capitalist urbanisation – mental and physical abuse, psychological dominance, victimisation, humiliation, insecurity, physical constraints and negative representation in the form of sexist imagery across all forms of media, to name but a few (Valentine 1990, 1995, Borisoff and Hahn 1997, Day 1997, 1999). The overall effect is to dominate, resist, oppose, undermine, threaten or express indifference, on a grand scale, to women's needs. The same is true to a varying degree with the queer world, ethnic minorities, children, the aged and the handicapped. The corollary is that, in order to generate the empowerment and necessary freedoms that reflect women's rights, space also matters. Not only does the system of power need to change, but also so do its methods in relation to spatial implications and consequences. This argument does not represent an unconscious vindication of physical determinism, quite the opposite. It stresses that the decisions that formed space were the controlling factors, along with their inherent ideological bias. Urban design decisions are not only material decisions about bricks and mortar; they also constitute political and moral decisions, frequently with effects that span centuries. There is no such thing as a value-neutral design process in cities, and this fact extends to every level of professional engagement (Roberts 1997, 1998).

Notwithstanding my comments about the existence of urban design as an independent region of knowledge, the research in architecture and planning about women's access to education and employment as the best method of bringing about gender equality is much better researched (Mackenzie 1988, 1989, Greed 1994, Loevinger *et al.* 1998, Madsen 1994, Adams and Tancred 2000, Weddle 2001). A seminal article on the methodology of gender planning was written by Moser and Levi (1986), with figurations for feminist methodologies more recently pursued (Olofsson 2008). Even the Royal Town Planning Institute has made its own contribution to gendered methodologies in publishing in its *Gender mainstreaming toolkit* (Reeves 2003), a belated recognition from twenty years earlier that something was amiss (RTPI 1985). The accompanying caveat, as noted above, is that research methods also tend to be gender biased, even if they are instigated by women (Grant *et al.* 1987). Indeed, the architectural profession has also been presented with its sexist history, in two fine books, *Designing Women* (Adams and Tancred 2000) and *Designing for Diversity* (Anthony

2001). Both make disturbing reading, in that they destroy all of our prejudices that somehow misogyny and discrimination have nothing to do with the civilised professional world, when patently they are equally rife, if better disguised, as elsewhere in society. Indeed, the architectural profession also qualifies significantly in racial and ethnic discrimination as well. Anthony's methodology was based on both primary and secondary research in Canada, using census material on women architects from 1921 to 1991, archival sources and interviews with various groups of registered female architects, including those who no longer belonged to the profession. Apart from many insightful outcomes, an overarching conclusion is that the few women who have become successful have had to do so by inserting themselves into a male-dominated profession and accepting its values, rather than belonging to one that was non-sexist and democratic. The critique of the professions is also paralleled by the critique of the academy, where ideological practices in the androcentric organisation of space and form are taught across gender boundaries (Sutton 1996). Similar sentiments have also been expressed about planning education (MacGregor 1995: 25).

Methodical discrimination through design takes on many forms, and professional bias at the institutional level is only the beginning. Countless other methods of gendering the built environment also exist, from the interior spaces of architecture to the construction of the public realm, monuments and art forms (Gardiner 1989, Weisman 1992). At its most elementary, women's underwear is fetishised as spectacle in boutiques, in countless public thoroughfares across the Western world. In certain places, it is the women themselves who are fetishised, placed in shop windows and sold in red light districts, in Amsterdam and Hamburg, for example. More subtle are the practices that have formed the domestic realm over time, the relationship between rooms, the form and location of contents, between inside and outside, and the gendered and social stratification of the inhabitants. Virginia Woolf is of the most perceptive of all writers, for example, in *Jacob's Room* and *A Room of One's Own*, where she undertakes a microscopic analysis of domestic space, along with the surgical dissection of its characters. As she demonstrates, gendered differences even apply to the use of furniture, its type, placement and materials. To take a single example, the most famous chairs of all time, by Thonet, Mies van der Rohe, Le Corbusier, Alvar Aalto, Gerrit Rietveldt and others, were all designed by men. Clearly, it is difficult to exclude furniture and fittings from an analysis of gendered space, as empty, unfurnished rooms can only transmit so much information (Colomina 1992, Leslie and Reimer 2003). Gendered domestic space can also be seen as a metaphor for domestic gendered social space, albeit at differing scales and contexts (Franck and Paxson 1989, Weisman 1992: 86). As men still dominate in the design professions, it is unsurprising that the contexts required for women's compliance are ideologically reproduced by men, in the absence of any awareness of the process.

At the level of policy, a diversity of methods have been initiated to accommodate women's need in cities, although only a fragment of what is actually required to restore some balance. In addition, such is the socialisation of women that there is no necessary correlation between more women and better outcomes. Nonetheless, European women planners started what is called *The Eurofem Initiative* in order to impose women on to the process of spatial and policy planning. This constitutes a major counter to the idea that so-called 'women's problems' have nothing to do with design and land use (Boys 1985, Huxley 1988, Sandercock and Forsyth 1992, Fainstein and Servon 2005). This initiative is also supported by a highly organised website that addresses planning issues: www.gendersite.org. Planning the non-sexist city has made slow but inexorable progress since 1980, when Dolores Hayden wrote her by now iconic article, 'What would a non-sexist city be like?'. Only a few initiatives can be mentioned here (see FOC6: 143). For example, the Royal Town Planning Institute denotes eight questions that should be incorporated at all levels in the planning process, in order to accommodate gender equality (this naturally includes men as well), namely:

- Who comprises the policy-making team?
- What is the representation of men and women? Minority groups?
- Who are the planners planning for? Men, women, workers, minorities?
- How are statistics gathered, and are they disaggregated by gender?
- What are the key values, priorities and objectives of the plan?
- Who is consulted, and who is involved in participation?
- How is the plan evaluated, by whom and on what basis?
- How is the policy implemented, managed and monitored?

While these are obviously not design criteria, they would clearly affect design outcomes through a more variegated input at the planning stage. Dolores Hayden also suggested a list of six properties for housing and residential neighbourhoods that a more egalitarian society should possess (Hayden 1980: 272). Added to this is a more recent taxonomy of priorities as a method of reducing gender bias in design:

- a well-developed network of services dealing with the issue of violence against women and children;
- elimination of public violence against women through a public agency with the mandate to ensure this [situation];
- friendly neighbourhoods through mixed use of space and lively streets oriented towards pedestrians rather than cars;
- a first-class public transportation system that is cheap, safe and efficient;
- an active social housing policy that includes cooperative housing, housing for women leaving transitional homes, and special housing for women with disabilities;
- good day-care in a variety of forms, from drop-in centres to full day-care;
- active encouragement of community-based economic development, with meaningful jobs for women, coordinated with day-care;

- a close physical relationship between services, residences and work-places, encouraged by mixed urban land use;
- a feminist planning process, working with the population rather than about the population;
- public art that is representative of women and women-centred activities.

(Eichler 1995: 16)

Other early initiatives include that of the London Planning Aid Service (1987) and urban planning and design in Toronto, where building women's needs into metropolitan planning has had a huge impact, much of it based in workshops to increase awareness, lobbying of politicians, meetings with community groups and general mobilisation of women to support their own best interests (Modlich 1994). Elsewhere, suggestions have been made that focus on gender equality by reclaiming public space for daily life, emphasising the local over the global, reintegrating culture, generating greater civic engagement and other qualities (Watson 1988, Ruddock 1996, Jaeckel and Geldermalsen 2006).

Conclusion

Along with nature, the fact of gender is arguably the most exploitive aspect of the capitalist system. Tragically, socialism has done no better. While gender equality makes glacial progress, along with the domestic mode of production, important inroads have been made into gender diversity and difference, from biochemistry to childhood education. The practical results are legion, illuminating such differences as learning capacity, physiology and perception in space. This naturally leads to the question of a distinctly feminist method, applied in our case to the built environment. Given that feminism is represented in all aspects of social science, arguably there can be no specifically feminist method. More significantly, the feminist contribution is oriented differently, to how entire fields of knowledge have been constructed within patriarchy, whatever theoretical bent is pursued. All of this impacts on the built environment, illustrated by the metaphor of the fl@neuse, which condenses a multitude of urban conflicts into a single concept. More specifically, it is transparent that, within the built environment disciplines as a whole, the entire gamut of prejudice and inequality has run rampant for many years. Gender bias has been exerted from education to employment and to professional activity. Hence, Dolores Hayden's question of thirty years ago, 'what would a non-sexist city look like?', may remain unanswered for some time to come.

7 Environment

By what right do we treat non-human species, from microscopic diatoms to 3000 year old Huon pines, as wholly subservient to human desires? This enslavement of other life forms, this debauching of a planet has brought us to the brink of ecocide.

(Barry Littlewood)

Introduction: market meltdown, density and urban form

Currently (October 2008), we are at the epicentre of the sub-prime mortgage crisis and market meltdown, a testament to greed, corruption, usury, speculation and downright stupidity. The private sector is now on social welfare, as the entire finance industry and private-sector corporations such as General Motors wait in line for handouts from the American government, with global ripple effects. So-called market capitalism, with its laissez-faire ideology, has vanished overnight, bailed out by Joe the Plumber and his savings. Driven by short-term economics, the built environment and its design expression remain a servo mechanism of state political expediency and private-sector profits, with significant cooperation or collusion between the two, depending on how one views state neocorporatism. The entire debacle had its predominant location in millions of suburban homes across the United States, where consumers had been allowed to own mortgages against no equity. American excesses were financed, not by their own government, but by borrowing the savings of other developed countries. This situation brought to the fore the importance of efficiency, not only in financial markets, but also in the built environment itself. It also illuminated the need for sustainability in all forms of enterprise, with principles directly linking the capitalist market system to our survival as a species.

In Chapter 7 of *The Form of Cities*, I outlined the framework of concepts that underpin current theory in sustainable development. I also indicated the clear relationship between these ideologies and urban form, the lynchpin being the debates over urban density (FOC7: 168–70). This relationship is inescapable, yet remains one that is unresolved today. Urban density is a direct reflection of the political economy of place and has been for millennia. Here, one of the most important and enduring conflicts influencing the development of cities in the Western world is the clash between advocates of urban consolidation and those who reify the suburbs. Below, I suggest that the debate is a form of false consciousness for all who endlessly pursue this struggle, and that the conflict itself is meaningless in the face of pre-existing capitalist urbanisation. It is clear that future trajectories in urbanisation will deploy a variety of strategies, as appropriate to geography, politics and other determinants of urban form. In the process, arbitrary analytical divisions of urban space into city, suburbs and countryside will become largely irrelevant, as to a large degree they have been for decades. New forms of technology, politics, social relations and sustainable development will influence how urbanisation develops, not the winners of a debate that has no meaningful outcome.

Suburb-urbs

At the risk of setting up two straw dogs, it seems apparent that nowhere is the debate on the method of building cities more intense than it is in the clash between suburban development and urban consolidation (Gottdiener 1977, Fishman 1987, Sharpe and Wallock 1994, Hayden 2003, Davison 2005). Without doubt it is the crucible round which conflict over policies on urban form and density become overheated. In the main, it would seem that the conflict originates round a singular confusion, that somehow pre-existing urban form is not a by-product of the capitalist world system; rather, it is a deliberate lifestyle choice. From this cultural world-view, Los Angeles, for example (or indeed London, Melbourne, Buenos Aires and other cities), is like it is because people preferred to live in suburbs, as they would have space for their families and clean air to breathe. The fact that they later breathed polluted air, existed miles from work in tract houses which forced them to spend a massive amount of their disposable income in support of the automobile and petrochemical monopolies, and used a large proportion of their tax dollars to pay for infrastructure in the form of freeways rather than public transport, all had to be the result of their own bad judgement.

Mike Davis's *City of Quartz* (1990) recounts in great detail a picture of the Los Angeles suburbs as an ecocidal, politically driven and corrupt process of land development motivated by nothing more than greed and exploitation (see also Rome 2001, Gwyther 2004, Lang *et al.* 2006). Riding on the back of this process, 'urban planning tends to be restricted to an after-the-fact search for "feasible" remedies to the negative outcomes of this contradictory process of land development' (Scott and Roweis 1977: 1109). The fact that urban planning had to resolve the resultant tension between the central city and suburban development generated an ideological 'planning' conflict represented in the opposing camps of suburbanisation or urban consolidation. Ultimately, all commitments to one form or the other are ideologically driven (Stretton 1970, Troy 2004, Searle 2007). This hiatus falsely displaced the root of the problem from being one of capitalist urbanisation to one of urban planning practice, guaranteeing a debate that could continue in perpetuity, without actually dealing with the issue – one that is compounded at the level of urban politics in confusions over growth, sustainability, profit, development, conservation and other factors.

The urban consolidation debate has been more heated in Australia than in many other countries, possibly owing to its sheer physical size and distance between urban centres, but more importantly because its major cities have gross residential densities lower than Los Angeles (Dawkins and Searle 1995). Given an arid climate to begin with, this fact makes them among the most wasteful on the planet, with a carbon footprint that leads the world in its excesses. Suburban expansion has been denoted as being at least partly due to a prevalent migrant ideology of home ownership, with the 'quarter acre block' representing the gold standard for many families. Owing to these and other factors, McLoughlin (1991) notes that, on average, Australian cities have about one-quarter the population density of European cities, making them among the lowest-density urban environments of any developed country. He notes that, per head of population, they have four times the length of roads, only three-quarters of the public transport route length, and half the journeys by foot or bicycle. He also mentions that Australians only make 12 per cent of recorded journeys by foot, bicycle or public transport, against 46 per cent in Europe (McLoughlin 1991: 148). No doubt this is part of the reason why Australians, along with Americans, are now on average the most obese people on the planet. Based on significant empirical research, his classic paper, 'Urban consolidation and urban sprawl' (1991), represents a singular defence of suburban living, as indeed does Hugh Stretton's paper, 'Density, efficiency and equity in Australian cities' (1996). McLoughlin's central point is that urban expansion is not limited by increasing densities [so we may as well build more suburbs]. After an extended study, McLoughlin concludes that the idea of saving urban land through consolidation is a fallacy, as 'increased residential densities save quite insignificant amounts even under the most favourable assumptions' (McLoughlin 1991: 155).

Hugh Stretton supports McLoughlin's thesis by attacking the idea that sprawling Australian cities are environmentally unsustainable, economically inefficient, inequitable and unsociable, the central arguments used to promote the idea of consolidation and sustainable development (Stretton 1996). He points to the fact that converting to European densities would only save around 6 per cent of total energy use, which would have to be offset against the benefits (both tangible and intangible) of having gardens. Although servicing suburban allotments is expensive, again this has to be offset against the cost of tearing up existing infrastructure, redeveloping existing areas and the provision of new services in highly dense environments to accommodate hundreds of thousands of new residents. Overall, Stretton's focus is on the somewhat unquantifiable idea of *community*, arguing that sociability will invariably remain with the upper and middle classes who can afford external space, which he considers to be the foundation of neighbourliness and which is lost as densities increase. Troy (1996) also supports the idea that most initiatives to generate consolidation are simplistic and are more likely to intensify environmental stresses rather than making them better. He maintains that increasing housing density:

- actually decreases our capacity to cope with domestic wastes and our opportunities for recycling;
- reduces our capacity to harvest or otherwise cope with the rainfall on urban areas and reduce run-off;
- makes it harder for urban residents to produce much of their own food;
- increases air pollution, because it reduces space for growth of trees and shrubs to purify air and cool the urban area;
- reduces chances of growth of wood for fuel and reduces habitats for birds and other native fauna; and
- increases congestion, which increases accidents and energy losses.

(Troy 1996: 129)

The opposing method of urban consolidation also has its supporters, who argue that consolidation conserves valuable agricultural land, is a more efficient use of existing urban infrastructure, and represents significant savings in terms of transportation and access to services. This concept of infrastructural efficiencies has been pursued in Munro (2005) in the context of the New Urbanism by comparing the various methods of creating communities at varying densities. Overall, the argument that housing land is most efficiently saved by increasing the density of low-density development has widespread support, as all other elements of collective consumption requirements represent a fixed proportion in the allocation of land for this purpose (universities, schools, parks, playing fields, medical facilities etc.). Therefore, 'an increase in density from 24 to 40 persons per acre (p.p.a.) saves almost ten times as much housing land as the much larger increase from 160 to 220 p.p.a.' (Dunleavy 1981: 73). Dunleavy argues that variations in building form on the overall size of the Greater London area, apart from increases in low-rise densities, had little or no effect, and there is no doubt that high buildings in nuclear centres only make sense in terms of real-estate speculation. Tall blocks increasingly diminish the space per habitable room vis-à-vis open space, and the real costs of providing and main-taining dwellings also rise more rapidly with increasing storey heights.

The current trend towards solving sustainability and the urban question centres on transit metropolises that favour public transit over private vehicle use (Newman and Kenworthy 1989, 1999, 2006, Cervero 1998, Newman 2006). This goes hand in hand with the overall method of increased densification into compact cities with sustainable agendas (Satterthwaite 1999, Jenks and Burgess 2000, Williams *et al.* 2000, Jenks and Dempsey 2005).

Cervero presents twelve case studies of major cities, arguing that free-market choices alone do not adequately answer for the success or failure of the chosen examples. The impacts of electronic communication via the Internet, economic restructuring and increased gender equality have all played a significant role (the implication being that the market does not automatically adapt to these movements). After 450 closely typed pages and the noted case studies, it is revealing that the book has no conclusion as to which method or methods of urban design generate the best solutions. By drawing on a variety of case studies, the author hopes that 'underlying patterns, common themes, and useful lessons emerge on how to build and maintain successful transit metropolises for the future' (Cervero 1998: 23).

Newman, on the other hand, suggests that there are three key models that can be used in assessing sustainability, namely population impact, ecological footprint and sustainability assessment. Although not supporting any particular set of policies, he suggests that only the sustainability assessment approach 'allows us to see the positive benefits of urban growth and provides policy options that can help cities reduce their local and global impact while improving their liveability' (Newman 2006: 275). Hence, although suburban expansion as a method of dealing with population increase would appear to possess a singular logic, the argument for the opposing method of urban consolidation is also convincing, facing us with the inevitable conclusion that, while both are equally compelling, the illusion remains that there is a choice between them.

Natural capitalism

In contrast to the ongoing rapture of capitalism, the term *natural capitalism* originates from a book by that name, subtitled *The Next Industrial Revolution*, and it signifies a purportedly new method of dealing with sustainability, from the global to the local (Hawken *et al.* 1999; see also McDonough and Braungart 1998). In that text, the authors ask us to accept that pre-existing capitalism, the system responsible for the financial crash of 2008, will gradually evolve into a more humane and greener system, despite the fact that the entire apparatus of capital remains unchanged. Natural capitalism is fundamentally a new method of extracting capital from nature and built form through a gradual transformation and improved efficiencies in the production and consumption of commodities. The concept is echoed across a whole series of texts, from business and the role of government, to education, transport and the greening of the built environment in both the developing and the developed world (Hamm and Pandurang 1998, Hargroves and Smith 2005, Benedict and McMahon 2006, Sorensen *et al.* 2004, Zetter and Watson 2006). The idea constitutes a major challenge to critics of the capitalist system and its constituent environment, as natural capitalism purports that the entire foundation of capitalist enterprise is shifting from one of profit based on exploitation, to one where sustainability is not only the adopted paradigm, it is also profitable. Ergo, the current system will be transformed and, along with it, a more democratic politics and equitable society will come about. All of these assumptions are questionable, given the last four centuries of capitalist exploitation.

As in the New Urbanism, and despite its appealing presentation, there is nothing *new* about natural capitalism. The term describes a utopian trajectory for pre-existing capitalist enterprises and sustainable initiatives, from reducing carbon dioxide emissions to hydrogen-fuelled and photovoltaic cells, to solar and wind farms or to earth-rammed and straw-baled homes. The underlying theory assumes that the prevailing methods through which capitalism exploits nature and the inherent inefficiencies and pollution that result will evolve into a new, sustainable, environment-friendly process and improved politics. When the entire product cycle is taken into account, sustainability is more profitable than pollution. New methods will allow the profit motive new territory to conquer, making as much out of eliminating pollution through green alternatives as it did in generating it. Hence, the focus of natural capitalism is enduringly towards a commercial–technical process, rather than one that is socio-political. In principle, business would state what society's problems are and then come up with technological solutions, rather than civil society stating which problems it needs to have resolved on the basis of a shift in urban politics. Natural capitalism describes the end state of this process. The overall schema of sustainable design alternatives is given in Table 7.1. However, leaving any further interrogation of a new, green, neocorporatist state to one side, the fundamental assumptions are nonetheless laudable and have been stated as follows:

- The environment is not a minor factor of production but is rather an envelope containing, provisioning and sustaining the entire economy.
- The limiting factor to future economic development is the availability and functionality of natural capital, in particular, life-supporting services that have no substitutes and currently have no market value.
- Misconceived or badly designed business systems, population growth and wasteful patterns of consumption are the primary causes of the loss of natural capital, and all three must be addressed to achieve a sustainable economy.
- Future economic progress can best take place in democratic, market-based systems of production and distribution in which all forms of capital are fully valued, including human, manufactured, financial and natural capital.
- One of the keys to the most beneficial employment of people, money and the environment is radical increases in resource productivity.
- Economic and environmental sustainability depends on redressing global inequities of income and material well-being.
- The best long-term environment for commerce is provided by the true democratic systems of governance that are based on the needs of people rather than business.

(Hawken *et al.* 1999: 9–10)

Table 7.1 Design briefs that highlight the difference between industrial, efficient and sustainable design

Design a building based on the Industrial Revolution's *system of production*	*Design a building based on the* Efficiency Revolution's *system of production*	*Design a building based upon a* Sustainable *system of production*
Puts millions of tons of toxic material into the air, water and soil every day.	Releases *fewer* tons of toxic material into the air, water and soil every day.	Introduces no hazardous material into the air, water or soil.
Measures prosperity by activity not legacy.	Measures prosperity by less activity.	Measures prosperity by how much natural capital we can accrue in productive ways.
Requires thousands of complex regulations to keep people and natural systems from being poisoned too quickly.	*Meets or exceeds* the stipulations of thousands of complex regulations that aim to keep people and natural systems from being poisoned too quickly.	Measures productivity by how many people are gainfully and meaningfully employed.
Produces materials so dangerous they will require constant vigilance by future generations.	Produces *fewer* dangerous materials that will require constant vigilance by future generations.	Measures progress by how many buildings have no smokestacks or dangerous effluents.
Results in gigantic amounts of waste.	Results in *smaller* amounts of waste.	Does not require regulations whose purpose is to stop us from killing ourselves too quickly.
Puts valuable minerals in holes all over the planet where they can never be retrieved.	Puts *fewer* valuable materials in holes all over the planet where they can never be retrieved.	Produces nothing that will require future generations to maintain vigilance.
Erodes diversity of biological species and cultural practices.	Standardises and homogenises biological species and cultural practices.	Celebrates the abundance of biological and cultural diversity and solar income.

Source: Retyped from W. McDonough and M. Braungart, *The Atlantic Monthly*, 1998, p. 85

In addition, by reorienting capitalism to support sustainable enterprises, it is assumed that natural capitalism will automatically provide greater social equity:

> Through this transformation, society will be able to create a vital economy that uses radically less material and energy. This economy can free up resources, reduce taxes on personal income, increase per-capita spending on social ills (while simultaneously reducing those ills), and begin to restore the damaged environment of the earth. These necessary changes done properly can promote economic efficiency, ecological conservation, and social equity.
>
> (Hawken *et al.* 1999: 2)

However, ten years later, and in the face of the above financial Armageddon, pre-existing capitalism is desperately trying to influence any and all agreements regarding global warming and environmental conservation, in order to recover its profits as it heads towards equity with the Great Depression, which started in 1929 and lasted a decade. True to the nature of capitalism, everything has its price, and the value of natural capital is assessed as being almost on par with a global GDP of US\$37 trillion. 'Valuing natural capital is an imprecise exercise at best. Nonetheless, several recent assessments have estimated that *biological services* flowing directly into society from the stock of natural capital are worth at least \$36 trillion annually' (Hawkin *et al.* 1999: 5). My stress here on so-called 'biological services' refers to the planet's life-support systems, and it is good to see that they are still worth something. As ideology, natural capitalism has four central strategies – radical productivity, biomimicry, service and flow economy and investment in natural capital. Briefly stated, the methods deployed refer to the improved efficiency of resource extraction, processing and consumption and closing the industrial cycle, so that demands on new resources will be severely limited. Biomimicry refers to industrial production that 'mimics' or emulates nature, where the concept of waste is unknown. The same closed-loop approach also applies to consumption, with a shift from an old-style industrial model geared up to produce goods and products, to one that delivers services without ownership. Products would degrade back either into natural or technical nutrient cycles. All of this potentially affects urban design in a multitude of ways.

While radical changes in agriculture are also demanded by an enveloping natural capitalism, as well as abandoning the absurd distinction between *urban* and *rural* processes, populations and locations, the crucible for its success lies in urbanisation and the future of cities. Once again, we are dealing primarily with technology-led development. In *natural capitalism*, it is revealing that words such as development, built environment, city and architecture do not exist in its somewhat extensive index. Nor is there any comment on the very source of most pollution, namely urbanisation. The sustainability and design of cities go hand in hand, from imaginative urban transformations (Landry 2000), to the creativity and innovation necessary to drive ideas (Florida 2003) and to the actual implementation of methods of sustainable design for cities (Jenks *et al.* 1996, Girardet 1999, Thomas 2003, Garde 2004, Moughtin 2004, Zetter and Watson 2006, Farr 2008). Today, cities remain the playground of industrial, commercial and finance capital, with innovative solutions to the sustainability of cities playing a part in profits from land development. Nonetheless, great inroads have been made into the problem by various local governments, often in the most curious places, such as Curitiba (Brazil) and Chattanooga (Tennessee). In addition, other more likely venues, such as Portland and Eugene (Oregon) and Vancouver (Canada), set standards for other cities to emulate. China's environmental-protection sector is projected to grow at 15 per cent per annum, and cities such as Shanghai and Beijing are fully conscious of the environmental and health benefits of sustainable urban practices (Diesendorf 2005). Even Goa is making

Table 7.2 Sustainable design principles for Goa 2100

Three goals for the susatinability transition

---

1   Sufficiency and equity: well-being of all people, communities and ecosystems
2   Efficiency: minimal throughput of matter–energy–information
3   Sustainability: least impact on nature, society and future generations.

Seven organising principles for sustainability

---

1   Satisfying the basic human needs of all people and providing them with an equal opportunity to realise their human potential.
2   Material needs should be met materially, and non-material needs met non-materially.
3   Renewable resources should not be used faster than their regeneration rates.
4   Non-renewable resources should not be used faster than their substitution rates by renewable resources.
5   Pollution and waste should not be produced faster than the rate of absorptions, recycling or transformation.
6   The Precautionary Principle should be applied where the 'response' time is potentially less than the 'respite' time.
7   'Free energy' and resources should be available to enable redundancy, resilience and reproduction.

Five strategies for land use management

---

1   Enable a long-term ecological recession from forest to cropland to city to forest.
2   Design the landscape first; situate the city in the interstitial niches.
3   Land-use transitions governed by the demand for ecosystem services, resource potential, natural ecological succession and contiguity.
4   Identify static and dynamic elements in the city, design the former and provide a dynamic vocabulary for the latter to co-evolve with the landscape.
5   Devolve governance and taxation to the lowest viable level.

Six tactics to manage physical stocks and flows

---

1   Use less with factor 4 technologies for supply and social limits of sufficiency and equity on demand.
2   Grow your own, topping harvestable yields as autonomously as possible.
3   Build two-way networks for security: every consumer is also a producer.
4   Store a lot, because renewable resource yields are often diurnal and seasonal.
5   Transport less over shorter distances, using least lifecycle technologies.
6   Exchange using intelligent wireless networks to enable real-time trade and delivery of goods.

A dynamic fractal morpholgy

---

1   Cellular structure: nuclei, cores, spines and skins.
2   Hierarchical networks adapting to topography.
3   Optimal densities, settlement structure and heights enabling security.
4   Contiguous and hyperlinked with interpenetration of living net.
5   Dynamic consolidation and nucleation around fractal boundaries and surfaces.

Source: C. Hargroves and M. Smith, *The Natural Advantage of Nations*. London: Earthscan, 2005, p. 311, Table 16.1

considerable advances towards sustainable practices that follow the thrust of natural capitalism, and the basic method of approach is given in Table 7.2.

While it is easy to be seduced by the utopian principles inherent in natural capitalism, we must face the fact that global inequalities in income and material well-being are socially manufactured. They are not accidental by-products of inefficient production. Scarcity is a problem of politics not sustainability, and so there is no reason to believe that the benefits of development, sustainable or otherwise, will not be captured by monopoly capitalism as they have always been, with the same unequal distribution of benefits. In addition, there is the tacit assumption that the market will remain the thermostat through which the process will operate, driven by firms and corporations. Given the meltdown in global financial markets described above, the idea of a homeostatic market system has been finally destroyed at both global and national levels. Therefore, even setting parasitic forms of capitalism aside, there is nothing in the economic equation that allows us to assume that natural capitalism could have prevented the meltdown of the world economy. Nor will it necessarily result in the equity expected from it, as the problem was with the ideology of capitalist enterprise, that is, with its system of practices, and not with its inefficiencies.

(Natural) ecology

> I spent my childhood and adolescence squarely between two diametrically different environments, the poles of man and nature. Almost ten miles from my home lay the city of Glasgow, one of the most implacable testimonies to the city of toil in all Christendom, a memorial to an inordinate capacity to create ugliness, a sandstone excretion cemented with smoke and grime. Each night its pall on the eastern horizon was lit by flames of the blast furnaces, a Turner fantasy made real.
>
> (McHarg 1969: 1)

The explosion of population during the twentieth century and new forms of destroying the earth's atmosphere, such as air travel and massive coal-burning power plants, left the worst efforts of prior eras looking benign and harmless. The concentration of populations into urban centres, while improving production, also magnified its effects. Few designers rallied to the principle of sustainable environments with new methods for building towns and cities. A rare occurrence was Ian McHarg's seminal book, *Design with Nature*, written over forty years ago (1969). It still represents a challenge to some of the debates noted above, with the preservation of nature being a prime objective. Lewis Mumford, in his introduction to this work, placed it in the same category of 'essential classics' as those of Hippocrates, Thoreau, Carl Sauer and his own mentor, Patrick Geddes. Returning to Glasgow from the ravages of World War Two, McHarg was moved by the destructive effects of urbanisation on the beautiful local countryside. His book was a reaction to this situation. It was entirely devoted to a new design methodology, whereby predatory industrialisation could move into a new symbiosis with the natural world, a somewhat similar idea to natural capitalism. It signified the first attempt to link urban form with ecologically sensitive development. What is usually glossed over, however, was his inclusion of human pathology and social deviance in the equation. Arguably, and for the first time, problems of development, human survival and design were seen to be interconnected. Transparently, McHarg's polemic contained immense implications for urban designers and the methodologies they deployed. He challenged their most closely held beliefs – physical determinism, abstract design concepts and aesthetics – replacing them with the governing mandates of nature.

> While admitting that every city 'has some testimony to perception, intelligence and art', the general pattern of urban growth 'is the expression of the inalienable right to create ugliness and disorder for private greed, the maximum expression of man's inhumanity to man'.
>
> (McHarg 1969: 5)

McHarg accepts as axiomatic that respect for natural processes represents survival, whereas their destruction constitutes extinction for mankind; within this paradigm, Darwin's definition of fitness prevails. Successful organisms and communities flourish, whereas others perish. Hence, there is a direct relationship between creativity, fitness and urban form (Lynch 1981). The generation of appropriate spatial systems is seen in these terms to be dependent upon a successful ecological analysis of existing pathologies, both natural and human, so that action can be taken to eradicate the causes through planning policy (Platt 1994, Gordon and Tamminga 2002, Register 2002).

McHarg's entire book constitutes one of the finest expositions of the ecological principle and is a testament to his design brilliance. His analysis of the Potomac River basin initiated a seminal study of the relationship between urban land use and natural process (McHarg 1969: 127–51), and its iconic methodology is represented in his matrix of compatibility (Figure 7.1). In his last two chapters, *The City: Process and Form*, and *The City: Health and Pathology* he addresses whether or not the existing city may be understood in the same terms as 'natural' environments. In his exemplary study of Washington DC McHarg demonstrates the usefulness of the ecological method in confronting a rural-metropolitan region in prospect of urbanisation. In that study the main components of natural ecosystems were replaced by major socio-economic determinants impacting on physical health (tuberculosis, diabetes, syphilis, cirrhosis of the liver, amoebic dysentery, bacillary dysentery, salmonellosis and heart disease). Social deviance was then added to the equation (homicide, suicide, drug addiction, alcoholism, robbery, rape, aggravated assault, juvenile delinquency and infant mortality). Mental disease was also considered albeit the slenderest of all categories based upon psychiatric inpatient admissions.

Also important was ethnicity (six population types) and environmental pollution. Economic factors noted were income, poverty, unemployment, housing

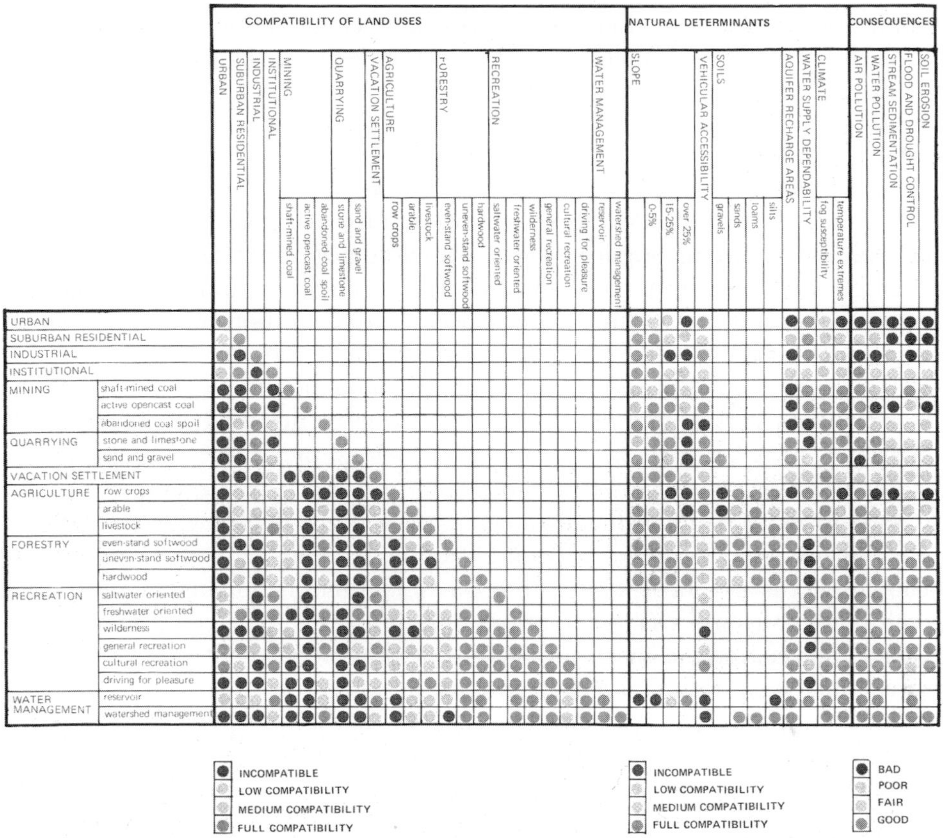

Figure 7.1 McHarg's matrix of compatible resources

Source: I. McHarg, *Design with Nature*. Garden City, NY: The Natural History Press/John Wiley, 1969, p. 144

quality, overcrowding and illiteracy. Density was considered to be an independent variable in the overall schema. Through a process of sieve mapping, McHarg was then able to overlay any or all sets of factors to determine specific interactions among and between groups. From this information, the spatial basis of urban inequalities was deduced, with appropriate recommendations for management of the urban system – an apparently objective basis for the practice of city planning and design.

McHarg canonises the importance of urban population density and draws an analogy between the work of Calhoun and Christian and the midtown Manhattan study conducted by the Cornell Medical School with regard to the mental health of area residents. McHarg substantiates his position in this respect by quoting from Leyhausen thus: 'the basic forces of social interaction and organisation are in *principle* identical and there is a true homology between man and animal throughout the whole range of vertebrates' (McHarg 1969: 194). Formally at least, this study reinforced the spatial relationship between mental health, urban density and a variety of other factors, where analogies between human and animal behaviour could no doubt claim singular reinforcement. The clear inference was that, beyond a certain point, urban density becomes pathological, as it does in animal communities.

Although McHarg's project can be respected for its methodological significance and, in principle, its contemporary relevance, the studies are by now close to half a century old, having been carried out several years before the book was written. The thrust of McHarg's synthesis of the urban spatial system derives much of its intellectual rigour from methodologies adopted by the Chicago School of Sociology, from ethology and medical research, and the strengths as well as the weaknesses of this cultural world-view are both contained within such a context (FOC3: 58–60). Hence, there are telling signs of age, not the least being references to negroes, social 'diseases', and homosexual behaviour as deviant. Whereas this approach provides a clear picture of the urban spatial matrix as it relates to pathologies and other factors, the synthesis is partial and incomplete. The effects of the urban system are spatially located, but causal aspatial processes are not defined, and it is assumed that planning exists to rectify these deficiencies. The total spectrum of political action, economic activity and social conflict is not incorporated into the model and is nowhere addressed. It therefore contains intrinsic assumptions and omissions that reflect a somewhat utopian approach to the urban problem – one that merely demands a homology between analytical techniques and planning action.

In addition, reliance on medical concepts of 'pathology' and 'disease' create categories of apparently neutral physical and mental states (nothing causes them), ignoring the basic fact that a high proportion of these conditions are socially reproduced by the urban processes established by Western capitalism. Because of the nature of the social relations within this system, one may argue that drug addiction, alcoholism, robbery, juvenile delinquency, infant mortality etc. are no more social 'diseases' than is ethnicity. The same holds true for mental 'disease', which ignores the immense part played in the formation of neuroses by the required repressive forces of socialisation and urbanisation. Therefore, an appropriate schema for urban spatial structure must demand a congruence between effects and causes, between the substance of the human condition and the economic circumstances of life from which it ensues.

Density: form fundamentals

> More particularly, capitalist urbanisation processes simultaneously require and resist planning; that is, the social and property relations of capitalism create an urban process which repels that on which its continued existence ultimately depends; collective action in the form of planning.
>
> (Scott and Roweis 1977: 1108)

Central to the 'urban' question is the defining factor of density, debated for over fifty years and encapsulated within a variety of theories and explanations of the built form of cities (Wirth 1938a, 1938b, Alonso 1965, Castells 1977, Newman 2006). Underpinning the high-rise, high-density scenario, there exist certain ideological assumptions that influence the political allocation of urban space in capitalist and socialist economies alike (Dunleavy 1981, Szelenyi 1983). In the 'Western' world, neoclassical economic theory has been most influential in directing the operation of urban land markets, implemented via planning policy and the mechanism of 'rent' (Lamarche 1976). In this system, architecture has been instrumental in articulating the structure of the built environment and in directing environmental benefits, as well as reinforcing class boundaries and contextual pathologies.

Methods of interpreting city form and structure have often related land use to economic and political realities on a two-dimensional basis, and in fact much planning methodology is rooted in this type of thinking. However, when we look at *formal* geometries (three- and four-dimensional), instead of *planar* geometries (dealing with flat surfaces), infinitely more sophisticated and complex methods of assessing the relationship between society, space and physical form become possible. Although it has been claimed that capitalist urbanisation processes are the most efficient use of land owing to price competition and the necessary maximisation of revenues from development, in effect this is not the case. The method is defied by the facts. The mechanisms that govern formal systems within economies not only extend and reproduce urban inequality, but may actually mitigate against the optimisation of productive land use, hence it is even against the stated interests of the development industry. Furthermore, these inefficiencies do not reflect the limitations of specific environmental geometries and patterns; instead, they mirror the intrinsic deficiencies of prevailing ideological values that underwrite socio-spatial factors within the economy as a whole.

The need for scientific investigation into form generation resulted in seminal approaches to the heterology of space and form some forty years ago, when the Centre for Land Use and Built Form Studies at Cambridge School of Architecture set out to test the idea that certain geometrical principles have profound spatial implications. Two books produced in the early 1970s were to remove many of the myths about the relationship between built form and spatial efficiency. Lionel March and Philip Steadman's book *The Geometry of Environment* (1971) and Leslie Martin and Lionel March's *Urban Space and Structures* (1972) represent landmarks in our understanding of the built form of cities. The research began with a range of population densities as a function of plot ratio and continued into the implications of a diverse range of building forms and structures (Figure 7.2). Many urban plans and buildings either built or proposed by famous architects were used as examples in order to demonstrate the relationship between science and intuition, from Ebeneezer Howard's garden city and Le Corbusier's Ville Radieuse to Frank Lloyd Wright's Chicago apartments and Mies van der Rohe's Seagram Building (Figure 7.3). Although the mathematics of this type of exercise can become exceedingly sophisticated (March 1976), nonetheless the basic principles are fairly straightforward and are best explained in Martin and March (1972: 1–54), in the two chapters on

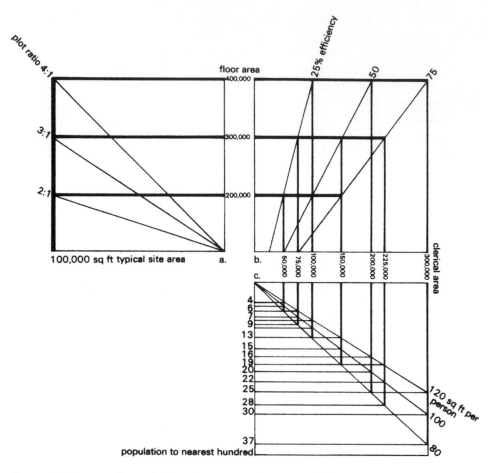

Figure 7.2 Range of population density as a function of plot ratio

Source: L. Martin and L. March (eds), *Urban Space and Structures*. Cambridge: Cambridge University Press, 1972, p. 34, Fig. 2.2

'The grid as generator' and 'Speculations'. What these studies demonstrate is that the relationship between the form of a building and the land upon which it is built is not arbitrary. Under specified conditions of exact light angles, the same number of floors and the same land area, one building can provide 50 per cent more floor area than another. Similarly, a given plot ratio of 3:1 can result in three-storey buildings in one situation and skyscrapers someplace else. When applied at the metropolitan level, the sum of total building, land configurations and relationships can result either in exacting efficiencies or the reverse, the unbelievable misuse of urban space. Therefore, the method by which spatial configurations are arrived at is deterministic of formal efficiencies.

In his chapter, 'The grid as generator', Leslie Martin uses Manhattan to demonstrate his point that spatial efficiency is *inversely* proportional to building height, given the basic principles of perimeter planning. Using the three

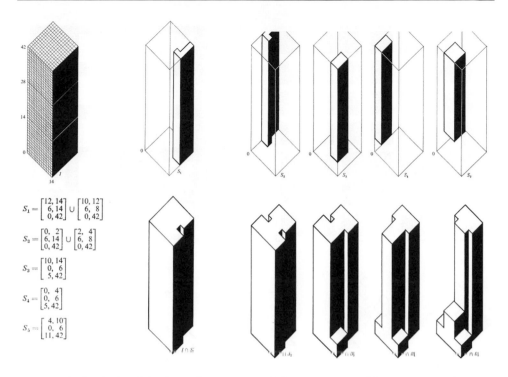

$$S_1 = \begin{bmatrix} 12,14 \\ 6,14 \\ 0,42 \end{bmatrix} \cup \begin{bmatrix} 10,12 \\ 6,\ 8 \\ 0,42 \end{bmatrix}$$

$$S_2 = \begin{bmatrix} 0,\ 2 \\ 6,14 \\ 0,42 \end{bmatrix} \cup \begin{bmatrix} 2,\ 4 \\ 6,\ 8 \\ 0,42 \end{bmatrix}$$

$$S_3 = \begin{bmatrix} 10,14 \\ 0,\ 6 \\ 5,42 \end{bmatrix}$$

$$S_4 = \begin{bmatrix} 0,\ 4 \\ 0,\ 6 \\ 5,42 \end{bmatrix}$$

$$S_5 = \begin{bmatrix} 4,10 \\ 0,\ 6 \\ 11,42 \end{bmatrix}$$

Figure 7.3 Analysis of the formal properties of the Seagram Building, New York.
Architect: Mies van der Rohe

Source: L. March and P. Steadman (eds), *The Geometry of Environment*. Methuen: London, 1971, pp. 142–3, Fig. 5.31

fundamental building types, the pavilion (tower), the street (linear development) and the court (square or rectilinear development), he plots a grid of forty-nine units, where development can either take place as towers in the centre of each block, or as courtyards occupying the perimeter, with 50 per cent site coverage in each case (Figure 7.4). Taking the pavilion as the basic form, he demonstrates that the anti-form (or the inverted mould of the pavilion) provides the same built form for one-third of the building height. These basic relationships are shown in Figure 7.5. He then applies the basic idea to the Manhattan grid, illustrating not only that twenty-one-storey towers could be replaced by eight-storey buildings, but that each courtyard would contain a central park equal to Washington Square. These examples clearly demonstrate the appreciable environmental benefits that accrue from using one structuring system over another, with no loss of floor space, and, since the early 1970s, the entire process of urban modelling has become infinitely more specialised (Steadman 2001). Overall, however, if we take a variety of high-rise, high-density environments, such as Manhattan or Hong Kong, it is generally true that only the pavilion is used in the majority of instances, in other words, the form that accrues the fewest spatial benefits to anyone except those who speculate on land. Therefore, the outcome of this research has been to establish a design method known as perimeter

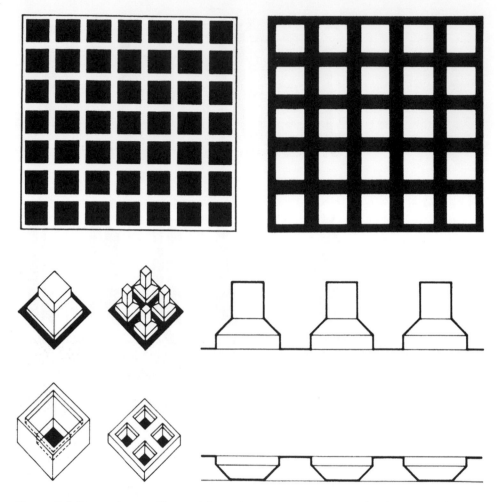

Figure 7.4 Forty-nine pavilions with 50% site coverage. Generalised pavilion form and its anti-form; modified anti-form of the generalised pavilion form at the same scale and containing the same amount of built volume on the same site; the heights are approximately in the ratio 3:1

Source: L. Martin and L. March (eds), *Urban Space and Structures*. Cambridge: Cambridge University Press, 1972, p. 34, Figs 1.6 and 1.7

planning, as its efficiency compared with the other two alternatives is monumental. Examples of this idea had already been expressed historically, for example in the Georgian New Town in Edinburgh (1750), where a basic gridiron plan provided open space both within and adjacent to the adopted tenement form of housing, or later, within modernism, in Bruno Taut's Hufeisensiedlung in Berlin, 1925–30 (Figure 7.6). More recently, architects looking for greater efficiency in housing form adopted the principle, in, for example, the Byker Wall in Newcastle, by Ralph Erskine.

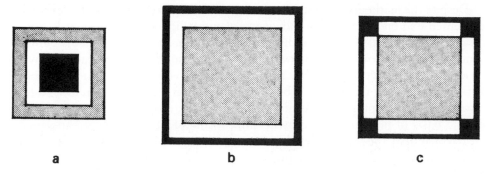

a   b   c

Figure 7.5 The illustration shows (a) pavilion development and (b) and (c) court
            developments, in which several proportions of site utilisation – coverage,
            built potential (bulk) and percentage of floor area without outlook – are
            the same. For the same number of storeys, the built potential will be the
            same for all three buildings

Source: L. Martin and L. March (eds), *Urban Space and Structures*. Cambridge: Cambridge
University Press, 1972, p. 34, Fig. 2.6

Figure 7.6 Example of perimeter planning: Bruno Taut's Hufeisensiedlung Project in
            Berlin, 1925–30

Source: AKG Images

Despite the mathematical integrity of the modelling process, all of the examples presented exhibit the inherent deficiency of modelling as a whole – it is not so much what is included in the model that is debatable, as much as what is omitted. One of the most obvious omissions in the kind of modelling indicated above is its degree of abstraction from any social, political or economic realities. Although perimeter planning may, in fact, be the most efficient method of building, a host of other factors impinge on this idea. To begin with, most cities are already built on the basis of prevailing land ownership, forms of title, leasing arrangements etc., which deny the wholesale adoption of perimeter-planning principles. Next, prevailing methodologies in the built environment professions are composed of a bibliography of concepts that are exceedingly vague and ill defined and frequently vary from country to country, agency to agency and firm to firm. In many cases, concepts have to be defined on a project-by-project basis simply to eliminate disparity and protect against legal and other contingencies. For example, there is frequent confusion over the relationship between density and building height, where high rise can be built at lower densities than low rise, and vice versa. It all depends on the size of individual units, how the idea of net density is defined in relation to open space, parking and sidewalks, and how spaces such as 'gardens' are attached to buildings and other factors. In addition to concepts of ownership and density, the built environment as conceptualised by most architects and planners relies on conventional and stereotyped (commodified) *architectural* forms, such as detached, semi-detached, terrace, low rise, high rise etc., whose deployment in congruence with their saleability implicitly denies the abstract efficiencies of building indicated by perimeter planning. In spite of the obvious merit of the concepts, they must impinge upon a set of historical conditions where the practical problems of ownership, existing infrastructure and buildings, administrative codes and regulations etc. are integrated. Overall, perimeter planning increases in efficiency with increases in physical scale, where escalating levels of material resources, capital and political power need to be deployed.

High-rise buildings or vertical architecture?

The use of roofs in high-rise buildings for recreational and domestic purposes has been promoted for decades, at least since Le Corbusier's *Unité d'Habitation* in Marseilles was built in 1947. This iconic building was conceptualised as a vertical village for 1,600 people, designed on the basis of communal living. It contained its own shopping street and community facilities, where the roof was used for a children's school and recreational purposes. Overall, modernism was a wholesale disaster for the practice of sustainability, where most if not all high rises had massive solar gain, no sunscreening, poor or no natural ventilation, little or no insulation, undue energy consumption with no production, and massive leaks due to poor curtain walling and other factors. However, the last twenty years have seen a more considered architectural approach to sustainable buildings, predominantly in low- to medium-rise structures. In urban areas, large expanses of roof space have been perceived as untapped resources for use in the generation of solar energy, significantly increasing the available urban land area for productive uses in recreation, and also for growing food. The principle involved here is simply to build an orthodox building of some description, one capable of supporting the additional dead and live loads in the form of people, soil, plants, water, solar panels and other forms of hardware. When we consider high-rise structures alone, it is clear that these ideas are insufficient, for the simple reason that the roof area is inadequate for much more than water storage, exhaust fans for air conditioning, telecommunications, infrastructure etc. Roofs are seldom useable for much more than storing the necessary servicing hardware that the building needs, although this can frequently be overcome by using lower floors for mechanical services and other functions. So, in order to advance truly sustainable development for the kinds of purpose available to low- and medium-rise developments, a revolution in the entire conception of high-rise structures had to occur.

Some indication of this new ideology was recorded at a London seminar on vertical architecture in May 2001, titled 'High places: the design of green skyscrapers'. Some of the outcomes were expressed as follows:

1   Eco towers are developing in cities around the world to deal with urban growth and migration from rural areas. They provide a way of coping with this and avoiding development on nearby arable land.
2   According to United Nations data, eco towers can reduce transportation costs, which will result in a reduction in energy consumption.
3   A 'green' method implies a balanced use of organic and inorganic mechanisms in order to achieve a balanced ecosystem. Designers conventionally tend to try and add on environmental features, instead of utilising passive methods that minimise the impact on the environment.
4   Designs should aim to create 'cities in the sky' instead of traditional high-rise developments, which create compartmentalisation. The challenge is to design in a thoughtfully organic and humane way, by integrating both horizontal and vertical aspects of the plan.
5   Ecological design is still young but complex and requires comprehension of the effects that one factor will have on another.
6   Owing to the past experience of receiving low funding and inadequate management arrangements in the public sector, ecological design might be unsuccessful. As a result of past experience, it can be a struggle to convince tenants that innovative methods will improve their quality of life.
7   Many planning authorities need to be persuaded of the advantage of developing towers.

(Eco Tower Seminar Proceedings,
www.sustainable-placemaking.org)

However, the idea of using towers has occurred before, resulting, for example, in the disastrous effects of post-war high-rise developments in Britain (Dunleavy 1981). Policy directives emanating from architectural ideologies, combined with professional influence, are powerful mechanisms for change, but are seldom founded on much more than the crudest social and political assumptions, if any, and even the basic physical geometry is misplaced. Physical determinism and the Eureka Principle once again hold sway, with a wholesale reliance on the promise that a good idea will always win out, which of course it usually does not. If we accept Martin and March's (1972) rather straightforward observations on built form and space discussed above, the tower is the most ineffective. Yet, even today, we are being presented with a 'born-again' form of the skyscraper, this time one supposedly based on sustainable principles as indicated above, incorporating high-rise farming, energy generation and urban space. We are asked to believe that planning authorities need to be persuaded that many benefits will ensue, without any contrasting arguments about other forms of housing, and the blame for failure is already anticipated to lie with the *tenants* of such projects, not the architects, and history looks set to repeat itself (see (6) above). However, leaving aside for the moment whether or not high rise in principle is a good thing, there is definitely a new awareness evolving about high-rise design that is somewhat superior to earlier models, and a precise summary of what is involved can be accessed at www. battlemccarthy.com/.

The iconic character in this respect is Ken Yeang, a Malaysian architect who currently has the highest profile in a new and revolutionary approach to the design of high-rise buildings, traditionally known as skyscrapers. Yeang was educated at the Architectural Association in London. It is also significant that in contrast to traditional architectural training, which concludes at the bachelor level with membership of the profession, Yeang went on to complete a doctorate in ecological design at Cambridge. He is the pioneer of low-energy passive design for high-rise structures and has a twenty-year history of published work in the field (Yeang 1987, 1994, 1995, 1996, 2002, Powell 1994). Yeang, therefore, has an immense base of academic material, as well as projects, with which to vindicate his ideas. In principle, his philosophy is to create a symbiotic relationship between his buildings and the surrounding environment.

Yeang claims his buildings are sustainable in terms of community, the recycling of all materials used in construction, energy use and dependency on existing infrastructure and services. As a result, the buildings adopt unique architectural forms that are radically different to other high rises in the effort to create a more stable and productive ecosystem, where requisite variety will flourish. The outstanding, unique feature is his approach to greening the skyscraper, using plants to improve the micro climate, solar gain, the absorption of carbon dioxide emissions, biodiversity, cross-ventilation and the overall aesthetic appearance of the buildings. He notes that high rises constitute a massive concentration of inorganic matter in a small space, and that,

Figure 7.7 Examples of integrated urban architecture that generates energy and food production. Vertical Architecture Studio (VAST) under the direction of Chris Abel at the Faculty of the Built Environment at the University of New South Wales, Sydney

Source: Chris Abel www.chrisabel.com

the concentration totally imbalances the ecology of the locality. To counteract this, the designer must introduce as much compatible organic matter in the form of diverse planting and landscaping (even including acceptable compatible fauna) into the skyscraper, both externally and internally.

(Yeang 1996: 100)

It is a short step from this position to include dedicated areas to permit gardening, hydroponics, fish farming and other food-growing activity, accepting the inevitable construction of skyscrapers in the form of vertical green and sustainable, productive urban space.

This theme is pursued by Chris Abel in several of his books and written articles, most notably in *Sky High* (2003), the source of the term 'vertical architecture'. The basic idea is portrayed beautifully by Abel in his Vertical Architecture Studio (VAST) undertaken at the University of New South Wales (Figure 7.7). Here, the idea of high rise is left behind, with a transformation of the concept of high-density dwelling to encompass complete communities, at least partially self-sustaining with the incorporation of food production, energy generation, parks and gardens and commercial facilities. The projects are pioneering works in the sense that they take a concept and pursue it relentlessly in a variety of physical manifestations. These may be accessed at www.chrisabel.com. Although such ideas may seem far-fetched, they contain the proposition that new architectural typologies require investigation, and their economic and social viability must be assessed. For example, we can see the embryo of a new architecture in the World Trade Centre in Bahrain, recently completed by Atkins Middle East, containing three immense wind turbines that will generate 15–30 per cent of its own energy requirements. Even more spectacular is David Fischer's wind-powered rotating skyscraper in Dubai, which is currently under construction. In addition, the relationship between biological systems of production and intelligent building design based on digital communication systems opens up another potentially unexplored field for high-rise technology devoted to such purposes. The new structures are indeed vast and complex and bear no relationship to traditional high-rise development.

The edible city

As we have seen, McHarg's heterology aimed to accommodate the conventional building of settlements, with minimum damage to natural process. Although laudable in intent, the city was still perceived as something built in *opposition* to nature, rather than inside it. In contrast, another position taken by environmentalists has been that urban development, particularly housing, should concentrate less on hypothetical conflicts between suburban development and urban consolidation (as above) and more on a concept of the city as a productive working organism that is capable of sustainable food production in concert with living space. In this model, the distinction between urban and suburban becomes blurred, and they merge together. Maintaining concepts such as *agriculture* and *urban* generates semantic barriers that defy new answers to questions of sustainability. This viewpoint, while accepting the artificial nature of all settlement, promotes a wholistic approach to community life based on a collective relation to the soil, sustainable energy, the capacity for each household to generate its own food, and a close-knit relationship between neighbours. It is a system that actively discourages waste, encourages the recycling of all materials, places people directly within the lifecycle of food production, generates health benefits and economic efficiencies, and ties local politics into something other than a reaction to developers' greed and state-imposed infrastructure expansion. To a large extent, it assumes decentralisation and village or small-town lifestyles, although these do not necessarily exclude new developments of the kind proposed by Ken Yeang.

These ideas were included in their entirety in an altogether more developed heterology, *The Edible City* (Britz 1981). The concept also reinforces the idea of the city as a nature reserve, where flora and fauna permeate urbanised regions along channels of natural landscape that encourage the settlement and migration of plant and animal communities (Wolch 1996, 2002, Beatley 2008, FOC7: 167, DC20: 254). Taken together, these three methods of visualising urban development – 'design with nature', 'the edible city' and 'zoopolis' – suggest a wholly sensible opposition to development based on a commodified and branded capitalism. They also deny the somewhat standardised and arbitrary zoning models of the New Urbanism. However persuasive the aesthetic of the New Urbanism, the system of production remains the same, albeit with a more acceptable patina. In contrast, Britz's vision promotes the concept of the city as one that provides most of its own energy and food, while simultaneously incorporating meaningful social change. The city therefore becomes a productive working landscape, even turning decorative street trees into ones that could grow fruit. Rather than rejecting agriculture as 'other', the city becomes a part of agricultural production, a sustainable life-support system that provides food in the form of vegetable gardens, fish farms, orchards, chicken coops etc. It is one that replenishes the soil by mulching, gathers and recycles water, generates electricity through solar and wind power, creates methane for gas supply and uses solar energy for electrical production. In the process, the generally promoted image of the suburbs as wasteful of agricultural land and infrastructure and stressful of public services, of atomic nuclear households living in isolation, and the wholesale erosion of community life is replaced with positive qualities that dispose of much of the criticism of future suburban development.

This type of urban agriculture clearly has revolutionary aspects, as it would also unplug many communities from local and state governments, at least as far as utilities are concerned. Such communities would constitute new tribal organisations, based on electronic communication and the benefits of modern technologies, but in a meaningful social and political environment that is community-centred and open to evolutionary change. It would effectively reduce taxation, erode localised political authority and reduce food provisioning from multinationals, along with the need to create 'frankenfoods', or genetically modified crops. The intention in *The Edible City* was to generate:

> a general system-based interdisciplinary approach to democratic decentral-isation of the land planning and design process ... it is premised on the hypothesis that individuals, families, and neighbours, in direct personal contact, working together for mutual improvement in their environmental and economic circumstances, can reverse the trend towards environmental entropy and social fragmentation.
>
> (Britz 1981: 92–3)

The overall aim is to stop the city feeding off nature, and instead to become a part of it. In the process, all life forms are respected and maintained,

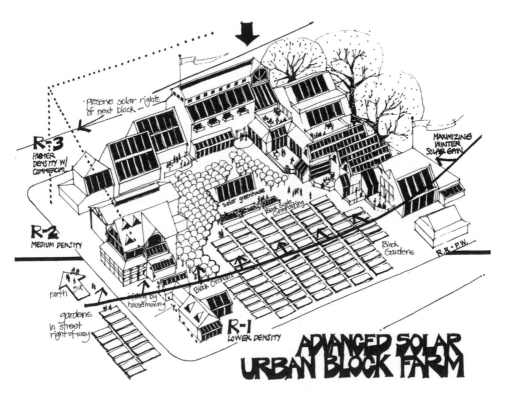

Figure 7.8 Richard Britz's advanced solar urban block
Source: R. Britz, *The Edible City*. Kaufmann Inc., 1981, p. 107

communities are enhanced, nature is replenished, and waste becomes deleted as a way of life, such as that proposed in his urban block farm (Britz 1981; Figure 7.8). Although there is no doubt a seriously utopian dimension to the method of urban agriculture, based on ideas not far removed from the utopian socialism discussed in the preceding chapter, the argument is infinitely more compelling than our current system of waste and dissolution. Ideas and practices contained in the edible city concept grew out of much empirical work on the bioregional ecosystem applicable to the neighbourhoods in Eugene, Oregon. Britz notes that it also emerges directly from 'our *evolving* political and economic atmosphere best illustrated by the Housing and Community Development Act [in the United States] of 1974'. Through strategies of self-sustaining sustainability (rather than state-controlled and -promoted sustainability), the densification of the suburbs happens automatically, but in an altogether more democratic fashion. Critically and most importantly, sustainable development and social change are seen to be interlinked, the implication being that, in order to survive, we must undertake radically different lifestyle choices. This is in total contrast to the concept of natural capitalism discussed above, or to high-rise industrial agriculture, where neocorporate reorganisation maintains profits, while society remains free to adapt. Since *The Edible City* was written, Britz's manifesto has seen widespread global accommodation, albeit fragmentary and uncoordinated at the level of the state. His work now involves a developed system of earth-sheltered housing for rural areas (see also Golanyi 1996).

What *The Edible City* contributed to the overall debate on sustainable development was, in the first instance, a semantic triumph. By combining two words that challenged our definitions of space and function, new relations became possible. In the process, a new model, based on the integration of food production and suburban residential development, was generated, one that detailed a synthesis of concepts and practices that, until that time (1980), had been locked into the separation of *urbs* and *agricultura*. Britz is also conscious that his ideas are part of an ongoing tradition, beginning with Howard's garden city, Wright's Broadacre City, Stein and Wright's Radburn and a host of others. The difference between Britz's ideas and these examples is that they all envision nature as land not yet used for agriculture, or as recreation and escapism from the deleterious effects of industrialisation, rather than as something to be entered on its own terms. Today, *greening the city* has become the mantra for many local authorities worldwide, particularly in Denmark, and Britz's ideas are now part of mainstream community development. As examples of this, Newman and Kenworthy (1999) note some forty-five sites in Copenhagen alone, including Oster Faelled, Korsgade 20 and Mariendalsveg Kolding, the latter of particular note. Samso Island is also a supreme example of ecological self-sufficiency. It has completely eradicated its carbon footprint and now exports energy to the national grid (*The Guardian Weekly*, 3 October 2008). Similar projects are also taking place around the world, for example in North America (Portland, Eugene, Ithaca, Jericho Hill Village), in Curitiba (Brazil), Viikki in Helsinki, Mole Hill in Vancouver, GLW Terrein in Amsterdam and Beddington in London. As Beatley remarks, 'Urban agriculture holds much promise, – from intensive commercial food production in downtown lots in Chicago, to rice paddies on high rise buildings in Tokyo' (2008: 194). Sustainable urban development has moved forward, from merely creating a sustainable transport net, to the incorporation of the edible city concept, albeit on a small but expanding scale (Jefferson *et al.* 2001). Consequently, much has now been added to Britz's seminal work in the area of urban agriculture (Martin and Marden 1999, Quon 1999, Bakker *et al.* 2000, Mougeot 2000, 2006, Vijoen 2005; see also bibliographies at www.ruaf.org/node/692 and https://idl-bnc.idrc.ca/dspace/handle/ 123456789/32959).

Hence, Richard Britz was one of the first to challenge the notion of high-density residential development having greater space efficiency than low-density, but in a manner that was entirely novel. Both forms of density had only one function, namely to house people. Britz's contribution is not one where technologies of form were manipulated to increase or decrease urban density; it is a strategy to change the entire function of residential space. By integrating housing with energy and food production, the efficiency of residential space was increased threefold, with the additional societal benefits of improved lifestyle, community, local politics and independence. It is this dimension of integrated social life that is wholly absent in the debate on high-rise agricultural communities today, and it is around this point that the debate will fail. In combination with the centripetal power of electronic communication and the increasing capacity for people to work at home, *The Edible City* also provides a viable alternative to traditional approaches in urban consolidation, which rely on the narrowest definition of land use to solve the functional problems of sustainable development.

Density and the New Urbanism

The New Urbanism by now constitutes a global ideology that has been lauded internationally for many fine projects and for the rigour of its methodology, one that claims to resolve the formal problems of urbanisation (see www.cnu.org/resources for all non-academic references, e.g. Charter, introduction, codes, databases etc.). Although the New Urbanism has had prior discussion in relation to branding and authenticity (see Chapter 5), another dimension of its philosophy is explored below. The extent to which the New Urbanism may be viewed as a generally adopted heterology for urban development, specifically in the realm of urban density, is the subject of this section. Although the ideology has produced many admirable architectural and urban design solutions to some intractable problems of form and aesthetics, the movement is now growing in such a manner that its claims far outstrip its capacity as an improved urban design technology, despite protestations to the contrary (Falconer 2001). In addition, the legitimation process required by this new ideology, its organisation and its institutions have moved far beyond what its so-called 'theory' can encompass. The medium simply cannot live up to the message.

In the latest, beautifully presented text *New Urbanism and Beyond*, world-class theorists and intellectuals such as Saskia Sassen, Ed Soja and Manuel Castells are now included, when in fact they have nothing at all to do with the movement (Haas 2008). As we shall see below, the New Urbanism rigorously avoids using the work of these scholars and others of a similar bent to legitimise its theoretical origins. In contrast to the enormous contribution of such individuals to the social sciences, the self-generated theory of the New Urbanism does not appear on the radar as anything other than a marginal attempt at legitimising a set of questionable physical relationships between town and country, on the basis of density guidelines and formal codes. However one may wish to phrase the problem, the New Urbanism has no significant theory of its own. Although this observation may be irrelevant to many, the fact that the New Urbanism presents itself as having a theoretical base lends credence to its legitimacy. Such a claim is unfounded, and yet lends many practices undue confidence in their work. As we shall see, even the claim to theory is actually rooted in three methodological principles. None of this denies the clear benefits of good architecture, urban design and urban planning, nor of having codes to govern development. What is transparent, however, is that the utopian ideals of the movement rigorously and systematically ignore the fact of capitalist urbanisation, as indeed the same theorists mentioned above have described in immense detail and with great erudition. Had they been read in any depth, the New Urbanism might have had a substantially more meaningful foundation. Therefore, the New Urbanism remains a methodology in search of a theory of capitalist urbanisation, branding and urban design.

Expediting the charter of the New Urbanism implies a heavy commitment to the idea of urban density and the linked concept of *the transect* (Brower 2002, Talen 2002b). The foundation for the transect principle has three claims to legitimacy, as noted in Duany (2002): first and foremost, Patrick Geddes's valley section, as illustrated in his seminal *Cities in Evolution* of 1914, and cited in much of the New Urbanist literature. Simply stated, it explains the evolved relationship between the geography of a region, its urbanisation and inhabitants (FOC9: 206). This section, upon which the New Urbanism builds its entire case, is described by Duany himself as being 'palpably inaccurate' and 'curiously useless as a model for an age well into the industrial revolution' (Duany 2002: 295). In other words, he claimed that it was no use, even when it was proposed, nearly 100 years ago.

To place this criticism in perspective, it is quite clear from a reading of *Cities in Evolution* what Geddes's intention actually was:

> The Valley section is the basis of *survey*. In such ways *we may work* out very many specific and definite civilisation values. *We can discover* that the

kind of place and the kind of work done in it deeply determine the ways and institutions of its people. *This is the real stuff of the economic interpretation of history.*

(1997 (orig. 1915): xv111; my italics)

Furthermore, in his introduction to his second Cities Exhibition of 1915 (the first being sunk by the Germans in 1914, near Madras in India), Geddes again makes explicit the function of the valley section 'as an introduction to the rational geography of cities in terms of their regional origins' (1997 (orig. 1915): 165–6). Hence, it is obvious that Geddes's use of the typical valley section was entirely different to that of the New Urbanism. As a strategy, it would have been more accurate to accept that, 'while historians and geographers use the transect to describe the way things *are*, he [Duany] uses it to describe how things *ought to be*' (Brower 2002: 314). It is transparent that Geddes's use of the valley section (he never used the word transect) was his adopted methodology for the purposes of survey-analysis, and, as he notes, further understanding of the economic interpretation of history, a place New Urbanist theory can never hope to reach, suffering as it does from what has been described as 'historical amnesia' (Saab 2007) and 'a lack of theoretical sophistication' (Grant 2002). In addition and probably most importantly, Geddes's entire vision in *Cities in Evolution* was based upon a vastly different perspective, formed as it was at the close of the industrial revolution. Whether or not he would have held the same philosophy today, in the light of globalisation, informational capitalism and potentially imminent ecocide, is a moot point.

The second claim to theory is on the basis of Ian McHarg's *Design with Nature* (see above), which is again used to justify the methodology of the transect:

> The transect is clearly articulated in an introductory chapter [of the book] by way of explaining the workings of ecosystems. The transect gradient was made operational in the body of the book by means of a series of transparent overlays designed to discover a transect gradient of the land.
>
> (Duany 2002: 254)

In fact, McHarg's book does nothing of the kind. The only section in the introductory chapters is of a sand dune, showing prototypical plant colonisation and succession. In addition, the remainder of the book is not devoted to discovering any transect gradients whatsoever, but constitutes a search by means of several in-depth case studies of regions and their natural ecology where urbanisation could safely take place, and to what degree. Duany is also misguided when he says that, 'McHarg's analysis was entirely a declension of natural, rather than social, habitas' Duany (2000: 254). In fact, the last chapter of *Design with Nature* is entirely devoted to a student project that he supervised, which was devoted to an in-depth analysis of social pathology in Philadelphia.

The third claim to legitimacy is on the basis that Duany selected four patterns from Christopher Alexander's famous *A Pattern Language* (1977), namely patterns (2) *The distribution of towns*, (13) *Subculture boundary*, (29) *Density rings* and (36) *Degrees of publicness*. He says that these were chosen from a total of 252 patterns (actually 253), claiming that they constituted a transect – 'a sideshow within that great work . . . which is lost among the other 252 patterns and has had little independent impact'. He could equally have chosen four others, let's say (4) *Agricultural valley*, which actually mentions McHarg, (8) *Mosaic of subcultures*, (14) *Identifiable neighbourhood* and (16) *Network of public transport*. The idea that the transect strategy was somehow hidden within Alexander's *A Pattern Language* and then had its buried meaning excavated makes no sense at all. The same is true of Duany's statement that the transect, 'is a fractal that allows design to integrate across scales; from regional tiers, to community codes to architectural standards' (Duany 2002: 258). Clearly, the transect methodology has little support either in the workings of major political economists or in its self-referential examples of McHarg, Geddes and Alexander. We are left with the observation that efforts to establish credibility for the movement constitute an attempt to justify a design methodology using sources that had entirely different purposes and objectives, and were in fact methodologies themselves, not theories.

Therefore, on the basis of some very dubious logic, the foundations of New Urbanism float clear of the analytical processes adopted by Geddes, McHarg and Alexander and instead retranslate the valley section into an imposed ideology of design. It is also clear from the above that although the transect is somewhat depthless in any theoretical rigour, it remains a persuasive methodology for many in the environmental professions owing to its promotion of sustainability and diversity, its attack on suburban sprawl, its capacity even to incorporate ethnicity into its vocabulary and, arguably and most importantly, its resurrection of physical determinism as a socially relevant strategy (Day 2000, Duany *et al.* 2000). The transect approach has been described as a 'pragmatic alternative system of zoning', based in 'a well established system of ecological analysis', and can be defined as 'a system that seeks to organise the elements of urbanism – building, lot, land use, street, and all of the other elements of the human habitat – in ways that preserve the integrity of urban and rural environments', with the intention that 'the transect has the potential to become an instrument of design' (Talen 2002b: 293–4); also, 'The correlation of the various specialised components by a common rural-to-urban continuum provides the basis for a new system of zoning, one that creates complex, contextually resonant natural and human environments' (Duany 2002: 255).

The methodology of the transect adopts what is claimed to be a generic or prototypical section from urban centres to peripheries or, to use an unfortunate descriptor from planning, the peri-urban fringe. Concepts of density, building type and building form are implicit. High density exists at the urban core, grading down to rural zones, which presumably have no density. The forms of

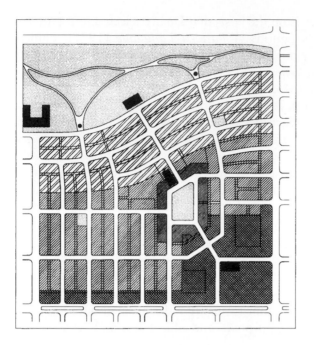

REGIONAL ZONES	LOCAL ZONES		
CIVIC	CS	CIVIC SPACE	
	CB	CIVIC BUILDING	
URBAN	T1	URBAN CORE	
	T2	URBAN CENTER	
	T3	GENERAL URBAN	
	T4	SUB-URBAN	
RURAL	T5	RURAL RESERVE	
	T6	RURAL PRESERVE	
DISTRICT	DN	DISTRICT BY VARIANCE	
	DE	DISTRICT BY EXCEPTION	

Figure 7.9 The New Urbanist transect

Source: Duany, Plater-Zyberk and Co. *The Lexicon of the New Urbanism*, 2001, p. 299, Fig. 3. Taken from an article by Emily Talen (2002) 'Help for urban planning: the transect strategy'. *The Journal of Urban Design*, 7(3): 293–312

buildings and spaces emanate from this density gradient, which is maintained as the natural order of towns and cities. Duany denotes seven main density zones and their functions, such as special districts for regional institutions, plazas and squares (Figure 7.9). Building forms shown in section are indicators of residential densities. Each zone would be subject to the constraints of a written code, which would be designed not only to conserve the rural-to-urban continuum, but also to transform it over time (Duany and Plater-Zyberg's 'Smart Code' is also available on the New Urbanist website). Codes would have to be translated to fit a diversity of regions, despite the accepted generic qualities of the transect itself. The methodology is therefore fairly straightforward – accept a generic section for all regions, which are divided into seven types, construct a code to control development in the relevant sector and accept the standard typology of building forms adopted by the New Urbanism as specified in each situation. In so doing, 'by tying its system of order to nature, not social processes, the transect resolves both issues simultaneously . . . it therefore eludes the criticism that the organisation of spatial form must be a search for control over moral and political order' (Talen 2002b: 305; see also Talen 2000).

Although it is undeniable that many projects that claim to be New Urbanist are excellent examples of urban design, it is dubious that this is owing to anything other than individual design talent and the intuitive ability to relate to a new aesthetic. The New Urbanist literature is also riddled with so many inconsistencies and undefined terminology that its success has to be based on simple solutions for those who refuse to think further. For example, how can one possibly accept Talen's statement (above) or Duany's remark that, 'The current dominant theory does not process authentic urbanism. An alternative based on the transect would' (Duany 2002: 257). Nowhere is it mentioned what this 'current dominant theory' is, what 'authentic urbanism' is supposed to be (as opposed to inauthentic urbanism) or, indeed, how the New Urbanism came to have a monopoly over authenticity. The New Urbanism is massively imbued with such rhetoric, to the detriment of the many excellent projects so far built around the world. Indeed, New Urbanist theorists could do worse than to revisit the prior work of Manuel Castells mentioned above, where he comments on the differentiation of urban form, definitions of spatial units and the rationale of separating rural from urban and town from country, the essence of the New Urbanist methodology:

> But is there not, then, to be any separation between 'town' and 'country'? Is it not a matter of 'generalised urbanisation'? In reality the problematic has no meaning (other than an ideological one) as such, posed in the terms in which it is generally posed. For it already presupposes the distinction and even the contradiction between rural and urban, an opposition and a contradiction that have little meaning in capitalism.
>
> (Castells 1977: 446)

Although the New Urbanism has no praxis, as it lacks theory, it offers a certain basic formal discipline to practitioners in architecture, urban design and urban planning. The idea of the transect itself is somewhat harmless and, if implemented, would no doubt be superior to the usual suburbification of capitalist urbanisation, if for the wrong reasons. It offers an easily understood set of principles and methodologies that attempt to synthesise the key elements which integrate the environmental disciplines into acceptable patterns of development, a laudable goal. In the same manner, the standardisation of development in accordance with certain basic urban forms, aesthetics, regulations and densities is positive, and we are forced to observe that, historically, many of the great urban centres in the Western world, Paris, London, New York and others, were built according to a similar, simple and uniform set of standards, including the use of materials, proportion and other design elements.

Conclusion

The debates that have fuelled planning and urban design for decades have focussed on whether high density is more efficient than low, or whether urban consolidation is more efficient than suburban expansion. Although this is a false dichotomy, the problems are nonetheless linked. Suburban America was not built because it was more efficient or desirable, but because it was the best available method of extracting capital from land and its improvements, facilitated by urban planning practice. Things are no different today. While the academic debate over high or low density goes on interminably, the system remains driven by capitalist interests, interests that have adapted to the prevailing profit-making urban system that they have created. Hence, academic debates over 'what kind of city should we promote' are as naive and utopian as they are ideological. The real problematic involves the degree to which planning is capable of resisting state neocorporatism and the so-called 'natural capitalism' of Amery Lovins, one that allows the capitalist system to claim legitimacy while, in principle, it remains unchanged. In the debate over urban structure, what seems to be lost is the fundamental question of what kind of community we wish to belong to, before deciding its form and working backwards.

The hiatus involves the absence of informed social planning to accompany the architecture, a conjuncture where a great many utopian ideas have come unglued, from Pruitt Igoe to the British New Town System. Studies that would merge new spatial forms with new forms of community are notably absent, and history looks set to repeat itself, unless physical determinism is finally abandoned as a method of planning human communities. Complex high-rise cities, of whatever configuration, are not merely a different form of living on the ground. New, three-dimensional, self-sustaining physical environments will bring with them new forms of social relations, equity, communication, crime, cultures, public space, waste disposal, recreation, shopping, opportunities for surveillance and social control, institutional frameworks, legal issues and a multitude of other circumstances. All of these need to be resolved before a new vertical architecture can be seriously contemplated. To this extent, the work of Richard Britz needs to be revisited, work that stands in direct opposition to conceptually new environments. Britz's project is one that seeks to integrate community, sustainability, lifestyle and gender equality, an exemplary approach that should, in principle, be incorporated into all urban design programmes and projects, at whatever density they occur.

8 Aesthetics

Art is a revolt against fate.

(André Malraux)

Introduction: issues in aesthetic judgement

The question central to the consciousness of every urban designer is surely the question, what makes a city beautiful? This automatically leads to greater specificity – how should we approach the design of beautiful urban spaces? What should we be thinking about *before* we initiate design strategies, i.e. the technologies that will implement our ideas? How should we deal with the evolution of the city in terms of aesthetic judgement (Porteous 1996, Bosselman 1998, Cinar and Bender 2002, Light and Smith 2005, Berleant 2007a, 2007b, Delafons 1998)? Although aesthetic experience is, in the last resort, a matter of individual discrimination and personal choice, it is also a conditioned event (Rappoport 1977, Wolff 1981, Weber 1995, Orr 2002). Travelling from one's own country to the one next door will immediately demonstrate that the aesthetic experience and how it is valued vary greatly from one place to another and from one generation to the next. Despite such difference, it is tempting to assume that some fundamentals remain that people hold in common. However, the idea that any generic or universal values exist must be seriously challenged (Graham 1997). For example, what could the term *aesthetic* possibly mean when applied to the original aboriginal inhabitants of Australia, who possessed neither settlements nor buildings? Was their aesthetic experience reducible to nature and the realm of the senses, or did an abstract concept of beauty in fact exist?

However, in today's commodity-producing society, the aesthetic experience is significantly integrated with, and conditioned through, the mass media, on the basis of commodity circulation on a global basis. Everybody across the planet can wear Levi jeans and find them aesthetically satisfying. We are continuously flooded with images, and indoctrinated on a moment-to-moment basis as to how beauty is constituted. Desire is cultivated, and aesthetic values are manipulated, so that mass markets in skin creams, perfume, clothes, automobiles, food, architecture and other commodities can prevail – this year's new car is always better looking (more desirable) than the last. So are there any universals that can inform our judgement of beauty in the realm of urban aesthetics, or are all values, like commodities, social products? More importantly, what methods of thinking about aesthetics have been used in the past, and are these same processes relevant for the present? As urban designers, which heterologies should inform our judgements about the aesthetics of space and form, beyond our own personal or collective 'intuition' about colour, dimensions, movement, form, purpose and the juxtaposition of objects in urban space?

Aesthetic values are progressively modified through modes of production, perception, history and individuation. Hence, each civilisation has provided many of its own answers, variously rooted in the development of biology, mathematics, philosophy, psychology, culture and other factors, and the search has been progressing, both individually and collectively, over millennia (Pickford 1972, Scruton 1974, 1979, Cosgrove 1984, Olsen 1986). In consequence, we must accept the fact that it is a search without any possible resolution, for the simple reason that culture, development, urbanism and the human imagination are dynamic processes, and so aesthetic values are always in a continuous state of flux. They evolve in step with society, as well as in relation to individual perception and experience, and, despite all of our best efforts, *the aesthetic* remains undefinable and evanescent. Although much of this might appear nihilistic (why bother with questions that have no resolution), it is clear that it is the unanswered and most intractable problems that lie at the centre of our existence and accord it value. Hence, the effort to resolve them – or at least to remain in a continuous state of awareness – remains crucial to the evolution of our humanity. Concepts of aesthetics are therefore rooted in philosophical debate, and questions fundamental to our aesthetic engagement with the world, such as 'What is beauty?', 'What is truth?', 'What is the nature of human experience?', also remain unanswered, despite John Keats' famous line in *Ode on a Grecian Urn* (1819): 'beauty is truth, truth beauty. That is all ye know on earth and all ye need to know'.

In *The Form of Cities* (FOC8), I suggested that three major building blocks were central to our understanding of aesthetics and the city. Collectively, they constitute a powerful and interacting conceptual system, within which the dynamics of aesthetic investigation may be played out. All three have an extensive theoretical grounding, and each constitutes a method of thinking about design issues. The first of these is *semiotics*, or the science of meaning. Given that meaning imbues our entire existence as a species, the methods by which meanings are either designed into spaces and places, or are accorded to them through human action, are critical to the designer's understanding and vocabulary (Harvey 1979, Krampen 1979, FOC3: 65–9). Second, *phenomenology* attempts to grapple with the realm of the senses, the direct experience we all undertake as we interact with the environment around us, where buildings and spaces constitute the governing dimension of urban life, and within which all experience occurs and coexists (FOC3: 69–72). Third, *political economy* allows us insight into how the apparent randomness of individuals, objects and processes is socially and spatially constituted in structuring the urban (FOC: 72–8). Clearly, these three positions interact in complex ways, and capitalist production over the last five centuries has had massive effects on consciousness. The nature of human experience has also shifted, as technology, labour, production and culture morph into increasingly diverse relationships. Meanings attached to these processes also result in new signs, associations, behavioural norms and aesthetic values, all of which affect the way we experience the city and, to a large extent, modify its construction. Importantly for urban designers, the built environment, as the major signifier of production, is simultaneously an aesthetic product by the mere fact of its dominant role in our daily life. So what is aesthetic?

Three main aesthetic determinants exist, related to environment, experience and communication. First, our external environment, created from the relationship between nature and human action, is the context within which the carnival of human experience takes place. This environment is subject to design in the broadest sense of the word, i.e. organised by human action. This would include everything, from slums to cathedral precincts or royal palaces. Second, at the level of individuation, we know that our aesthetic experience is conditioned, on the one hand, through the five senses – sight, hearing, touch, taste, smell – and, on the other, by our environment. In many cultures, what we refer to as 'a sixth sense', unrelated to these other five, is also claimed, an unconscious understanding or anticipation of events that evades our rational minds. Third, the aesthetic experience is fundamentally a form of communication between media, individuals and environments. Art, in all of its forms, is a method of transmitting information in a highly specialised manner, as it depends on individual participation and interpretation. In regard to individuation, I have also suggested that we need to add a seventh sense in order fully to appreciate the urban aesthetic, that of kinaesthesia, or the feeling of movement (FOC6: 13). Without the joy of movement, a universal experience of great beauty is removed, as well as several important methods of understanding urban form. The *flâneur*, for example, symbolises the seventh sense in the urban realm, where perambulation through space and the experience of openness and enclosure, vista, landscape and architecture constitute the essence of *flânerie*.

An elementary problem with terminology, however, is that 'aesthetic' usually relates to perceived beauty, art, pleasure and sensuality. *The New Oxford Dictionary of English* defines *aesthetic* in various different senses, all of which are concerned with the appreciation of beauty, with an aesthete denoted as 'a person who is appreciative of or sensitive to art and beauty'. Indeed, the Greek verb *aesthesthai* only means 'to perceive', from the root *aestheta*, meaning 'perceptible things' (Pearsall 2001: 28). Therefore, there was nothing in the original meaning that related to beauty, an attribution that was imported from German into English usage at the beginning of the nineteenth century. Hence, the connection between aesthetics and beauty is a recent construct, unrelated to its origins. This begs the question as to whether the aesthetics of urban form massively exaggerate the visual aspect of cities (predominantly owing to architectural education) and downplay the experiential. Given a definition of aesthetic that relates predominantly to the senses, as in phenomenology, there is nothing to indicate that aesthetic experience should not also be uncomfortable, insulting, dominating, ugly, painful, sinful or terrifying. Consequently, there is no necessary homology between art and aesthetics, despite the fact that there is a homology between aesthetics and beauty. Clearly, much art is designed to shock, and there need not be anything beautiful about it. Aesthetics can also be seen as a set of principles that guide or otherwise influence artistic production, raising the problematic as to whether aesthetic principles and creative processes are transferable from one art form to another.

This idea leads us inevitably into the question of aesthetics and form – music, sculpture, painting, literature, the theatre, poetry, film, architecture and the inevitable cross-fertilisation between them. Each form adds additional vectors to the problematic of aesthetics as a whole, for example 'a vast number of clichés and commonplaces, nurtured by centuries of theatre, have unfortunately also found a resting place in the cinema' (Tarkofsky 1986: 24). Even within any chosen art form, the process of arriving at a final aesthetic statement varies immensely, depending on a host of other factors embedded within the creative process. Johann Wolfgang Von Goethe famously described architecture as 'frozen music', posing the question, 'so what does the building sound like?'. The great American painter Mark Rothko also gave his own answer to the production of art in an address at the Pratt Institute in 1958. He offered what he considered to be the essential formula for a work of art (note that he did not say 'painting'):

- There must be a clear preoccupation with death – intimations of mortality . . . Tragic art, romantic art etc., deals with the knowledge of death.
- Sensuality. Our basis of being concrete about the world. It is a lustful relationship to things that exist.
- Tension. Either conflict or curbed desire.
- Irony. This is a modern ingredient – the self-effacement and examination by which a man for an instant can go on to something else.
- Wit and play . . . for the human element.
- The ephemeral and chance . . . for the human element.
- Hope. Ten per cent, to make the tragic concept more endurable.

Rothko's statements are not unique in their reflections on darkness and hope, and his sentiments parallel those in the conclusion to *Sculpting in Time*, the great Russian filmmaker Andrei Tarkovsky's flaying of himself, where he discusses the aesthetics of film:

What is art/is it good or evil? From God or from the devil? From man's strength or from his weakness? Could it be a pledge of fellowship, an image of social harmony, Might that be its function? Like a declaration of love: the consciousness of our dependence on each other. A confession. An unconscious act that none the less reflects the true meaning of life – love and sacrifice.

(Tarkovsky 1986: 239)

It is interesting, given these two examples of the aesthetic content of art and aesthetics, with regard to their direct application to the aesthetics of cities, whether or not in the urban designer's toolkit such questions ever arise. Whether these ideas are relevant to designing cities I leave to others to judge, but even a preliminary glance at Rothko's seven elements raises significant questions as to the aesthetics of urban design. In order to ground the form of the city and the city beautiful as heterology, much of this chapter will focus on what was in the designer's mind as he/she considered the aesthetics of urban form. This will be continued in the final chapter, where the manifestos of various influential movements in art and architecture suggested what the city meant and how it should be formed.

Aesthetic production, art and the city

So, how do we understand the methods used by designers in generating the aesthetics of urban form? Given the designer's need to create beauty, what insights do we have available that can inform the designer's actions? Roger Scruton, in his classic text *The Aesthetics of Architecture* (1979), suggested three central heterologies from which architectural and urban space come about. These derive from Freud, Saussure and Marx and have had a wide range of application. The governing heterology common to all three was, of course, the methods of structuralist thought that pervaded the twentieth century (see also his chapter on the aesthetic attitude in *Art and Imagination* (1974)).

Freud

Sigmund Freud, arguably the seminal psychologist of the twentieth century, has been eulogised and despised with equal fervour. Famous for inventing the method of psychoanalysis, Freud had an immense impact, not only on social science in its entirety, but also on literature and the arts. His investigation into the structure of the human psyche is unparalleled in the modern world, with the possible exception of Carl Gustav Jung, who was his student. The structure of the mind (id, ego and superego), the development of sexuality (anal, oral and genital), archetypal forms such as the Oedipus and Electra complexes, and even the term *psychology*, all owe their origins to Freud. The concept of critical theory originating in the Frankfurt School pays as much homage to Freud as it does to Marx, given that its central focus was to generate an encompassing formulation of civilisation and its discontents through a marriage of psyche and economy. If aesthetics is indeed embedded in the realm of the senses, then it is clear that Freud's influence had few boundaries. A central theme of Freud's psychology was the repressive principle in society, and his great contribution was in developing a sociology of the unconscious mind, maintaining that society's institutions and personal neuroses were interlinked. There was no point in unravelling individual neurosis and returning a healthy person to a society whose institutions were fundamentally sick. In this context, Robert Bocock says:

> The social institutions of traditionalism, such as religion and ideology, can also be seen as deformed, pathological modes of communication.

He goes on to quote directly from Freud:

> Knowledge of the neurotic afflictions of individuals has well served the understanding of the major social institutions, for neuroses ultimately reveal themselves as attempts to solve, on an individual basis, the problems of wish compensation that ought to be solved socially by institutions.
>
> (Bocock 1976: 31)

Central to Freud's method was the analysis of neurosis by way of deconstructing the meanings embedded in dreams. Neurotic behaviour, fundamentally a conflict between thoughts and feelings, could be understood and treated by revealing its sources. In this process, the relationship between fantasy and reality, repression and sublimation, the real and the surreal, and the nature of longing and desire, are all suspended in a dynamic balance (frequently imbalance) – between instinct, awareness and sacrifice. Probably the best and most direct example of Freud's effect on aesthetics is in the surrealist and Dada movements of modern art, exemplified in the paintings of artists such as Salvador Dalí, Joan Miró, René Magritte, Max Ernst and a host of others. However, this reduces the scale of Freud's influence to one particular form of expression. The overall impact of Freud's method on aesthetics is the manner in which his basic conceptual system is used in analysis or design in the execution of aesthetic judgement, in architecture and urban design as in other dimensions of human endeavour – in literature, painting, poetry, film, music and other art forms.

Roger Scruton's book *The Aesthetics of Architecture* was groundbreaking when it was published in 1979, and Chapters 6 and 7 are instructive. The psychoanalyst Hannah Segal and the poet/painter Adrian Stokes had already suggested the connection between psychoanalysis and aesthetics, but Scruton was among the first to connect architectural aesthetics directly to theories central to social theory: psychology, language and historical materialism, reflecting his belief that 'the cultivation of aesthetic experience, without corresponding adoption of a critical point of view is nothing more than self-deception' (Scruton 1979: 137). He goes on to state that Freud himself was critical of a psychoanalytic aesthetics, considering that, while psychoanalysis might have much to say about creativity, it was unable to say much about the results. This opinion was not shared by one of Freud's acolytes, Melanie Klein, and the architectural critic Adrian Stokes. Scruton notes that great architecture is capable of generating profound emotion in individuals, and that the sources of such emotion are to be found in the psychoanalytical depth of individual consciousness: 'to describe those sentiments psychoanalytically is at the same time to describe their value. We are therefore one step on the way to an account of success in architecture' (Scruton 1979: 146).

Of all repressed desires, sexuality probably takes pride of place in any hierarchy. Sexualising buildings and spaces therefore constitutes a prime mode of operation, and the relation between Freud and sexuality is universally recognised. The Freudian approach considers the ego/personality to be a mask, with the real impetus driving individual action coming from the (repressed) unconscious mind. Therefore, unless designers are extremely aware of their own hidden repressions and desires (almost never), then clearly urban form becomes a major outlet for the subconscious to assert itself in the built environment. Architecture and urban form therefore represent a potentially fertile canvas for designers to express their favourite neurosis (conflict) or psychosis (fantasy), and I can only begin to mention here a few of the most obvious Freudian traits that appear in three-dimensional form. Dominant among these is fetishism, a fetish being defined as any object that substitutes for perceived castration, real or otherwise: 'Fetishism is a refusal of loss: the fetish object blocks or displaces this traumatic discovery of loss. By nature a fetish is also preoccupied with surface appearances that conceal a deeper anxiety, a more profound sense of loss' (Pouler 1994: 182). Pouler goes on to suggest that the resultant insecurity encourages a retreat to the imaginary world of the past, where the facts of the present are substituted in a surreal return to the happy certainties of yesterday. History then becomes a method of counteracting the insecurity of the present. He maintains that a fetishistic mentality is the method of postmodern architecture, where:

> historical styles are revived against the realities of the contemporary; style is inherently concealed with an image, in the surface quality of the architecture, in facades, masks, and decorated sheds (what is seen dominates what is known); and buildings and plazas – that is, form and space – substitute for a legitimate phenomenology of place that once provided for the ontological needs of individuals and groups.
>
> (Pouler 1994: 182)

While we can interpret postmodern history as fetishistic, fetishism has more direct and obvious effects. The most obvious expression here is in high-rise development, where phallic symbolism and penis-fixation have been held responsible for the ongoing obsession with skyscraper architecture. Beginning most notably with architect Frank Lloyd Wright's visionary Mile High Skyscraper of 1956 (which was never built), half a century later the endless competition by urban authorities for tallest building in the world still continues. The corollary that women's subconscious expression of their own sexuality would reflect womb-like spaces, all curves, nurturing, cloistered and close to the earth, is the parallel. Likewise, the association of women with elaborate decoration and chintzy ornament was an aesthetic stigma that placed them in contravention with the modernist project and its architecture. Overall, such interpretations do nothing for gender equality. They are crudely symbolic and deny the complexity of gender differences, which have more to do with politics than skyscrapers. It assumes that the male fixation with erections, architectural or otherwise, is so absolute that all central business districts, from Manhattan to Hong Kong, owe their existence to the idea. This is clearly ridiculous, ignoring, as it does, such things as urban politics, market forces, urban densities and planning action, and the fact that many famous cities, such as Haussmann's Paris, did not have any buildings over five storeys in height. Freud's famous dictum that 'sometimes a cigar is just a cigar' appears to have been overlooked, though some writers still cling to phallic symbolism:

> Female urban form means the end of 'the phallus' as architect of all those oppositions and hierarchies – male over female, youth over age, beauty over ugliness, all those oppositions and hierarchies upon which Classical value and meaning depend. Female urban form means the death of architecture as phallic differentiation.
>
> (Bergren 1998: 89)

Saussure

The important theoretical aspects of semiology and semiotics were covered in FOC 3: 65–9. The discipline had a curious beginning, with the simultaneous framing of the science of meaning first in the United States in the work of Charles Sanders Pierce, who used the term *semiotics*, and in Europe in the work of Ferdinand de Saussure, who named his own philosophy *semiology*. Strictly speaking, the terminology should be applied discriminately. Here, the term semiotics will be applied heterologically to encompass the general methodology of analysing or integrating meanings in built forms. I have also included two articles that describe the semiotic method in Mark Gottdiener's article, *Recapturing the Centre: A Semiotic Analysis of Shopping Malls* (DC3), and Sarah Chapin's *Heterotopia Deserta*; (DC9: 26), which analyses Las Vegas and other places. Semiotics considered as heterological to design is a method whereby meanings incorporated into built form and space may be deconstructed (and therefore understood) or, alternatively, consciously designed. Around 1980, when postmodernism had gained a firm footing, three seminal works appeared on semiotic method – Krampen's book *Meaning in the Urban Environment* (1979) and two books by Preziosi, *The Semiotics of the Built Environment* (1979a) and *Architecture Language and Meaning* (1979b). These were updated by Gottdiener in *Postmodern Semiotics* (1995). Each is a seminal study in the method of urban semiosis, deriving formal meanings from linguistic interpretations and using the vocabulary of semiotic analysis – pragmatic, syntactic, semantic, sign, image, symbol, langue and parole. The overall process constitutes an attempt to clarify the way 'in which architectural objects are processed cognitively, if not as signs of communication, at least as meaningful instruments, in order for the urban environment to become viable for human beings' (Krampen 1979: 1).

The importance of semiotics for architecture and urban design cannot be overestimated, as it constitutes a major factor in distinguishing between modernism and postmodernism. To be pragmatic for a moment, modernism as structural functionalism used the method of eliminating meanings incorporated into architectural form and detailing as a way of expressing beauty. By this means, it was thought that the true function/beauty of a building could be accessed and fully expressed, as exemplified in the work of the great modernists such as Le Corbusier, Mies van der Rohe, Walter Gropius etc. (Figure 8.1). However, the idea that the complexity of buildings such as hospitals, schools and city halls

Figure 8.1 The Barcelona Pavilion by Mies van der Rohe
Source: © age fotostock/SuperStock

could be reduced to a single apparent function was absurd. Most buildings had multiple functions to perform, which made the idea of functionalism as an appropriate form of expression somewhat tenuous, unless the concept was wholly limited to technology. Postmodernism, on the other hand, reversed this process, by deliberately incorporating referents from other contexts, meanings, places, histories etc. It argued that buildings, monuments, spaces and other urban elements had multiple functions to perform over the mechanical, witness Charles Moore's Piazza D'Italia in New Orleans (Figure 8.2). Indeed, the more referents a building incorporated, the richer it seemed to become. The adopted method was that of the text. The built environment could be viewed as a multiplicity of texts that could then be constructed or deconstructed in accordance with reference to the methods of linguistic analysis. As texts are, by definition, cultural products, the built environment had the capacity, not only to reveal hidden meanings, but also, more importantly, to consciously link architecture and culture. Despite the fact that Pierce and Saussure were the progenitors of structuralist semiotic method, it was up to others to advance methods of deconstruction within postmodernism. The linguistic theory referred to was that of the structuralists (Piaget, Chomsky and Helmsjev) but also of its extension into poststructuralist semiotics – Gottdiener, Barthes, Kristeva and others. What we can say, however, is that the aesthetic process set in place by modernist

Figure 8.2 The Piazza D'Italia in New Orleans, by Charles Moore. A supreme
          example of the use of semiotics in postmodern urbanism
Source: © Robert Holmes/Corbis

urbanism was one where beauty was conflated with function. In postmodernism, we can say speculate that beauty is based in communication, and how much of the text is stored, revealed, transformed or hidden.

Needless to say, there is no one method of analysis or design, and there are a multiplicity of methods from which to choose. Many of these are difficult to follow, and only a flavour of what is involved may be given here. Krampen, for example, follows the heterology of Saussurian method, whereby meanings are revealed in the relationship between the signifier and signified. He demonstrates the experiential aspect of what is signified, for example, in relation to his study of various types of building facade (Figure 8.3) and illustrates, in a multiplicity of ways, the semiotic structure of architectural connotation that lies behind the aesthetic experience of individuals in relation to various aspects of architectural and urban form (Figure 8.4). Aesthetic values are not determined by abstract ideas of beauty and are seldom mentioned. The inference is that aesthetic value is based on the relationship between individual perception and the satisfaction

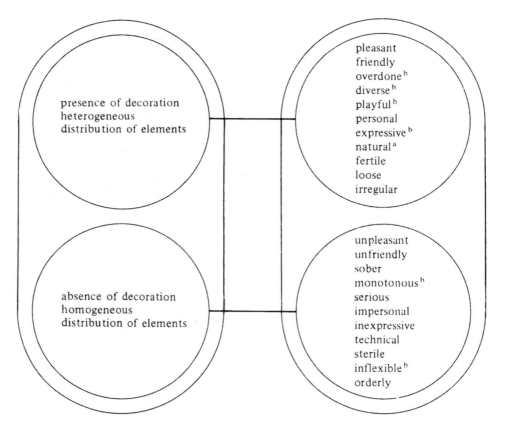

Figure 8.3 The semiotic structure of architectural connotation. In this structure, the universe of the signified is coordinated with the universe of the signifier, in which two kinds of facade are opposed

Source: M.K. Krampen, *Meaning in the Urban Environment*. London: Pion, 1973, p. 299, Fig. 5.29

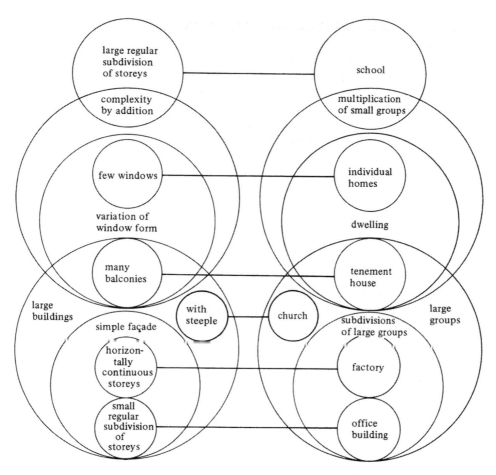

Figure 8.4 The hypothetical semiotic structure between the level of the signified, namely small-group and large-group activities defining the social functions of buildings (on the right), and the level of the signifier, namely building design features (on the left)

Source: M.K. Krampen, *Meaning in the Urban Environment*. London: Pion, 1973, p. 177, Fig. 4.63

that results from the sign formation of buildings. Figure 8.5 illustrates the method of layering in an architectural facade that results from a correlation between individual satisfaction and semiotic content.

Marx

While it might seem a stretch of the imagination to conjoin Marx and aesthetics, there is a significant body of literature that explores Marx's philosophy of aesthetic production, albeit mostly embedded in more general texts on social theory, art or ideology. The subject is more directly tackled in Vazquez (1973),

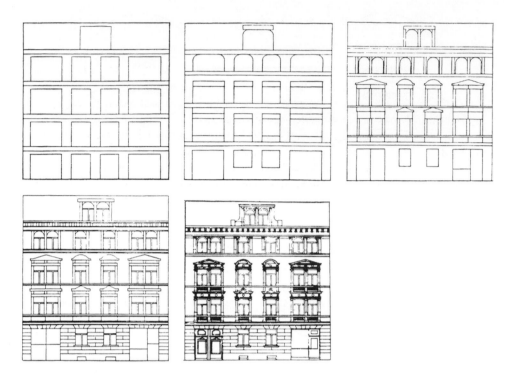

Figure 8.5 Five successive stages in 'supersign' formation of an architectural facade
Source: M.K. Krampen, *Meaning in the Urban Environment*. London: Pion, 1979, p. 249, Fig. 5.18

Zis (1977) and Marcuse (1968). Raphael (1981), Johnson (1984), Eagleton (1990), Graham (1997) and I have also covered Marxist economic theory and political economy in relation to politics, ideology and urban planning at length, in FOC3: 72–81 and FOC4: 85–9. In contradistinction to other theories of art, the clue to Marxist and neo-Marxist aesthetics lies in understanding the mechanisms that structure aesthetic production as part of economic production as a whole. Therefore, the most obvious relation of Marxism to aesthetic method is in the capacity of works of art to resist or otherwise comment on those forces that Marx identified as being oppressive, or, alternatively, in their capacity to critically appraise and portray methods of resistance against class oppression. To this extent, Marxist aesthetics are revolutionary in spirit and operate within a moral compass that considers art in the context of ideology and history. As a prime objective, art should focus on the amelioration of society by resisting oppression in all of its forms, commenting on social injustice and providing a radical critique of bourgeois society. In other words, true art should not constitute yet another bourgeois method of storing capital. However, within capitalism, artistic production is tied into the market mechanism, and the artist (read architect or urban designer) is in turn affected by the historical circumstances within which his/her work is produced. Art then becomes a highly specialised form of surplus value within the overall labour process.

Overall, Adolfo Sanchez Vazquez's essays on Marxist aesthetics remain the most comprehensive treatment of the subject. His analysis is complex and fragmented, owing to the construction of the book from twenty-four essays, but a few key features of his argument need to be elaborated. Vazquez notes that, although Marx did not write a definitive treatise on aesthetics, nonetheless he was keenly interested in all aspects of the subject, and it was left to others such as Kautsky, Lafargue and Plekhanov, and later to Althusser, Lukacs, Gramsci, Benjamin, Jameson and Eagleton, to elucidate the Marxian method. Unfortunately, capitalist ideology has demonised Marx's name as a primeval version of 'the great Satan' (in Indonesia, for example, his three volumes of *Capital* were only removed from censorship in 2008, a century and a half after they were written). Hence, there is a somewhat universal tendency to associate his views on aesthetics with all things socialist and communist, forgetting that his lifetime's work was a critique of capitalism, not socialism, about which he did not have much to say. However, the association sticks, and there is a similar tendency to view Marxist aesthetics as *method*, coming to fruition in the realist art of socialist societies (see Figure 8.6). Marxist aesthetics then becomes associated with that of the Soviet Union in the mid 1930s or, by extension, the art of all so-called socialist societies and the social realist art of China, Cuba, North Vietnam and Albania etc. in the course of the twentieth century. Nothing could be further from the truth. This is, indeed, an extremely crude interpretation of Marx's conception of aesthetics and the relationship between aesthetic production, material production, ideology and moral values.

> However, the favourable conditions created in the Soviet Union in the early thirties, in which a thorough and creative study of Marx's aesthetic ideas might have provided the foundation for a scientific, open minded, non-normative Marxist aesthetic, were seriously undermined when the Stalinist regime began to give rise to increasingly dogmatic, sectarian and class subjectivist methods in aesthetic theory and artistic practice.
>
> (Vazquez 1973: 19)

In that context, literature, painting, graphic design, sculpture and architecture were concentrated exclusively in the service of the state, glorifying its accomplishments, celebrating labour and censoring non-conformity to these ideals with great vengeance. Nonetheless, and despite these overpowering limitations, iconic art and indeed entire genres (constructivism, futurism etc.) still managed to emerge, producing artists such as Popov, Rodchenko, Tatlin, El Lissitsky, Leonidov, Krinsky, Miljutin, Malevitch, Tarkovsky etc. The art of the Soviets in the mid 1930s would likely constitute the high point of the genre:

> But in the same way that capitalism, being hostile to art, has known great works of art, socialism does not by itself guarantee an art superior to that

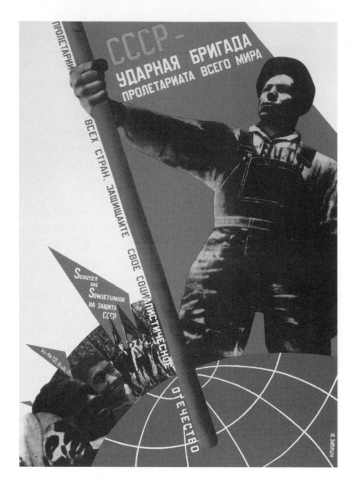

Figure 8.6
Example of Soviet
socialist realist art: poster
Source: IAM/AKG Images

created under capitalism; numerous factors, both objective and subjective, have a bearing on this matter. In short the law of the uneven development of art and society, from a qualitative point of view, always presents a constant need for art to transcend its limits, thus preventing artists from completely settling down under the accomplishments of the society as a whole.

(Vazquez 1973: 103)

Hence, there is no necessary relation between the methods used in artistic production, the political form of the state and the historical processes of capital accumulation. There are several reasons for this, the most fundamental being that all modern societies, communist, socialist or capitalist, are hostile to the production of works of art, simply because of their inherent capacity for resistance to social and political inequality, whatever system prevails. One could also argue that there has been a greater reflection of the spirit of Marxian aesthetics within capitalism than there has been in any so-called socialist states during the twentieth century, owing to a greater relative autonomy of art and therefore of the artistic freedom that Marx supported. On the other hand, as material production alienates the worker from his/her object, so the process of artistic production as a means of subsistence within capitalism automatically undermines the objective capacity of artistic production – the artist has to survive within the market and is affected by the logic of commodity production as a whole, and this clearly applies to architecture and urban design. Whereas Freud's method concentrated on the incarceration of individual aesthetics within the psychological body, Marx's concern was with those methods by which capitalism turns the human body into an object in the process of producing commodities, and how the same body becomes alienated from the work process by becoming commodified itself. Or, as Terry Eagleton puts it:

> Marx is most profoundly 'aesthetic' in his belief that the exercise of human senses, powers, and capacities is an absolute end in itself, without the need of utilitarian justification; but the unfolding of this sensuous richness for its own sake can be achieved, paradoxically, only through the rigorously instrumental practice of overthrowing bourgeois social relations. Only when the bodily drives have been released from the despotism of abstract need, and the object has been similarly restored from functional abstraction to sensuously particular use value will it be possible to live aesthetically.
>
> (Eagleton 1990: 202)

In other words, the human body is atomised within capitalism and both legally and existentially reduced to an item of property. Like others, the artist is caught within this frame of reference. Only by escaping from this context can Freud's pleasure principle be realised, thus liberating the capacity for true aesthetic experience unsullied by oppressive mechanisms that are devoid of moral content.

The contextualist method and aesthetic production

The two great design traditions of the twentieth century were those of contextualism and rationalism (FOC: 179–86). Risking oversimplification, we can say that contextualism is an appeal to the heart, to emotion, to the senses and to experience, and is closely related to phenomenology (particularly that of Norberg-Schulz). Needless to say, both movements are themselves rooted in historical antecedents stretching back over millennia, having clear methodological principles that continue to affect the design of cities today. The contextualist tradition as a conscious design idiom stems more recently from Gian Battista Nolli's plan for Rome (1768) and Camillo Sitte's classic *The Art of Building Cities* (1945 (orig. 1889)). The movement was given renewed impetus in Britain when the ravages of the industrial revolution, combined with the blitzkrieg of the Second World War, created outrage in the general population. This general feeling was first expressed publicly in two issues of *The Architectural Review*, aptly called 'Outrage' and 'Counter attack' (Nairn 1955, 1956). These were followed by *The Concise Townscape*, arguably the seminal publication that dealt directly with the aesthetic qualities of towns and cities in England, with strategies for their improvement, concentrating on the principle of serial vision (Cullen 1961; see Figures 8.7 and 8.8). Thereafter, the methods of creating good 'townscapes' became embedded as a strategic method both for analysing and promoting good urban design. A plethora of other 'townscape' publications followed, such as *British Townscapes* (Johns 1965), *Townscapes* (Burke 1976), *The Aesthetic Townscape* (Asihara 1983), *How to Design the Aesthetics of Townscape* (Goakes 1987) and *Making Townscape* (Tugnutt and Robertson 1987). Other classics of the period (1955–85), not using the term *townscape* in the title, must also include *The Image of the City* (Lynch 1960), *Man-made America: Chaos or Control?* (Tunnard 1963), *God's Own Junkyard* (Blake 1964), *Place and Placelessness* (Relph 1976) and *Great Planning Disasters* (Hall 1982). More generally, others have echoed the same sentiment up to the present time (Bacon 1965, Jellicoe and Jellicoe 1987, Gindroz 2003).

Despite their impact, few of the preceding texts actually prescribe a method of approach to the question of contextualism in practice, choosing to lead by example rather than any specific methodology, and many appealing to sentiment as much as to logic, i.e. think how lovely the world would be if we could all live in a wonderful English/American village or small town. In addition, it is also notable how many texts are stuck in the question of scale at the level of the village or town, and it is an open question as to whether or not the inherent principles of the townscape tradition are relevant for today's Internet-driven, neocorporate global cities. To put things in perspective before looking at *Townscape* (1961), and given that the book took several years to produce, Cullen was separated from Camillo Sitte (1889) by a distance comparable with that between himself and today's designers.

Hence, *Townscape* now possesses an aura of antiquity, somewhat exaggerated by the edition, which is cramped, disorganised, archaic in its language, overflowing with subjectivity and somewhat unreadable. Nonetheless, it stands as a masterful piece of intuition that clearly exposes a particular vision of the essential features of beautiful towns and cities. It fits neatly into the three design strategies traditionally used by architects, namely the inertia, scientific or intuitive methods. Smith notes that elements of each approach are inherent in the other two, so that the methods are not shrink-wrapped within their own logic. The inertia method is ubiquitous, reflecting the status quo almost everywhere, a process encouraged by standardisation in order to reduce design and construction costs. The scientific method utilises the laws of reason and logic, an approach significantly reflected in the structural functionalism of the modernist period. The intuitive method 'allows unconscious information processing to dictate a conscious solution' (Smith 1974: 228). It is this latter method that characterises the townscape tradition, and Cullen's *Townscape* is a case in point.

Figure 8.7 Example of the principles of serial vision
Source: G. Cullen, *The Concise Townscape*. London: The Architectural Press, 1961, p. 6

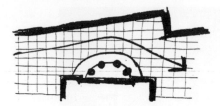

14 Wren's plan at the north portico of St Paul's.

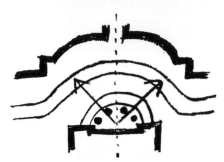

15 The Beaux Arts solution.

16 Royal Academy scheme.

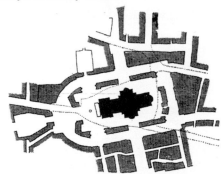

17 *Architectural Review* scheme.

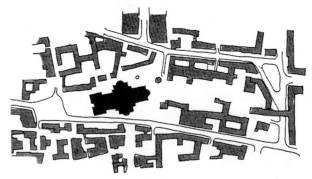

Figure 8.8 Four schemes for St Paul's Cathedral precinct, London

Source: G. Cullen, *The Concise Townscape*. London: The Architectural Press, 1961, p. 296, Figs 14–17

His book is divided into four parts. The first provides a casebook of studies, where three specific elements are highlighted, namely serial vision, place and content, along with what he calls 'the functional tradition', which has little bearing on modernism. His entire analytical method in the book is based almost exclusively on these three dimensions. Second, he undertakes a series of general studies of elements of townscape in England. Third, eight town studies are provided of, for example, Ludlow, Shrewsbury and Shepton Mallet. Finally, Cullen brings his prior considerations to bear on proposals for a variety of urban contexts, including cathedral precincts, urban redevelopment areas, new towns and other projects. His method of analysis (and implied method of aesthetics and design) is based almost exclusively on serial vision, place and content. Cullen's adopted method is unabashedly nationalistic (English), relative, highly subjective and personal. Aesthetic experience is reduced almost exclusively to what is seen, and, in this regard, science is rejected as a method of generating visual interest:

> Firstly we have to rid ourselves of the thought that the excitement and drama that we seek can be born automatically out of the scientific research and solutions arrived at by the technical man (or the technical half of the brain). We naturally accept these solutions but are not entirely bound by them ... this means that we can get no further help from the scientific attitude, and that we must turn to other values and other standards ... We turn to the faculty of sight, for it is almost entirely through vision that the environment is apprehended.
>
> (Cullen 1961: 10)

Having rejected science as insufficiently accommodating, Cullen then focusses almost exclusively on optics and the visual dimension, specifically the method implied in what he terms *serial vision*. By this, he refers to the shifting complexity of the visual experience that is present in many organic towns and cities, i.e. those that have largely resisted any form of planning. Clearly, this does not necessarily exclude other forms of planned development, such as Haussmann's plan for Paris, but most of Cullen's extensive examples would suggest that this is a rare occurrence. The overall implication is that urban design must be organised in such a manner that the citizen's movement through space provides a constantly shifting kaleidoscope of visual interest, an objective few would disagree with. Also implied is the idea that such complexity enriches human experience, stimulates the memory and imparts emotional content. Hence, from moment to moment, we may be enthralled, pacified, stimulated, amazed, seduced, challenged or filled with wonder by the environment around us. Such effects are historically generated through the organisation of space and materials that collectively form the built environment. Moreover, the basic argument is that, through understanding of the emotional effects of buildings and spaces, they may be reproduced to create complex and interesting environments rather than the sterile wastelands that constitute many cities worldwide.

After serial vision, Cullen then deals with *place* in terms of kinaesthetics and the positioning of the body in space. Important to this idea are the experiences of exposure and enclosure, which in their extreme forms result in agoraphobia or claustrophobia. Although these experiences can be generated in all of us through extreme enclosure in space, being in a cave, a tunnel, a tiny room or a small passage between two buildings, or through exposure, as in hill towns in Greece, Italy or Spain, where dwellings can be built on the top of cliffs that drop off several hundred metres, most urban spaces do not offer such extremes. Nonetheless,

> If we design our towns and cities from the point of view of the moving person, (pedestrian or car-borne) it is easy to see how the city becomes a plastic experience, a journey through pressures and vacuums, a sequence of exposures and enclosures, of constraint and relief.
>
> (Cullen 1961: 12)

This method of approach was amplified specifically in regard to the automobile in *The View from the Road* (Appleyard *et al.* 1964), *Freeways* (Halprin 1966) and *Road Form and Townscape* (McCluskey 1979), and, for the *flâneur*, Macauley (2000). The possession of place in the mind of the observer is fundamental to Cullen's consideration, frequently echoing the writing of Norberg-Schulz's phenomenology when he says, 'he is in IT or entering IT or leaving IT, we discover that no sooner do we postulate a HERE than automatically we must create a THERE, for you cannot have one without the other' (Cullen 1961: 12). Perhaps the idea was expressed most succinctly in Gertrude Stein's famous remark about her own home in Oakland, California, that, 'there is no there, there.'

The final element in Cullen's method is what he calls 'content'. By this, he means traditional referents familiar to all architects, namely colour, texture, scale, style, character, personality and uniqueness, the palette from which designers draw inspiration. Serial vision, place and content embrace the basic elements that, collectively, underwrite the methods intuitively adopted by urban designers. Despite the fact that Cullen leaves little to the imagination, he also abandons the designer to a completely blank canvas when it comes to a stated set of elements or processes that designers can reference. Notably, Kevin Lynch's *Image of the City* was published one year before *Townscape* (1960) and is significantly more useful in guiding designers after their intuition has been exhausted (see Bannerjee and Southworth (1990) for a full account of Lynch's work). Lynch later refined his theoretical work in the *Image of the City* with regard to the actual planning of the site (Lynch 1971) and to a more encompassing urban process in Lynch (1981). Lynch's five elements of good urban form – paths, edges, districts, nodes and landmarks – are known to all architects as the key method to bring about a legible built environment. In turn, methods of classifying each have been studied, and typologies have been suggested. For example, a typological method for districts or tourist precincts is given in Hayllar *et al.* (2008: 41, 54), as follows:

- recreation or tourism business districts
- tourist shopping villages
- historic or heritage quarters
- ethnic precincts or quarters
- cultural precincts or quarters
- entertainment precincts
- red-light districts or bohemian quarters
- waterfront precincts
- festival marketplaces.

An exemplary methodology for urban precinct development is also given in Ritchie (2008), which shows the extent to which the concept of urban image is embedded within the development process (Ritchie 2008: 168; Figure 8.9). In addition, he also suggests a functional typology of precincts in terms of use and character:

- meeting places
- places of orientation
- comfort zones
- places of respite or refuge
- play spaces
- encounter zones
- zones of intimacy
- zones of authenticity
- zones of distinctiveness and contrast.

This typological approach to method has its origins in the work of Cullen and Lynch half a century ago. Cullen and Lynch's seminal contribution to contextualist methodology was also given further legitimation in Peter Smith's groundbreaking texts, *The Dynamics of Urbanism* (1974) and *The Syntax of Cities* (1976), two texts on the methodology of aesthetic appreciation in urban design that have yet to be bettered. Smith added an entirely new dimension to contextualist thought by applying the principles of environmental psychology to the townscape tradition. The examples used in *The Dynamics of Urbanism* are drawn almost exclusively from the traditions noted by Cullen, where he dissects the urban schema on the basis of forms of learning, subliminal perception, symbols and archetypes, in order to establish value systems and an agenda for design methods (Smith 1976: 225–47). Curiously, what Smith basically does is apply the scientific method to Cullen's ideas, a process that Cullen himself had rejected as invalid. However, taken together, Gordon Cullen's *Townscape* and Kevin Lynch's *Image of the City* formed a powerful critique and set of strategies to guide urban designers until the present time. The latter work is mentioned by Norberg-Schulz as emblematic of the urban design process, despite the fact that at least one critic saw Norberg-Schulz's own contribution as a 'classic failure', owing to its dependence on structural rules. From about

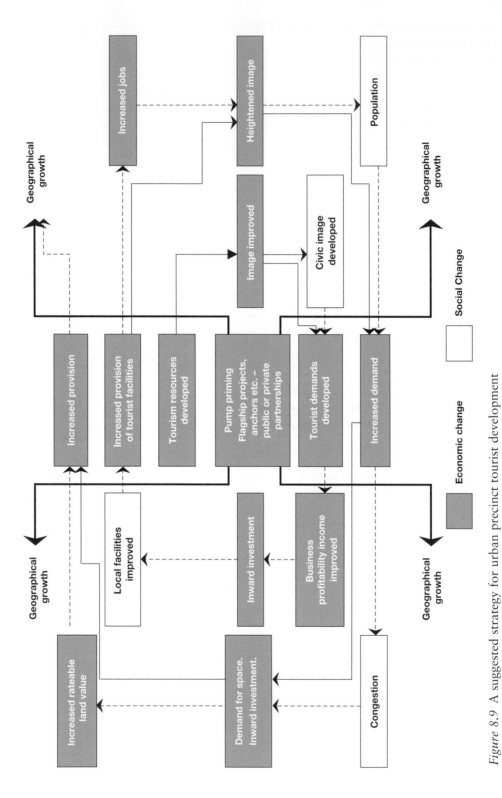

Figure 8.9 A suggested strategy for urban precinct tourist development

Source: Redrawn by G.A.M. Suartika from B. Hayllar, T. Griffin and D. Edwards (eds), *City Spaces, Tourist Places: Urban Tourism Precincts*. Oxford: Butterworth-Heinemann, 2008, p. 168, Fig. 8.2

1980, neo-traditionalism in Britain and New Urbanist design methods originating in the United States owe much to the cultural world-view emanating from the townscape tradition, recently brought up to date in Frers and Meier (2007), Watson and Bentley (2007), Hayllar *et al.* (2008) and Marshall (2009). Even greater levels of detail have been plumbed in *Urban Design: Ornament and Decoration* (Moughtin *et al.* 1995), where the embellishment of buildings and spaces is theorised and recounted in a series of layers, from skylines to the city floor. Here, the basic method used is to outline the physical variables of decoration, which are given as unity, proportion, scale, harmony, balance and symmetry, rhythm and contrast, principles that apply across the range of urban spaces and places.

The rationalist method and aesthetic production

The rationalist school of thought in urban design is welded to the concept of structuralist-functionalism, a philosophy that was to dominate, not only the social sciences throughout much of the twentieth century, but also the environmental disciplines. In politics, it manifested itself as National Socialism, a political movement not only limited to the right-wing working class of the Weimar Republic. In anthropology, it was expressed in Levi Strauss's method of structural anthropology, which demonstrated the universality of mythic structures in human societies, and in the structural linguistics of Jean Piaget. In contrast to the contextualist appeal to the heart, rationalism as method makes its appeal in the first instance to the head, to logic, deductive thinking, calculation and science. The clash between rationalism and contextualism in urban design, personified as a conflict between Camillo Sitte (an architect) and Otto Wagner (an engineer), began at the *fin de siècle*, around 1900, and has continued over the last 100 years (FOC: 55–6, 184–6). Over much of this time, the relationship between architectural design and urban design was so embedded that little distinction was drawn between them, and indeed this remains true in many circles today. Even town planning (as it was then called) was largely the domain of architects, and it was not until the mid 1960s that a surge of social scientists and geographers demonstrated that much planning and urban design might have superior stewardship somewhere else.

   Culture envelops aesthetic production, and, as in most ideological processes, the environmental disciplines contribute without necessarily understanding the role they are playing in the overall scheme of things. Ideologies constitute lived systems of values that seldom embed themselves in our conscious minds. For example, we all obey the law, without having much comprehension of its practices and black-letter regulation. The same is true of aesthetic production. Rationalism, as part of this event, is no different. Although the rationalists produced many manifestos throughout the twentieth century (see Chapter 9), individual architects did not necessarily conform to any specific 'rationalist code of practice', despite the fact that the concept pervaded their ethos. So, what did the practice of rationalism entail as a method of approach to aesthetics? Which heterologies were deployed, consciously or otherwise, in the creation of aesthetics in architectural and urban design? The interdependence of rationalism and scientific enquiry has a history that goes back millennia and was most clearly exemplified by the ancient Greeks. Rationalist architecture has evolved over the subsequent 2,500 years, copying its original details and principles in numerous ways, and arguably reaching its zenith during the Renaissance period, centuries before modernism. Systems of mathematics and proportion structured the design of buildings, along with principles derived from optics, perspective and other devices (Figure 8.10). The scientific principles of observation, experimentation, deduction and the formation of hypotheses across the field helped to impact rationalism as a design method. In architecture, Gottfried Semper had allocated functionalism as a fundamental premise of architecture as early as the middle of the nineteenth century:

> Semper clearly attempted to make the process of design analogous to the resolution of algebraic equations. The 'variables' represented the manifold aspects of reality that architecture had to take into account: The solution was simply a 'function' of these variables. This reductionist strategy has since become the fundamental framework of architectural theory.
> (Perez-Gomez 2000: 469)

For rationalist methodology, therefore, function was the vector directly connecting method to form, and the aesthetic projection of beauty depended on how well this process was accomplished.

Although a rationalist ideology pervaded the twentieth century, it accelerated as a design strategy in the 1960s. Until that time, there existed what we might call *intuitive* rationalism, that is, rational thinking without any generalised research that would integrate architectural theory on the basis of scientific investigation. All that was required as a methodology was a regression to a few happy homilies, best exemplified at the *fin de siècle* in the great Louis Sullivan's famous dictum 'that form ever follows function'. Somewhat later, the most influential design school of all time, namely the Bauhaus, adopted the principles of *form follows function* and *ornament is a crime* as its basic mandates. On this basis, some of the most ghastly urban design projects ever to grace the face of the earth were proposed by architects such as Le Corbusier, Ludwig Hilberseimer, Mies van der Rohe and others. Here, new levels of abstraction and standardisation were plumbed in the pursuit of a rational architecture. Intuitive rationalism *qua* method also produced massively inefficient architecture in terms of today's sustainable building practices. Intuitive rationalism advanced as a glacial disaster zone over the next half a century, until pseudo science was finally revoked as legitimising design.

While Charles Jencks has fixed the beginning of postmodernism as 15 July 1972, on the basis of the dynamiting of the modernist Pruitt-Igoe housing

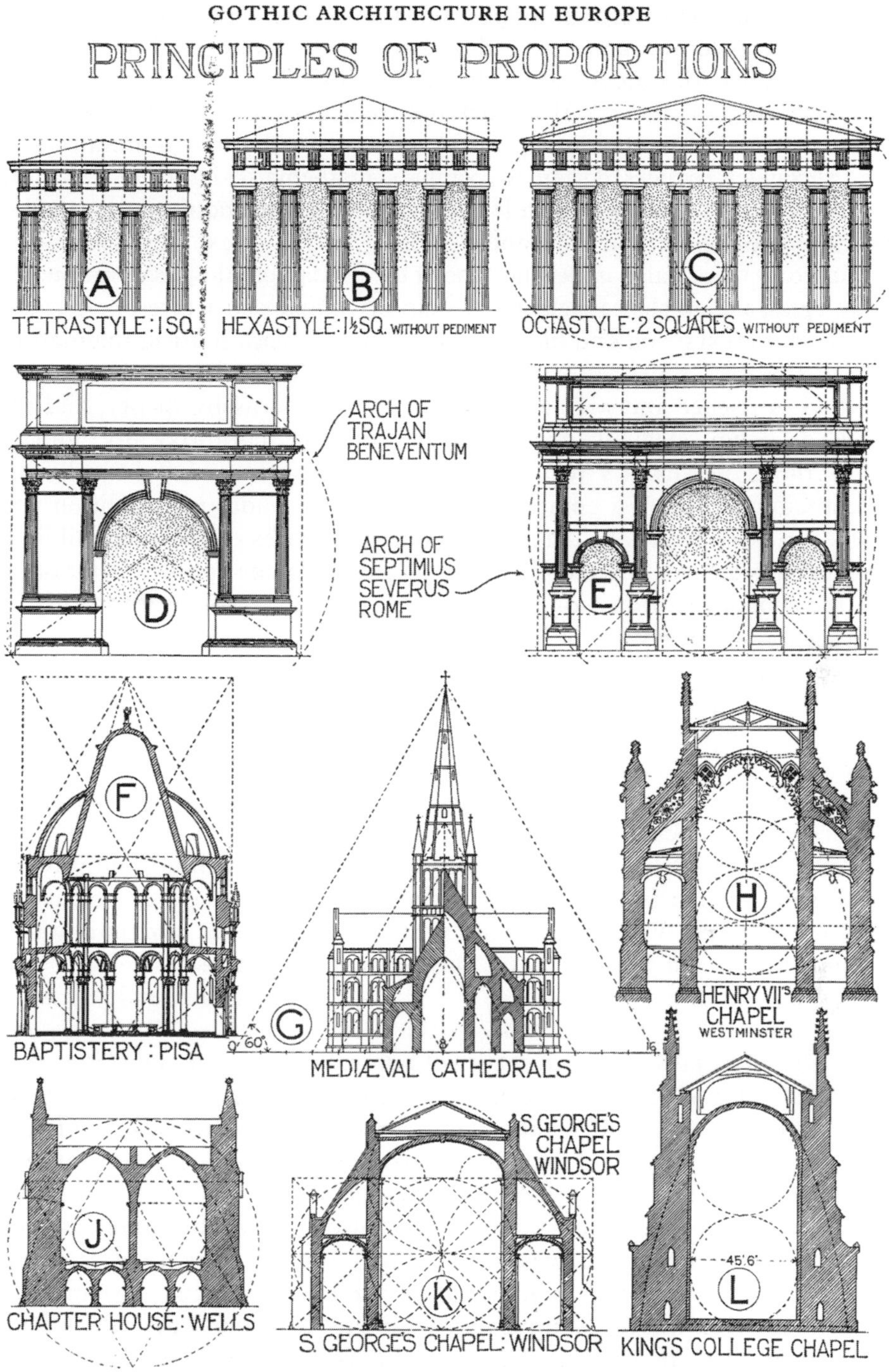
GOTHIC ARCHITECTURE IN EUROPE
PRINCIPLES OF PROPORTIONS
A
TETRASTYLE: 1 SQ.
B
HEXASTYLE: 1½ SQ. WITHOUT PEDIMENT
C
OCTASTYLE: 2 SQUARES. WITHOUT PEDIMENT
ARCH OF TRAJAN BENEVENTUM
D
ARCH OF SEPTIMIUS SEVERUS ROME
E
F
BAPTISTERY : PISA
G
60°
MEDIÆVAL CATHEDRALS
H
HENRY VII'S CHAPEL WESTMINSTER
J
CHAPTER HOUSE: WELLS
S. GEORGE'S CHAPEL WINDSOR
K
S. GEORGE'S CHAPEL: WINDSOR
45'6"
L
KING'S COLLEGE CHAPEL

Figure 8.10 Proportional systems used in historic forms of architectural design: classical Greek and Gothic periods

Source: Sir B. Fletcher, *A History of Architecture on the Comparative Method*. The Royal Institute of British Architects and the University of London: The Athlone Press, 1961, p. 377

project in St Louis, it is also tempting to denote as the beginning of a *logical* rationalism a classic in architectural thought, namely *Notes on a Synthesis of Form*, Christopher Alexander's groundbreaking work that came as a revelation to architects in 1964. Indeed Alexander's introduction is explicitly titled 'The need for rationality'. In this book, one that became a legend in architectural circles, Alexander reduces design to complex mathematical formulae. In the appendix, the social structure of an Indian village is expressed through calculus as his chosen design method (Alexander 1964: 136–91). Alexander's persistent use of hierarchy theory also underlines one of the fundamental rules of rationalist methodologies, namely the capacity to decompose complex structures, both social and physical, into systems and hierarchies of various types (lattice, semi-lattice etc.). In this process, the intuitive approach of the contextualist is given over to the method of science and mathematics, system and hierarchy theory, and the synthesis of design elements from logical processes. Paradoxically, and at the same time, Alexander's text constitutes a eulogy for what he calls the 'unselfconscious process', a combination of inherited traditions, intuition and experience. By this, he means the time-honoured practices of creating buildings and spaces (this did not include modernism). So, while he supports intuition in design, the support is offered on the basis of logic, not emotion, thus bridging the gap separating intuitive and scientific rationalism:

> The use of logical structures to represent design problems has an important consequence. It brings with it the loss of innocence. A logical picture is easier to criticise than a vague picture since the assumptions it is based upon are brought out into the open. Its increased precision gives us the chance to sharpen our conception of what the design process involves. But once what we do intuitively can be described and compared with non-intuitive ways of doing the same things, we cannot go on accepting the intuitive method innocently. Whether we decide to stand for or against pure intuition as a method, we must do so for reasons that can be discussed.
>
> (Alexander 1964: 8)

Whether Alexander falls into the category of rationalist or contextualist is a moot point, possibly not worth debating in the context of forty years of professional output. However, it is clear from the statement above that, in promoting intuition and the timeless way of building, Alexander remains committed to a rational method that allows logic to prevail over intuition.

Another iconic text from the same period, also adopted by architects and reflected in their design ideologies, was Herbert Simon's *The Sciences of the Artificial* (1969), where Simon laid out the rules of artificial systems (i.e. architecture) in a clear and unambiguous manner. He claimed that all systems obeyed universal laws of whatever origin – social, political economic, mechanical etc. Each possessed five irreducible properties – structure, environment, resources, objectives and behaviour. From that point onwards, the idea of *design methods* became fashionable, and the literature was swamped by the jargon of science –

input–output, black boxes, system theory, hierarchic structures, rule systems, synectics, data logging, problem structure etc. – all became part of the prevailing vocabulary in architecture and urban design. As Peter Smith has remarked:

> Urban design is increasingly becoming the province of rational sciences. Because in the past, architects have tended to be regarded as unscientific, economists, geographers, surveyors etc, are now entering the lists in order to redress the balance. The life force of the town and city is being cleverly analysed so that its essence may be extracted, encapsulated in order to distribute it to all urban designers. The sphere of planning is being monopolised by scientific people who honestly believe good design can emerge from atomistic analysis of the many factors which compose the urban environment.
>
> (Smith 1974: 227)

Nonetheless, the blame for an accelerating rationalism could not be placed on the 'other'. The above quotation ignores the fact that the rational–functional approach to architecture, planning and urban design had been swallowed wholeheartedly by much of the architectural profession, and that many architects, e.g. Christopher Alexander, Bill Hillier, Christopher Jones and others, were leading the field in the pursuit of logical and rational approaches to design aesthetics. Like Alexander, Christopher Jones's book, *Design Methods*, was the first solid text to pursue rationality in design (1970), followed by a revised version twenty-two years later in 1992 (see also Cross 1984, Oxman 1987, Albin 2003, Laurel 2003). The extent to which rationalism in design has evolved is evident in the journal *Design Methods*, which had its inception in 1976 and is still in circulation. On the other hand, we could also argue that '*plus c'est la même chose*', exemplified in the following two quotations separated by nearly thirty years:

> The city has almost no characteristic geometry. It is not like an atom, an orange, or a table, or an animal. It is more like the pattern of pieces on a chess board, half way through a game of chess.
>
> (Alexander and Poyner 1967: 6)

> A city is like a game of chess, in that the location of each piece is the product of a rational decision, but the overall effect may look chaotic, and is unpredictable in advance. A city plan – like the plan of a chess game in progress – is a snapshot of a continuously changing process.
>
> (Marshall 2009: 186)

While the use of analogy as a design method remains undiminished, neither statement comes to any real conclusion, and the following probably has more generic significance to urban design, reinforcing the relationship between rationality and identity in the organisation of meaning, and therefore the aesthetic content of urban form:

Thus one can say that the units of the game of chess have no material identity; there are no physical properties necessary to a king etc. Identity is wholly a function of differences within a system.

(Culler 1976: 28)

The idea of language and syntax begun by Peter Smith (1976) was taken to new levels in the work of Hillier and Leaman (1976) and Hillier and Hanson (1984) and has been restated in S. Marshall (2009). The idea that the aesthetics of the urban order emerge from mathematics is still deeply rooted in the psyche of most architects and urban designers, and Alexander's concept that the city is not a tree continues to be abused in the planning lexicon. Although design methods in architecture have been addressed for nearly half a century, the question of language, or more accurately languages, still remains. A seldom-addressed question is whether not the vocabularies of architecture and town planning are adequate to convey urban design concepts and ideas, a problem that has only been addressed by a few designers and one that will be expanded upon below.

Regulation and design control

There can be no more thorny issue in the aesthetic governance of the built environment than the concept of design guidelines as the accepted method of controlling form, function and taste (Scheer and Preiser 1994, Parfect and Power 1997). It is a region of urban administration totally riddled with confusion, where power, ideologies, culture and professional endeavour all collide. Superficially, all that is required is a mechanism to guarantee the city beautiful. Yet so many vested interests exist that it is questionable whether design guidelines have any capacity whatsoever to control aesthetics or to set standards of design that are democratic and free of vested interests. Beyond the limitations of method, larger questions arise, such as whose city is it anyway? What is to be aestheticised? Whose version of aesthetics should be sanctioned? What should be the objects of aesthetic consideration? Whose design interests or standards should be adopted? What methods are most appropriate under which circumstances?

The aesthetic control of cities is not a new idea and has been evolving for centuries. Louis XIV adopted a code of practice for the redevelopment of Paris; New York had to adopt a basic set of rules for skyscrapers in 1916; and the first New York Zoning Ordinance was set in place in 1961. In Britain, however, the first 'Design Guide' as such was published by Essex County Council in 1973 and remains the seminal document on the subject. A year later, a groundbreaking work emerged that suggested a new method of approach to design guidelines, namely *Urban Design as Public Policy* (Barnett 1974). Up to date, the American Planning Association recently published a 700-page tome called *Planning and Urban Design Standards*, which leaves little to the imagination as to how aesthetics should be governed (Sendich 2006). Despite this seeming control, such an immense variety of design guidelines exists for cities across the developed world that there is little congruence as to method, and the aesthetic dimension is impossible to separate from functionality, speculation, cost-effectiveness and other criteria. Guidelines exist at different urban scales (national, regional, local, project-based); they also reflect a varying pallet of objectives (to promote public safety, enhancement of community, historical preservation, sustainability, amenity, neighbourhood character etc.). They use a diversity of statutory and non-statutory controls to achieve objectives (zoning, development control, design guides, design review panels, competitions, fine arts commissions etc.). Then there is the omnipresent 'public interest' to be considered. Despite such complexity, John Delafons makes the point that:

> In Britain, the index to Butterworth's 760 page *Planning Law Handbook* contains no references to 'design', 'aesthetic control', or external appearance. Nor does the index to the 728 pages of Professor Malcolm Grant's standard work *Urban Planning Law*. This is very odd because the British Town and Country Planning Acts have contained (at least since the Planning Act of 1932) explicit provisions enabling the local planning authority to control the height, design, and external appearance of buildings.
>
> (Delafons 1994: 13)

One reason for the absence of aesthetic criteria is the fact that, in the UK, design guidelines are not codified into law. They are non-statutory, and local authorities have a wide range of discretion as to how they are interpreted and applied. Delafons goes on to comment that traditional zoning powers, which are used to implement aesthetic controls for a variety of purposes, all end up reflecting one major consideration – the preservation of property values. He notes that, in the United States, aesthetic controls are exercised through a variety of methods and suggests a possible typology as follows:

- the regulatory mode
- the stylistic imperative
- the proprietorial injunction
- the authoritative intervention
- the competitive alternative
- the design guidelines.

Briefly stated, the regulatory mode refers to traditional zoning ordinances, which apparently serve an aesthetic function but do not incorporate design objectives. The stylistic imperative refers to the necessary use of a specific form of vernacular or architectural style. The proprietorial injunction represents a form of self-imposed control by developers in order to further their own specific interests. The authoritative imperative is used by local authorities to confer decision-making powers on an expert committee or commission on artistic matters. The competitive alternative uses the well-worn device of the architectural competition in order to select the best of available design options for a given project, as is the case, for example, with all public buildings in France. Design guidelines supplement the mode of regulation by adding a detailed code, which is frequently prescriptive (elaboration of style and detail), rather than a more enlightened, qualitative approach that encourages the enhancement of distinctive character, identity and experience (Delafons 1994: 14–17).

From all of the above, it may be argued that urban planning retains significantly greater control over the aesthetics of the built environment than architects, a point that the latter bemoan on a daily basis. The crucial question here is, 'who does the planning system represent and under what circumstances?'. Setting aside the nature of planning as a state enterprise (discussed in FOC3: 75–6), it is clear that the method of aesthetic regulation, in the form of development control, design control and design guidelines, has a political substructure based on significant economic influence and interests. In many cases, a superstructure of aesthetic controls masks a deeply embedded economic rationalism, a process whereby state neocorporatism, in collusion with the private sector in 'public–private partnerships', allows developers basically to write their own rules. As David Harvey remarks:

> Public–private partnerships are favoured in which the public sector bears all of the risk and the corporate sector reaps all of the profit. Business interests get to write legislation and to determine public policies in such a way as to advantage themselves.
>
> (Harvey 2007: 29)

The same sentiment is echoed more directly in relation to aesthetic control, as follows:

> Aesthetic decision making is ultimately not founded upon objective or mutual standards of judgment, nor in consensus, but simply reverts back to those in control, the same forces that control much of the public realm; the political, capitalist, and cultural elite. Those groups outside the dominant power matrices – the disenfranchised and marginal – are characteristically excluded from the important decision making processes. Furthermore, the trend towards homogeneity, toward the violent elimination of difference through control, of regionalism and nationalism, are all trends towards domination.
>
> (Pouler 1994: 185)

In order to promote the project-based planning favoured by developers, there is a tendency for aesthetic regulation to devolve into functional and material considerations, whose primary objective is to accellerate the accumulation of capital from land development. In addition, the methodological progression towards non-uniform design regulations, reflecting what Lang calls 'all of a piece' urban design, sits well with this overall philosophy (Lang 2005). The stress on design guides by the New Urbanism is a manifestation of this position, where design codes are assembled on a project-by-project basis, by the architect, for the developer. Consequently, most design guidelines tend to focus on density, plot ratio, building envelope, fenestration, colour, use of materials, sign control, parking provision and restrictions, building setbacks, sight lines, height restrictions, resource transfer etc. (Barnett 1974). Even greater flexibility is added by the fact that design guidelines are usually advisory rather than statutory, leaving significant room for negotiation and 'to promote the watchword of the neo-liberal state, "flexibility" . . . it trumpets the virtues of competition while actually opening the market to centralised capital and monopoly power' (Harvey 2007: 25). This process is one that clearly mitigates against any qualitatively biased outcomes (e.g. contextualist) and, to a large degree, any significant aesthetic impact whatsoever.

Problematically, and despite the clear need for expediency in the development process, the lack of resistance to the needs of capital is manifested in the myth of community. It is in the interests of this nebulous 'community' that design controls are implemented. Although traditional concepts of community based on the machinations of industrial capital are now obsolete, perpetuating the myth of community is an extremely useful device in the context of design guidelines – it allows them to be written for an imaginary form of social organisation, an avatar for the interests of development capital. In *Disciplinary Society and the Myth of Aesthetic Justice* (1994), Patrick Pouler points to the erosion and decay of the extended family, as well as notions of neighbourhood and community:

> The myth of community differs from an authentic community in the way in which exhausted ideals are artificially resurrected in order to elicit unity from the chaos of a society desperate for security and stability. Here the invocation of myth supersedes concrete and productive social activity: the image attempts to overcome the reality. In this sense, architecture is the perfect medium by which to perpetuate the dominant power structures.
>
> (Pouler 1994: 177)

Pouler goes on to enunciate the tendency for design guidelines to retreat into 'a new pathos of preservation', whereby 'existing character, neighbourhoods (a morphological delusion) and political organisation are reinforced and the status quo is perpetuated' (Pouler 1994: 177). In addition, the same existing forms of speculation, based on short-term profits, rampage across the landscape. Hence, design and aesthetic controls formally ascribe to the same objectives, where only a limited number of outcomes are possible. This can easily result in an aesthetic monotony of places, using the same visual language and structure and fetishising history, as in many New Urbanist projects.

It is therefore plausible to argue that as methodology, design guidelines generate little, if any, democratic control over development, and instead fulfil many other purposes on the basis of fictitious concepts of community interest and ideals. At best, they look to the past and, in the process, seek to conserve property values, using the myth of community in housing to preserve self-interest and autonomy of control over the design process.

Conclusion

Of all urban design heterologies, the concept of aesthetics predominates in the mind of the designer. The creation of the city beautiful is the designer's mandate, in opposition to the developer's focus on capital. Significant economic interests always rule. Although there is an ongoing debate among designers over how to 'control' aesthetics, the single-minded, inexorable path to profit remains. In addition to a confused rhetoric, the mainstream urban designer's position is also weakened by learning based on intuition and uninformed by substantial theory. The academy seldom includes courses on urban aesthetics into urban design programmes, and most learning is based on osmosis or mimesis, with a liberal dose of Kevin Lynch, Gordon Cullen and Peter Smith as models. Original definitions of the word *aesthetics* suggest that the process has as much to do with morality and ethics as it does with arbitrary concepts of beauty, something to be taken seriously in class-divided society (FOC8: 173). Understandably, confusion exists as to how control should be exercised over aesthetic judgement in urban design – Whose taste? Whose morality? Whose gender? Whose right? The chosen method, for decades, has relied on the idea of design guidelines, a process whereby desirable physical attributes are meant to reflect an aesthetic-ally improved judgement on the basis of fictitious concepts of community. Also meaningful is that design guidelines are seldom statutory documents, leaving room for 'flexibility' and 'negotiation', euphemisms for how best to accommodate private-sector requirements. Invariably, this process tends towards homogeneity and the exclusion of difference, increased social control by the private sector, and commodity aesthetics. Although the designer will almost always remain in the service of capital in one form or another, an improvement in the designer's position might occur through a transition from the mainstream to *heterologies* of design, to sources that most designers would not recognise as influential – to Freud, Jung, Saussure, Marx, Wittgenstein and others discussed above.

9 Typologies

If the space of flows is truly the dominant spatial form of the network society, architecture and [urban] design are likely to be redefined in their form, function, process and value in the coming years.

(Manuel Castells)

Introduction: form and process

In the last two volumes of this series, the overall purpose of exploring typologies was to cement the relationship between economic and social processes and urban forms. They stressed that such forms are produced and reproduced in accordance with social development, rather than pursuing the cul-de-sac offered in mainstream concepts such as *the elements of townscape*, which has traditionally dominated the palette of urban designers and their understanding of social space (Taylor 1999). The latter approach suggests that urban forms and spaces are independent factors in urbanisation, and as such are manufactured by a combination of historical accident and design imagination. On this basis, new spaces tend to be retrofitted to historical templates and typologies, governed only by the design awareness of firms and individuals. Rob Krier has gone so far as to suggest that all of the forms of space we can consider have already been invented (Krier 1979), a fraternal trend (Krier 1985). By this logic, another 'end of history' has been reached, that of architectural and urban space. This ideology not only limits the designer's capacity to find some congruence with urban development as a whole, it is also a deeply stultifying process that has little capacity to explain how such elements (both objects and spaces) arose in the first place, or indeed, how new elements of townscape surface from a global morass of politicised urban space and 'neo-con' politics. The 'townscape tradition' as practised was also ethnocentric, introverted, historicist and class ridden, given that professions are solidly middle class in composition and conservative in outlook. In addition, the entire aesthetic has concentrated on restating the past, rather than explaining the present or anticipating the future (Isaacs 2000).

Paradoxically, none of this denies that such elements of form do exist – streets, squares, arcades, crescents, monuments and fountains etc. – components that are axiomatic and have formed the building blocks of the designer's palette for centuries. Nor does it deny that much of the early work done on the subject was enlightening and useful (see Chapter 8), as was the actual specificity of research on typologies such as streets (Rudofsky 1969, Celik *et al.* 1994, Hebbert 2005), arcades (Geist 1985), squares (Krier 1979, Webb 1990, Kostoff 1992) and patterns (Alexander 1977). However, from the position of spatial political economy, we are left with a one-dimensional explanation as to how urban forms arise, mutate, are transformed and morph into other dimensions. The mainstream interpretation of this entire scenario has stressed the elements of architectural content and composition, rather than tackling the more involved problem of social space and form, as for example in relation to architectural aesthetics as a form of economic currency (Clarke 1989), typological theory as it relates to the consumption of authenticity in architecture (Goode 1992), or indeed *Global Architecture and Its Political Masquerades* (Easterling 2005). Hence, the ability to generate a complex and wholistic appreciation of urban design has been driven by considerations of building form, with spaces peripheral to, or in support of, the *edifice*. In contrast, urban design, the real object of which is the public realm, is essentially concerned with *spaces* and informed by social theory (Lofland 1998). Although the overlap between them is clearly significant, and one cannot live without the other, mainstream architectural, planning and urban design perspectives have vectors that start and finish at altogether different points. Heterology in regard to urban design typologies seeks to answer the question, 'what are the specific urban processes from which the elements of townscape arise today, and which typologies of form are consequent upon these processes?'.

At the largest compass, global development is replete with attempts to generate an appropriate vocabulary as a method of describing its own mutations. Adopting a starting date of 1938, when Lewis Mumford coined the phrase *Megalopolis* in his book *The Culture of Cities*, a plethora of descriptors have since been offered to encapsulate the morphing of *Megalopolis* and its components into entirely new combinations of space and place. Later, Jean Gottmann wrote a book that adopted the concept of *Megalopolis* (1961), using it to describe the region from Boston to Washington (Boswash) on the eastern seaboard of the United States. About the same time, the Greek city planner Constantinos Doxiadis had expanded these descriptors in the concept of *Eperopolis* (continent city), used to define massive urbanisation in Europe that stretched across entire countries, from London to the Ruhr in Germany. By 1967, he had joined up his continent cities into a single giant entity, which he named *Ecumenopolis*, meaning the world city. Doxiadis did not use *Ecumenopolis* as it is commonly used today, to imply a city that has world-class status in accordance with a basket of desirable performance specifications. He used it to mean the urban form of the entire planet. Since then, there has been an avalanche of new terminology that tries to situate urbanisation at a global level, either in its components or as a total phenomenon. Hence, we now have mega-projects, mega-cities, mega-regions, edge cities, world cities, multinucleated urban regions, the informational city, postmetropolis, shifting cities, carceral cities and many others. As a result, the 'city' as a distinguishing unit in the context of global urbanisation is a seriously contested idea (Sudjic 1991, Swyngedouw 1996, Davis 2005, Taylor *et al.* 2007). In the meantime, Gottmann's original study has been revisited, noting massive inner suburban decline and a much more fully suburbanised agglomeration, increasing polarisation between central city and suburban cores and within suburban areas themselves, and the return of mass immigration, not witnessed in *Megalopolis* for over a century (Vicino *et al.* 2007: 363). Lewis Mumford coined the term *Megalopolis* to describe ancient Rome, and he drew the analogy between development 2,000 years ago and what he saw happening when *The City in History* was written:

> Every overgrown megalopolitan centre today, and every province outside that its life touches, exhibits the same symptoms of disorganisation, accompanied by no less pathological symptoms of violence and demoralisation. Those who close their eyes to these facts are repeating, with exquisite mimicry, the very words and acts, equally blind, of their Roman predecessors.
>
> (Mumford 1961: 239)

As we shall see later, Mumford's original prediction has largely materialised, with monumental poverty and demoralisation taking place in third-world cities around the globe. What all of this suggests is that typologies can only ever approximate development and will inevitably lag behind it. Although cities do not morph into new forms overnight, urban research is invariably historical – it deals with events that have already passed. In addition, the tools at the planner's disposal to control these phenomena appear woefully inadequate, both legally and conceptually. The traditional 'land-use planning' of prior decades cannot even begin to encompass development that characterises global capitalist enterprise. Vast swathes of the planet have no planning of any kind. Many countries have no planning systems, and those that do struggle to maintain some semblance of order and control in the face of urbanisation. Therefore, instead of attempting new descriptors for emergent forms of global development, a more productive method for understanding form is to examine the heterologies from which these forms emanate (FOC3: 72–8, FOC4: 79–89).

Globalisation and urban form

The literature on globalisation is now massive, reflecting its importance as the governing paradigm of the third millennium. Nonetheless, research into the actual geography of globalisation is relatively new, with much definitive work appearing in the last twenty years (King 1990, 2004, Sassen 1991, Castells 1998, Marcuse and Van Kempen 2000, Scott 2000, Minca 2001). Given the complexity of defining *globalisation*, it is probably safer to say that many globalisations exist – economic, spatial, cultural and technical – qualified by the significant and evolving dimensions of gender and sustainability (Yang 1999). The picture is rendered even more complex by the inherent tendency of capitalism to uneven geographic development. What is certain is that globalisation represents a new deepening in capitalist social relations and the forms of consciousness necessary to sustain them. As such, the fundamental dynamics of capitalism are simultaneously extended and entrenched – commodity production, social class, the exploitation of nature and the Third World, the growth of monopolies, a reserve army of labour (as well as reserve armies of non-labour in the Fourth World of the dispossessed, in China, Africa, India etc.), conflict between social classes, and among and between capitals – all heralding new levels of exploitation or advantage. Immanuel Wallerstein, who first proposed the idea of a world system, was of the opinion that globalisation represents the extension of forced dependencies inherent in historic forms of imperialism and colonisation (Wallerstein 1974, 1980, 1988, King 1990). Hence, the old forms of global oppression have not disappeared. Instead, they have evolved into more advanced forms of post-colonial and post-imperialist ideologies, structures, institutions and spaces, more recently addressed in Hardt and Negri (2000) and Harvey (2003). The mechanisms used to implement the ideology of neocorporatism (both state and private-sector) include evolving organisational forms such as the transnational corporation, a new international division of labour and the public sphere, and the absolute reliance on electronic information. At the same time, traditional concepts of social class need to be re-examined (Embong 2000). However, the instantaneous movement of capital via the Internet also underlines the fundamental instability of the capitalist world economy, as the financial crisis of 2008 amply demonstrated, along with the enduring principle that wealth is socially produced but privately expropriated. At the time of writing, the largest global corporation, General Motors, has just declared bankruptcy, owing US$88 billion. Sixty per cent of the debt was purchased by the state, i.e. the taxpayer footed the bill for corporate incompetence. Never before has this private appropriation been more in evidence, to the extent that postmodern urbanism may be described as a *privatised* urbanism, where control over entire swathes of social reproduction are being transferred to private-sector interests – health, education, recreation, housing and, most importantly, the public realm.

Operating in a symbolic space largely outside the management of individual nations, transnational corporations have relative freedom to operate largely as they wish. This situation is facilitated by the monopolistic authority of the transnational corporation and its persuasive power over the entire range of state bureaucracy. Of the world's top economic entities in the year 2000, there were more corporations than states represented. There can be no more chilling reminder of the erosion of the state as the guardian of civil society, its rights and obligations. No doubt the recent global depression has modified these relationships somewhat. Nevertheless, while nation-states still possess significant autonomy, this independence is being rapidly eroded by the ideology of neocorporatism, which aligns public and private interests, based on state fiscal crises and the rise of public–private cooperation across all forms of development:

> Many of the concepts dear to postmodernists and postcolonialists find a perfect correspondence in the current ideology of corporate capital and the world market ... As the world market today is realised ever more completely, it tends to deconstruct the boundaries of the nation-state. In a previous period, nation-states were the primary actors in the modern imperialist organisation of global production and exchange, but to the world market they appear increasingly as mere obstacles.
>
> (Hardt and Negri 2000: 150)

Corporations no longer need to wait passively for the state to generate rule systems within which business and civil society can coexist as distinctly separate entities, as they are now actively involved in creating the environment within which they can function most effectively. Consequently, there is also a transfer of political authority from the state to the private sector, a situation that allows the private sector to penetrate more deeply into the privatisation of public assets, spaces and government. While this influence penetrates many aspects of daily life at the local level, it also has global consequences for those in the Third and Fourth Worlds, where, in many cases, new forms of empire are more ravaging than the old. While the First World wallows in surplus production, its excesses are supported by a new and different empire, where individual imperialist nations no longer seek to carve up the world into separate ownerships for the plunder of raw materials and labour and as captive markets for commodities. This is accomplished by entirely different means, and with arguably worse effects. The spatial effects of these global processes on settlement and urban form are profound.

As social processes do not occur 'on the head of a pin', it is axiomatic that the global political economy is simultaneously economic and spatial. The main driver of this approach is the world capitalist system, now in divergent forms in the former socialist states of China and the Soviet Union (Sklair 2002, King 2004). Globalisation has had an immense effect, as a new political economy reorganises space to entirely different needs and agendas. In this process, the effects of electronic communication have been paramount, as a new dimension of human experience came into being. Manuel Castells, in his visionary *The Rise of the Network Society*, characterised globalisation as a transition from 'the space of places' into what he called 'the space of flows' (Castells 1996: 378). Because of this new order, prior structures of human association exchange face-to-face relationships for electronic messages and images – e-mail, skype, Facebook, Twitter, blogs etc. all replace human relations with electronic impulses. Although this has multitudinous spatial effects, four are paramount.

First, local and regional ties to the nation are being rapidly eroded, as the global economy establishes a higher order of control, albeit in a legal and political vacuum, and 'a new regionalism' is undermining the traditional authority and responsibilities of the nation-state. The new network of communication ignores traditional concepts of scale and hierarchy, as communication can take place 'from the global to the local'. Second, a new spatial hierarchy is formed, where global or world cities concentrate economic and social prosperity by monopolising the command and control functions of the world economy (Davis 2005). At the same time, a massive dispersal of other functions also occurs, particularly those that introduce electronic communication to replace face-to-face contacts. The implications are for high-density, multinodal centres in global or world cities, surrounded by a massively lower, uniform grid of low-density development. In between, many cities will decay in what Castells calls 'the black hole of marginality' (Castells 1996: 379, Gospodini 2002). Third, because of continuing centripetal forces, social capital is similarly concentrated in what Florida has called *the creative class*, who are drawn to urban centres by the high order of facilities and quality of life they provide (Florida 2003, 2005, McCarthy 2006). Hence, a multinodal urbanisation replaces the traditional forms associated with material production based on heavy industry with one based on informational capital. Fourth, because traditional concepts of space–time shift owing to the instantaneous nature of electronic communication, a key implication for environmental designers is the tendency of the space of flows to deterritorialise existing human relationships and, consequently, the forms of space that have traditionally supported them.

In a passage headed 'The architecture of the end of history', Castells states:

> If the space of flows is truly the dominant spatial form of the network society, architecture and design are likely to be redefined in their form, function, process and value in the coming years . . . My hypothesis is that the coming of the space of flows is blurring the meaningful relationship between architecture and society. Because spatial manifestations of the dominant interests take place around the world, and across cultures, the uprooting of experience, history and specific culture as the background of meaning is leading to generalisation of ahistorical, acultural architecture . . . this is why, paradoxically, [it is] the architecture that seems most charged with meaning.
>
> (Castells 1996: 418)

Castells goes on to imply that the transition into the space of flows, while offering massive improvements in communication and the generation of wealth, also results in a massive loss of identity (Castells 1997). He stresses that, more than ever, society needs to evolve a new architecture of space and form that exposes the new reality 'without faking beauty from a transhistorical repertoire' (Castells 1996: 420). Although this task is clearly immense, he offers several prototypes that encapsulate this evolution: Ricardo Bofill's Barcelona airport;

Rafael Moneo's new Madrid AVE station; Rem Koolhaas's Lille Grand Palais Convention Centre; and Steven Holl's offices on West 57th Street in New York for D.E. Stuart and Company (Figures 9.1 and 9.2). Castells is of the opinion that the expression of the new architecture should lie in its neutrality, where its forms do not pretend to say anything:

> And by not saying anything they confront the experience with the solitude of the space of flows. The message is the silence … either the new architecture builds the palaces of the new masters, thus exposing their deformity hidden behind the abstraction of the space of flow; or it roots itself into places, thus into culture and into people. In both cases, under different forms, architecture and design may be digging the trenches of resistance for the preservation of meaning in the generation of knowledge. Or, what is the same, for the reconciliation of culture and technology.
>
> (Castells 1996: 420–3)

Although the new architecture of resistance may point to a faceless neocorporate authority, others are not so sure that the actual spaces that result

Figure 9.1 Rem Koolhaas: Lille Grand Palais Convention Centre
Source: Hans Werleman (Hectic Pictures)/OMA

Figure 9.2 Steven Holl: offices on West 57th Street, New York
Source: © Paul Warchol

have the same potency. Using the example of branded chain hotels, Yakhlef promotes the idea that the detachment of global brands from cultural settings results in generic spaces that are place-constrained and have no referents except the commodity:

> Generic spaces are deterritorialized, disembedded, and lifted out from their context. Once cut loose from the joints of time and space, they take on features that are associated with the logic of flows (such as money, airports, hotels, information, etc.), which turns them into a direction rather than a reference that anchors them into a specific organizational culture or a specific nation . . . Brands as generic spaces do not refer to any particular place (Casey, 1997) or context. For Lash (2002), generic spaces can be seen as prototypes of natural, physical spaces that are contextless and identity-less.
>
> (Yakhlef 2004: 239)

Collectively, these issues hold profound significance for urban designers who wish to understand the forces that affect their art. The physical forms and spaces that result from this complexity, in one form or another, directly reflect the demands of the neocorporatist agenda in regard to space. Location, function, dimensions and appearance are not arbitrary. Their most important characteristics and features are frequently decided before designers can even reach for their latest computer-aided design software. At the epicentre of these changes exists the concept of the commodity. In the past, commodity production was centred on fulfilling basic human needs through the provision of use values, thus placing constraints on socially necessary production. In developed countries, however, basic needs have now been met. Today, need has been retranslated into the limitless aspirations of desire, and consumption has become an activity undertaken for its own sake. In transcending its material function, commodification has also been extended from production into *consciousness*. What we are and what we desire fuse together. Hence, individual consciousness merges into that of the commodity. In the process, three things happen. First, the ideological potential of capital is vastly increased, as the symbolic universe of commodity production is its sole constituency. Not only this, but capital also controls the rationality and methods through which desire comes about, from the design and manufacturing process to control over the mass media. Second, and in consequence, individual autonomy shrinks, as the material need to seek food, shelter and community outside is replaced inside by the psychological associations of a limitless world of desire. Third, none of this can take place (as yet) without a vast array of spaces and places designed specifically to host commodity transfer. Although history has accrued a huge physical plant of towns and cities, the transformation of their original functions, ownership and management, as well as the generation and design of new urban spaces, is transforming the face of cities worldwide. As a result, 'the dialectic of design movements is intimately connected to the development of capitalist markets' (Jenkins 2006: 195).

The mega-project and the spectacle

It is important to distinguish between 'traditional' mega-projects and those emerging from the spectacular production of postmodernity. In order to do this, we have to look at the forces that preceded the spectacle as form-giving to urban design and contemporary life as a whole. With the growth of the (post-)industrial state, a chasm began to appear over time between its income and the social costs it was required to finance. As revenues dwindled, corporate monopoly power resisted expenditures on the social good, as the ideology of the market system and its so-called 'trickle down effect' invariably demanded business expansion, not social welfare as the panacea. The gradually increasing fiscal crises of states in the Western hemisphere, particularly from the mid 1970s onwards, was exacerbated by the enduringly parasitic function of private capital (O'Connor 1971).

As its economic burden increased, the fiscal authority of the state continued to decline, offering private capital the opportunity to exert increasing influence on state politics through public–private sector partnerships. Under neo-liberalism, 'Public–private partnerships are favoured where the public sector bears all the risk and corporate sector reaps all the profit. Business interests get to write legislation and to determine public policies in such a way as to advantage themselves' (Harvey 2007: 26). The accumulated pool of capital is then used to bankroll project-based development using state finances, land, social capital and legitimation, all of which development capital is then in a position to manipulate with even greater sophistication than in previous eras. More importantly, its *political* authority has increased in line with its economic advantage, allowing significantly greater manipulation of government policy, legislation, public expenditures on social reproduction and other functions. This allowed a pernicious leverage over state planning practice, which traditionally had development plans extending up to twenty-five years into the future, with reviews every five years. Along with the control over the public realm, the lag in development between initiation and profit offered serious resistance to private capital, which demanded a more immediate return on investment. Over the last twenty years, the alignment of neocorporatist ideology in both the state and private sectors has encouraged short-to-medium-term, project-based planning practice, based on urban design rather than policy planning. At least part of this was a reaction to the negative consequences of physical planning over the years from 1960 to 1990, much of which was state driven owing to post-war reconstruction, redevelopment and the emergence of urban social movements that offered significant resistance against the oppression of modernist architecture and design by private capital and state alike (Orueta and Fainstein 2008).

This shift in the power and control of private-sector interests over the state was not merely material, a lascivious if neutral process of improving profits to shareholders and increased market share to successful corporations. Neocorporatism also represents collusion between state and capital, aligned in their common interest, a bargain that the state, as the representative of the people, had little choice but to accept. In the process, an improved method of commodifying and controlling the built environment in its totality – commodified architecture, a commodified public realm, commodified institutions and a commodified experience of urban life – was advanced. In the process, traditional concepts of social class were both trashed as forms of resistance and enhanced in their reality, popular culture was gradually absorbed by the ideology of neocorporatism, and social life enduringly falls under the hammer of commodity production. Significantly, capital is increasingly consolidated as a political force, that is, in its ideological command, and labour is even further marginalised and alienated.

Given the possible range of mega-projects, it is clear that the attempt to generate a significant typology is a difficult task, and a diversity of methods may apply, from sheer physical scale, to economic investment, forms of ownership and funding, activity mix and many other factors (Home 1989, Diaz and Fainstein 2009). To begin with, it would appear axiomatic that mega-projects are first and foremost planning projects. Sub-elements are basically urban design projects, and smaller projects are architectural in scale. This form of distinction has little analytical use and does not get us very far, as it then begs the question as to how we divide projects according to professional intervention, and whether size itself is of any significance at all. Other efforts have been made to classify mega-projects where form and location are seen to be significant:

- regeneration of waterfronts;
- recovery of old manufacturing and warehouse zones;
- construction of new transport infrastructures or extensions of existing ones;
- renovation of historic city districts, usually to meet the special consumer demands of middle- and upper-class sectors.

(Orueta and Fainstein 2008: 761)

Elsewhere, generic urban design projects have been classified in relation to the function of the urban designer or the urban design team, the nature of the design process or the overall function of the project:

- total urban design, where the urban designer is part of the development team that carries the scheme through from inception to completion;
- all-of-a-piece urban design, where the urban design team devises a master plan and sets the parameters within which a number of developers work on components of the overall project;
- piece-by-piece urban design, in which general policies and procedures are applied to a precinct of a city in order to steer development in specific directions;
- plug-in urban design, where the design goal is to create the infrastructure so that subsequent developments can 'plug in' to it, or, alternatively, a new element of infrastructure is plugged into the existing urban fabric to enhance a location's amenity level as a catalyst for development.

(Lang 2005: 28)

Naturally, this process of classification could range endlessly over all kinds of physical scale, typological feature and variant, and so it is important to distinguish here the sense in which the concept of the spectacle relates to the mega-project, and where big plans represent both the allure and folly of urban design practice (Kolson 2001, Moor and Rowland 2006). Mega-projects, of which the spectacle is part, have seen resurgence in recent years and across a wide range of economies, particularly in Europe and the United States (Swyngedouw *et al.* 2002, Flyvbjerg *et al.* 2003, Flyvbjerg 2005), but also in the so-called economies of the 'Pacific Rim' (Yeung and Li 1999, Olds 2001, R. Marshall 2003, Douglas *et al.* 2008) and in Australia (Stevens and Dovey 2004). These range from distinctly architectural projects such as Berlin's new Reichstag building (Figure 9.3), across all intermediate geographic scales, through to Toronto's 46-kilometre waterfront project (Lehrer and Laidley 2009), or the Thames Gateway, a project extending some 70 kilometres east from Canary Wharf in central London into Essex and Kent. Nesting within these vast projects are many smaller elements that are themselves enormous. For example in an immigrant area close to Canary Wharf, is included the athletes' village for the London 2012 Olympic Games, along with a 175,000 square metre regional shopping mall, 120,000 square metres of hotel and conference space, 13 hectares of open space and over 485,000 square metres of office space, offering the potential for thousands of permanent jobs (Fainstein 2009: 776). Fainstein goes on to note that only three types of construction generate big profits, namely luxury residences and hotels, large-footprint office towers and shopping malls. She comments on the similarity between European and American cities in this respect, where locations seek land outside core areas and have common product mixes and also lack the vibrancy and interest of the central city.

Although scale is a distinguishing feature of mega-projects, they are not necessarily 'spectacular' in Debord's sense, despite the fact that many adopted

Figure 9.3 The revamped Reichstag building in Berlin
Source: © Matthew Dixon/iStockphoto

Figure 9.4 The London Eye
Source: © Emma Brown

forms of the spectacle are also mega-projects. Scale of itself is not the defining feature of spectacular production in urban development. In a very real sense, scale is immaterial, as the spectacle is a form of social development contingent with postmodern life, across all functions and scales. Nonetheless, the intersection of a mega-project with the spectacle is now a branding feature of cities; witness the London Eye (Figure 9.4), Dubai's CDN$1.2 billion waterfront project by ZAS Architects (Figure 9.5) or the West Edmonton Shopping Mall, which occupies the equivalent of forty-eight city blocks (Figure 9.6). In addition, the incorporation of mega-events into the overall picture is also a defining feature of urban branding. Frequently, but not necessarily, these two functions coincide, as in the Olympic Games, held every four years, where huge construction projects, from rapid transit systems to 60,000-seat stadia, set the stage for spectacular physical prowess and accomplishment. This basic principle extends to, for example, the World's Fair in Shanghai in 2010, World Cup football matches, Formula One Grand Prix, Grand Slam tennis, international conventions and similar events. In many of these projects, the spectacle has the dual function of promoting massive luxury consumption as well as national and urban identity. The hosting of spectacular mega-events is by now a desirable feature of postmodern urbanism and is perceived as part and parcel of a successful urban

Figure 9.5 Dubai waterfront project valued at CDN$1.2 billion by ZAS Architects
       Inc.

Source: Dubai Promenade – Marina + Beach Towers. Dubai Marina, Dubai, UAE. Architect: ZAS
Architects International. Rendering: ZAS Architects Inc.

Figure 9.6 West Edmonton shopping mall, Winnipeg, Canada
Source: © William Manning/Corbis

economy, although frequently with disastrous results. More importantly, these events only highlight a process that also pervades daily life, in malls, shopping centres, iconic buildings and spaces. By offering cash to financially strapped local councils for the 'temporary' rental of public space, the use values to the public are turned into the exchange values of the commodity production. Even in the absence of ownership, the colonisation of the public realm continues. Significantly, however, none of the above typologies considers social change a prime distinction in any system of classification. Scale, function and form are all viewed as independent factors in urbanisation, more important than the functions they contain and the ideologies they pursue. In other words, apart from the extension of the historical processes of capital accumulation in regard to land and its improvements, as indicated in mega-projects, what else is going on?

Debord's concept of the spectacle allows us to identify a specific form of mega-project that does not merely target quantitative increases in the scale of accumulation, or classify its organisational forms and functions, or link it to global development, but associates mega-projects with a qualitative shift in the ideology of social control. Of direct interest to our pursuit of heterology, therefore, are those projects that accommodate the nature of spectacular consumption in the postmodern marketplace, the born-again equivalent of the world's first supermarket, the Roman Coliseum. Although the idea of the spectacle has a long history, its most significant recent incarnation is expressed in a small book called *The Society of the Spectacle* (Debord 1983 (orig. 1967)). It was first published in Paris in 1967 and translated into English in 1970. Although the book was undoubtedly sensationalist in its attack on commodity capitalism, the significance of Debord's thesis was that it heralded an important feature of postmodernity before the process had actually been christened as the dominant ideology in the latter quarter of the twentieth century. Debord used the term to characterise the tightening grip of private capital over the totality of social life. So 'the spectacle' was simultaneously a political and economic process, an ideology, an aesthetic, a way of life, a general process of urbanisation and territory, as well as a symbolic event of postmodernity, with social relations reified as commodities:

> The society which rests on modern industry is not accidental or superficially spectacular, it is fundamentally *spectaclist*. In the spectacle, which is the image of the ruling economy, the goal is nothing, development everything. The spectacle aims at nothing other than itself ... As the indisputable decoration of the objects produced today, as the general exposé of the rationality of the system, as the advanced economic sector which directly shapes a growing multitude of image-objects, the spectacle is the main production of present day society.
>
> (Debord 1983 (orig. 1967): theses 14, 15)

Despite Debord's philosophical grounding, the political economy of the spectacle and its expression in mega-projects had some fairly clear origins, which only gathered speed some ten years after the book was written. Although Debord's 'society of the spectacle' has clearly not progressed at the speed he may have anticipated, it is undeniable that the process is ubiquitous and that:

> The world at once present and absent which the spectacle makes visible is the world of the commodity dominating all that is lived. The world of the commodity is thus shown for what it is, because its movement is identical to the estrangement of men among themselves and in relation to their global products.
>
> (Debord 1983: thesis 37)

Although Debord made the ideology absolutely clear in his book of 221 theses, he did not address forms of space, and it has been left to others to give form to his ideas. Twenty years ago, a landmark article appeared called 'Landscape as spectacle: world's fairs and the culture of heroic consumption', which used the 1986 World's Fair in Vancouver to mark the undeniable arrival of the spectacle as a new form in the development of urban space (Ley and Olds 1988). In this process, the promotion of the brand image of the city coincides with the brand image of products. For example, the City of Sydney recently granted the right to turn its Olympic Park into a racetrack for the premier grand auto event of the year, thus enhancing the urban brand 'Sydney', while simultaneously promoting the automobile industry, oil companies, financial and other institutions and a host of others. Much public dissatisfaction with this idea was simply ignored in the interests of promoting the brand *Sydney*. Hence, the brand becomes synonymous with the political appropriation of urban space as a general rule. Ownership of the image, branding and urban design become welded together in the interest of commodity production and the consciousness that supports this coalition (Kumic 2008). Thus, Marshall McLuhan's concept that *the medium is the message* becomes redundant, as the medium and the message fuse together (Baudrillard 1981, 1997).

Several methods then nest within this idea. Closely related is the idea of theming to promote consumption, challenging traditional concepts of reality and authenticity (Mitrasinovic 2006, Van Melik *et al.* 2007). Building on the somewhat spectacular existing brand, even the 'old style' Las Vegas has been recently rethemed, to a fake version of its fake original with a family focus, and the urban design of themed environments now occupies an increasing proportion of the public realm and commodity circulation (Sorkin 1992, Chaplin 2003 (orig. 2000), Rothman 2002) (Figure 9.7). This overall process occurs in two major dimensions: first, the theming of space, and, second, the theming of its individual components. The theming of space through urban design projects is not new, and it could be argued that the concept is integral with the discipline. Any large-

Figure 9.7 A rethemed, family-oriented Las Vegas, complete with Eiffel Tower and Roman Pantheon lookalikes

Source: © Trombax – Fotolia.com

scale design is 'thematic', in that L'Enfant's plan for Washington or Walter Burley Griffin's plan for Canberra imposed *themes* on nature. The difference is that neither was designed as an integral strategy to promote luxury consumption and commodity fetishism, as is the case, for example, in the extension of the Disney franchise to Florida and Paris. Second, branding is now strategically accomplished through the process of iconic architecture and franchising. Therefore, the fact that the spectacle has existed historically in a variety of forms is no indication that the process today is of the same order, and it is distinguished by several significant features that pervade the provision of spectacular space:

- First, the sacrifice of all prior qualities traditionally associated with the public realm to the promotion and sale of the commodity, either as experience, image or product (Starbucks was only recently thrown out of the Forbidden City in Beijing).
- Second, concepts of branding and theming are implicit, from the revamping of Las Vegas, for example, to the character of individual stores and their products on a global basis.
- Third, reality is challenged in the sense that *authentic* social life disappears, and the simulacra offered by commodity production hold sway. Authenticity loses its more absolute qualities for a total relativity.
- Fourth, history is suspended, and time is measured by the shifting images of the commodity.
- Fifth, behaviour within spectacular spaces is, in the majority of cases, under the total surveillance and control of the private sector.
- Sixth, iconic architecture, branding and ambiguous spaces all play dominant roles in developing the spaces of the spectacle.
- Seventh, reality, fantasy, Utopia and dream become intermingled, as images replace the harsh realities of social life, and individuals become their own avatar in a wonderland of unfulfilled promises.

Sarah Chaplin refers to such spaces as heterotopias, a concept borrowed from Michel Foucault and first discussed in his classic *Les Mots et Les Choses* (*The Order of Things*, 1966, Chaplin 2003 (orig. 2000), DOC: 26). Foucault denotes the cruise ship, a floating extravaganza of desire and indulgence, as the ultimate example of heterotopic space, but Chaplin suggests that:

Las Vegas would seem a yet more perfect example of the heterotopia, combining the attributes of theatre, cinema, garden, museum, holiday camp, honeymoon motel, brothel and colony, as well as that of the ship. In Las Vegas, heterochronism exists in the form of a multitude of themed resorts which borrow from other places and other times and are then juxtaposed along the Strip without any logical historical or geographic ordering . . . Recent ambitious resort developments have begun to reproduce Las Vegas as a collective spectacle or a series of spectacles, in which the Strip functions as a flow of spaces between which pedestrians can move from one fantasy to the next at timed intervals: from a Caesar's forum shopping mall where the sun sets every hour and the statues come to life, to an erupting volcano at the Mirage, then on to a full scale pirate battle at Treasure Island, before experiencing the computerised extravaganza of Fremont Street.

(Chaplin 2003 (orig. 2000): 344–8)

Whether Las Vegas is a 'real' town or merely a theme park that includes the lives of its permanent occupants is a moot point (Rothman 2002), but nowhere is the world of the spectacle more apparent than in Dubai's strategic plan for the year 2015. In the process, much of the world's carboniferous resources, in the form of oil, are being turned into a theming extravagana of pan-national dimensions in order to create a 'genuine' economy that will continue to generate revenue after oil is superseded as the world's main source of energy. In Bawadi area, the world's largest shopping and hospitality boulevard is being created, with entertainment and tourist facilities and fifty-one hotels, one of which will have 6,500 rooms.

Even this development, however, fades against the sheer scale of Dubailand, the world's biggest theme park, currently under construction. This will also dwarf the neighbouring 2,500-acre Ferrari Land in Abu Dhabi, only sixty minutes away by car and part of a $40 billion facelift to its tourist image. Dubailand consists of forty-five mega-projects, which encompass theme parks, hotels, all supporting services and, arguably, the international airport, which is only ten minutes away. The world's largest theme park company, Unites States-based Six Flags Inc., has been hired 'to develop thrill driven theme parks across the Arab world, and . . . a five million square feet multi-billion dirham theme park within the world's largest tourism, leisure and entertainment destination' (Dubai-livethedream.com). As Mike Davis remarks:

The biggest project, Dubailand, represents a vertiginous new stage in fantasy environments. Literally a 'themepark of themeparks' it will be more than twice the size of Disney World and employ 300,000 workers who, in turn, will entertain 15 million visitors per year (each spending a minimum of $100 per day, not including accommodation). Like a surrealist encyclopaedia, its 45 major 'world class projects' include replicas of the Hanging Gardens of Babylon, the Taj Mahal, and the Pyramids, as well as a snow mountain with ski lifts and polar bears, a Nubian village, 'Eco Tourism World', a vast Andalusian spa and wellness complex, golf courses, autodromes, racetracks. 'Giants' World, Fantasia, the largest zoo in the Middle East, several new 5 star hotels, a modern art gallery and the Mall of Arabia.

(Davis 2006b: 50)

However, the spectacle as theme park, with the foremost examples of the genre in Las Vegas and Dubai, is closely related to the production of spectacular and iconic architecture, from the Millennium Dome in London to the world's tallest building, in a permanent state of supercession wherever it may be found. Architecture apart, the most important aspect of such locations is that they do not merely suggest new forms of urban organisation and urban space, they also point to the evolution of humanity and to the development of human consciousness in ways never before encountered:

> A *hyperkitsch-human* would be immersed in an ideology of escapism, subjugated to the hallucinatory effects of the mystification of reality, hardly capable of either facing the challenges and responsibilities involved in a real urban experience, or worse yet, indifferent to finding a *real* urban experience in the midst of a hyperreal world.
>
> (Irazabal 2007: 219)

Therefore, in order to deepen our understanding, the concept of the iconic building and iconic space as an inherent part of the spectacular neocorporatist project need discussion.

Iconic space and neocorporatism

Today, globalisation is itself a generator of culture, based on the universalisation of products, informational capital and the mass media. A singular feature of this process is the significance of iconic architecture and urban design to the branding of towns and cities and, in many cases, as a potential stimulus to economic development. The generic process of 'branding', inherent in the neocorporatist agenda of commodification as the basis of wealth creation, now begins at the national level and descends to the construction of individual buildings and spaces and the events that they accommodate. The psychology is well demonstrated in the following quotation:

> A group of prominent businessmen is pushing for the creation of a panel to advise business and government on how *Australia Inc.* can market itself more aggressively overseas, amid growing recognition that the country risks losing its hard-fought position as a *global brand* on the world stage.
>
> (*Sydney Morning Herald*, 25 June 2009: 25; my italics)

The overall power of the commodity expressed in the image of the city and its promotion through neocorporatist ideology results in designed environments that mirror production. This begins with what Kumic refers to as *the master brand*, branding the city within which branded architecture and urban design coexist. Reflecting commodity fetishism, the brand represents a galaxy of desires compressed into physical space. Hence, the sign language of brand and image progressively colonises all public places, from Times Square in New York, to the Ginza in Tokyo, to local shopping centres, public buildings and spaces, deepening in its compass from year to year (Chmielewska 2005). The concept of the brand and the accompanying logo (think Sydney Opera House) has been extended from shoes and perfume to cities, and *the city brand* is sought after and promoted by all urban administrations:

> The branding of commercial entertainment products and leisure shopping together presents a synthesis of the physical and symbolic economies of urban consumption spaces which public culture has now emulated. Hard branding the city through cultural flagships and festivals has created a form of *Karaoke* architecture where it is not important how well you can sing, but that you do it with verve and gusto.
>
> (Evans 2003: 417)

The concept of 'hard branding' is a highly politicised event whose unstated purpose is to align the private interests of capital with a mass public psychology of the brand. It is an insidious process that moves inexorably forward, one where individuals subconsciously begin to incorporate the concept of branding with belonging and personal aspirations and thus involuntarily participate in a process that will slowly swallow their autonomy as free thinking human beings. Therefore, along with the need to provide a spectacular public realm comes the threat of ownership and/or colonisation by neocorporate interests and the threat this poses to civil society (Cuthbert 1995, Cuff 2003). On the way, cultural and historical processes, structures and events are all packaged in the interests of wealth generation, and the development of cities becomes dependent on their capacity to commodify themselves through the branding and image generation associated with urban design and the public realm (Zukin 1995). Not only this, but the success of the urban brand in providing spectacles, artistic venues, cappuccino environments and overall amenity in the form of improved urban design becomes a magnet for the tourist dollar and the cultural capital of the creative class. The objectives of the private sector for a karaoke architecture of place and space then clash with the political function of the public realm to reinforce social life and its evolving culture, heritage and traditions.

Hence, a core strategy in the manifesto of postmodern urbanist neocorporatism is that the success of cities and nations is dependent on the degree that brand, image and taste are promoted and the public realm becomes a seriously contested space. The corollary is that those cities that are unsuccessful are likely to perish in a landscape of decaying institutions, infrastructure and derelict buildings, as they are deserted by capital seeking the most profitable locations. As a result of neocorporatism controlling development through public–private partnerships, with its emphasis on mega-projects offering quick returns on investment, urban design has come to the fore as the discipline most suited to delivering large-scale physical planning projects with more rapid rewards.

Although the idea of branding an entire nation may be new (as in Australia Inc.), urban spaces and iconic architecture have symbolised both cultures and nations for millennia, though there is no necessary congruence between them (Betsky 1997). Iconic spaces may exist without iconic buildings, and vice versa. The Parthenon on the Acropolis in Athens, the Coliseum in Rome, the Forbidden City in Beijing, Borobodur in Jogjakarta, Buckingham Palace in London, Sydney Opera House, the Temple Mount in Jerusalem, the Empire State Building in New York, The Hong Kong and Shanghai Bank or the Ise shrine in Japan, all have great significance, without being embedded in iconic urban spaces. Similarly, Trafalgar Square in London, the Piazza del Campo in Sienna, Times Square in New York, Pershing Square in Los Angeles or Tiananmen Square in Beijing are internationally significant, in the absence of iconic architecture. When they coincide, however, the synergy is quite extraordinary, such as in St Mark's Square in Venice, with the Doge's Palace, the Piazza de San Pietro with Bernini's colonnade and the Cathedral, or the Louvre or the Pompidou Centre in Paris, where building and space form a single consolidated event (Heinich 1988). Today, things are different. In prior epochs, iconic architecture and urban spaces were constructed by church and state and, in a very real sense, belonged to the people and the practice of culture in daily life. However, in today's economy, there is a new dimension to the conscious creation of iconic architecture and urban space as symbolic capital in the service of neocorporatism (McNeill 2005, 2008, Jencks 2005, Jencks and Sudjic 2005).

Leslie Sklair (an economist) discusses the role of iconic architecture and trans-nationalist neocorporatism as follows:

> Iconic architecture is defined as buildings and spaces that are (1) famous for professional architects and/or the public at large and (2) have special symbolic/aesthetic significance attached to them. Architects can also be iconic in these senses. Also introduced [in Sklair 2006] are distinctions between professional and public icons; local, national and global icons; and historical as contrasted with contemporary icons. The argument is located within a diachronic thesis suggesting that in the pre-global era (roughly the period before the 1950s) most iconic architecture was driven by the interests of the state and/or religion, while in the era of capitalist globalization the dominant force driving iconic architecture is the transnational capitalist class.
>
> (Sklair 2005: 485)

Prior to the emergence of postmodernism, the corporate phase of modernist capitalist development had its own icons – the Guggenheim Museum in New York (Frank Lloyd Wright), the Sydney Opera House (Jorn Utzon), the World Trade Center in New York (Minoru Yamasaki and Emery Roth) and the Pompidou Centre in Paris (Piano and Rogers), built in 1977 and probably the last of the era. Postmodernity heralded the era of electronic communication and the age of globalisation. Iconic architecture in the sense that I discuss it below belongs to this period, which is from the mid 1970s up until today; it is ubiquitous, and there are countless examples in major cities around the world

(Sklair 2002, 2006, McNeill 2007). Important among these are the 'Bird's Nest' at Beijing's Olympic Park (Herzog and De Meuron), the Chinese Central Television Building, also in Beijing (Rem Koolhaas), Bahrain's World Trade Centre (Shaun Killa), the Swiss Re building in London and the Reichstag in Berlin (Norman Foster), the Disney Concert Hall in Los Angeles and the Guggenheim Museum in Bilbao (Frank Gehry), and the Getty Center (Richard Meier), also in Los Angeles. What is significant here is not what form these buildings take, but their overall role within transnational neocorporatism, as the production of architectural and urban form is now generated from entirely different circumstances to that of modernity. One of the most important features is the emergence of buildings and spaces from a new class formation situated as part of an emergent polity. Sklair delineates four fractions of this new class, as follows:

1   Corporate fraction: those who own and/or control the major transnational corporations and their local affiliates. In architecture, these are the major architectural, architecture–engineering and architecture–developer–real-estate firms, listed in the magazine *World Architecture*.
2   State fraction: globalising politicians and bureaucrats. These are the politicians and bureaucrats, at all levels of administrative power and responsibility, who actually decide what gets built where, and how changes to the built environment are regulated.
3   Technical fraction: globalising professionals. The members of this fraction range from the leading technicians centrally involved in the structural features and services (including financial services) of new buildings to those responsible for the education of students and the public in architecture.
4   Consumerist fraction: merchants and media (these are the people responsible for the marketing and consumption of architecture in all of its manifestations).

(Sklair 2005: 486)

Hence, the essential feature of branded iconic architecture is not merely its economic stimulus to the city brand. It has produced a new social class involved with the branding of the city, using the built environment as its medium. A second major aspect of branded architecture and urban design is the effect of transnational franchise architecture, for example McDonald's, Starbuck's, Burger King etc.; global commodity corporations such as Aldi and Ikea; and upmarket brand stores such as those of famous fashion houses and couture outlets (Gucci, Chanel, Armani, Zena etc.). Third, the overall process is enhanced by transnational architectural practices and their supporting retinue of firms – engineering, accounting, surveying, building services etc.

Probably the best example of branded iconic architecture to date is Frank Gehry's Guggenheim Museum in Bilbao (1997), a desolate industrial city in the Basque region of Spain (Del Cerro 2007). It constituted an attempt to 're-narrate the region', if not to re-narrate the city in the process (McNeill and Tewdwr Jones 2003). It was designed to be a museum of modern art, of supreme importance as the container of the region's history and cultural heritage. Although the building is without doubt a masterpiece of postmodernism, its primary purpose was to put Bilbao on the map and stimulate an entire process of urban regeneration that would restore economic vitality to the city:

> The Guggenheim Museum Bilbao was not constructed simply as an iconic building; it was built to address a number of serious problems. At the time the city suffered an extremely high unemployment rate, up to 25%. Traditional Industries had become obsolete, and the city centre hosted a riverport plagued by severe traffic congestion. Other troubles included violence from extremist Basque separatists, urban deterioration, pollution and a poor public transport system.
>
> (Plaza 2008: 506)

Needless to say, the €166 million paid by the public for the building constituted a massive piece of advertising that would generate significant revenues to the private sector. Much of this was to be accomplished via the tourist dollar, with 800,000 people from around the world flocking, on an annual basis, to gaze on an icon the likes of which did not exist anywhere else in Europe. Apart from drawing the uniqueness of Gehry's design into question, as he has a style that was already in evidence in prior work and post-Bilbao projects (one was already planned for New York), the issue of the capacity of the building to accomplish its economic and political aims has since been raised (Plaza 1999, 2006, 2008, Gomez and Gonzales 2001). Despite the museum's success as an icon, the Guggenheim Bilbao had a limited capacity as an economic generator, as it is beyond the potential of any building to replace sound economic management targeting investment strategies, marketing and transport. Plaza notes that the building did indeed assist the hotel and restaurant sector, with Bilbao gaining 4,000 new employees from 1995 to 2005. She remarks that, although cultural tourism no doubt increased, the methods of quantifying the tourist sector statistically involve business travel as well, which accounted for significant seasonal fluctuations in trade. In consequence, she suggests that cultural heritage investments must go hand in hand with productivity improving policies (Plaza 2008: 517).

Ambiguous space and the citizen

Because of the significance of the commodity, as noted above, there is no limit to the application of the commodity principle. The fact that the commodity is first and foremost a social relation between seller and buyer means that the ownership, design and control of privatised commodity production now exerts enormous power over the behaviour of populations at a global level. The theoretical endgame is a wholly privatised environment where the commodity principle permeates all walks of life, one within which the production, circulation and exchange of goods are wholly under the control of corporate power (Kohn 2004). In addition, capital has gradually entered the arena of collective consumption, not merely in privatising institutions and facilities once thought to be the sole purview of the state, but also in absorbing the last barrier to control over urban space, namely the public realm (Mitchel 2003, Low and Smith 2006, de Cante 2008). Most important, however, is the capacity to exercise control over symbolic capital and therefore to manufacture and manipulate the psychology of entire populations. With desire now the driving force behind shopping till you drop, neocorporate institutions are well placed to create the perfect market – total control over space, the production of commodities and the means to direct luxury consumption into commercially acceptable pathways via increasing command over education and the mass media. In the process, individuals gradually relinquish their autonomy as reasoning human beings to the sublimation of manufactured desires.

In fact, things are not that simple. There are a myriad checks and balances within the global economy that deny validity to a wholly commodified planet, one of them being global warming. Uneven development also means that the private sector will be more interested in the public realm in some regions than others. Urban social movements are not yet devoid of authority, nor are local councils totally bereft of the public interest. In addition, and by the very nature of commodity exchange, people must have access to goods, and so corporations must, of necessity, provide space for human circulation, the mall being a good example of a global typology of privatised space with public access (Kayden 2000). Nonetheless, and however much we refine the argument, the public realm represents a spatial barrier to accumulation and is therefore under threat, either directly or passively, from state neocorporatism. The central heterology here hinges on the concept of rights and the methods through which rights are exercised, and I have set out the significant theoretical considerations in FOC4: 82–6. Briefly stated, the right to a public realm is by no means assured in any bill of rights, statutes or other legislation. Owing to the diversity of political systems, there is no uniform, universal acceptance of the idea that a public realm is necessary. In the Universal Declaration of Human Rights, adopted by the United Nations in 1948, everyone has the right of freedom of movement and residence within the borders of each state. As in every manifesto, however, the actual adoption and implementation of principle are left to each country to interpret however it wishes. More significantly, although individuals have the right to freedom of movement, there is nothing to suggest that rights and ownership should coincide. At this point, concepts of public realm, public space and commons retain a tenuous relation to civil society as a whole (Dandeneker 1990).

In 1995, I wrote an article called 'The right to the city', which explored the concept of right in application to Hong Kong, and I later elaborated on this in 'Ambiguous space, ambiguous rights' (Cuthbert and McKinnell 1997). These papers explored in some depth how social space in Hong Kong is configured by a private sector unrestrained by the public good, where various brands of corporatism are all the population has ever known. An imperialist mandate, a system of laissez-faire economics, a political system with no effective political parties, monumental penetration by the private sector into the executive and legislative assemblies of government, and a supine population disinterested in urban politics, all contributed to the situation where, for all practical purposes, public space did not exist (and still does not exist) as an inalienable right of the people. Tragically, this right is almost impossible to trace, in any political system at any level of development, as a legally constituted right mapped out in physical space. The result is that an essential feature of *public space* is its very ambiguity. You never know whose space you are in, what rights you have, or what forms of behaviour are sanctioned. To a large degree, the same principles apply to entire systems of transportation that have been farmed out to private-sector ownership – tollways, tunnels, bridges, ports, subways, airports etc.

On Hong Kong Island, the downtown area has been constructed and controlled by the private sector, with the entire system of individual movement on walkways and through buildings controlled by the private agency of large corporations. Hong Kong Land, the property arm of Jardine's, owns some twelve tower blocks in central Hong Kong and is the largest landowner. It also designed and built the system of second-level walkways linking its properties into one vast emporium. Not only this, but a ubiquitous modus operandi of development, which is by now a universal practice, exemplifies this concept of ambiguous space. Developers not only privatise their own commercial spaces, but they also manage to have the public pay for spaces to which they have no rights of access. In Hong Kong, Citibank Plaza/Asia Pacific Tower is a commercial development in the central district that was developed by Great Eagle Properties. The development consists of two towers, reaching a maximum height of forty-seven storeys. In return for an increase in plot ratio from 15 to 18, the developers agreed to dedicate space to the public on both lower- and upper-ground floors. However, the Deed of Dedication agreement states that the total area dedicated to the public is for the purpose of pedestrian passage only, with the developer maintaining control over the space. In simple terms, the state grants even higher densities than those allowed in its own development plans to encourage developers to allocate space for the circulation of pedestrians. In order to reduce costs to the state, dedicated space is then returned to the developer for maintenance and surveillance, where the only sanctioned activity is for the citizen to keep moving or stop and shop.

Two other important items are significant for urban design in the context of ambiguous spaces. First, the environmental professions (architecture, landscape architecture, urban planning) are complicit in the policing and design of urban space generally, in gated communities, shopping malls, theme parks and other urban spaces. In spaces of commodity exchange, design strategies not only delineate and control movement and rest, they also promote commodity circulation by channelling consumers into pathways that cement a permanent gaze on products and encourage purchase.

Second, these design strategies coincide and reinforce both active surveillance, via private security operations, and passive surveillance, through the use of closed-circuit television (CCTV) in 'public' spaces such as malls, shopping centres, franchises, walkways, overpasses, elevators, corridors, lifts etc. In the United Kingdom, the British government's information minister has expressed the fear that Britain would sleep-walk into a surveillance society, as the country now has in place some 5 million CCTV cameras, one for every twelve people. Moreover, the traditional typologies of urban space design, such as landscaping, public art, sculpture, fountains, waterfalls, monuments, staircases etc., now serve a dual purpose in controlling and channelling pedestrian movement. Paradoxically, CCTV covers both the space of pleasure and the space of terror (Fainstein 2002, Marcuse 2006). The evolution of the informational society has allowed governments to track individual movement, expenditure, contacts, medical records, personal preferences and many other aspects of life via a plethora of means – satellites, credit cards, electronic road pricing, mobile phones, Internet cookies and other devices. In the aftermath of the World Trade Center attack – 9/11 – physical design, active policing and passive surveillance have become closely integrated, not to mention the architectural design of buildings and the surrounding space (Lyon 2003, Molotch and McClain 2003). Hence, spaces of terror now stretch around the world, particularly in those locations where terrorist attacks are either anticipated or have actually occurred. Ambiguous space, ambiguous rights, surveillance and policing now play a significant role in the organisation of the public realm. Unfortunately, the threat of terrorism has served a dual purpose, namely a legitimate need to protect individuals, along with the potential abuse of individual rights. Peter Marcuse elaborates on the distinction between safety and security when he remarks that, 'the treatment of public space illustrates the pattern: a possible increase in safety but an increase in insecurity. Manipulated false responses restrict and pervert the uses of public space, both directly limiting political uses and indirectly restricting popular functions' (Marcuse 2006: 919).

Hence, issues connected to branding, themed urban design, iconic architecture, the creative class and the economic success of cities are all deeply interconnected with the new urban form and neocorporatist strategies in regard to urban space, its occupation, use and image.

Invisible space and the global migrant

This section and the one following raise a significant issue for urban designers. As we have seen, many urban design projects in prior chapters allude to large-scale projects conceptually organised by the environmental disciplines, primarily architecture and urban planning. Problematically, urban design is to a large degree defined as such in the Western world. So far, the same has been true for this chapter on typologies. However, the concept must be challenged as an elitist, monopolistic and somewhat racist definition of urban design knowledge, as it leaves out most of the developing world, except for a few spectacular examples of historic grandeur. Urban design cannot be constrained to large-scale,

predominantly architectural projects in developed Western nations, leaving out
the rest of the planet. For this and other reasons (involving social class, racism,
nationalism etc.), I have chosen to conflate urban design with the generation of
urban form. Although most urban designers may not be involved in the 'design'
of many forms of urban space, such as Foucault's heterotopias, the spaces of
the global migrant, slums, squatter settlements and refugee camps, it is our
responsibility to recognise that all forms of space are designed by human action,
and, therefore, as designers, we are either tacitly or knowingly involved (Dennis
2004, Rao 2006).

As in many regions of intellectual theory and debate, cities in the developed
world dominate enquiry, owing to their vastly superior economic power and the
political authority that comes with it. Globalisation is, however, burdened with
a serious semantic problem. The overall tendency when globalisation is discussed
is to locate the problematic in the context of the benefits that accrue to the rich
– as nations, regions and individuals – not in terms of the handicaps that remain
with the poor – as nations, regions and individuals. Part of the problem of
accommodating globalisation as heterological to the generation of urban space
is the idea that many globalisations exist. It seems to me that the only appropriate
way to study globalisation is in a manner similar to the total lifecycle approach
advocated by the best analysts in the field of sustainable development. No clear
picture of globalisation can ever emerge if only the short-term interests of the
Western world are taken into account, without encompassing in some manner
the potential disasters on the horizon posed by global warming, massive
emigration, refugee settlements, poverty and disease. This would be akin to an
assessment of the wealth of Britain in the eighteenth and nineteenth centuries
that ignored the reality that colonisation and imperialism had harnessed one-
third of the world in its own interest. Today, altogether new forms of colonisation
and imperialism exist, along with an entirely new dynamic caused by post-
colonialism, a new international division of labour, global warming, crony
capitalism, dictatorships, AIDS and so on. One way or another, global wealth
cannot be accommodated without counting the costs of global poverty, and we
can safely say that all nations are delinquent in their responsibilities in this respect
(Smith 2001). Overall, we tend to forget that over half the world now lives in
cities, and half of those in cities that are neither 'world', 'global' nor 'mega'.
Even the tendency to split research activity into urban studies and development
studies alienates developing countries and tacitly suggests that they have nothing
to do with globalisation, are not affected by it, and are somehow self-contained
in a permanent recycling of oppression and poverty. 'Where the global city
approach generalises the successful locales of high finance and corporate city
life, the developmentalist approach builds towards a position of all poor cities
as infrastructurally poor and economically stagnant yet (perversely?) expanding
in size' (Robinson 2002: 540).

Although imperialism may have morphed into new forms, traditional forms
of exploitation remain. The old and the new share the same need to exploit the
developing world for resources, markets and labour. Today, the export of people

from the core economies to the periphery (colonisation) has undergone a massive reversal, with the developed world now importing labour from the Third World, a phenomenon made possible by enormous wage differentials between working classes in both locations (Benton-Short *et al.* 2005). This is illustrated, for example, by the number of foreign-born individuals in various cities, e.g. New York. It has been estimated that remittances from exported labour back to the country of origin could have reached as much as US$200 billion in 2003 (Sander 2003). The extent to which global cities absorb migrant labour is now a widespread feature of global development, and the conditions under which labour is exploited are diverse. For example, the importation of Philippina (female) labour into Hong Kong and the importation of Indian and Pakistani labour into the United Arab Emirates do not entitle individuals to any rights of citizenship. Although contracts may be renewed, migrants have no more rights after twenty years of labour than they did when they arrived. The right to citizenship is also marked by the absence of any right to space, and migrant workers in the millions, resulting from internal migrations (as in China) or emigration of labour to Hong Kong, Dubai, Los Angeles and other places, make their unstated claims by virtue of their weight of numbers. In turn, this impacts on globalising cities, both in terms of residential accommodation and of the impact on the public realm, and therefore indicates an important, if unrecognised, urban design phenomenon.

In 'The right to the city', mentioned above, I addressed this issue in relation to the Philippina population in Hong Kong, a group currently numbering 142,000. Philippinas are preferred by local, middle-class Chinese families, as they all speak English (in addition to Philippino, the national language based on Tagalog, and at least one dialect such as Cebuano, Ilokano, Hiligaynon, Bikol, Pangasinan etc., of which there are literally hundreds). These women have only contractual rights, which are exceedingly difficult to claim when problems arise, and, as a distinctly separate ethnic group, they have no spatial existence as a community as they are accommodated in the residences of their employers. Nonetheless, they manage to create a one-day-a-week world, on Sunday, that transforms the central district of Hong Kong Island into a different kind of business district, where hundreds of one-person businesses and sundry services – currency exchange, loans, the sale of clothes, perfumes and beauty products, fortune telling, hairdressing etc. – are set up in the interstitial spaces between buildings, those ambiguous spaces mentioned above (see Figures 9.8–10). In order to protect the privately owned public realm, however, many central areas are closed to pedestrian activity, i.e. Philippinas, with racial overtones. To its credit, the Hong Kong Bank, designed by Norman Foster, accommodates for the day, at street level, a squatting population of over a thousand women, who confirm their collective experience in a symbolic yet temporary city of their own creation.

Today's migrations into developed countries have altogether different dynamics to those of the past, sponsored by globalisation and new structures of economic development. The United States, the European Union and Middle Eastern countries, as well as places such as Hong Kong and Singapore, would

Figure 9.8 Sunday colonisation of public space in central district, Hong Kong by Philippina population

Source: The author

Figure 9.9 Hong Kong: detail of tape used to prevent Sunday access to pedestrian network

Source: The author

Figure 9.10 Hong Kong: normal weekday access to pedestrian network, banned on
Sundays by certain central district corporations

Source: The author

be seriously challenged economically if immigrant labour, legal or illegal, were
to be withdrawn overnight. Historically, few cities have been able to ignore this
phenomenon. For example, in Hong Kong, prior to the Japanese occupation,
the resident population of 1 million added another 800,000 persons in the space
of three years, from 1937 to 1940. Today, the problem of the global migrant
and the provision of spaces that reflect both culture and needs is ubiquitous,
exemplified by the vexed issue of migrant space in Dubai. Owing to the extreme
nature of the situation, we can learn from an exaggerated picture of what occurs
when immigrant populations make demands on the public realm, and residential
accommodation in particular. The concept *theme park* probably best describes
development across the entire state, not merely its attempts to become the
world's number-one tourist attraction. However, artificial islands, luxury hotels,
marinas, a plethora of iconic buildings, vast emporia of luxury consumption,
the world's tallest building (Burj Dubai, by Skidmore, Owings and Merrill) and
the largest theme parks are made possible only through the exploitation of
migrant labour and enduring poverty in such countries as India, Sri Lanka,
Pakistan and the Philippines. For all practical purposes, such labour has no rights
of any kind, and the only difference between slavery and their conditions of
existence is that they are paid for their work, albeit meagerly. They are also
banned from accessing ambiguous spaces owing to racism, regulation, physical
surveillance or distance, as many locations demand private transport:

Nor are the bleak camps on the city's outskirts – where labourers are crowded six, eight, even twelve to a room, often without air conditioning or functioning toilets – part of the official tourist image of a city of luxury, without poverty or slums.

(Davis 2006b: 66)

While the spaces of luxury consumption and tourism are stressed, Dubai's immigrant population constitutes 82 per cent of its population of 1.5 million people, inhabiting what has been referred to as 'transient urbanism' (Elsheshtawy 2008). Most of the territory's 300,000 construction workers live in labour camps in marginal areas and are transported to work by their employers, and half a million single men (both married and unmarried) live in the city. Observing that, in Dubai, a genuine urban realm was conspicuously absent, Elsheshtawy studied four key sites, and the following is a brief summary of his work. As might be expected, the main settings that corresponded to migrants' need for some form of social intercourse were concentrated round important bus stops, surrounded by poor-income areas that also had high levels of commercial activity. Despite the fact that migrant labour is the lifeblood of the country's economy, and that migrants have no other places to go, in the public spaces they inhabit such as Sabhka and Baniyas Square, where 'hanging about' is the main activity, there are prominent notices on display informing them that waiting is forbidden. In the same locations, the global nature of immigration is reinforced by the high level of Internet cafes, cellphone use and foreign-exchange outlets. Despite the apparent need for a class of labour unavailable locally, enclaves have been established, such as those of stateless Arabs. The underclass of the Arab world is housed in metal shacks called *bidoon*. Another area is known as Little Quiapo, after a busy commercial district in Manilla. Elsheshtawy notes that all of the settings exhibit common features such as the dominance of male users (except Karama district), the absence of 'locals', the portrayal of such areas as 'authentic', in contrast to the sterile wastelands of shopping centres and malls, and the occupation of incidental spaces that were not planned for use by immigrants. These spaces are also most easily accessible and welcoming by day, but turn into environments for illegal activities in the late evening – prostitution, gambling, drug use etc. A predominant quality exhibited in these spaces, an invisible public realm, is the association with place, despite the transitory nature of its occupants. Despite all of this, by such occupation,

A subtle form of resistance emerges, in which the formal settings of the city are rejected in favour of another kind of publicness that allows migrants to gather with their compatriots and display their ethnicity. These elements do constitute a significant aspect of transnationalism whereby these immigrants are able to give meaning to these spaces by navigating both a local space (the city) and a global space (their home country).

(Elsheshtawy 2008: 985)

Although Dubai is without doubt a somewhat special case, it nonetheless highlights the otherness of public space and represents a challenge to urban designers to broaden traditional conceptions of the public realm, particularly where multiculturalism is a claimed benefit of the social structure, e.g. in Australia, the United States and other countries. Although both migrant and immigrant labour and the environments it inhabits around the globe are depressed and disadvantaged, they represent luxury accommodation for many in slum areas (usually urban) and the world's dispossessed, who occupy the largest transitory spaces on the planet (usually in rural areas), and it is to these two phenomena that I now turn.

Slum and superslumspace

In rough figures, the current world population is nearing 7 billion, and the world's population of slum dwellers approaches 1 billion. It is hard to accommodate the sheer scale of the slum, but, retranslated, this figure is more than twenty times the entire population of Spain, or forty-five times that of Australia. If, as urban designers, we ignore the concept *slum* as *other*, then we automatically exclude the shelter of some 15 per cent of the world's population – 'Slum dwellers of the new millennium are no longer a few thousand in a few cities of a rapidly industrializing continent. They include one out of every three city dwellers, a billion people, a sixth of the world's population' (www.unfpa.org/swp/2007). Despite the fact that our designs do not stretch to slum environments, designers in India, Bangladesh or Ethiopia, for example, cannot avoid the fact that the slum population constitutes, in most cases, the predominant influence on the form of cities. Hence, slums constitute a significant urban form in cities, almost eradicated in some, and almost totally dominant in others. Few cities in developed countries can claim to have completely eradicated the problem, and a variety of terms envelop the concept of slum, such as shantytown, squatter settlement, deprived area etc., with countries and regions each maintaining its own particular linguistic terminology – *colonias populares* (Mexico), *pueblos jovenes* (Peru) *kampung* (Indonesia), *gececordas* (Turkey) – and even Paris still retains its *bidonvilles* ('garbage can towns'). Western cities, however, pale into irrelevance when we consider Africa and Asia. In Africa, for example, 99.4 per cent of the population of Ethiopia are slum dwellers, 98.5 per cent in Afghanistan, and around 12 million in Mumbai. The following extracts from Mike Davis's apocalyptic text *Planet of Slums* indicates the dimensions of the problem:

> A point of no return is reached when a reserve army waiting to be incorporated into the labour process becomes stigmatised as a permanently redundant mass, an excessive burden that cannot be included now or in the future, in economy and society.

> Altogether the global informal working class (overlapping with but not identical to the slum population) is about one billion strong, making it the fastest growing, and most unprecedented social class on earth.

By 2015 Black Africa will have 332 million slum dwellers, a number that will continue to double every fifteen years.

(Davis 2006a: 198,178, 19; see also Davis 2004)

Although academics make a significant contribution to the conceptualisation and analysis of the slum, most of the data come from the United Nations habitat reports, specifically *The Challenge of Slums* and *Slums of the World* (2003a, 2003b), the World Bank/UNCHS (Habitat) *Cities Alliance for Cities Without Slums* (2000) and subsequent updates. However, even 'the data' are suspect, owing to one simple fact, that there is no universally accepted definition of the phenomenon. The sheer diversity of political regimes, fixed capital in existing buildings, geography, climate, available materials and other factors combine to create a problem unknown in other urban typologies. How does one know that one inhabits a slum? Scholars have been tackling the problem for at least 100 years, since Engels' seminal *The Condition of the Working Class in England* appeared in 1892. It has also been nearly fifty years since Charles Abrams wrote his classic, *Man's Struggle for Shelter in an Urbanising World* (1964), and more recently there have been other significant contributions, such as those by Perlman (1976), Angotti (1993), Seabrook (1996) and Breman (2003). Engels, of course, never bothered with defining the word *slum* and went straight from conditions in cities to the actual causes of exploitation and poverty, and it is clear that the definitions of poverty and that of the slum are closely related. In his *Planet of Slums*, Mike Davis offers a typology of slum housing (Davis 2006a: 30). He makes two basic geographic distinctions, of the Metro Core and of the Periphery, dividing each in turn into formal (F) and informal sectors (I), adding refugee camps to the periphery as a separate category. The Metro (F) category contains tenements, which include hand-me-downs, those built for the poor and hostels etc. The informal sector includes squatters, whether authorised or not, as well as pavement dwellers. Periphery (F) includes both private rental as well as public housing. Periphery (I) contains two classes: first, what he terms 'pirate subdivisions', either owner-occupied or rental, and squatters, either authorised, including site and service, or unauthorised. Although this is a workable framework to begin with, it is problematic, as it ignores the multitude of diverse economic and cultural settings that exist around the world. Hence, any application of this system would have to undergo rather selective scrutiny and adaptation to be effective.

Slums are characterised by a basket of conditions that vary in importance from place to place – insecurity of tenure or ownership; the absence of basic services, such as electricity, gas or water, sanitation, waste collection, safe infrastructure including roads, sidewalks, drainage and open space; the absence of social services, such as clinics, schools, support for the elderly; and the presence of crime – extortion, prostitution, street gangs, drugs and other ills. In the worst cases, child labour and child prostitution are rife, as well as the sale of human organs in places such as Manilla and Chennai in India. Being built on the cheapest land available, slums are also more exposed to natural disasters such as flooding, mudslides and excessive damage from earthquakes and typhoons.

Overall, it is futile to try to arrive at an absolute definition of a slum. Even relative definitions are rendered more complex by the fact that, within many slums, there may be a huge variance in income and the quality of dwelling space, or secure tenure in some parts and none in others, piped water in a few locations but a general absence elsewhere.

In *The Return of the Slum*, Gilbert raises the problematic of the slum as a semantic issue:

> The 'cities without slums' initiative has resuscitated an old and dangerous term from the habitat vocabulary. Use of the word 'slum' will recreate many of the myths about poor people that years of careful research have discredited . . . the campaign implies that cities can actually rid themselves of slums, an idea that is wholly unachievable. The word is also dangerous because it confuses the physical problem with the characteristics of the people living there.
>
> (Gilbert 2007: 619)

Gilbert's anxieties are rooted in a generalised acceptance by planners and local government that slum clearance is a necessary part of social development, ignoring the fact that, in the process of moving residents, their economic and social infrastructure is destroyed and seldom replaced. In many cases, the land is simply sold by government to developers. Given that slums, like the public realm, represent a barrier to accumulation from land, the practice remains ubiquitous. Gilbert goes on to illustrate that many studies have demonstrated the capacity of slums to evolve gradually into consolidated and serviced communities, and that the United Nations' campaign for cities without slums constitutes a 'combination of genuine altruism and bureaucratic opportunism . . . using headlines to compete for funds . . . a victory for the banner headline and tabloid thinking' (Gilbert 2007: 710). Both Gilbert and Angotti (2006) attack Davis's obvious penchant for hyperbole and the apocalyptic future he predicts. Nonetheless, many of Davis's statements, such as 'Indeed the one billion city-dwellers who inhabit postmodern slums might well look back with envy at the ruins of the sturdy mud homes of Catal Huyok in Anatolia, erected at the dawn of life nine thousand years ago', do not seem any more fatalistic than the current rhetoric on global warming, a force that could magnify even the most conservative forecasts on slum dwellings beyond recognition.

Conclusion

Beginning with Çatal Huyuk in Anatolia some 9,000 years ago, urban design has used typologies to catalogue form into streets, squares, avenues, boulevards, embarcaderos, arcades and other features. Over time, evolution has dictated massive requisite variety across the formal spectrum, sufficient for at least one scholar to suggest that all possible urban forms are already in existence (Krier 1979). All we have to do is be aware of each vocabulary and use it in design. No new urban forms are required, nor perhaps are even possible. In contrast, and as a basic design principle, I maintain that urban forms do not spring arbitrarily from the Eureka Principle. Typologies evolve in concert with socio-economic requirements. To take a somewhat extreme example, the refugee camps of the disposessed, now housing millions of people, constitute a new urban form that has no historical referents. Although we can debate the idea that historically derived urban forms are adaptive to new circumstances and therefore possess over-capacity in terms of design concepts, nonetheless evolution has a long way to travel, and we have no idea what the future holds, except for the glaring possibility of ecocide. However, it is undeniable that the growth of cities is mutating faster than our imagination can accommodate, and Debord's idea of the spectacle, a futuristic prediction some forty years ago, is already looking dated. Already, his vision is a way of life for many. In the society of the spectacle, the idea that the interests of capital are congruent with the needs of the people has been sufficiently persuasive to allow a neocorporatist agenda to evolve and infuse the state with its ideologies and manifestos. These strategies are diffuse and usually hidden, ranging from the direct impact of monopolistic control over the media and creating a transnationalist capitalist class, to the branding of cities and the theming of fifth space. However, if the public realm is to be colonised by neocorporatism, it will not fall to something as crude as the sale of land, but to a multivalent strategy that uses the state as a willing mechanism in the exchange process, where rights are conferred without the need for ownership. In addition, many of the proposed encroachments will be supported by the general public itself, where agreement to allow certain forms of activity creates precedents for others. All of this assumes a certain level of development. In other situations, the space of the slum, the global migrant and the globally dispossessed are generating a whole new formal vocabulary of urban space.

10 Pragmatics

Sociological concepts are, in Alfred Schutz's words, 'second level constructs'; the first level constructs are those through which social actors have already prestructured the social world prior to its scientific investigation. Understanding the latter is a necessary point of departure for constructing the former.

(Thomas McCarthy)

Introduction: the power of polemic

Pragmatics can be defined as the study of the way in which language is used to express what is really meant in particular situations, given that the actual written word may imply something different. In a more general context, *The New Oxford Dictionary of English* defines pragmatism as 'the doctrine that evaluates assertions solely by practical consequences' or, alternatively, 'thinking about solving problems in a practical and sensible way rather than having fixed ideas and theories'. In my last two volumes, I concentrated on the two most pragmatic influences on urban design. These were, first, the design professions and their direct link to cultural capital, focussing on the political economy of professional practice (DC2; FOC: 214–45). Second, the teaching of urban design knowledge within tertiary education was assessed (DC: 28). More importantly, the triadic relationship between professions, the institutional arrangement within universities and the actual transmission and accumulation of cultural capital within educational programmes was also elaborated at length (FOC: 10). What were not explored were the origins from which both the academy and the professions sourced their ideologies. Where did their ideas originate?

Neither of these institutional arrangements invented themselves. They resulted from a long period of gestation where ideas became sufficiently condensed that they could be stated with conviction, with the aspiration that they would result in some form of social action. Some were short lived. Others have lasted a thousand years or more. Hence, given my use of the adopted term 'heterology' as 'the method behind the method', we need to look for the origins of polemic and debate that have informed both professional action and the academy. In this realm, both are united in grids of practices that have collectively affected the design professions and their knowledge base for at least a century, with sources stretching back over two millennia. We call these forms of knowledge *manifestos* – statements that have been inherited over time from a variety of sources: imperial mandates, political ideologies, institutions, individuals and a myriad of urban social movements that shared the same philosophy and aspirations in respect to particular forms of oppression, lifestyle, art, religion, politics and social change. It is impossible to say for certain when manifestos as a form of social practice came into being, as their formation clearly depended on a diverse combination of phenomena – modes of production, the form of labour and the state, the nature of government, types of religious freedom or bias, prevailing philosophies or ideologies, concepts of law, punishment and opportunity. Therefore, we cannot state with any conviction that, 'the first manifesto was issued at this particular moment'. Even a brief investigation reveals the complexity of the problem, as manifestos can be found on issues ranging from the construction of entire political systems to the detailed complexity of individual interests – manifestos on blogging, Avant-Pop, cyborgs, fractals, freedom, culture, waffle, the Communist Party, folk art, humanism, Mozilla, cannibalism and a myriad of others. Given this diversity, one almost begins to think in terms of Tristan Tzara's Dadaist manifesto of 1918 (Caws 2001: 5).

> I am writing this manifesto and I don't want anything. I say however certain things and I am on principle against Manifestos, as I am also against principles . . . I am writing this manifesto to show you that you can do contrary actions together, in one single fresh breath; I am also against action; for continual contradiction; for affirmation also. I am neither for nor against and I don't explain because I hate common sense.

The origins of the word 'manifesto' are in two Latin words, *manifestus* ('obvious') and *manifestare* ('to make public'), but also in the word for hand *manus*, implying a written document or statement, and it is defined in *The New Oxford Dictionary of English* as 'a public declaration of policy and aims, especially one issued before an election by a political party or a candidate'. This is clearly an extremely limited definition and has been variously elaborated, starting from its origins within legal documents, and progressing through an enormous variety of interpretations, such as 'The manifesto was from the beginning, and has remained, a deliberate manipulation of the public view' and, elsewhere, 'The manifesto is an act of *démesure* going past what is thought of as proper, sane and literary' (Caws 2001: ix, xx). Again, we have the idea that a manifesto 'is a curious art form, like the Haiku, with its own rules of brevity, wit and *le mot juste'* (Jencks and Kropf 1997: 6). Hence, a standard definition of *manifesto*, which adopts such a diversity of forms in addition to being an evolutionary event, is a somewhat daunting task, if not, in the end, self-defeating. It is probably more productive to situate the manifesto as a form of social action in the origins of capitalism, the Enlightenment and the age of reason, if for no other reason than capitalism offered more individual freedom of expression than prior modes of production, and that rationality, to a degree, had finally triumphed.

This, of course, would leave out such epochal statements as Magna Carta (1215), a document that would forever alter the course of British history and, by extension, that of one-third of the world, through British imperialism. Magna Carta was the origin of constitutional law and was continually updated well into the eighteenth century. It also had a significant effect on the *Constitution of the United States*. There is no doubt, however, that the twentieth century became the age of the manifesto, with an effusion of manifestos across all regions of human interest and activity, with individuals, social movements and institutions of all types vying to have their case heard and legitimated by as many people as possible. The crisis of modernity and the transition from industrial capitalism to commercial and informational capitalism generated conflict sufficient for all to participate. Overall, however, the age of reason also brought with it the idea that undiluted authority was no longer acceptable, and that economic and political power had to be enshrined within stated manifestos and legal sanction. The limits to authority, and the rights and obligations that went with it, specifically the rights of citizens, were no longer a matter of opinion or personal whim, but were made concrete in text and statute. However, the age of reason also accommodated new forms of unreason. The legitimation of capitalism in terms of its capacity for self-regulation and its ability to solve an entire range of social problems that emerged from the exploitation of labour and nature became seriously challenged. In other words, the structural features of capitalism remained, with the capitalist state being unable to resolve its own internal contradictions. Jürgen Habermas condensed the arguments in his *Legitimation Crisis* and argued that the hiatus did not issue from a lack of belief in the system. In contrast, it was 'the result of people still believing the promises in the political manifestos and feeling betrayed when they are not kept' (Noble 2000: 212).

There is no realm of human activity that remains unaffected by manifestos of some kind, either by direct influence or by implication. Philosophy, science, religion, art, politics and culture have all been changed (sometimes savaged) by manifestos that set out to challenge or, in some manner, alter the course of the established order. To this extent, manifestos are dialectic, as they exist in the dynamic space between theory and practice, affecting both simultaneously. They also constitute ideological constructs, if we accept the idea that all theory is ideological, beginning as it does with certain fundamental assumptions that are incomplete, thus involving a commitment to ideas that are debatable and thus manifestly capable of refutation. Mary Ann Caws, in her book *Manifestos* (2001), relates the manifesto to 'isms' – where public statements were made about some new movement, for example manifestos in art that relate to Impressionism, Cubism, Surrealism, Dadaism, Vorticism, Suprematism and countless others. Architecture was likewise affected by a diversity of schools of thought – Constructivism, Functionalism, Brutalism, Neo-traditionalism, Deconstructivism, Neo-modernism, Postmodernism, as well as much less well known 'isms' such as Noisism, Acmeism, Rayonism and others. Many such 'isms' were frequently nested within other movements. The Bauhaus, one of the inspirations for all forms of design in the twentieth century, is a good example. Within the overall ideology of craft-based learning and the master–student approach to teaching, a variety of manifestos were issued by its directors over the course of its existence, as each expressed their own orientation to the political and economic forces of the time. Although we identify manifestos through the use of the suffix 'ism', there are many other forms of manifesto that omit this (Caws 2001). While the classic manifesto was an inspirational and polemical document that stated some new ideology such as 'workers of the world unite!', it came in a variety of forms, which included charters, covenants, edicts, mandates, tenets (commandments) and other discourses. Part of the problem with all of these, of course, is that they frequently represent narrow, sectarian interests. Hence, manifestos tend to be self-serving. The ideology of an era or adopted movement always synthesises a diversity of ideas and principles that are not necessarily inclusive or politically correct. While the environmental professions and academia alike are similarly affected, nonetheless the manifesto constitutes concrete evidence of the ideologies that construct our cultural world-view, adopted professional mandates and the ideas transmitted to the next generation of ideologues.

What manifestos 'mean' is a process subject to monumental scrutiny, misinterpretation, manipulation and abuse, exemplified in arguably the greatest manifestos of all time, the Bible and the Koran. Not only have these texts been a work in progress over centuries, there are as many interpretations as individuals who believe in them. In the process of attempting to create a certain type of social order (one where everybody believes in the same ideology, but in different ways), they have also been used to create vast fortunes, raise great armies, destroy other civilisations, dominate populations, suppress scientific enquiry, repress imagination and undermine democracy, confusing private beliefs with the politics of religion, the state and collective social life. It then becomes difficult to disentangle the intended aims of a manifesto from its practical consequences, as, for example, in the Chinese and Russian revolutions. At the core of this problem is the idea that language is not merely a simple means of communication. It has political manifestations, owing to the multiplicity of meanings that can be attached to the written word. Jürgen Habermas used the term '*distorted communication*' to refer to this feature of language, implying that linguistic interpretation was so fraught with subjectivity that language was almost incapable of conveying what we might refer to as 'the truth' (Habermas 1970). For example, semantic problems leave vast amounts of space for confusion and manipulation. Terms such as *freedom*, *right*, *autonomy*, *democratic* and *law* will never have any uniform meaning and must be tied to an entire system of thought whenever they are used. Even when they are embedded in statute and code, they remain subject to interpretation and possibly to meanings they were never meant to contain. Political life spends much effort in simply coming to grips with what is meant when such terms are deployed as the basis for agreements. Manifestos are therefore highly politicised and subjective statements about the world and require to be deconstructed within the political economy of the time in order for their aspirations and potential future effects to be comprehended.

In order to demonstrate the heterological influences of manifestos on the environmental professions and urban design, we must further deconstruct some of their essential features. Other factors will have to be taken into account, far beyond the mere assembly of historical documents, as in the major sources available to date, namely Jencks and Kropf (1997), Conrads (1970), Caws (2001) and the website http://manifestos.net/titles/. Collectively, these sources contain some 680 manifestos, mostly from the arts and architecture and with some degree of overlap. Even this is only a fragment of what is potentially available. If other fields were to be included, many from the social sciences, politics etc. are conspicuously absent. Although I have already stated that the manifesto is extremely difficult to define, I prefer a much narrower definition of manifesto than that adopted by Caws. Many inclusions in her book are, in the larger scheme of things, of overwhelming insignificance and of such variety that the manifesto becomes indistinguishable from other forms of writing. I prefer to look at the manifesto as a piece of writing the objective of which is in some manner profoundly political in its intentions, despite its focus on art, architecture, urbanisation etc., and bearing in mind Habermas's principle of distorted communication. Hence, I will concentrate, as a matter of choice, on those that possess such qualities.

Language and communication

Language and communication are not only fundamental to the practical day-to-day operation of professions, they are arguably central to any systematic analysis of modern life. Professional activity on a daily basis is conducted using a variety of codified systems – speech, computer software, drawings, sexuality, body language etc. – as means of communication central to the tasks of dealing with clients, negotiating contracts, resolving disputes and conducting discourse between staff, management, consultants and others. Therefore, business operates pragmatically through negotiation at a variety of levels and using a diversity of media, where the concept of *language* reigns supreme in both original and applied forms. However, owing to the process of socialised education, individuals, families, companies and other forms of social organisation communicate using language that is assumed to have standard meanings, and yet, in every case, meanings are applied to words on an individual basis. Around this idea revolve the twin concepts of language and speech as central to the evolution of society and the problems that are generated on the way. To realise its significance to

the manifesto as 'method', we must briefly turn to a few theoretical principles
not previously discussed.

Important to the idea of pragmatics is the concept of language and its role in
the construction of social life. Indeed, it is so significant that Jürgen Habermas,
a major figure in twentieth-century social theory, devoted much of his writing
to the process he called *universal pragmatics* (Habermas 1979). Habermas
played a central role in the development of the critical theory of the Frankfurt
School, which sought a marriage between the ideas of Freud and those of Marx.
Therefore, Habermas offered a major challenge to pre-existing social theory:
Marx, who maintained that all social relations were explainable in terms of
productive forces, and Freud, who argued that the unconscious mind was where
society forged its elementary structures. Habermas maintained that all social
processes, including Freud's unconscious ones, were dependent on language, as
thought and communication between people were impossible without it.
Although he generated a withering critique of Marx and Freud, Habermas
nonetheless remained committed to both methods of understanding society and
saw his own work as a process of synthesis rather than as a rejection of these
other two theorists. His conflict with Marx was over what Habermas considered
to be his circular and self-serving logic, which had come under attack both within
Marxist thought and from other fields:

> The most interesting of these attacks rejects Marx's paradigm of production
> altogether because it remains totally within the context of bourgeois thought
> and practice. From this perspective Marx's 'productivist ideology' and the
> orthodox Marxist idea of history as progress do not challenge the current
> order of exploitation and alienation but rather reinforce it. A truly radical
> theory will conceive of a socialist transformation as a total break with the
> inhuman continuity of history as 'progress', and not as a consummation
> of it. Habermas' project was to identify the processes of universal
> understanding that structure the known world, – *a universal pragmatics.*
>   (Roderick 1986: 152)

Therefore, Habermas tried to displace production, as the foundation of
economy and society, with communication, particularly language and certain
forms of grammar. He maintained that all strategic action and the social processes
involved, conflict, competition, argument and debate – all seeking the level playing
field of understanding – were rendered difficult, frequently impossibly so, by
the inherent capacity of language for distortion. This occurs at all levels of
communication, from the practice of ideology as distorted communication at its
largest compass, to the psychoanalytic process of individual therapy. Habermas
argued that because the adopted method of psychoanalysis (the talking cure) was
welded to speech and was therefore wholly dependent on language, de facto, its
origins must also exist in linguistic distortions and the meanings attached to
them by individuals, a process central to the post-Freudian psychoanalytical
methods adopted by Jacques Lacan. In Lacanian psychoanalysis, the Saussurian

distinctions between *La Langue* (the system of forms that constitutes a language) and *Parole* (the individual's use of language and the meanings attached to it) are maintained, but with the imprimatur that the unconscious 'is the sum of the effects of the parole on a subject' (Turner 1996: 180). Habermas therefore viewed universal pragmatics as the mediation process between self and society, between the world of the instincts and modes of production. For Habermas, therefore, language is the mother-lode of social organisation, defining both the mental and the material aspects of our existence. Despite its capacity for distortion, language shapes both our thoughts and our reality. Language is also assembled into specific discourses, which reflect philosophies, interpretations of history, systems of value and other modes of thought that contour the evolution of social structures. Manifestos therefore constitute a particular form of discursive practice, and although we cannot conflate the terms manifesto and discourse, clearly there is a significant overlap in the terminology.

To the extent that manifestos are statements of a belief in something, they are also synonymous with a certain kind of power and attraction. For Habermas, discourse politicises language as a method of control, persuasion, obligation or demand and locks it into an interlinked network of ideologies that are synonymous with social life. Language as the object of linguistics has specific internal structures that give it a relative autonomy and a system of rules that serve as the medium for discursive practices. Language is therefore a strategic instrument and a method through which beliefs are shaped and manipulated. Therefore, the integration of discourse, language and ideology plays a dominant role in social control. However, the questions as to where power originates, and how it acts, are the source of much debate. These are exemplified by the different positions adopted by Michel Foucault and Michel Pêcheux. Discussing Foucault, Lukes points to what he calls the 'how' of power, namely the triadic relationship between power, rights and truth. Power is delineated by rules (rights), but is also subject to the effects that it transmits based upon a concept of 'truth'. He points out that power cannot be exercised and maintained without the production of specific discourses and their accumulation over time. 'In the end we are judged, condemned, classified, determined in our undertakings, destined to a certain mode of living or dying, as a function of true discourses which are the bearers of the specific effects of power' (Lukes 1986: 230). Foucault's concept of power cannot be detached from its foundation in knowledge, hence his preferred use of the dyad power/knowledge. Nor could it be separated from the methods of subjugation that it initiates. These are simultaneously multivalent, decentred and discontinuous, where the social field 'is constituted by a grid of technologies of power which act upon the body' (Poster 1984: 52). Therefore, Foucault was resistant to concepts of power being derived from a juridical–liberal or a Marxist conception based in class power, one that also rejects a concept of domination deriving from the idea of labour rooted to industrialised production and the factory system. For Foucault, history contained no essential meaning, it was not rooted in subjects and could not be understood in terms of any totalising set of constructs.

On the other hand, in a classic study, *Language Semantics and Ideology* (1982), Michel Pêcheux takes the concept of discourse into the same realm of analysis, but with entirely different premises and conclusions. He suggests that, although the system of language is the same for everyone, people will not hold the same discourse. In contradiction to Foucault, he suggests that every discursive process is inscribed in an ideological class relationship, and he sets out to establish a materialist theory of discourse. As meanings are generated from context, and as this context reflects the class struggle within capitalism, discourses are embedded within, and obtain their meaning from, the particular class, class fraction, institution or other social formation that forms their environment (see also Bernstein 1973, 1977, Atkinson 1985). Pêcheux maintains that language mobilises meanings that support class-centred domination. While meanings clearly suffuse both individual and society, they are embedded in ideologies that constitute discursive practices and reinforce the class system on which capitalism depends. Whereas Marx and Engels viewed language purely as a method of communication, Pêcheux maintained that language allowed both communication and non-communication. As controlling forms of discourse reflect class practices within which endemic conflict between classes is embedded, discourses must embody the contradictions and antagonisms that erase as well as encourage communication. Clearly, Habermas stands at the centre of this overall debate, and the one dimension in common is the power of historical materialism as an intellectual construct against which the battering rams of alternative philosophies are set, frequently with great authority and persuasion. Manifestos variously incorporate an entire array of concepts and ideas that reflect the above considerations – ideology, social class, oppression, conflict, desire – whose embedded meanings require to be deconstructed so that hidden meanings may be accessed. In addition, methods of understanding discourses cannot be boiled down to a single viewpoint, and, in varying degrees, the understanding offered by Marx, Foucault, Freud, Habermas and others forms the grids of practices through which manifestos may be understood.

How language becomes politicised is an important dimension of manifestos, and a few potent observations from Basil Bernstein (1973, 1977), Murray Edelman (1977) and Clark and Dear (1984) are useful. With regard to rhetoric and the text, Bernstein distinguished between *visible* and *invisible* pedagogies. The former reflect a process of explicit and exacting rules, whereas, in the latter, the criteria are assumed: 'The visible pedagogy reflects: explicit hierarchy, explicit sequencing rules, and explicit and specific criteria of assessment. The invisible pedagogy reflects implicit and specific criteria of assessment, implicit sequencing rules and implicit criteria' (Atkinson 1985). Pedagogic discourse can be assembled from a mixture of both elements, and Bernstein further refined this idea by suggesting instructional discourse, which transmits competencies, whereas the latter dictates social order and identity. Edelman focusses on the use of the official language of bureaucracies and professions primarily from the perspective of subjects or subject populations. Through his analysis of language, he strips away the hidden agendas and sheer duplicity of social organisations in general:

In politics as in religion, whatever is ceremonial or banal strengthens reassuring beliefs regardless of their validity, and discourages sceptical enquiry about disturbing issues. From the beginnings of recorded history to the present day, governments have won the support of large numbers of their citizens for policies that were based on delusions: belief in witches, in non-existent internal and external enemies, or in the efficacy of laws to regulate private power, cope with destitution, guarantee civil rights or rehabilitate criminals that have often had the opposite effect from their intended ones. Large numbers of people continue for long periods of time to cling to myth, to justify it in formulas that are repeated in their cultures, and to reject falsifying information when prevailing myths justify their interests, roles and past actions, or assuage their fears.

(Edelman 1977: 3)

Edelman concentrates on the duplicity of language as used by public officials and professional organisations, and the methods they use to capture, maintain and extend their authority. To this extent, he does not examine the language of resistance, but the official languages of persuasion and control. He goes, in some detail, into the linguistic structuring of social problems, professional imperialism and the language of bureaucracy. He is concerned with the idea of so-called *public opinion*, pointing out that there can be no such thing, as there are, as we know, multiple *publics*. The term is only useful to politicians who wish to legitimise their stance through an anonymous audience whose support cannot be disproved. Edelman also refers back to Bernstein's work on several occasions, noting the usefulness of his terminology of formal language categorised by abstraction denoting things, and public language as a method of analysing political language forms denoting processes, the former epitomised in mathematics, the latter in the infamous 'White House Tapes' of Richard Nixon (Edelman 1977: 108). Linguistic structuring also has impacts on the manner in which debates are conducted. In addition to the specific use of particular forms of language, bureaucracies in general, and the state bureaucracy in particular, seek to constrain debate in ways that are conducive to outcomes that they have anticipated in advance, and a great many manifestos are written that, in principle, follow the same rules – if they are up for discussion, it is on the terms of reference of those who are in command. Clark and Dear (1984: 96) suggest that this process is facilitated according to three main principles:

- to control entry to debate, as, if you cannot speak the language, you cannot participate in the process of politics;
- to limit the nature of debate, because, in the absence of certain concepts and categories, political discourse surrounding these concepts is limited or even impossible;
- to condition the judgement of political outcomes, as we tend to view political issues in separate, linguistically segmented ways.

I have stressed here the political dimension of language, for the simple reason that, as a general rule, all manifestos by their very nature are political, whether or not they are actually promoted by governments, the private sector, individuals or groups. They can be in turn persuasive, conflictual, malign, oppressive, uplifting or critical, but they are seldom neutral in intent. Even basic statements of rights carry the expectation and obligation that, overall, people will conform to the principles of the manifesto. I have already discussed the *flâneur* as both symbol and icon, embodying a constellation of socio-spatial problems, from gender and social class to the configuration of, and access to, the public realm. The manifesto serves a similar function, in that it encapsulates an array of politicised social contexts expressed in discourse, many of which have relevance to culture and space and, thence, represent a necessary part of the designer's understanding of the dynamics of those social movements. Having indicated some of the undercurrents structuring the operation of the manifesto, I now turn to concrete examples of manifestos noted for their impact on society in general and urban development in particular.

Origins

Although constitutions *qua* manifestos would seem far from the practice of urban design, they are heterological to its very existence. In *The Form of Cities*, I suggested that the theoretical object of urban design was civil society and its real object was the public realm. Hence, the actual constitution of a physical public realm is central to the political constitution of societies and is at the core of urban design practice. Where otherwise does the citizen actually have a right to exist as a public? Despite this clear requirement, there is almost no institutional context for the delineated material existence of a public realm in any of the great manifestos from which nations arose. In most cases, the physical public realm is assumed as the reflection of certain other human rights, such as *liberté*, *égalité* and *fraternité*, but is not delineated. Presumably, brotherhood and sisterhood must have space to occur, and de facto, a public realm must exist in some form. Here, the concept of the state is problematic. In communist societies as the state is, in theory, owned by the people, the public realm coincides with national boundaries. In capitalist societies, based on class divisions, no such simple assumption can be made, as indeed they can no longer be made in previously socialist societies today. As a public realm is assumed rather than delineated, the role of the state is critical, as it has varying degrees of support for, and influence over, the private sector and labour power. Here, the public realm is negotiated rather than assumed as a right. Given the rise of state neocorporatism in contemporary society, this process of negotiation is problematic, owing to the embeddedness of private-sector influence in state policy formation and the barrier to accumulation that public space represents. What follows are a few examples of manifestos adopted in the establishment of nations, along with some of the limitations they maintain.

One undeniable origin for manifestos in the Western world was Magna Carta (1215), otherwise known as *The Great Charter of Freedoms*. As it went through several revisions in the thirteenth century, it is the 1297 version that is legally deployed in England and Wales. Magna Carta established the principle of *habeas corpus* and the concept of due process of law. Most importantly, it initiated the constitution of the commons, and its lesser-known companion, *The Charter of the Forest*, established for the first time the subsistence rights of the poor. Magna Carta can be interpreted two ways: first, that rights were given by the king and granted to the common people, but second, in fact, it was about the people claiming their rights as citizens, a process of 'commoning' or collective action in feudal society (Linebaugh 2008). As such, it represented a pinnacle of achievement in the establishment of what would later be referred to as 'democracy'. The principle of the commons implied rights over land that was not collectively owned, and the term 'common' was a concept close to the idea of 'use value', for example the right of access to land or to use it for grazing animals in the absence of ownership. However, the concept of the commons stemming from Magna Carta has gradually been expanded over the last 700 years to contain the idea of a regime of common property, particularly land as common property, held by the state in perpetuity for the people. At the time Magna Carta was written, it only applied to England and Wales, and did not extend to Scotland or Ireland, which had their own forms of common land, despite similarities between them. The gradual loss of these rights accelerated post-1945, when,

> After the Second World War, most lowland commons became neglected because commoners, who could find better paid work in other sectors of the economy, largely stopped exercising their rights. When open habitats are no longer grazed, they start to develop scrub and then dense woodland, losing the grassy or heathland vegetation which may have occupied the land continuously for many centuries.
>
> (http//en.wikipedia.org/wiki/Commons)

A reading of the website is extremely enlightening as to the specific types of rights people had prior to the seventeenth century in comparison with their rights today. Our current use of the word 'public', as in *public space*, the *public realm*, are in fact adaptations of the term 'common', stemming from Magna Carta some seven centuries ago.

Since America was not yet discovered when Magna Carta was written, three other great manifestos or charters of freedom evolved in the United States: Thomas Jefferson's *Declaration of Independence* from Britain of the thirteen 'United States' (1776); the *Constitution of the United States*; and the *Bill of Rights*, all of which act together as statements of what citizens may expect in terms of rights as well as obligations. Jefferson's statement contains the historic lines, 'We hold these truths to be self evident, that all men are created equal, that they are endowed by their Creator with certain unalienable Rights, that among these are Life, Liberty and the pursuit of Happiness.' The declaration also allows for social revolution, so that, for the people in the face of absolute despotism, 'it is their right, it is their duty, to throw off such a government and to provide new guards for their future security'. Indeed, the *Declaration of Independence* had as its central target and cause that, 'The history of the present King of Great Britain is a history of repeated injuries and usurpations, all having in direct object the establishment of an absolute tyranny over these states'. Eleven years after the *Declaration of Independence* was made, the *Constitution of the United States* was established in 1787. Amendments 11–27 to the Constitution are known as the *Bill of Rights*, formed in 1789 and implemented in 1791. Paradoxically, the American *Bill of Rights* was influenced by the English *Bill of Rights* of 1689, rights emanating from the country they now sought to overthrow. Despite the care taken in the drafting of these three manifestos forming the American Constitution, it is clear that the lofty principles it contained were hard to implement, with much disagreement on content and interpretation. For example, certain fundamental disagreements between northern and southern states remained over the Constitution, where slavery had been the order of the day since 1619, resulting in the American Civil War of 1861–5. More up to date, the Second Amendment – 'the right of the people to keep and bear arms' – now means that, out of every 100 citizens, 90 own guns, making it the most heavily armed citizenry on the planet. Similarly, the Fifth Amendment allows a witness to refuse to testify against accusations of crime, as he shall not be compelled to be a 'witness against himself', but, significantly for our purposes, also states that 'nor shall private property be taken for public use without just compensation'. Not only was the *Constitution of the United States* built in reference to English law, where the commons was implicit, but many subjects of the New World Constitution were there because they had been forced off the land in England. However, unlike Magna Carta, the *Constitution of the United States* contains no legal protection for the commons, despite the fact that 'public space' remains a general form of expression. Clearly, manifestos, even at the highest level, are subject to significant operational difficulties. Although rights may exist, acquiring them remains problematic.

On the other side of the political spectrum, one of the most controversial polemics ever written was Marx and Engels' *Manifesto of the Communist Party* (1999, orig. 1848), for it threatened the entire edifice of capitalist production, and with good reason. Given the context of the industrial revolution in Britain and the appalling human misery it generated, Marx and Engels' manifesto was a necessary expression of the outrage they felt at what was clearly an iniquitous institution based on violence and human misery. The logic of the argument was clear and compelling, and the urge to social revolution was difficult to resist. It is indeed one of the masterpieces in the history of manifestos, unfortunately debased *in extremis* by those societies that have purported to implement its mandate. To place the *Manifesto of the Communist Party* in context, a few quotations regarding *The Condition of the Working Class in England* (1973 (orig. 1892)) from Engels' text of the same name may suffice, particularly concerning 'Northern England (referred to as Scotland by the locals)'. Part of the cause of the abject decay of the built environment in Edinburgh and Glasgow was the higher densities resulting from deployment of tenement housing of up to seven storeys, whereas, in England, individual housing tended to be the norm; as a result:

> The poor in Scotland, especially in Edinburgh and Glasgow, are worse off than any other region in the three Kingdoms.
>
> The wynds of Glasgow contain a fluctuating population of fifteen to thirty thousand human beings. This quarter consists wholly of narrow alleys and square courts, in the middle of every one there lies a dung heap . . . in some of the sleeping places we found a complete layer of human beings stretched upon the floor, often fifteen to twenty, some clad, others naked, men and women indiscriminately . . . No one seemed to take the trouble to cleanse this Augean stable, this Pandemonium, this tangle of crime, filth and pestilence.

and in Edinburgh:

> On the bed posts chickens roost at night, dogs and horses share the dwellings of human beings, and the natural consequence is a shocking stench, with filth and swarms of vermin . . .
>
> In this part of the city there are neither sewers or other drains, nor even privies belonging to the households. In consequence, all refuse, garbage and excrements of at least fifty thousand persons are thrown into the gutters every night, so that in spite of all street sweeping, a mass of dried filth and foul vapours are created.
>
> (Engels 1973: 68–9)

It is therefore unsurprising that, having found themselves in the middle of the most appalling exploitation and human misery caused by a bourgeoisie whose sole interest was profit, they sought an alternative form of social order. Central to the entire manifesto were the following principles:

1 Abolition of property in land and the application of all land rents to public purposes.
2 A heavy progressive or graduated income tax.
3 Abolition of all rights of inheritance.
4 Confiscation of the property of all emigrants and rebels.
5 Centralisation of credit in the hands of the state, by means of a national bank with state capital and an exclusive monopoly.
6 Centralisation of the means of communication and transport in the hands of the state.

7   Extension of factories and instruments of production owned by the state; the bringing into cultivation of waste-lands, and the improvement of the soil generally in accordance with a common plan.
8   Equal liability of all to work. Establishment of industrial armies, especially for agriculture.
9   Combination of agriculture with manufacturing industries; gradual abolition of all distinction between town and country by a more equable distribution of the populace over the country.
10 Free education of all children in public schools. Abolition of children's factory labour in its present form. Combination of education with industrial production etc.

This document provided the inspiration for many other manifestos, such as the *Manifesto of the Communist International to the Workers of the World* (Leon Trotsky 1919), the *Manifesto of the Chinese People's Liberation Army* (Mao Tse Tung 1947), and some much lesser-known manifestos, such as the *Manifesto of Libertarian Communism* (George Fontenis 1953), the *Declaration to the Citizens of Russia* (Vladimir Lenin 1917), and more individual offerings such as *The Society of the Spectacle* (Guy Debord (1983 (orig. 1967)), not to mention Labour Party manifestos (UK) over the last century. In Russia, the revolution of 1905 resulted in two key manifestos, the *October Manifesto* (1905) and the first *Russian Constitution* (1906). While promising freedom of religion, speech, association and assembly, absolute power still rested in Tsar Nicholas II, and it was not until the Second Revolution, usually referred to as the *October Revolution* that Lenin's plans for socialist reconstruction came to the fore. These were short lived, as the civil war followed, ending in the establishment of the Soviet Union in 1922, when Leninism was revived under the rule of Joseph Stalin, one of history's great mass murderers. In modern history, the influence of Marxist-Leninism has been enormous, the tragedy being the vast distance between the theory of socialist democracy and the reality of its application by tyrants and dictators. Nonetheless, the overall impact has been immense, and, as we shall see below, several significant movements in twentieth-century art, architecture and urbanism, for example the Bauhaus, the establishment of The Royal Town Planning Institute, the City Beautiful movement, and the New Towns movement, were influenced by socialist principles, and, in the case of the Bauhaus, by the communism of the Soviets.

These preceding manifestos, all of which sought in their own way to move society forward, remained rooted in nationalist sentiment, despite the expressed universality of, for example, the *Communist Manifesto*. It was not until 1948 that the *United Nations Charter* (UNC) was established, and that a *Universal Declaration of Human Rights* (UDHR) was adopted by the United Nations after the horrors of the Second World War. The overall intention was to have a declaration by all member states to agree implicitly to common principles of justice and government. The sixtieth anniversary of the agreement was held in 2008. The third part in the establishment of the United Nations was the creation of the *International Bill of Human Rights*, which contained two legally binding covenants that came into effect in 1966. It is clear, however, that huge ideological barriers exist at the highest level, and there exists a separate *Universal Islamic Declaration of Human Rights*, established in 1980 to celebrate the commencement of the fifteenth century of the Islamic era and signed by fifty-four Muslim countries. Unlike the Islamic version, the *UDHR* itself has no signatories and is not binding under international law. The main principles of the *UDHR* are:

- the right to life, liberty and security of person;
- the right to education;
- the right to participate fully in cultural life;
- freedom from torture or cruel, inhumane treatment;
- freedom of thought, conscience and religion.

Urbanism and the manifesto

Manifestos in art, culture and urbanism come in an immense range of forms and substance, and it is impossible to do justice to even a fragment of these. A few examples in the realm of culture indicate this complexity – *The Black Woman's Manifesto* (La Rue 1970); *The Street is their Home: The Hobo's Manifesto* (Ward 1979); *A Green Manifesto* (Irvine and Ponton 1988), *Reflective Teaching in the Postmodern World: A Manifesto for Education in Postmodernity* (Parker 1997); *The Politics of Subversion: A Manifesto for the Twenty-First Century* (Negri 1989); *The Sustainable Cities Manifesto* (Yanarella and Levine 1992); *Delirious New York: A Retroactive Manifesto for Manhattan* (Koolhaas 1994), *Manifesto for the Earth* (Gorbachev 2006); *Get to Work: A Manifesto for Women of the World* (Hirshman 2006); *The Atheist Manifesto* (Onfray 2005); *Fans of the World Unite: A (Capitalist) Manifesto for Sports Consumers* (Szemanski 2008); and also *An Anti-capitalist Manifesto* (Callinicos 2003). Race, homelessness, education, politics, sustainability, religion, sport, anticapitalism and other facets of modern culture are all represented. However, there has never been an equivalent period to that of 'the great manifesto moment' in art from 1909 to 1919, which Mary Ann Caws refers to as 'a ten year period of glorious madness', including manifestos beginning with Marinetti's Futurism, through Cubism, Collage, Rayonism, Suprematism, Vorticism, Imagism, Dadaism, Surrealism and De Stijl (Caws 2001: xxii). More recently, architecture itself has seen several book-length manifestos published (Allen 2003, Betsky and Adigard 2000). While we are concerned with the design of cities, great movements in art seem to parallel and accompany social change more immediately than architecture and urban design. In addition, they would appear to be even more deeply politicised, strident and engaged than those written by architects. The reason for this is possibly as simple as it appears, that the practice of architecture is ideologically compromised owing to its connections to the state and the private sector, which fund most projects. In addition, once expressed, a movement in painting and other art forms does not possess the same time inertia as changes to the urban fabric. The process is, however, more integrated than this might suggest, given the interrelationship between art and architecture, one that is both complex and enduring, as demonstrated for example in Constructivism, De Stijl and the Bauhaus (FOC3: 60–3). I will use these three examples to express the complex interrelationship between art, culture and political change, leaving their implications for architecture and the built environment for the following section. Important here is the inclusion of De Stijl. Despite the fact that it influenced, and was influenced by, Constructivism and the Bauhaus, it is significant for its total exclusion of any kind of social agenda whatsoever, a paradox that, on the one hand, it was influential in the development of modern art, and, on the other, that it was dispossessed of any social conscience. To this extent, it remains suspended on a tightrope between the two pillars of Russian Suprematism and Constructivism and that of the Bauhaus.

The manifesto: 1900–45

The professionalisation of architecture began in the UK when it was awarded a Royal Charter in 1837. It was first named the Royal Institute of British Architects in London, later dropping the London reference in 1892. What we must bear in mind, therefore, when we investigate manifestos in architecture, urban design, urban planning, and landscape architecture is that, historically, all four disciplines have in the past been subsumed under the term 'architecture' and have arguably emerged from it. This continued throughout the nineteenth and twentieth centuries. Even after the inception of the Royal Town Planning Institute in 1914, it was still dominated by architects, and this remained so until the early 1970s, when 'town planning', as it was still called, was rapidly taken over by the social sciences in response to the massive failure of modern architecture to understand urbanisation beyond its actual physical presence. Architecture had by then colonised urban design and urban planning for one and a half centuries. Some of the problems this created are readily apparent in many of the manifestos to be discussed below.

Previous reference lists of manifestos all suffer from the same problem, in that they are listed chronologically, with no further distinctions or organisation in accordance with any typological system, e.g. in terms of responses to politics, technology, aesthetics, culture etc. Ulrich Conrads covers the period from 1903 to 1963. Overall, the twentieth century is full of significant detail, and it is interesting to note that roughly the first half of the century is distinguished by manifestos that issue from collective protest and commentary. The second half reverts to the cult of the individual architect, and there are no collective statements included, a clear indication of the anarchy of postmodernity. Jencks and Kropf justify the lack of any solidarity or concrete response to specified climacteric social developments by suggesting that a somewhat mystical *Zeitgeist* was inherent in the manifestos, revealing 'an impending sense of crisis' and 'the feeling of imminent catastrophe' (Jencks and Kropf 1997: 12).

Beginning with the *fin de siècle* period, there were more material considerations to be made, with populations in Europe crawling out of one of the darkest ages in the history of environmental squalor and degradation. In this context, two great movements emerged, the first being that of the Garden City, the second of the Arts and Crafts movement, both originating in the latter quarter of the nineteenth century, with reverberations into the present. The expanding wasteland of the industrial revolution noted above was being met with diverse forms of resistance, from feminism to philanthropic capitalism. It also spawned one of the most significant influences for urban design in the twentieth century, namely the Garden City movement, promoted by Ebeneezer Howard. His manifesto, *Tomorrow: A Peaceful Path to Real Reform* (1898) was renamed and published as *Garden Cities of Tomorrow* (1902), initiating a concept that would reverberate throughout the twentieth century. Beginning with the first new town at Letchworth (1904), outside London, he later founded Welwyn Garden City (1920), where he lived until his death in 1928. His influence continued through the Second World War reconstruction of London with the New Towns movement, finally morphing into the New Urbanism and the gated communities of today. Importantly, Howard's agenda was not merely to improve general health and welfare, it was also politically motivated to decentralise power, in line with his beliefs as a Utopian Socialist.

The late nineteenth century also gave rise to the Arts and Crafts movement in England, whose main proponents were John Ruskin (a writer) and William Morris (a writer and designer, as well as a Marxist and revolutionary socialist, and a leading figure in the anti-war movement). Both proposed a renewed respect for traditional arts and crafts as a method of combating the alienation of the worker from the objects of his/her labour and of counteracting the alienation associated with mass production. Morris's manifesto was called *To the Working Men of England*, a diatribe significantly influenced by Marx. In addition to arts and crafts, the movement also permeated architecture and soon extended to North America and the rest of Europe, influencing architects such as Edward Lutyens, Frank Lloyd Wright and Charles Rennie Mackintosh, and movements such as the Vienna Secession, De Stijl and Art Nouveau. However, the influence of the Arts and Crafts movement on architectural and urban design was nowhere more strongly felt than in Germany.

The Bauhaus

The inheritance of William Morris expressed itself in the Deutscher Werkbund (1906), whose key exponents were Henry van de Velde and Herman Muthesius, the latter being in charge of design education for the German government. In 1911, he wrote the first manifesto of the Werkbund, in which he railed against the poverty of architectural expression as an indication of the hopelessness of prevailing artistic culture. Muthesius saw in mass production the promise of a standardisation of good taste to combat prevailing anarchy. Whereas van de Velde held on to his belief that a return to the medieval forms of building and designing through craft-based skills was necessary, Muthesius realised that the way forward had to be through mass production, a conflict that would later repeat itself in the Bauhaus. The first manifesto of the Staatliches Bauhaus in Weimar (1919–24) was written by its founding director, Walter Gropius, and its first line was 'The complete building is the final aim of the visual arts!', a comment that needs no reprise. At that time, Gropius remained committed to craft training, despite his inclusion of courses for apprentices, journeymen and junior masters and the overall orientation of the Bauhaus to mass production. It was influenced in no small part by Expressionism, Cubism and other contemporary art movements. For political reasons, the Bauhaus moved to Dessau in 1925. Hannes Meyer took over the directorship from Gropius in 1928. Meyer was committed to Marxist socialism, continuing a tradition started by Gropius and ending with Mies van der Rohe, after Meyer was himself replaced (see FOC: 60–3). In addition to Futurism and De Stijl described above, a marked influence on the Bauhaus (established 1919–33) arose in the form of the Russian State School of Art and Technics, called Vkhutemas, originating one year later in 1920. Vkhutemas accommodated three major vectors in modern architecture, namely Constructivism, Rationalism and Suprematism; several iconic figures in modern architecture taught at Vkhutemas, including El Lissitsky, Kazimir Malevitch and Vladimir Tatlin. As a result, apart from the political influence of Bolshevism on the founding fathers of the Bauhaus, it was also heavily affected by the art and architecture of a new society in the making. The defeat of Germany in the First World War, the liberalism established by the Weimar Republic and modernist culture were at the root of the Bauhaus success.

Constructivism

Constructivism originated in Russia around 1913 with the Russian artist Vladimir Tatlin, half way between the two Russian revolutions. There still remained a modicum of free artistic expression, and, since then, the movement has been influential in architecture and urban design up until the present. Apparent from its name, constructivism refers to the interrelated ideas of machine technology, structure and social development. Its adopted method was the politicisation of art, directed towards social and economic change as its primary object. Tatlin's Russian Constructivism grew out of Russian Futurism, which in turn was influenced by, and overlapped with, Futurism in Italy. Marinetti wrote *The Futurist Manifesto* in 1909, attacking Neo-classicism as 'that idiotic flowering of stupidity and impotence' and declared that he despised:

1 all the pseudo-architecture of the avant-garde, Austrian, Hungarian, German and American;
2 all classical architecture, solemn, hieratic, scenographic, decorative, monumental, pretty and pleasing;
3 the embalming, reconstruction and reproduction of ancient monuments and palaces;
4 perpendicular and horizontal lines, cubical and pyramidical forms that are static, solemn, aggressive and absolutely excluded from our utterly new sensibility; and
5 the use of massive, voluminous, durable, antiquated and costly materials.

(www.unknown.nu/futurism/architecture.html)

However, Russia also adopted its own brand of Futurism more appropriate to the social demands of the post-1917 regime. Like Constructivism, Futurism in Italy was focussed on socio-technical traits – construction, technology, flight, speed and industrialisation, but without the constraints imposed by the rigid ideology of the Soviets. The difference between the two movements is well expressed on the one hand in Umberto Boccioni's sculpture *Unique Forms of Continuity in Space* (Figure 10.1) and Tatlin's Tower (Figure 10.2), or in the futurist architecture of Antonio Sant'Elia (Figure 10.3) and that of Kasimir Malevitch, whose art is usually classified as *Suprematism*. Other artists of the same orientation include Alexander Rodchenko and El Lissitsky, as well as Naum Gabo and Antoine Pevsner, who wrote their own *Realistic Manifesto* of 1920. This movement was later sanctioned by Stalin as bourgeois, as he considered that it was insufficiently aligned with the promotion of the proletariat, resulting in its condemnation in 1935 for its supposedly reactionary leanings. However, the clear orientation of constructivism, with its inherent need to connect art with collective social life, is transparent in the fifth and sixth theses of his manifesto:

Art, always being connected with life at the moment of change in the political system (change of the Collective-consumer) and being cut off from the collective in the person of the artist, goes through an acute revolution. A revolution that strengthens the impulse of invention.

Invention is always the working out of impulses of the collective and not the individual.

(Caws 2001: 401)

While its intentions were socially focussed and its intentions genuine, a chasm existed between constructivist architecture and urbanism and their application to any social purposes (Collins 1998). Hence, the year 1935 marked a symbolic end to their development in Russia, arguably from then into the twenty-first century. Around the same time, another significant influence on art and architecture appeared in Holland, by the name of De Stijl.

Figure 10.1 Umberto Boccioni: *Unique Forms of Continuity in Space*, 1913
Source: The Metropolitan Museum of Art/Art Resource/Scala, Florence

De Stijl

The De Stijl movement originated in Leyden in the Netherlands in 1918, under
the leadership of Theo Van Doesburg, and owed its rise in no small part to Dutch
politics, as the Netherlands had remained neutral in the period 1914–18, and it
was able to continue its traditions undisturbed by the horrors of the First World
War. In contrast to other manifestos of the time, De Stijl had no social agenda
and remained a somewhat isolated and introverted aesthetic ideology, whose
central figures were a cabinetmaker by the name of Gerrit Rietveld (Figure 10.4),
the designer and critic Theo Van Doesburg and the painter Piet Mondrian. From

Figure 10.2 Tower designed by Vladimir Tatlin to commemorate the Third
         International of the Communist Party (1919). It was planned to be 400
         metres tall and designed in the constructivist style. It was never built

Source: Moderna Museet, Stockholm

Figure 10.3 Italian futurist Antonio Sant'Elia: *Vision for a New City*
Source: Private Collection/Bridgeman Art Library

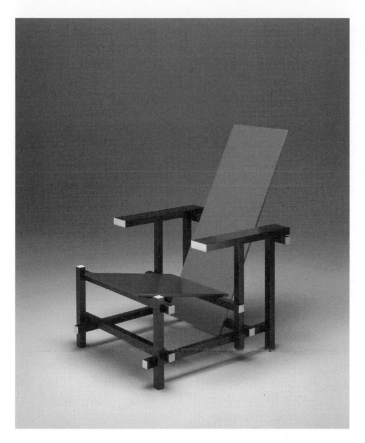

Figure 10.4
The spirit of De Stijl:
the Red–Blue chair, by
Gerrit Rietveld, 1923

Source: DeAgostini
Picture Library/Scala,
Florence

Van Doesburg's own manifesto, *Towards a Plastic Architecture* (1924), it is easy to see the the impact he had on the Bauhaus, which was sympathetic to his aesthetic. Van Doesburg and Mondrian wrote several manifestos of their own, but the collective manifesto of De Stijl was promoted in 1918. Van Doesburg's manifesto focussed totally on the actual building itself and its properties – elemental, economic, functional, formless, open, anti-cubic were some of the adjectives used to generate architecture within which 'Euclidean mathematics will be of no further use' (Conrads 1970: 78). Piet Mondrian was concerned with what De Stijl called neoplasticism in painting, where his concerns focussed on the alienation of man from nature, the universal basis for aesthetic emotion and the idea of art as a purely 'plastic' form of expression. Hence, despite the fact that De Stijl did not have social development as a significant concern, it was otherwise engaged in relating art to the growth of consciousness.

During the last few years of the Bauhaus and the decline of De Stijl and Russian constructivism, a historic moment was struck in 1928, when a group of architects (including Meyer) assembled in Switzerland to discuss the collective ideas of Le Corbusier (a practising architect) and Sigfried Giedion, a major historian and author of the iconic text *Space, Time and Architecture* (1941).

Given his prolific output, Le Corbusier constituted a movement all by himself and had already written a major essay on *Urbanisme* (town planning) in 1925. Nonetheless, the meeting founded one of the most important architectural events of the twentieth century, namely CIAM – *Congrès Internationaux d'Architecture Moderne* – an organisation that was to set the international stage for some of the most important debates about architecture and urbanism in the twentieth century. Nothing quite like it has happened since: 'It remained for over thirty years the medium of a world-wide interchange of ideas. It was the CIAM Congresses which brought the objectives of "town planning" into perspective' (Conrads 1970: 109). The manifesto produced from this original CIAM conference was called 'The Saraz declaration', which was indeed groundbreaking in three main ways. First, it was international, indeed *global* in its reach, responding to the social conditions of an era in an attempt to bring about an awareness of architecture and urbanism in the first machine age. Second, it brought architecture out of the realm of personal taste and aesthetic monopolies into the realm of production, where the declaration was divided into four key divisions: the general economic system; town planning; architecture and public opinion; and architecture and its relations to the state. Third, it was *anti* the academy and *pro* statism – 'Modern architects having the firm intention of working according to the new principles can only regard the official academies and their methods tending towards aestheticism and formalism as institutions standing in the very way of progress' (Conrads 1970: 112). Altogether, eleven CIAM conferences were held across European countries, the last being held in Otterlo in Holland to disband the organisation. The most famous of these assemblies was held in 1933, in Italy, and had as its main topic the idea of *the functional city*, later included in a copy, heavily edited by Le Corbusier, of what came to be known as 'The Charter of Athens' (1942). This was the first time in modern history that an international agreement had been reached on the planning and building of so-called rational cities, a process that would be in some demand with the end of the Second World War, three years later.

The manifesto: post-1945

Heterologies prior to the Second World War can therefore be characterised by certainty of the future, of great hope, possibility, social conscience, and the strident polemic of movements, institutions and collective action; they are driven by a large dose of revolutionary socialist ideology in a variety of forms. The post-war period has had very different leanings. The inheritance of two world wars (one nuclear), a period of rapid population expansion and the growth of cities, massive social and political upheaval, globalisation and the diffuse effects of the Internet have all affected the manifestos of the late twentieth century. What was immediately striking about the pre-Second World War period in architecture/urbanism, however, was a general trend for individuals and firms to speak on behalf of a movement, as spokesperson. In the latter part of the twentieth century, individuals tended to speak for themselves, and my own preference is for the integration of social ideals and the manifestos that issued in the former, an altogether more politically engaged approach to urbanism than what followed. After the war, there was never any equivalent of the Werkbund, De Stijl, Bauhaus, Vkhutemas or CIAM, and the very nature of postmodernity after 1975 seemed to revel in its own dissonance. Even the categories proposed by Jencks and Kropf are blistered with inconsistency, as well as those relating to individual architects, some of whom could arguably appear in several of them at the same time (Christopher Alexander, Peter Eisenman, John Hedjuk etc.). Only at the end of the century did a major movement come into being in the shape of the New Urbanism, with a charter ratified by its members in 1996, arguably in response to crises, like so many other manifestos (see Figure 10.5). This time, the crises were perceived as the erosion of community and the need for sustainable building practices at all levels, from planning to construction.

Introduction to the charter of the New Urbanism

The Congress for the New Urbanism views disinvestment in central cities, the spread of placeless sprawl, increasing separation by race and income, environmental deterioration, loss of agricultural lands and wilderness, and the erosion of society's built heritage as one interrelated community-building challenge.

We stand for the restoration of existing urban centers and towns within coherent metropolitan regions, the reconfiguration of sprawling suburbs into communities of real neighborhoods and diverse districts, the conservation of natural environments, and the preservation of our built legacy.

We recognize that physical solutions by themselves will not solve social and economic problems, but neither can economic vitality, community stability, and environmental health be sustained without a coherent and supportive physical framework.

We advocate the restructuring of public policy and development practices to support the following principles: neighborhoods should be diverse in use and population; communities should be designed for the pedestrian and transit as well as the car; cities and towns should be shaped by physically defined and universally accessible public spaces and community institutions; urban places should be framed by architecture and landscape design that celebrate local history, climate, ecology, and building practice.

We represent a broad-based citizenry, composed of public and private sector leaders, community activists, and multidisciplinary professional. We are committed to reestablishing the relationship between the art of building and the making of community, through citizen-based participatory planning and design.

We dedicate ourselves to reclaiming our homes, blocks, streets, parks, neighborhoods, districts, towns, cities, regions, and environment.

We assert the following principles to guide public policy, development pratice, urban planning, and design: ...

Figure 10.5 Introduction to the charter of the New Urbanism
Source: The Congress of New Urbanism

In their book *Theories and Manifestos of Contemporary Architecture*, Charles Jencks and Karl Kropf propose five major typologies, namely: post-modern; post-modern ecology; traditional; late modern and new modern (Jencks and Kropf 1997: Contents). Briefly stated, *traditional architecture* uses classical forms and vernacular methods of building to recreate the past as a desirable context for the present. In some ways, the style was overtly political, in that the alienation of labour using modern construction methods and materials was reversed. A return to craft-based building re-emancipated workers, giving them back the objects of their labour and pride in their work. This genre is adopted by, for example, Christopher Alexander, Leon Krier, Quinlan Terry and the Prince of Wales. Terry's office specialises in high-quality, traditional building, continuing a tradition begun by Raymond Erith in 1928. *Late modern architecture* takes the technical aspects of modernism into new realms of extravagance and expression, characterised by architects such as Archigram, Alison and Peter Smithson, and Peter Eisenman. *New modern architecture* 'is deconstructive of modern forms and ideas, hermetic in coding, often fragmented and dissonant in form, self-contradictory by intention, anti-humanist and spatially explosive' (Jenks and Kropf 1997: 10). *Post-modern architecture* is a truly hybrid form that borrows indiscriminately across the previous three forms and pieces them together to convey meanings that would otherwise remain hidden. It builds meanings rather than traditions, as exemplified by, for example, Bernard Tschumi, Zaha Hadid and Tom Mayne of Morphosis. *Post-modern ecology* once again begins prior to its own definition, with Ian McHarg and his seminal book *Design with Nature*, and is focussed primarily on the marriage of ecological and sustainable principles with postmodern forms of expression. To a degree, this is the realm of landscape architects such as McHarg and Anne Whiston Spirn, but individuals such as Ken Yeang are opening up new possibilities in the new high-rise 'bioclimatic architecture'.

The authors denote these, not as evolutionary periods (diachronic), but as distinct types that have frequently overlapped in the post-war period. Curiously, given that Charles Jencks is a co-editor and the person who actually invented the term *postmodern*, they include manifestos from an entire range of architects, beginning in 1955 with James Stirling, seventeen years before postmodernism was canonised by Jencks himself in 1972. The title of the book also raises the issue of whether a theory is a manifesto or vice versa, and there is no easy answer to this. It is, however, worth considering that a theory may become a manifesto, depending on the extent to which it attempts to politicise its possibilities, for example in exhorting others to join a movement of some kind. A manifesto is seldom a theory, although theory will presumably inform the best manifestos.

The immediate post-war period in Europe was, of course, focussed on rectifying the destruction of its major cities, with London, Coventry, Birmingham and others demanding serious rebuilding. It was not until ten years after the war's end, however, that the first manifestos emerged to protest the remaining detritus as well as the inheritance of decaying landscapes from the industrial revolution. These came in the form of two special issues of *The Architectural*

Review, named *Outrage* and *Counter Attack* (1956), manifestos that initiated a public campaign to rectify the urban landscape, their titles indicative of the polemic inside. Modernist urbanism was in serious strife and was attacked 'from the outside' by several notable figures who were not architects by training. Kevin Lynch, a planner who had trained with Frank Lloyd Wright at one point, made significant advances on the emotional polemic of *Outrage* and *Counter Attack* (Nairn 1955, 1956), with his text *The Image of the City* (1960). Jane Jacobs, who had no professional education, wrote one of the most memorable books of twentieth-century urbanism, *The Death and Life of Great American Cities* (1961). Christopher Alexander, whose article 'A city is not a tree' (1965) was revolutionary in its impact, first trained as a mathematician. Although it would be wrong to describe these texts as manifestos, nonetheless they remained as *stellae* in the wreckage of modernist urbanism, in both theory and practice. They had similar effects in shifting awareness of architectural and urban design away from form and back to society. Indeed, it was Jencks himself who said, in his denotation of postmodern architecture:

> No doubt modern architecture has ended as a serious body of theory – no one believes in it after twenty years of sustained attack – but it continues, for want of an alternative, as actual practice. The only way to kill off the monster is to find a substitute beast to take its place and decidedly 'Post-Modern' won't do the job. We need a new way of thinking, a new paradigm based on broad theory, which enjoys a large consensus.
>
> (Jencks and Kropf 1997: 6)

The 1970s was the period where postmodernity originated, was named and developed into a significant movement. Despite its importance to twentieth-century architecture, a manifest approach to postmodern architecture and urban design was a rare occurrence, with the exception of personal testaments by individual architects. Among the best known are Venturi, Brown and Izenour in *Learning from Las Vegas* (1972); Jencks's *The Language of Postmodern Architecture* (1977); Rowe and Koetter's *Collage City*; Rob Krier's *Urban Space* (1975); and Manfredo Tafuri's *Architecture and Utopia* (1976), although this may do a disservice to much of the fine writing of the period, for example, that of Aldo Rossi, Leon Krier, Joseph Rykwert, Giancarlo de Carlo and others. Of these, I would single out the titles of Manfredo Tafuri, and Rowe and Koetter as coming closest to my definition of a manifesto. Both launch a serious attack on the social place of architecture. The one movement that does stand out from this period, through the 1970s, is that of the *Archives d'Architecture Moderne* (AAM), by a group of European architects (Krier 1978). Their interests were collectively expressed in a document called the Brussels Declaration, of 1978, the key promoters of which were Maurice Culot and Leon Krier, whose manifesto is best expressed as follows:

> [We] denounce functionalist architecture and urbanism because it has destroyed the European city in response to the exigencies of public and

private capitalist industrial purposes; equally [we] denounce the compliance
of architects and their professional organisations in accepting the conditions
of production, an attitude that has substantially contributed towards the
state of things; [we] consider that the only possible way towards the
reconstruction of the European city is the development of a labour force
with improved professional qualities and the rejection of industrial methods
developed solely for the profit of their promoters.

(Jenks and Kropf 1996: 177)

The Brussels Declaration constituted a collective anti-modern manifesto,
seeking a return to the traditional European city. The two key publications that
expanded the basic manifesto of the group were *Rational Architecture* (1978)
and *The Reconstruction of the City* (1975). As a return to European urban
traditions was being promoted at the beginning of the 1980s, in the United States
a new manifesto was taking shape, calling for a return to small town USA, in
the form of Seaside in Florida in 1982 (Katz 1994). Seaside provided the model
for a certain kind of Utopia, based on traditional architecture and patterns of
living, but to a degree it also reflected what Kenneth Frampton was to call 'a
critical regionalism', in his own manifesto of 1983. Shortly after Seaside was
built, an urban design manifesto was proposed by two senior academics in the
United States, namely Allan Jacobs and Donald Appleyard. This manifesto was
written as a reaction to the New Towns and Garden City movements in the
United Kingdom, as well as the Charter of Athens and the CIAM of Europe. In
contrast to the highly politicised documents issued by European scholars, Jacobs'
and Appleyard's manifesto is a singularly unfocussed document, though
incredibly well intentioned. It wanders along, uninformed by theory, a weak-
kneed piece of liberal thought filled with platitudes and disconnected from any
social causes. Hence, a clutch of 'problems for modern urban design' begins with
poor living environments, gigantism and loss of control, large-scale privatisation
and loss of public life; it then traverses 'centrifugal fragmentation', ending in
placelessness and rootless professionalism, where 'Supported by semiology and
other abstract themes, much of architecture has become a dilettantish and
narcissistic pursuit', and where 'The planning profession's retreat into trendism
under the positivist influence of social science has left it unable to resist the
pressures of capitalist economy' (Jacobs and Appleyard 1987: 114–15). The
document is littered with cloying sentences, such as:

Buildings tend to be islands, big or small. They could be placed anywhere.
From the outside perspective, the building, like the world of art it was intended
to be, sits where it can be seen and admired in full. And because it is large it
is best seen from a distance (at a scale consistent with a moving auto).

(Jacobs and Appleyard 1987: 113)

This kind of vacuity, over ten pages of close-typed text, is exactly why urban
design as a discipline has remained in its own, self-imposed stone age since the
Second World War.

The charter of the New Urbanism, however, remains the most recent manifesto. It addresses urban design directly and is an entirely different document. Ratified by its members in 1996, it has been adopted by hundreds, if not thousands, of environmental practices throughout the world, and it has been translated into a variety of other cultural and ethnic typologies, both in the United States and elsewhere (FOC5: 122–6). The Congress for the New Urbanism is not limited to just architects as members, but encompasses a variety of professional groups who are committed to the overall ideology. The first paragraph in the charter says, 'The Congress for the New Urbanism views disinvestment in central cities, the spread of placeless sprawl, increasing separation by race and income, environmental deterioration, loss of agricultural lands and wilderness, and the erosion of society's built heritage as one interrelated community building challenge' (www.cnu.org/charter). While recognising that 'physical solutions of themselves will not solve social and economic problems', the answers remain uncompromisingly in the realm of physical design, with policies enunciated at three levels – 'the metropolis, city and town; the neighbourhood, district and the corridor; the block, street and building'. To the extent that any manifesto can of itself produce change, the charter of the New Urbanism goes far as a coherent document. Although it has drawn much criticism, this of itself may be viewed positively, as the best ideas usually do. Although the limitations of the New Urbanism are all too apparent, it is a significant improvement on anything emanating from the planning profession, where a reliance on development control mechanisms and design briefs has clearly failed to control the form and design of cities in any significant manner.

Conclusion

Urban planning and urban social movements have equivalences in monuments and manifestos. As urban planning depoliticises urban conflict and is, therefore, suspect in its strategies, so the representation of social history in monuments erected by the state and private sector must also be interrogated for their real meaning. As urban social movements signify the direct needs of individuals for planning action, so manifestos make similar demands of the state and other citizens for wider recognition. Urban planning and urban monuments are, in essence, ideologically driven dimensions in the construction of social space. On the other hand, urban social movements and manifestos, sometimes one and the same thing, are a direct expression of the demands by various publics for social change. Urban design is inextricably locked into this web of relationships. Our capacity to implement our mandate – the symbolic attempt to express an accepted urban meaning in certain urban forms – totally depends on our willingness to excavate the archaeology of meanings that lie beneath the superficial expression of urban form. Here, language and its dynamics are crucial tools. Dominant heterologies in the codification of symbolic meaning are associated with several contemporary social theorists, such as Bernstein, Pêcheux,

Lacan and Foucault, but prime in this respect is Jürgen Habermas, whose concepts of universal pragmatics and distorted communication reign supreme. Although a variety of heterologies assist in deconstructing symbolic meanings in the built environment, it should also be noted that this process is not linear but cyclical. The understanding that comes from deconstruction becomes the complex knowledge that is required to infuse urban space with structures of symbolic meaning that enhance social life. This process will not necessarily produce good design, but the overall effect of such understanding is exemplified by Le Corbusier's analysis of his own proportional system, called the *Modulor* (1980). When asked if the Modulor would guarantee good architecture, he responded, no, it would not. But it would make bad architecture more difficult.

Postscript

The progression from *The Form of Cities* to *Understanding Cities* represents a transition from theory to method, or more accurately meta-method, using a basic concept derived from Michel de Certeau, that of 'heterology'. The latter term seems confusing, as it is not in general use, despite its fundamental simplicity. Because the terms *method* and *methodology* are frequently, and wrongly, conflated with each other, and the concept of meta-method or heterology appears even more arcane, I recently used an analogy from *The Guardian Weekly* to clarify the latter problematic. Every two months, the newspaper has a section on learning English. Clearly, to teach or learn English, the structure and form of the language must be communicated, with the varying teaching and learning techniques that can be used, the differences between syntax, semantics and semiotics must be understood, and problems of dialect, speech and writing etc. must be revealed. This is analogous to mainstream urban design, where basic material relationships prevail. Most of the section, however, focusses on an entirely 'other' system of knowledge that informs these elementary technologies and methods, and their social context. Some of the articles include, for example, the contribution of multilingualism to creativity; the relationship between political language and government; English-medium degrees in the Eurozone; the assessment of linguistic fluency by computers; the relationship between racism and dialect; and a myriad of other subjects. Simply stated, the latter are heterological to the former (methods and techniques), offering insight and a critical basis for the entire universe of linguistic fluency. Mainstream urban design is characterised by the former grouping, the New Urban Design by the latter. Hence, mainstream urban design represents an evolutionary stage of development that has largely outlived its use, despite the fact that the new heterology would redefine and absorb mainstream knowledge, rather than eliminate it. Fortunately, the required paradigm shift in urban design consciousness has been gradually taking shape over at least the last ten years, despite the fact that it has remained insufficiently formulated to become the dominant discourse.

Understanding Cities completes a trilogy begun in 2002. The task I set myself was to outline a unified field for urban design. Rightly or wrongly, I felt that the discipline was in a state of total dissolution. Time-worn definitions, the enduring lack of significant theory, an arthritic dependence on physical determinism, the cult of personalities over principles, and a stagnating position within the culture of environmental education, all were contributing to its dissolution. That urban design was still seen as a colony shared between architecture and urban planning, to be plundered at will for whatever resources it had to offer, seemed to be the root cause of its demise. On the one hand, state planning systems are forced to view urban design in relation to their *raison d'être*, namely planning law, without which they could not survive. Urban design in this context cannot be inherently defined and exists only insofar as it plays a role in the regulation of state planning practices, i.e. in managing capital accumulation from land and its increasingly marginal role in social reproduction. This effectively embeds urban design as a function of development control regulations and design guidelines, which in many cases the private sector writes for itself. On the other hand, the capacity to design and construct buildings allowed the architectural profession to claim sovereignty, not only over individual buildings, but also over the built form of cities in its entirety. Naturally, this included urban design. Overall, architecture exists as a monopoly practice embedded within the general framework of capitalist enterprise. In order to operate within these rules, therefore, urban design has to be conflated with architectural design, a product of signature architects, firms, corporations and supporting legislation; and with an evolving transnationalist class structure of its own. Only on the insistence of architects that design implies both authorship and ownership can urban design remain commodified and within their purview.

Over time, the joint colonisation of urban design by these two processes has left it, as in most colonies, with its identity savaged, its resources plundered, and its capacity for reconstruction seriously undermined. I felt the much-touted ideas that urban design did not require its own profession, and that such an open system of participation in urban design ('anything goes') actually enriched the 'discipline', were the consequence of intellectual sloth and opportunism. None of it seemed to add up. Furthermore, such generously democratic and libertine ideologies had brought the coherence and integrity of urban design close to collapse. The mainstream position had seemingly reached its nadir.

As in most post-colonial environments, prior ideologies must be rejected, and new norms must be established. I felt therefore that the only way forward was to reconstruct urban design as an independent *field* of knowledge, one that demanded serious catharsis and a reconstitution of prevailing norms. The third millennium required better than the second. Clearly, this was a task that had to recognise the realities of interdisciplinarity and the necessary blurring of boundaries between the environmental disciplines. However, I did not see this situation as a mandate to continue defining urban design as a satellite of architecture, urban planning and, to a lesser extent, landscape architecture. If boundaries were to be blurred, urban design had to start in a position of equality, not inferiority. Hence, the problem became 'what is that position?'.

In order to answer this question, I needed to start unencumbered and relatively free from the emballage of past history. Incremental change was not working, and a paradigm shift was required. The first step, therefore, was to rethink the problem from first principles, rather than retracking a so-called 'history' of a fragmented discipline that appeared to have a decreasing degree of relevance. This effort was greatly assisted by the fact that I had completed my doctoral studies at the London School of Economics and Political Science. In the process, my mind had rotated 180° from my 'traditional' academic and professional qualifications in architecture, urban design and urban planning, and I am endlessly grateful for the experience. Rather than being locked into the solitude of professional self-interest, I was now able to look afresh at how the material field of urban design morphs out of the social field of human relationships, using the insights allowed by political economy, critical theory, cultural studies and human geography. From this perspective, nothing looked quite the same as it used to. In *Designing Cities* (2003), therefore, I sketched out a new theoretical framework for urban design, illustrated by a collection of articles from these disciplines. Among a dozen or so urban design readers that have followed, to date, this is the only one to present an extended theoretical and organising framework at the outset, rather than leaving the reader to invent his/her own. The book was structured on the basis of ten irreducible categories, with examples from various authors writing from within these paradigms. As a result, a theoretical scaffolding with specific building blocks constituted my initial sketch, to be elaborated in two subsequent volumes. The fundamental distinction in the reader was that social and economic forces generated a political economy of space, which in turn configured the form of cities and the field we call urban design.

Transparently, urban design and architectural design were not the same thing. Cities in their totality are never 'designed' by anyone, and for those that are *supposedly* designed this is usually limited to some basic organising framework (usually infrastructure). These preconceptions are subsequently completed by a multitude of disparate human interventions (e.g. Paris, Canberra, Brasilia, Cumbernauld etc.) and seldom comply with their designer's original blueprint. Transparently, many environments hailed as consummate examples of urban design have no obvious creators, from the Italian hill towns of Umbria and the Greek Cyclades, to the medieval environments reified by Camillo Sitte and the magnificent adobe settlements of Africa, such as Kano in Nigeria or San'a in the Yemen. One of the greatest masterpieces hailed by one and all, including the architectural profession, is St Mark's Square in Venice, which took 600 years to evolve. Paris, one of the most beautiful cities in the world, is also an urban design masterpiece, with magnificent monumental architecture, and I note here that there is no necessary relation between the two. Paris was created largely on the basis of layering the schematic infrastructure of a tyrant (Napoleon III), and a demagogue (Baron Haussmann) on top of a medieval city. The rationale had little to do with aesthetics and a lot to do with the fact that the French economy was going under, and its competitor, England, was forging ahead. Commodity circulation in Paris was grinding to a halt in the chaos of medieval streets and lanes. The new Paris and its residential architecture of tenements that define the great boulevards evolved on the basis of a few simple rules regarding building heights, prevailing architectural styles, the use of materials (stone, slate and wood) and the cultural practices of the French. Hence, Paris was not 'designed' as a result of any controlled architectural plan; it was the consequence of the political economy of the time, and the vexed issues of design as 'urban' and design as 'architecture' require some additional elaboration.

I have written elsewhere that all cities, towns and villages are designed in some manner by human action, and broadly speaking this remains my position in regard to urban design. Although this statement may seem so general as to make urban design wholly undefinable, I hope that I have been sufficiently explicit in my other work not to be misunderstood. In the trilogy, the focus has been on how urban design problems are approached, how they are constituted, and how answers are promoted, not how they are built. In addition, although a myriad different decisions are made by individuals, the state, the private sector and others such as urban social movements, this in no way implies that the process is chaotic, random or necessarily out of control. Nor does it suggest that a design process is absent. Quite the contrary. Even in the realm of the urban dispossessed, squatter settlements and refugee camps are 'designed' on the basis of fear, corruption, available resources, expediency, social relations, defence and other factors. A good urban designer would understand why this is the case and perhaps see the futility of drawing up an architectural plan to solve the problem, despite the fact that a preconceived plan might be the correct answer under different circumstances. How mature 'design' features emerge is therefore dependent on the resolution of a multitude of factors over time and cannot be defined by a single significant concept off a drawing board.

Such an approach, generalisable to the production of space and place in cities, stands in direct opposition to the mainstream. It reverses the idea that urban design is the sole domain of the architectural profession, including the idea that all other aspects of global development, while interesting, do not register as design activity. This position has little to do with the traditional architectural imagination, or indeed with the bureaucratic procedures of planning practice, and a lot to do with how socio-spatial structures arise and are transformed over time. Unavoidably, urban design and urban evolution possess a necessary coincidence, a relationship that architectural design cannot accommodate. Indeed, this need to see *evolution* and *design* as opposing forces is not merely a point of debate; it constitutes a necessary ideological construct in the survival of the architectural profession. Moreover, only by maintaining this position can the ownership of urban design be perpetuated. Hence, singular differences exist between architecture and urban design as to their varying recognition and/or acceptance of four integrated processes, namely design, evolution, preconception and control. As these ideas exist at the juncture where architectural design and urban design part company, they need some elaboration.

For most architects, *design* implies working out some preconceived plan or concept of what should be constructed or how people should live, the critical word here being 'preconceived'. Hence, there is a real hiatus in the architectural lexicon, as preconception and evolution stand in direct opposition to each other. Architectural design is the earthly form of 'intelligent design', because it implies a creator with a final plan that anticipates and then governs human activity. Evolution, in these terms, lasts as long as the building takes to build. Therefore, individual buildings, the result of architectural design, must of necessity be conceived as totalities and contain no evolutionary prospect except decay. As an extension of this idea, because urban design is composed of buildings, it too must have a designer and should be conceived as large-scale architecture, despite the fact that urban design focusses on the public realm, not architecture per se. Therefore, the inherent nature of *architectural* design denies concepts of transformation so vital to *urban* design. Nonetheless, most architects recognise that other forms of design exist, provided the concept of evolution is set to one side. What this does is to conflate architectural design with product design, albeit at the largest physical scale, reflecting the same *Weltanschauung* as watch design, automobile design, furniture design, aerospace design etc. and, on occasion, incorporating technologies derived from these disciplines. Even with these simple facts, it is obvious that serious questions exist as to the possibility of any free discussion of urban design as an evolutionary process that is formative in the design of cities.

Within this paradigm, it is also transparent that preconception and control are mandatory. As the predominant feature of architectural design is control, it is inevitable that the evolution of urban space must be seen as a random process, with outcomes that cannot be predicted, and for this reason cannot constitute design in any form. Furthermore, this position is sustained by the fact that urban evolution is an incremental process, involving a multitude of disparate factors, organisations and individuals, whose actions are in theory unpredictable. *Ipso facto*, as design relies on certainty within this paradigm, urban design cannot possibly have anything to do with urban evolution. The inexorable assumption, therefore, is that urban design is large-scale architecture and must be subject to individual authorship. Trapped within the dual concepts of creation and control, architects therefore conflate project design with urban design and are caught within a Gordian knot of their own creation.

However, the method of unravelling the knot is simple. It merely demands the recognition that architectural design deals with objects (buildings), and urban design deals with spaces and places – the public realm, a domain that cannot possibly be conceived of as a one-off event, but nonetheless may incorporate all kinds of physical projects. Similarly, urban design is concerned fundamentally with processes of transformation. By some accident of history, individual buildings may, for example, be transformed in their use, but seldom is this ever part of the original design. Taking urban space as a whole, it is, however, paradoxical that the transformation of built form, an unintended consequence of social development and unanticipated in individual projects, has played a greater part in the design of cities than the combined authorship of individual architectural creations. For example, in Edinburgh, where I went to college, the entire Georgian New Town has undergone major transformations in use that were never part of its original residential concept. Urban design deals at its core with growth and change. Evolution is inherent. The fact that some architects may not like the term 'design' being used more generally is unfortunate, an ideology that this trilogy has tried to liberate.

Although it is irrefutable that architectural design is an evolutionary part of urban space, urban design continues as a phenomenon, whether or not architects are present. This does not mean that we have to believe in 'intelligent design', whereby evolution is seen to have a creator, but, if evolution is to be eliminated, as suggested, from the urban design process as 'not design', then we are left with a corollary that is absurd – that all urban design must be conceived and built by a designer. The evidence of 10,000 years of urban evolution denies this idea. Unfortunately, resistance by many architects to concepts of urban design outside those of preconception, control and ownership has been one of the great limiting factors on the development of a theoretically robust and convincing urban design consciousness. Indeed, it is tempting to remove the idea of urban design from architecture in its entirety, replacing it with a more appropriate terminology – project design. As I have done in *The Form of Cities*, it is then possible to move unencumbered in redefining the discipline, leaving such ideological blindness behind.

Fundamental to any understanding of the seemingly chaotic, random and unrelated processes of urban development and design is an understanding of spatial political economy, used in varying degrees across all three volumes of the trilogy. From this starting point, the *field* of urban design can access significant social theory and escape from the prevailing physical determinism and design ideologies of the environmental disciplines. On this basis, pre-existing relationships can be restructured, and new forms of respect can be generated between disciplines on the basis of redefined knowledge and responsibilities. As a necessary foundation for the New Urban Design, a sound understanding is required as to how space emanates from specific modes of production, with their inherent structure of social and property relations, ideologies and history, as well as the class, ethnic and gender struggles that configure the urban realm. The spatial structures so produced morph on a daily basis to accommodate incremental or traumatic social and environmental influences, resulting in the design of cities. For a reconstructed urban design, it is axiomatic that the educational process of urban designers must be radically different from that of architects. It includes design, but is not of it.

I also need to clarify, in the face of my own tirade, my great commitment to, and respect for, the science and art of architecture. In my personal life, I have made many pilgrimages to visit both historical and contemporary architectural masterpieces across four continents and have frequently been overwhelmed at the ineluctable magnificence and genius exhibited by the architectural imagination. But this is not the point. The architectural profession bears the brunt of responsibility in its role as caretaker of urban design knowledge, as indeed it did with urban planning up until the early 1970s, when it was routed by social science. In generating new theory, the best of the old must be brought into question, and much of this is represented in the dominant discourse of architecture with regard to urban design. There is no doubt that we need the best architects society can educate, so that great architecture can be reproduced as one of the predominant features of great cities. However, as the New Urban Design gathers momentum, the space it occupies will necessarily encroach on the territory of other environmental disciplines as decolonisation occurs. This implies that architects will concentrate on what they do best – designing buildings; that planners will do what they do best – implementing national and state policies; and that landscape architects will continue to reinforce the urban landscape by inserting nature (now conceived of as a multitrillion-dollar service industry) into urban space. Although the name will stay the same, there will be a realm of design that claims its own territory, and that is the New Urban Design.

Finally, in urban design as in science, Heisenberg's thesis prevails, that everything changes in the act of observation, both the observer and the object. No doubt this has happened to me in the process of completing three integrated books. Indeed, an additional volume could be written on each of the ten categories I have used to outline the field of urban design, and I am also cognisant of the fact that one more text needs to be completed, on case studies that elaborate on practices in each dimension. Although I remain convinced that the overall approach I have outlined is both necessary and valid, I also recognise that only the rough contours of an overall field for urban design have been sketched out. I accept that this could have been done in a variety of other ways. Had I to start from the beginning again, I might do things differently, and I am only too conscious of the limitations of the trilogy, despite the 1,000 pages of text involved in its exposition. My sincere hope is that others will take up the challenge of creative destruction that all new knowledge demands and improve on my somewhat speculative offering.

Alexander Cuthbert
Gandapura, Bali, June 2010

References

Abel, C. 2003: *Sky High: Vertical Architecture*. London: The Royal Academy of Arts.

Abrams, C. 1964: *Man's Struggle for Shelter in an Urbanising World*. Cambridge, MA: MIT Press.

Adams, A. and Tancred, P. 2000: *Designing Women: Gender and the Architectural Profession*. Toronto: University of Toronto Press.

Adorno, T. and Horkheimer, M. 1979: *The Dialectic of Enlightenment*. London: Verso, p. 163. (Originally published as *Dialektik der Aufklärung*. Amsterdam: Querido, 1947.)

Agrest, D., Conway, P. and Weisman, L. (eds) 1996: *The Sex of Architecture*. New York: Harry N. Abrams.

Akkerman, A. 2006: 'Feminism and masculinity in city-form: philosophical urbanism as a history of consciousness'. *Human Studies*, 2(29): 229–316.

Al Hindi, K.F. and Staddon, C. 1997: 'The hidden histories and geographies of neo-traditional town planning: the case of Seaside, Florida'. *Environment and Planning D: Society and Space*, 15(3): 349–72.

Albin, S. 2003: *The Art of Software Architecture: Design Methods and Techniques*. Hoboken, NJ: Wiley.

Alexander, C. 1964: *Notes on a Synthesis of Form*. Cambridge, MA: Harvard University Press.

Alexander, C. 1973: 'A city is not a tree'. In John Thackaray (ed.), *Design After Modernism*. London: Thames and Hudson, pp. 67–84.

Alexander, C. 1977: *A Pattern Language*. Oxford: Oxford University Press.

Alexander, C. and Poyner, B. 1967: *The Atoms of Environmental Structure*. London: Ministry of Public Buildings and Works.

Alexander, E.R. 2000: 'Rationality revisited: paradigms in a postmodernist perspective'. *Journal of Planning Education and Research*, 19(3): 242–56.

Allen, J. 2003: *Parasite Paradise: A Manifesto for Contemporary Architecture*. Rotterdam: NAI Publishers.

Alonso, W. 1965: *Location and Land Use*. Cambridge, MA: Harvard University Press.

Althusser, L. 1965: *For Marx*. London: Allen Lane.

Althusser, L. 1984: *Essays on Ideology*. London: Verso.

Althusser, L. and Balibar E. 1970: *Reading Capital*. London: New Left Books.

Andrew, C. and Milroy, B.M. (eds) 1988: *Life Spaces, Gender, Household, Employment*. Vancouver: University of British Columbia Press.

Angotti, T. 1993: *Metropolis 2000: Planning, Poverty and Politics*. New York: Routledge.

Angotti, T. 2006: 'Apocalyptic anti-urbanism: Mike Davis and his planet of slums'. *International Annual Review of Sociology*, 19(3): 301–20.

Anthony, K.H. 2001: *Designing for Diversity. Gender, Race and Ethnicity in the Architectural Profession*. Urbana, IL: University of Illinois Press.

Appleyard, D., Lynch, K. and Myer, J. 1964: *The View from the Road*. Cambridge, MA: MIT Press.

Arato, A. and Gebhart, E. 1982: *The Essential Frankfurt School Reader*. New York: Continuum.

Ardener, S. (ed.) 1981: *Women and Space*. London: Croom Helm.

Arendt, H. 1958: *The Human Condition*. Chicago, IL: Chicago University Press.

Arrighi, G. 1994: *The Long Twentieth Century*. London: Verso.

Ashcroft, B. and Ahluwalia, P. 1999: *Edward Said: The Paradox of Identity*. London: Routledge.

Asihara, Y. 1983: *The Aesthetic Townscape*. Boston: MIT Press.

Atkinson, P. 1985: *Language, Structure and Reproduction*. London, Methuen.

Audirac, I. and Shermyen, A.H. 1994: 'An evaluation of neo-traditional design's social prescription: postmodern placebo or remedy for suburban malaise?'. *Journal of Planning Education and Research*, 13(3): 1161–73.

Azarayahu, M. 1986: 'Street names and political identity: the case of East Berlin'. *Journal of Contemporary History*, 21(4): 581–604.

Azarayahu, M. 1996: 'The power of commemorative street names'. *Environment and Planning D: Society and Space*, 14(3): 311–30.

Bacon, E. 1965: *The Design of Cities*. New York: The Viking Press.

Bakker, N., Dubbeling, S., Sabel Koschella, U., Gundel, S. and Zeeuw, H. (eds) 2000: *Urban Agriculture in the Policy Agenda*. The German Federation for International Development. Feldalig: DSE.

Balaben, O. 1995: *Politics and Ideology: A Philosophical Approach*. London: Avebury Press.

Ballard, J.G. 1973: *Crash*. London: Vintage.

Ballard, J.G. 2006: *Kingdom Come*. London: Harper Collins.

Banai, R. 1996: 'A theoretical assessment of "neotraditional" settlement form by dimensions of performance'. *Environment and Planning B: Environment and Design*, 23(2): 177–90.

Banai, R. 1998: 'The New Urbanism: an assessment of the core commercial areas with perspectives from (retail) location and land-use theories, and the conventional wisdom'. *Environment and Planning B: Environment and Design*, 25(2): 169–85.

Bannerjee, T. and Southworth, M. (eds) 1990: *City Sense and City Design: The Writings and Projects of Kevin Lynch*. Cambridge, MA: MIT Press.

Barnacle, R. 2001: *Phenomenology*. Melbourne: RMIT University Press.

Barnett, J. 1974. *Urban Design as Public Policy: Practical Methods for Improving Cities*. New York: The Architectural Press.

Baron-Cohen, S. 2004: *The Essential Difference*. London: Penguin.

Battle, G. and McCarthy, C.: www.battlemccarthy.com/Sustainable%20Towers%20Website/sustainable%20towers%20_%20Definition.htm.

Baudrillard, J. 1981: *For a Critique of the Political Economy of the Sign*. St Louis, MO: Telos Press.

Baudrillard, J. 1990: *Cool Memories*. London: Verso.

Baudrillard, J. 1996: *Cool Memories II*. Cambridge: Polity Press.

Baudrillard, J. 1997: *Cool Memories III: Fragments*. London: Verso.

Baum, A. and Epstein, Y. 1978: *Human Response to Crowding*. New York: Halstead Press.

Baum, H.S. 1996: 'Why the rational paradigm persists – tales from the field'. *Journal of Planning Education and Research*, 15(4): 263–78.

Beatley, T. 2008: 'Green urbanism: a manifesto for re-earthing cities'. In T. Hass (ed.), *The New Urbanism and Beyond: Designing Cities for the Future*. New York: Rizzoli, pp. 190–6.

Bell, D. and Jayne, M. 2004: *City of Quarters: Urban Villages in the Contemporary City*. Aldershot: Ashgate.

Benedict, M.A. and McMahon, E.T. 2006: *Green Infrastructure: Linking Landscapes and Communities*. Washington, DC: Island Press.

Benevolo, L. 1967: *The Origins of Modern Town Planning* (Vols 1–7). Cambridge, MA: MIT Press.

Benevolo, L. 1980: *The History of the City*. Cambridge, MA: MIT Press.

Benevolo, L. 1993: *The European City*. Oxford: Blackwell.

Benjamin, W. 1997: *Charles Baudelaire*. London: Verso.

Benjamin, W. 1999: *The Arcades Project*. Cambridge, MA: Harvard University Press.

Benton-Short, L., Price, M.D. and Friedman, S. 2005: 'Globalisation from below: the ranking of global immigrant cities'. *International Journal of Urban and Regional Research*, 29(4): 945–59.

Bergren, A. 1998: 'Female fetish, urban form'. In D. Agrest, P. Conway, and L. Weisman (eds), *The Sex of Architecture*. New York: Harry N. Abrams, pp. 73–92.

Berlant, L. and Warner, M. (eds) 1993: 'Sex in public'. In S. During (ed.), *The Cultural Studies Reader*. London: Routledge, pp. 271–91.

Berleant, A. 2007a: 'Cultivating an urban aesthetic'. In A. Berleant and A. Carlson (eds), *The Aesthetics of Human Environments*. Sydney: Broadview Press, pp. 79–91.

Berleant, A. 2007b: 'Deconstructing Disney World'. In A. Berleant and A. Carlson (eds), *The Aesthetics of Human Environments*. Sydney: Broadview Press, pp. 139–49.

Berman, M. 1982: *All that is Solid Melts into Air*. Harmondsworth: Penguin.

Bernstein, B. 1973: *Class Codes and Control: Theoretical Studies Towards a Theory of Language* (Vols 1 and 2). London: Routledge and Kegan Paul.

Bernstein, B. 1977: *Class Codes and Control: Theoretical Studies Towards a Theory of Language* (Vol. 3). London: Routledge and Kegan Paul.

Betsky, A. 1997: *Icons: Magnets of Meaning*. San Francisco: Chronicle Books.

Betsky, A. and Adigard, E. 2000: *Architecture Must Burn: A Manifesto for an Architecture Beyond Building*. London: Thames and Hudson.

Blaikie, N. 1993: *Approaches to Social Enquiry*. Cambridge: Polity Press.

Blake, P. 1964: *God's Own Junkyard. The Planned Deterioration of America's Landscape*. New York: Holt, Rinehart and Winston.

Blanco, H. 1984: 'Comment'. *Journal of Planning Education and Research*, 3(2): 91.

Bleier, R. 1986: *Feminist Approaches to Science*. London: Pergamon.

Blum, D. 1997: *Sex on the Brain*. New York: Viking Press.

Boardman, P. 1944: *Patrick Geddes, Maker of the Future*. Chapel Hill, NC: University of North Carolina Press.

Bocock, R. 1976: *Freud and Modern Society*. Wokingham, Berkshire (UK): Van Nostrand Reinhold.

Bohl, C.C. 2000: 'The New Urbanism: potential applications and implications for distressed inner city neighbourhoods'. *Housing Policy Debate*, 11(4): 761–801.

Borisoff, D. and Hahn, D.F. 1997: 'The mirror in the window: displaying our gender biases'. In S.J. Drucker and G. Gumpert (eds), *Voices in the Street: Explorations in Gender, Media and Public Space*. Cresskill, NJ: Hampton Press, pp. 149–63.

Bosselman, P. 1998: *Representation of Places: Reality and Realism in City Design*. Berkeley, CA: University of California Press.

Bottomore, T. 1983: *A Dictionary of Marxist Thought*. Oxford: Blackwell.

Bourdieu, P. 2000: *Pascalian Meditations*. Cambridge: Polity Press.

Bowlby, S., Lewis, J., McDowell, L. and Ford, J. 1989: 'The geography of gender'. In R. Peet and N. Thrift (eds), *New Models in Geography*. London: Routledge, pp. 157–75.

Boyer, M.C. 1983: *Dreaming the Rational City: The Myth of American City Planning*. Cambridge, MA: MIT Press.

Boyer, M.C. 1994: *The City of Collective Memory*. Cambridge, MA: MIT Press.

Boyle, D. 2003: *Authenticity: Brands, Fakes, Spin, and the Lust for Real Life*. London: Flamingo.

Boys, J. (1985) 'Women and public space'. In Matrix (ed.), *Making Space: Women and the Man-made Environment*. London: Pluto Press, pp. 37–54.

Bracken, I. 1981: *Urban Planning Methods: Research and Policy Analysis*. London: Methuen.

Breman, J. 2003: *The Labouring Poor in India*. Oxford: Oxford University Press.

Bressi, T.W. 1994: 'Planning the American dream'. In P. Katz, *The New Urbanism*. New York: McGraw-Hill, pp. xxv–xlii.

Britz, R. 1981: *The Edible City*. Los Angeles: Kaufmann Inc.

Brizendine, L. 2006: *The Female Brain*. New York: Morgan Road Books.

Brower, S. 2002: 'The sectors of the transect'. *The Journal of Urban Design*, 7(3): 313–20.

Browne, J. (ed.) 2007: *The Future of Gender*. Cambridge: Cambridge University Press.

Browne, K., Lim, J. and Brown, G. (eds) 2007: *Geographies of Sexualities*. Aldershot: Ashgate.

Bubner, R. 1988: *Essays in Hermeneutics and Critical Theory*. New York: Columbia University Press.

Burgess, E.W. 1925: 'The growth of the city'. In R.E. Park, E.W. Burgess and R. McKenzie (eds), *The City: Suggestions of Investigation of Human Behaviour in the Urban Environment*. Chicago, IL: University of Chicago Press, pp. 47–62.

Burke, G. 1976: *Townscapes*. London: Penguin.

Calhoun, C. (ed.) 1992: *Habermas and the Public Sphere*. Cambridge, MA: MIT Press.

Callinicos, A. 2003: *An Anti-capitalist Manifesto*. Oxford: Blackwell.

Camus, A. 1965: *The Plague*. New York: McGraw-Hill.

Camus, A. 2000: *The Rebel*. London: Penguin.

Camus, A. 2006: *The Fall*. London: Penguin.

Cannadine, D. 2002: *What is History Now?* Hampshire: Palgrave McMillan.

Canovan, M. 1983: 'A case of distorted communication: a note on Habermas and Arendt'. *Political Theory*, 2(1): 105–16.

Casey, E.S. 1997: *The Fate of Place: A Philosophical History*. London: California University Press.

Castells, M. 1976: 'Is there an urban sociology?'. In C. Pickvance (ed.), *Urban Sociology: Critical Essays*. London: Tavistock, Chapter 1, pp. 27–42.

Castells, M. 1977: *The Urban Question*. London: Arnold.

Castells, M. 1983: *The City and the Grassroots: A Cross-cultural Theory of Urban Social Movements*. Berkeley, CA: University of California Press.

Castells, M. 1990: *The Shek Kip Mei Syndrome: Economic Development and Public Housing in Hong Kong and Singapore*. London: Pion.

Castells, M. 1996: *The Rise of the Network Society*. Oxford: Blackwell.

Castells, M. 1997: *The Power of Identity*. Oxford: Blackwell.

Castells, M. 1998: *End of Millennium*. Oxford: Blackwell.

Castells, M. 2000: 'Toward a sociology of the network society'. *Contemporary Sociology*, 29(5): 693–9.

Caws, M.A. (ed.) 2001: *Manifesto: A Century of Isms*. Lincoln, NB: University of Nebraska Press.

Celik, Z., Favro, D. and Ingersoll, R. (eds) 1994: *Streets: Critical Perspectives on Public Space*. Berkeley, CA: University of California Press.

Cenzatti, M. 1993: *Los Angeles and the L.A. School: Postmodernism and Urban Studies*. Los Angeles, CA: Los Angeles Forum for Architecture and Urban Design.

Cervero, R. 1998: *The Transit Metropolis: A Global Inquiry*. Washington, DC: Island Press.

Chalmers, A.F. 1999: *What is This Thing Called Science?*. Indianapolis, IN: Hackett.

Chapin, S. and Kaiser, E.J. 1979: *Urban Land Use Planning*. Urbana, IL: University of Illinois Press.

Chaplin, S. 2003 (orig. 2000): 'Heterotopia deserta: Las Vegas and other places'. In A. Cuthbert (ed.), *Designing Cities: Critical Readings in Urban Design*. Oxford: Blackwell, pp. 340–61.

Childe, V.G. 1935: *Man Makes Himself*. London: Watts.

Chmielewska, E. 2005: 'Logos or the resonance of branding: a close reading of the iconosphere of Warsaw'. *Space and Culture*, 8(4): 349–80.

Cinar, A. and Bender, T. (eds) 2002: *Imaginaries: Locating the Modern City*. Minneapolis, MN: University of Minnesota Press.

Clark, G.L. and Dear, M. 1984: *State Apparatus: Structures and Language of Legitimacy*. London: Allen and Unwin.

Clarke, P.W. 1989: 'The economic currency of architectural aesthetics'. In M. Diani and C. Ingraham (eds), *Restructuring Architectural Theory*. Evanston, IL: Northwestern University Press, pp. 48–59.

Clarke, V. and Peel, E. (eds) 2007: *Out in Psychology: Lesbian, Gay, Bisexual, Trans and Queer Perspectives*. Chichester: Wiley.

Cohen, G.A. 1978: *Karl Marx's Theory of History*. Oxford: Clarendon Press.

Collins, G.R. and Collins, C.C.C. 1986: *Camillo Sitte: The Birth of Modern City Planning*. New York: Dover.

Collins, P. 1998: *Changing Ideals in Modern Architecture 1750–1950*. Montreal: McGill–Queens University Press.

Colomina, B. (ed.) 1992: *Sexuality and Space*. New York: Princeton Architectural Press.

Comte-Sponville, A. 2005: *The Little Book of Philosophy*. London: Vintage.

Conrads, U. 1970: *Programs and Manifestos on 20th Century Architecture*. Cambridge, MA: MIT Press.

Conzen, M.P. and Greene, R.P. 2008: 'All the world is not Los Angeles or Chicago: paradigms, schools, archetypes and the urban process'. *Urban Geography*, 29(2): 27–100.

Cosgrove, D. 1984: *Social Formation and Symbolic Landscape*. Madison, WI: University of Wisconsin Press.

Cross, N. (ed.) 1984: *Developments in Design Methodology*, Chichester, NY: Wiley.

Cuff, D. 2003: 'Immanent domain: pervasive computing and the public realm'. *Journal of Architectural Education*, 57(1): 43–9.

Cullen, G. 1961: *The Concise Townscape*. London: The Architectural Press.

Culler, J. 1976: *Saussure*. Glasgow: Collins.

Cuthbert, A.R. 1984: 'Conservation and capital accumulation in Hong Kong'. *The Third World Planning Review*, 6(1): 102–12.

Cuthbert, A.R. 1995: 'The right to the city: surveillance, private interest and the public domain in Hong Kong'. *Cities*, 12(5): 293–310.

Cuthbert, A.R. (ed.) 2003: *Designing Cities: Critical Readings in Urban Design*. Oxford: Blackwell.

Cuthbert, A.R. 2006: *The Form of Cities: Political Economy and Urban Design*. Oxford: Blackwell.

Cuthbert, A.R. 2007: 'Urban design: requiem for an era – review and critique of the last 50 years'. *Urban Design International*, 12(4): 177–223.

Cuthbert, A.R. and McKinnell, K. 1997: 'Ambiguous space, ambiguous rights?: corporate power and social control in Hong Kong'. *Cities*, 12(5): 295–313.

Dalton, L.C. 1986: 'Why the rational paradigm persists: the resistance of professional education and practice to alternative forms of planning'. *Journal of Planning Education and Research*, 15(4): 279–88.

Dandeneker, C. 1990: *Surveillance, Power and Modernity*. New York: St Martin's Press.

Davis, D.E. 2005: 'Cities in global context: a brief intellectual history'. *International Journal of Urban and Regional Research*, 29(1): 92–109.

Davis, M. 1990: *City of Quartz*. London: Verso.

Davis, M. 2004: 'Planet of slums'. *New Left Review*, 26(1): 5–34.

Davis, M. 2006a: *Planet of Slums*. London: Verso.

Davis, M. 2006b: 'Fear and money in Dubai'. *New Left Review*, 41(1): 47–68.

Davison, G. 2005: 'Australia: the first suburban nation', *Journal of Urban History*, 22(1): 40–74.

Dawkins, J. and Searle, G. 1995: *The Australian Debate on Urban Consolidation 1985–1994: A Selective Bibliography*. Sydney: Faculty of Architecture, Design and Building, University of Technology.

Day, K. 1997: 'Better safe than sorry? Consequences of sexual assault prevention for women in urban space'. *Perspectives on Social Problems*, 9: 83–101.

Day, K. 1999: 'Embassies and sanctuaries: women's experiences of race and fear in public space'. *Environment and Planning D: Society and Space*, 17: 307–28.

Day, K. 2000: 'The New Urbanism and the challenges of designing for diversity'. *Journal of Planning Education and Research*, 23(1): 83–95.

De Beauvoir, S. 1972: *The Second Sex*. Harmondsworth: Penguin.

De Botton, A. 2002: *The Art of Travel*. London: Penguin.

De Botton, A. 2004: *Status Anxiety*. London: Hamish Hamilton.

De Cante, L. 2008: *Heterotopia and the City: Public Space in a Post Civil Society*. Oxford: Routledge.

de Certeau, M. 1984: *The Practice of Everyday Life*. Berkeley, CA: University of California Press.

de Certeau, M. 1988: *The Writing of History*. New York: Columbia University Press.

de Certeau, M. 1993: 'Walking in the city'. In S. During (ed.), *The Cultural Studies Reader*. London: Routledge.

Dear, M. 2000: *The Postmodern Urban Condition*. Oxford: Blackwell.

Dear, M. 2002: 'Los Angeles and the Chicago School. Invitation to a debate'. *City and Community*, 1(1): 5–32.

Dear, M. 2003: 'The Los Angeles school of urbanism: an intellectual history'. *Urban Geography*, 24(6): 493–509.

Dear, M. and Dishman, J.D. (eds) 2002: *From Chicago to L.A.: Making Sense of Urban Theory*. Thousand Oaks, CA: Sage.

Dear, M. and Flusty, S. 1998: 'Postmodern urbanism'. *Annals of the Association of American Geographers*, 88: 50–72.

Debord, G. 1983 (orig. 1967): *The Society of the Spectacle*. London: Practical Paradise Publications.

Del Cerro, G. 2007: *Bilbao: Basque Pathways to Globalisation*. London: Elsevier.

Delafons, J. 1998: 'Democracy and design'. In B. Scheer and W.F.E. Preiser (eds), *Design Review: Challenging Urban Aesthetic Control*. New York: Chapman and Hall, pp. 13–19.

Demeterio, F. 2001: www.geocities.com/philodept/diwatao/critical_hermeneutics.htm.

Dennis, R. 2004: 'Slums'. In S. Harrison, S. Pile and N. Thrift (eds), *Patterned Ground: Entanglements of Nature and Culture*. London: Reaktion Books.

Diaz, O.F. and Fainstein, S. 2009: 'The new mega-projects: genesis and impacts'. *International Journal of Urban and Regional Research*, 32(4): 759–67.

Diesendorf, M. 2005: 'Growth of municipalities: a snapshot of sustainable development in China'. In C. Hargroves and M. Smith, *The Natural Advantage of Nations*. London: Earthscan, pp. 303–6.

Douglas, M., Ho, K.C. and Ooi, G.L. 2008: *Globalisation, the City and Civil Society in Pacific Asia: The Social Production of Civil Spaces*. London: Routledge.

Downey, J. and McGuigan, J. (eds) 1999: *Technocities*. Thousand Oaks, CA: Sage.

Drucker, S.J. and Gumpert, G. (eds) 1997: *Voices in the Street: Explorations in Gender, Media and Public Space*. Cresskill, NJ: Hampton Press.

D'Souza, A.D. and McDonough, T. 2006: *The Invisible Flâneuse*. Manchester: Manchester University Press.

Duany, A. 2000: 'A new theory of urbanism'. *The Scientific American*, 283(6): 90–1.

Duany, A. 2002: 'Introduction to the special issue: the transect'. *The Journal of Urban Design*, 7(3): 251–60.

Duany, A. and Talen, E. (eds) 2002: 'The transect'. *The Journal of Urban Design* (Special Issue), 7(3).

Duany, A., Plater-Zyberk, E. and Speck, J. 2000: *Suburban Nation: The Rise of Sprawl and the Decline of the American Dream*. New York: North Point Press.

Duany, Plater-Zyberk and Co. (2000) *The Lexicon of the New Urbanism*. C3.1–C3.2.

Dunleavy, P. 1981: *The Politics of Mass Housing in Britain 1945–75*. Oxford: Clarendon.

During, S. (ed.) 1993: *The Cultural Studies Reader*. London: Routledge.

Eagleton, T. 1990: *The Ideology of the Aesthetic*. Oxford: Blackwell.

Easterling, K. 2005: *Enduring Innocence: Global Architecture and Its Political Masquerades*. Cambridge, MA: MIT Press.

Eaton, R. 2001: *Ideal Cities*. New York: Thames and Hudson.

Eco, U. 1986: *Travels in Hyper-reality*. London: Picador.

Edelman, B. 1977: *Political Language: Words that Succeed, Policies that Fail*. New York: Academic Press.

Eichler, J. (ed.) 1995: *Change of Plans: Towards a Non-sexist Sustainable City*. Toronto: Garamond Press.

Ellis, C. 2002: 'The New Urbanism: critiques and rebuttals'. *The Journal of Urban Design*, 73(3): 261–91.

Elsheshtawy, Y. 2008: 'Transitory sites: mapping Dubai's "forgotten" spaces'. *International Journal of Urban and Regional Research*, 32(4): 968–88.

Embong, A.R. 2000: 'Globalisation and transnational class relations: some problems of conceptualisation'. *The Third World Quarterly*, 21(6): 989–1000.

Engels, F. 1973 (orig. 1892): *The Condition of the Working Class in England*. London: Lawrence and Wishart.

Eran, B.J. and Szold, T.S. 2005: *Regulating Place: Standards and the Shaping of Urban America*. London: Routledge.

Evans, G. 2003: 'Hard branding the city: from Prado to Prada'. *International Journal of Urban and Regional Research*, 27(2): 417–40.

Fainstein, S.S. 2002: 'One year on: reflections on September 11th and the "war on terrorism": regulating New York City's visitors in the aftermath of September 11th'. *International Journal of Urban and Regional Research*, 26(3): 591–5.

Fainstein, S.S. 2009: 'Mega-projects in New York, London and Amsterdam'. *International Journal of Urban and Regional Research*, 32(4): 768–85.

Fainstein, S.S. and Servon L.J. 2005: *Gender and Planning: A Reader*. New Jersey: Rutgers University Press.

Falconer, A.K. 2001: 'The New Urbanism: where and for whom? investigation of a new paradigm'. *Urban Geography*, 22(3): 202–19.

Fann, K.T. 1969: *Wittgenstein's Conception of Philosophy*. Berkeley, CA: University of California Press, p. 37.

Fanon, F. 1965: *The Wretched of the Earth*. Farringdon, London: Macgibbon and Kee.

Fanon, F. 1967: *Black Skin, White Masks*. New York: Grove Press.

Farr, D. 2008: *Sustainable Urbanism: Urban Design with Nature*. Hoboken, NJ: Wiley.

Fauque, R. 1986: 'For a new semiological approach to the city'. In M. Gottdiener, P. Alexandros and A. Lagopoulos, *The City and the Sign: An Introduction to Urban Semiotics*. New York: Columbia University Press, pp. 137–60.

Fernandez-Armesto, F. 2002: *The World, a History* (Vol. 1). Upper Saddle River, NJ: Prentice Hall.

Feyerabend, P. 1975: *Against Method*. London: Verso.

Feyerabend, P. 1987: *Farewell to Reason*. London: Verso.

Feyerabend, P. 1995: *Killing Time: The Autobiography of Paul Feyerabend*. Chicago, IL: University of Chicago Press.

Fishman, R. 1987: *Bourgeois Utopias: The Rise and Fall of Suburbia*. New York: Basic Books.

Fletcher, Sir B. 1961 (orig. 1897): *A History of Architecture on the Comparative Method*. London: B.T. Batsford and New York: C. Scribner's Sons.

Florida, R. 2003: *The Rise of the Creative Class*. Melbourne: Pluto.

Florida, R. 2005: *The Flight of the Creative Class*. New York: Harper Collins.

Flyvbjerg, B. 2005: 'Machiavellan megaprojects'. *Antipode*, 37(1): 18–22.

Flyvbjerg, B., Bruzelius, N. and Rothengatter W. 2003: *Megaprojects and Risk: An Anatomy of Ambition*. Cambridge: Cambridge University Press.

Fogelson, R.E. 1986: *Planning the Capitalist City: The Colonial Era to the 1920's*. Princeton, NJ. Princeton University Press.

Ford, L.R. 1999: 'Lynch revisited: New Urbanism and theories of good city form'. *Cities*, 16(4): 247–57.

Foucault, M. 2002 (orig. 1966): *The Order of Things: Archaeology of the Human Sciences*. London: Routledge.

Frampton, K. 2000: 'The status of man and the status of his objects: a reading of the human condition'. In M. Hays (ed.), *Architecture Theory Since 1968*. Cambridge, MA: MIT Press, pp. 362–77.

Franck, K. and Paxson, L. 1989: 'Women and urban public space'. In I. Altman and E. Zube (eds), *Public Spaces and Places*. New York: Plenum, pp. 121–46.

Frankel, B. 1983: *Beyond the State*. London: Macmillan.

Franklin, B. and Tait, M. 2002: 'Constructing an image: the urban village concept in the U.K.' *Planning Theory*, 1(3): 250–72.

Fraser, N. 1990: 'Rethinking the public sphere: a contribution to actually existing democracy'. *Social Text*, 25/26(1): 56–9.

Frers, L. and Meier, L. (eds) 2007: *Encountering Urban Places: Visual and Material Performances in the City*. Aldershot: Ashgate.

Fritzsches, P. 2004: *Stranded in the Present*. Cambridge, MA: Harvard University Press.

Fukuyama, F. 2006: *The End of History and the Last Man*. New York: The Free Press.

Fulbrook, M. 2002: *Historical Theory*. London: Routledge.

Fulton, W. 1996: 'New Urbanism as sustainable growth?: a supply side story'. *Environment and Planning D: Society and Space*, 15(3): 349–72.

Gadamer, H.G. 1989: *Truth and Method*. New York: Crossroad.

Galinsky.com: www.galinsky.com/buildings/marseille/index.htm.

Gans, H. 2005 (orig. 1962): 'Urbanism and suburbanism as ways of life'. In J. Lin and C. Mele (eds), *The Urban Sociology Reader*. London: Routledge, pp. 42–50.

Garde, A. 2004: 'New Urbanism as sustainable growth: a supply-side story and its implications for sustainable growth'. *Journal of Planning Education and Research*, 24(2): 154–70.

Gardiner, C.B. 1989: 'Analysing gender in public places: rethinking Goffman's vision of everyday life'. *American Sociologist*, 20(1): 42–56.

Garreau, J. 1991: *Edge City: Life on the New Frontier*. New York: Anchor.

Geary, D. 1998: *Male, Female: The Evolution of Human Sex Differences*. New York: The American Psychological Association.

Geddes, P. 1997 (orig. 1915): *Cities in Evolution: An Introduction to the Town Planning Movement and the Study of Civics*. London: Routledge.

Geist, J.F. 1985: *Arcades. The History of a Building Type*. New York: Oxford University Press.

Gibberd, F. 1953: *Town Design*. New York: Praeger.

Gibson-Graham, J.K. 1996: *The End of Capitalism (as we knew it): A Feminist Critique of Political Economy*. Oxford: Blackwell.

Giddens, A. 1974: *Positivism and Sociology*. London: Heinemann.

Giedion, S. 1941: *Space, Time and Architecture*. Cambridge, MA: Harvard University Press.

Gilbert, A. 2007: 'The return of the slum: does language matter?'. *International Journal of Urban and Regional Research*, 31(4): 697–713.

Gindroz, R. 2003: *The Urban Design Handbook: Techniques and Working Methods*. New York: W.W. Norton.

Girardet, H. 1999: *Creating Sustainable Cities*. Dartington: Green Books.

Gleber, A. 1999: *The Art of Taking a Walk; Flânerie, Literature, and Film in Weimar Culture*. Princeton, NJ: Princeton University Press, pp. 3–63.

Goakes, R.J. 1987: *How to Design the Aesthetics of Townscape*. Brisbane: Boolarong Publications.

Golanyi, G.S. 1996: 'Urban design morphology and thermal performance'. *Atmospheric Environment*, 30(3): 455–65.

Gomez, M.V. and Gonzalez, S. 2001: 'A reply to Beatriz Plaza's "The Guggenheim Bilbao museum effect"'. *International Journal of Urban and Regional Research*, 25(4): 898–900.

Goodchild, B. 1997: *Urban Planning*. Maiden, MA: Blackwell Science.

Goode, T. 1992: 'Typological theory in the United States'. *The Journal of Architectural Education*, 46(1): 2–14.

Gorbachev, M.S. 2006: *Manifesto for the Earth: Action Now for Peace, Justice and a Sustainable Future*. Forest Row: Clairview.

Gordon, D.L.A. and Tamminga, T. 2002: 'Large scale traditional neighbourhood development and pre-emptive ecosystem planning: the Markham experience'. *Journal of Urban Design*, 7(3): 321–40.

Gosling, D. 2003: *The Evolution of American Urban Design: A Chronological Anthology*. Hoboken NJ: Wiley-Academy.

Gospodini, A. 2002: 'European cities in competition and the "uses" of urban design'. *Journal of Urban Design*, 7(1): 59–73.

Gottdiener, M. 1977: *Planned Sprawl: Private and Public Interests in Suburbia*. Beverly Hills, CA: Sage.

Gottdiener, M. 1985: *The Social Production of Urban Space*. Austin, TX: University of Texas Press.

Gottdiener, M. 1986: 'Recapturing the centre: a semiotic analysis of the shopping mall'. In M. Gottdiener and A. Lagopoulos (eds) 1986: *The City and the Sign: An Introduction to Urban Semiotics*. New York: Columbia University Press.

Gottdiener, M. 1994: *The New Urban Sociology*. New York: McGraw-Hill.

Gottdiener, M. 1995: *Postmodern Semiotics*. Oxford: Blackwell.

Gottdiener, M. 1997: *The Theming of America: Dreams, Visions and Commercial Spaces*. Boulder, CO: Westview.

Gottdeiner, M. and Klephart, G. (eds) 1991: 'The multinucleated metropolitan region'. In R. Kling, O. Spencer and M. Poster (eds), *Postsuburban California: The Transformation of Orange County since World War II*. Berkeley, CA: University of California Press, pp. 31–54.

Gottdeiner, M. and Lagopoulos, A. (eds) 1986: *The City and the Sign: An Introduction to Urban Semiotics*. New York: Columbia University Press.

Gottdeiner, M., Collins, C. and Dickens, D. 1999: *Las Vegas: The Social Production of the All-American City*. Maiden, MA: Blackwell.

Gottmann, J. 1961: *Megalopolis: The Urbanised North-Eastern Seaboard of the United States*. New York: Twentieth Century Fund.

Graham, G. 1997: *Philosophy of the Arts: An Introduction to Aesthetics*. London: Routledge.

Grant, J. 2002: 'Exploring the influence of New Urbanism'. *Journal of Planning Education and Research*, 20(3): 234–53.

Grant, J. 2005: *Planning the Good Community: New Urbanism in Theory and Practice*. London: Routledge.

Grant, J. 2008: 'Planning the new community: the New Urbanism in theory and practice'. *Planning Theory*, 7(1): 103–15.

Grant, L., Ward, K.B. and Rong, X.L. 1987: 'Is there an association between gender and methods in sociological research?'. *American Sociological Review*, 52(6): 856–62.

Gray, J. 2002: *Straw Dogs*. London: Granta.

Greed, H. 1994: *Women and Planning: Creating Gendered Realities*. London: Routledge.

Greenberg, M. 2003: 'The limits of branding: the world trade centre, fiscal crisis and the marketing of recovery'. *International Journal of Urban and Regional Research*, 27(2): 386–416.

Guhathakura, S. 1999: 'Urban modelling and contemporary planning theory: is there a common ground?'. *Journal of Planning Education and Research*, 18(4): 281–92.

Gutkind, E.A. 1964: *The International History of City Development* (8 vols). New York: The Free Press of Glencoe.

Gwyther, G. 2004: 'Paradise planned: community formation and the master planned estate'. *Urban Policy and Research*, 23(1): 57–72.

Haas, T. (ed.) 2008: *The New Urbanism and Beyond: Designing New Cities for the Future*. New York: Rizzoli.

Habermas, J. 1970: 'Towards a theory of communicative competence'. *Inquiry: An Interdisciplinary Journal of Philosophy*, 13(1): 360–75.

Habermas, J. 1971: *Towards a Rational Society*. London: Heinemann.

Habermas, J. 1972: *Knowledge and Human Interests*. Cambridge: Polity Press.

Habermas, J. 1979: *Communication and the Evolution of Society*. Toronto: Beacon Press.

Habermas, J. 1989: *The Structural Transformation of the Public Sphere*. Cambridge: Polity Press.

Hacking, I. 1983: *Representing and Intervening: Introductory Topics in the Philosophy of Natural Science*. Cambridge: Cambridge University Press.

Haggerty, E.H. and McGarry, M. (eds) 2007: *A Companion to Lesbian, Gay, Bisexual, Transgender and Queer Studies*. Oxford: Blackwell.

Hall, K. and Porterfield, G. 2000: *Community by Design: New Urbanism for Suburbs and Small Communities*. New York: McGraw-Hill.

Hall, P. 1982: *Great Planning Disasters*. Harmondsworth: Penguin.

Hall, P. 1988: *Cities of Tomorrow: An Intellectual History of Urban Planning and Design in the Twentieth Century*. Cambridge, MA: Basil Blackwell.

Hall, P. 1998: *Cities in Civilization*. London: Weidenfeld and Nicholson.

Hall, S. and Gieben, B. (eds) 1992: *Formations of Modernity*. Cambridge: Polity Press.

Halprin, L. 1966: *Freeways*. New York: Reinhold.

Hamm, B. and Pandurang, K.M. (eds) 1998: *Sustainable Development and the Future of Cities*. London: Intermediate Technology Publications.

Hammond, M., Howarth, J. and Keat, R. (eds) 1991: *Understanding Phenomenology*. Oxford: Blackwell.

Hanson, J. 2003: *Decoding Home and Houses*. Cambridge: Cambridge University Press.

Haraway, D.J. 1991: *Simians, Cyborgs, and Women. The Reinvention of Nature*. London: Routledge, pp. 271–91.

Haraway, D.J. 1993: 'A cyborg manifesto'. In S. During (ed.), *The Cultural Studies Reader*. London: Routledge, pp. 271–92.

Harding, S.G. (ed.) 1987: *Feminism and Methodology*. Bloomington, IN: Indiana University Press.

Harding, S.G. 1991: *Whose Science, Whose Knowledge? Thinking for Women*. Ithaca, NY: Cornell University Press.

Harding, S.G. 1998: *Is Science Multicultural?: Postcolonialisms, Feminisms and Epistemologies*. Indianapolis, IN: Indianapolis University Press.

Harding, S.G. (ed.) 2004: *The Feminist Standpoint Reader: Intellectual and Political Commentaries*. London: Routledge.

Hardt, M. and Negri, A. 2000: *Empire*. Cambridge, MA: Harvard University Press.

Hardt, M. and Negri, A. 2005: *Multitude*. London: Penguin.

Hargroves, C. and Smith, M. 2005: *The Natural Advantage of Nations*. London: Earthscan.

Harloe, M., Issacharoff, R. and Minns, R. 1974: *The Organisation of Housing*. London: Heinemann.

Harrill, R. 1999: 'Political ecology and planning theory'. *The Journal of Planning Education and Research*, 19(1): 67–75.

Harris, C.D. and Ullman, E.L. 1945: 'The nature of cities'. *Annals of the American Academy of Political and Social Science*, 242: 7–17.

Harris, N. 1990: *The End of the Third World*. London: Penguin.

Hartsock, N.C.M. (ed.) 1991: *The Feminist Standpoint Revisited, and Other Essays*. Oxford: Westview Press.

Harvey, D. 1973: *Social Justice and the City*. London: Arnold.

Harvey, D. 1979: 'Monument and myth'. *Annals of the Association of American Geographers*, 68(3): 362–81.

Harvey, D. 1982: *The Limits to Capital*. Oxford: Blackwell.

Harvey, D. 1985: *The Urbanisation of Capital*. Oxford: Blackwell.

Harvey, D. 1989: *The Condition of Postmodernity*. Oxford: Blackwell.

Harvey, D. 2003: *The New Imperialism*. Oxford: Oxford University Press.

Harvey, D. 2007: *Spaces of Global Capitalism: Towards a Theory of Uneven Geographical Development*. London: Verso.

Hashimoto, K. 2002: 'The new urban sociology in Japan: the changing debates'. *Journal of Planning Education and Research*, 26(4): 726–36.

Hawken, P., Lovins, A. and Lovins, L. 1999: *Natural Capitalism: The Next Industrial Revolution*. London: Earthscan.

Hay, I. (ed.) 2005: *Qualitative Research Methods in Human Geography*. South Melbourne: Oxford University Press.

Hayden, D. 1976: *Seven American Utopias: The Architecture of Communitarian Socialism 1790–1975*. Cambridge, MA: MIT Press.

Hayden, D. 1980: 'What would a non-sexist city be like? Speculations on housing, urban design and human work'. In C. Stimpson, E. Dixler, M. Nelson and K. Yatrakis (eds), *Women and the American City*. Chicago, IL: Chicago University Press, pp. 266–81.

Hayden, D. 1981: *The Grand Domestic Revolution: A History of Feminist Designs for American Homes, Neighbourhoods and Cities*. Cambridge, MA: MIT Press.

Hayden, D. 1984: *Redesigning the American Dream: The Future of Housing, Work and Family*. New York: W.W. Norton.

Hayden, D. 2003: *Building Suburbia: Green Fields and Urban Growth 1820–2000*. New York: Pantheon.

Hayles, K. 1999: *How We Became Posthuman. Virtual Bodies in Cybernetics, Literature, and Informatics*. Chicago, IL: Chicago University Press.

Hayllar, B., Griffin, T. and Edwards, D. (eds) 2008: *City Spaces, Tourist Places: Urban Tourism Precincts*. Oxford: Butterworth-Heinemann.

Hays, M. 2000 (ed.): *Architecture Theory since 1968*. Cambridge, MA: MIT Press.

Hebbert, M. 2005: 'Street as a locus of collective memory'. *Environment and Planning D: Society and Space*, 23(4): 581–96.

Hegel, G.W.F. 1977: *The Phenomenology of Spirit*. Oxford: Oxford University Press.

Heidegger, M. 1952: *Being and Time*. New York: Harper.

Heinich, H. 1988: 'The Pompidou Centre and its public. The limits of a utopian site'. In R. Lumley (ed.), *The Museum Time Machine*. London: Comedia.

Held, D. 1980: *Introduction to Critical Theory: Horkheimer to Habermas*. Berkeley, CA: University of California Press.

Hesse-Biber, S., Gilmartin, C. and Lydenberg, R. (eds) 1999: *Feminist Approaches to Theory and Methodology: An Interdisciplinary Reader*. Oxford: Oxford University Press.

Highmore, B. 2006: *Michel De Certeau: Analysing Culture*. London: Continuum.

Hilberseimer, L. 1955: *The Nature of Cities*. Chicago, IL: Paul Theobald.

Hillier, W. and Hanson, J. 1984: *The Social Logic of Space*. Cambridge: Cambridge University Press.

Hillier, W. and Leaman, A. 1976: 'Space syntax'. *Environment and Planning B*, 3(2): 147–85.

Hines, M. 2004: *Brain Gender*. Oxford: Oxford University Press.

Hirshman, L.R. 2006: *Get to Work: A Manifesto for Women of the World*. New York: Viking.

Home, R. 1989: *Planning around London's Megaproject: Canary Wharf and the Isle of Dogs*. Oxford: Butterworth.

Howard, E. 1898: *Tomorrow: A Peaceful Path to Real Reform* (1898), reissued as *Garden Cities of Tomorrow* (1902). Original publisher unknown.

Hoyer, M. 2008: 'See why McNeil's so hot right now'. *The Sunday Telegraph*, Sydney, 15 June: 6.

Hoyt, H. 1933: *One Hundred Years of Land Values in Chicago: The Relationship of the Growth of Chicago to the Rise of Its Land Values, 1830–1933*. Chicago, IL: University of Chicago Press.

Hoyt, H. 1939: *The Structure and Growth of Residential Neighborhoods in American Cities*. Washington, DC: United States Federal Housing Administration.

Huang, E. and Yeoh, S. (eds) 1996: 'Gender and urban space in the tropical world.' *Singapore Journal of Tropical Geography* (Themed Issue).

Huang, M. 1996: *Walking Between Slums and Skyscrapers*. Washington, DC: University of Washington Press.

Hudson, B.M. 1979: 'Comparison of current planning theories. Counterparts and contradictions'. *Journal of the American Planning Association*, 45(4): 387–98.

Hulser, K. 1997: 'Visual browsing: auto flâneurs and roadside ads in the 1950's'. In Lang and Miller (eds), *Suburban Discipline*. New York: Princeton Architectural Press, pp. 26–39.

Husserl, E. 1969: *Ideas: General Introduction to Pure Phenomenology*. London: Allen and Unwin.

Huxley, A. 1960: *Brave New World*. London: Chatto and Windus.

Huxley, M. 1988: 'Feminist urban theory: gender, class and the built environment'. *Transition*, Winter: 39–43.

Huxley, M. 2000: 'The limits to communicative planning'. *Journal of Planning Education and Research*, 19(4): 369–77.

Illich, I. 1983: *Gender*. London: Marion Boyers.

Ince, M. 2003: *Conversations with Manuel Castells*. London: Wiley.

Irazabal, C. 2007: 'Kitsch is dead, long live kitsch: the production of hyperkitsch in Las Vegas'. *Journal of Architectural and Planning Research*, 24(3): 199–219.

Irvine, S. and Ponton, A. 1988: *A Green Manifesto: Policies for a Green Future*. London: Optima.

Isaacs, R. 2000: 'The urban picturesque: an aesthetic experience of urban pedestrian places'. *Journal of Urban Design*, 5(2): 2000.

Jacobs, A. and Appleyard, D. 1987: 'A manifesto'. *American Planning Association Journal*, November.

Jacobs, J. 1961: *The Death and Life of Great American Cities*. New York: Random House.

Jaekel, M. and van Geldermalsen, M. 2006: 'Gender equality and urban development: building better communities for all'. *Global Urban Development Magazine*, 2(1).

Jefferson, C., Rowe, J. and Brebbia, C. (eds) 2001: *Street Design and Management*. Michigan: WIT Press.

Jellicoe, S. and Jellicoe, J. 1987: *The Landscape of Man: Shaping the Environment from Prehistory to the Present*. London: Thames and Hudson.

Jencks, C. 1977: *The Language of Postmodern Architecture*. London: Academy.

Jencks, C. 1993: *Heteropolis: Los Angeles, the Riots, and the Strange Beauty of Hetero-architecture*. New York: St Martin's Press.

Jencks, C. 2005: *The Iconic Building: The Power of Enigma*. London: Francis Lincoln.

Jencks, C. and Kropf, K. (eds) 1997: *Theories and Manifestos of Contemporary Architecture*. Sussex: Wiley.

Jencks, C. and Sudjic, D. 2005: 'Can we still believe in iconic buildings?'. *Prospect*, June: 22–6.

Jenkins, B. 2006: 'The dialectics of design'. *Space and Culture*, 9(2): 195–209.

Jenks, J., Williams, B. and Burton, W. (eds) 1996: *The Compact City: A Sustainable Urban Form?* London, Melbourne: Spon.

Jenks, M. and Burgess, R. 2000: *Compact Cities: Sustainable Urban Form in Developing Countries*. London: Spon.

Jenks, M. and Dempsey, N. (eds) 2005: *Future Forms and Design for Sustainable Cities*. Oxford: The Architectural Press.

Jensen, O.B. 2007: 'Cultural stories: understanding urban branding'. *Planning Theory*, 6(3): 211–36.

Johns, E. 1965: *British Townscapes*. London: Arnold.

Johnson, N. 1994: 'Cast in stone: monuments, geography and nationalism'. *Environment and Planning D, Society and Space*, 14(1): 51–65.

Johnson, P. 1984: *Marxist Aesthetics: The Foundations Within Everyday Life for an Emancipated Consciousness*. Boston: Routledge and Kegan Paul.

Jones, J.C. 1992(1970): *Design Methods: Seeds of Human Futures*. New York: Wiley-Interscience.

Jordanova, J.L. 2000: *History in Practice*. New York: Oxford University Press.

Joyce, J. 1960(Orig. 1922): *Ulysses*. London: Bodley Head.

Joyce, J. 1992(Orig. 1939): *Finnegan's Wake*. London: Penguin

Kagan, R. 2008: *The Return of History and the End of Dreams*. New York: Knopf.

Katz, C. 2006: 'Power space and terror: social reproduction and the built environment'. In S. Low and N. Smith, *The Politics of Public Space*. London: Routledge, pp. 105–21.

Katz, P. 1994: *The New Urbanism*. New York: McGraw-Hill.

Kayden, J.S. 2000: *Privately Owned Public Space*. New York: Wiley.

Keil, R. 1998: *Los Angeles: Globalisation, Urbanisation and Social Struggles*. New York: Wiley.

Kennicott, P. 2007: 'The meaning of a marker for 100 million victims'. *The Washington Post*, 13 June: CO1.

Kimmel, M.S. 2008: *The Gendered Society*. Oxford: Oxford University Press.

Kimura, D. 1993: *Neuromotor Mechanisms in Human Communication*. New York: Oxford University Press.

Kimura, D. 1999: *Sex and Cognition*. Cambridge, MA: MIT Press.

King, A. 2004: *Spaces of Global Cultures: Architecture, Urbanism, Identity*. London: Routledge.

King, A.D. 1990: *Urbanism, Colonialism and the World Economy: Cultural and Spatial Foundations of the World Urban System*. London: Routledge.

Kitchen, P. 1975: *A Most Unsettling Person: An Introduction to the Ideas and Life of Patrick Geddes*. London: Gollancz.

Klein, H. 2007: *Project Planning*. Zurich: Birkhauser.

Knaap, L., Hopkins, D. and Kieran, P. 1998: 'Do plans matter? A game-theoretic model for examining the logic and effects of land use planning'. *Journal of Planning Education and Research*, 18(1): 25–34.

Kogler, H.H. 1996: *The Power of Dialogue: Critical Hermeneutics after Gadamer and Foucault*. Cambridge, MA: MIT Press.

Kohn, M. 2004: *Brave New Neighbourhoods: The Privatisation of Public Space*. London: Routledge.

Kolson, K .2001: *Big Plans: The Allure and Folly of Urban Design*. Baltimore, MD: Johns Hopkins University Press.

Koolhaas, R. 1994: *Delirious New York: A Retroactive Manifesto for Manhattan*. New York: Monacelli Press.

Korn, A, 1953: *History Builds the Town*. London: publisher unknown.

Kostoff, S. 1991: *The City Shaped*. London: Thames and Hudson.

Kostoff, S. 1992: *The City Assembled*. London: Thames and Hudson.

Krampen, M.K. 1979: *Meaning in the Urban Environment*. London: Pion.

Krier, L. 1975: *The Reconstruction of the City*. Brussels: Archives d'Architecture Moderne.

Krier, L. 1978: *Rational Architecture: The Reconstruction of the European City*. Brussels: Archives d'Architecture Moderne.

Krier, L. 1985: *Houses, Palaces, Cities*. London: Academy/St Martin's Press.

Krier, R. 1979: *Urban Space*. New York: Rizzoli.

Kuhn, T. 1962: *The Structure of Scientific Revolutions*. Chicago, IL: University of Chicago Press.

Kumic, I. 2008: 'Revealing the competitive city: spatial political economy and city brands'. Doctoral thesis, Faculty of Architecture, Design and Planning, The University of Sydney, Australia.

Kundera, M. 1985: *The Unbearable Lightness of Being*. London: Faber and Faber.

La Rue, L. 1970: 'The black movement and women's liberation'. *The Black Scholar*, 1: 42.

Lagopoulos, A. 1986: 'Semiotic urban models and modes of production'. In M. Gottdiener, P. Alexandros and A. Lagopoulos, *The City and the Sign: An Introduction to Urban Semiotics*. New York: Columbia University Press, pp. 176–202.

Lamarche, F. 1976: 'Property development and the economic foundation of the urban question'. In C. Pickvance (ed.), *Urban Sociology*. London: Methuen, pp. 45–68.

Landry, C. 2000: *The Creative City*. London: Earthscan.

Lang, J. 2005: *Urban Design: A Typology of Procedures and Products*. New York: Elsevier.

Lang, J.T. 1994: *Urban Design the American Experience*. New York: Van Nostrand.

Lang, R., LeFurgy, J. and Nelson, A.C. 2006: 'The six suburban eras of the United States'. *Opolis*, 2(1): 65–72.

Lash, S. 2002: *Critique of Information*. London: Sage.

Latham, R. 2001: 'A journey towards catching phenomenology'. In R. Barnacle, *Phenomenology*. Melbourne: RMIT Press, pp. 45–57.

Lather, P.A. 2007: *Getting Lost: Feminist Efforts toward a Double(d) Science*. Albany: State University of New York Press.

Laugier, M.A. 1985 (orig. 1763): *Essay on Architecture*. New York: Hennessy and Ingalls.

Laurel, B. (ed.) 2003: *Design Research: Methods and Perspectives*. Cambridge, MA: MIT Press.

Lay, J. 2004: *After Method: Mess in Social Science*. London: Routledge.

Le Corbusier 1980: *Modulor 1 and Modulor 2*. Cambridge, MA: Harvard University Press.

Lechte, J. 1994: *Fifty Key Contemporary Thinkers from Structuralism to Postmodernity*. London: Routledge.

Lefebvre, H. 1976: *The Survival of Capitalism: Reproduction of the Relations of Production*. London: Alison and Busby.

Lefebvre, H. 1991 (orig. 1974): *The Production of Space*. Oxford: Blackwell.

Lehrer, U. and Laidley, J. 2009: 'Old mega-projects newly packaged? Waterfront redevelopment in Toronto'. *International Journal of Urban and Regional Research*, 32(4): 768–803.

Leslie, D. and Reimer, S. 2003: 'Gender, modern design and home consumption'. *Environment and Planning D: Society and Space*, 21(2): 293–314.

Lewis, J. 2002: *Cultural Studies: The Basics*. Thousand Oaks, CA: Sage.

Ley, D. and Olds, K. 1988: 'Landscape as spectacle: worlds fairs and the culture of heroic consumption'. *Environment and Planning D: Society and Space*, 6(2): 191–212.

Light, A. and Smith, J. (eds) 2005: *The Aesthetics of Everyday Life*. New York: Columbia University Press.

Lin, J. and Mele, C. (eds) 2005: *The Urban Sociology Reader*. London: Routledge.

Linebaugh, P. 2008: *The Magna Carta Manifesto: Liberties and Commons for All*. Berkeley, CA: University of California Press.

Lippa, R. 2002: *Gender, Nature, Nurture*. Mahwah, NJ: Lawrence Erlbaum.

Little, J., Peake, L. and Richards, P. 1988: *Women in Cities: Gender in the Urban Environment*. New York: New York University Press.

Llosa, M.V. 2003: *The Way to Paradise*. London: Faber and Faber.

Loevinger, R., Rahder, B.L. and O'Neill, K. 1998: 'Women and planning: education for social change'. *Planning Research and Practice*, 13(2): 247–65.

Lofland, L. 1998: *The Public Realm: Exploring the City's Quintessential Social Theory*. New Jersey: Transaction Publishers.

London Planning Aid Service 1987: *Planning for Women: An Evaluation of Consultation in Three London Boroughs*.

Low, S. 2000: 'How private interests take over public space'. In S. Low and N. Smith, *The Politics of Public Space*. London: Routledge, pp. 81–103.

Low, S. and Smith, N. (eds) 2006: *The Politics of Public Space*. Oxford: Routledge.

Lucarelli, M. 1995: *Lewis Mumford and the Ecological Region: The Politics of Planning*. New York: Guildford Press.

Lukes, S. 1986: *Power*. New York: New York University Press.

Lynch, K. 1960: *The Image of the City*. Cambridge, MA: MIT Press.

Lynch, K. 1971: *Site Planning*. Cambridge, MA: MIT Press.

Lynch, K. 1981: *A Theory of Good City Form*. Cambridge, MA: MIT Press.

Lyon, D. 2003: 'Technology vs "terrorism": circuits of city surveillance since September 11th'. *International Journal of Urban and Regional Research*, 27(3): 666–78.

Lyotard, J.F. 1991: *Phenomenology*. New York: State University of New York Press.

McCann, E.J. 1995: 'Neo-traditional developments: the anatomy of a new urban form'. *Urban Geography*, 16(2): 210–33.

MacCannell, D. 1992: 'The Vietnam memorial in Washington DC'. In D. MacCannell, *Empty Meeting Grounds*. London: Routledge, pp. 280–2.

McCarthy, J. 2006: 'Regeneration of cultural quarters: public art for place image or place identity?'. *Journal of Urban Design*, 11(2): 243–62.

Macauley, D. 2000: 'Walking the city: peripatetic practices and politics'. *Capitalism, Nature, Socialism*, 11(1): 3–43.

McCluskey, J. 1979: *Road Form and Townscape*. London: The Architectural Press.

McDonough, W. and Braungart, M. 1998: 'The next industrial revolution'. *The Atlantic Monthly*, 282(4): 82–92.

MacGregor, S. 1995: 'Deconstructing the man-made city: feminist critiques of planning thought and action'. In J. Eichler (ed.), *Change of Plans: Towards a Non-Sexist Sustainable City*. Toronto: Garamond Press, pp. 25–49.

McHarg, I.L. 1969: *Design with Nature*. Garden City, NY: The Natural History Press.

Mackenzie, S. 1988: 'Building women building cities: towards gender sensitive theory in environmental disciplines'. In C. Andrew and B. Milroy (eds), *Life Spaces: Gender, Household, Employment*. Vancouver: University of British Columbia Press, pp. 126–48.

Mackenzie, S. 1989: 'Women in the city'. In R. Peet and N. Thrift (eds), *New Models in Geography*. London: Winchester, pp. 109–26.

McKeown, K. 1987: *Marxist Political Economy and Marxist Urban Sociology: A Review and Elaboration of Recent Developments*. Basingstoke: Macmillan.

McLoughlin, J.B. 1970: *Urban and Regional Planning: A Systems Approach*. London: Faber and Faber.

McLoughlin, J.B. 1991: 'Urban consolidation and urban sprawl: a question of density'. *Urban Policy and Research*, 9(3): 148–56.

McNeill, D. 2005: 'In search of the global architect: the case of Norman Foster (and partners)'. *International Journal of Urban and Regional Research*, 29(3): 501–15.

McNeill, D. 2007: 'Office buildings and the signature architect: Piano and Foster in Sydney'. *Environment and Planning A*, 39(2): 487–501.

McNeill, D. 2008: *The Global Architect: Firms, Fame and Urban Form*. London: Routledge.

McNeill, D. and Tewdwr-Jones, M. 2003: 'Architecture, banal nationalism and re-territorialisation'. *International Journal of Urban and Regional Research*, 27(3): 738–43.

Madsen, K. (ed.) 1994: 'Women, land, design'. *Landscape Journal* (Themed Issue), 13(2).

Mairet, P. 1957: *Pioneer of Sociology: The Life and Letters of Patrick Geddes*. London: Lund Humphries.

Makarova, E. 2006: 'The New Urbanism in Moscow: the redefinition of public and private space'. Paper presented at the Annual Meeting of the American Sociological Association, Montreal Convention Center, Montreal, Quebec, Canada. University of Virginia: Department of Sociology.

Mandelbaum, S.J., Mazza L., Burchell, R.W. (eds) 1996: *Explorations in Planning Theory*. New Jersey: Rutgers, State University of New Jersey: Centre for Policy Research.

March, L. 1976: 'A Boolean description of a class of built forms'. In L. March (ed.), *The Architecture of Form*, Cambridge: Cambridge University Press, pp. 41–73.

March, L. and Steadman, P. (eds) 1971: *The Geometry of Environment*. London: Methuen.

Marcuse, H. 1978: *The Aesthetic Dimension: Toward a Critique of Marxist Aesthetics*. Boston: Beacon Press.

Marcuse, P. 1962: *Eros and Civilisation: A Philosophical Enquiry into Freud*. New York: Vintage Books.

Marcuse, P. 1968: *Negations: Essays in Critical Theory*. New York: Beacon Books.

Marcuse, P. 2006: 'Security or safety in cities? The threat of terrorism after 9/11'. *International Journal of Urban and Regional Research*, 30(4): 919–29.

Marcuse, P. and Van Kempen, R. (eds) 2000: *Globalising Cities: A New Spatial Order?* Oxford: Blackwell.

Marshall, R. 2003: *Emerging Urbanity: Global Urban Projects in the Asia Pacific Rim*. London: Spon.

Marshall, S. (ed.) 2003: 'New Urbanism'. *The Journal of Urban Design*, Themed Issue, 29(3): 185–271.

Marshall, S. 2009: *Cities, Design and Evolution*. London: Routledge.

Martin, L. and March, L. (eds) 1972: *Urban Space and Structures*. Cambridge: Cambridge University Press.

Martin, R. and Marden, T. 1999: 'Food for urban spaces'. *International Planning Studies*, 4(3): 389–412.

Marx, K. 1959: *Capital* (Vol. 3). London: Lawrence and Wishart.

Marx, K. and Engels, F. 1999 (orig. 1872): *The Communist Manifesto with Related Documents*. Boston: Bedford/St Martin's Press.

Massey, D. 1984: *Spatial Division of Labour: Social Structures and the Geography of Production*. London: Methuen.

Massey, D. 1994: *Space, Place and Gender*. London: Wiley.

Mazlish, B. 1994: 'The *flâneur*: from spectator to representation'. In K. Tester (ed.), *The Flâneur*. London and New York: Routledge.

Meller, H.E. 1990: *Patrick Geddes: Social Evolutionist and City Planner*. London: Routledge.

Mendez, M. 2005: 'Latino New Urbanism. Building on cultural preferences'. *Opolis*, 1(1): 33–48.

Merleau-Ponty, M. 1962: *Phenomenology of Perception*. London: Routledge.

Merrifield, A. 2002: *Metromarxism*. London: Routledge.

Miliband, R. 1973: *The State in Capitalist Society*. New York: Basic Books.

Milicevic, A.S. 2001: 'What happened to the new urban sociology?'. *International Journal of Urban and Regional Research*, 25(4): 759–83.

Miller, D.W. 2000: 'The new urban studies'. Research and Publishing section: A15. Available online at: http://chronicle.com.

Millet, J.M. (ed.) 2004: *Research Methods: A Qualitative Reader*. Upper Saddle River, NJ: Prentice Hall.

Millett, K. 1971: *Sexual Politics*. London: Rupert Hart-Davis.

Minca, C. 2001: *Postmodern Geography: Theory and Praxis*. Oxford: Blackwell.

Mitchell, D. 2003: *The Right to the City: Social Justice and the Fight for Public Space*. New York: Guilford Press.

Mitrasinovic, M. 2006: *Total Landscape, Theme Parks, Public Space*. New York: Ashgate.

Modlich, R. 1994: 'Women plan Toronto'. *Women and Environments*, 14(Spring): 27–8.

Moholy-Nagy, S. 1968: *The Matrix of Man*. London: Pall Mall.

Molotch, H. 2002: 'Schools out: a response to Michael Dear'. *City and Community*, 1(1): 39–43.

Molotch, H. and McClain, N. 2003: 'Dealing with urban terror: heritages of control, varieties of intervention, strategies of research'. *International Journal of Urban and Regional Research*, 27(3): 679–98.

Moor, M. and Rowland, M. 2006: *Urban Design Futures*. Abingdon: Routledge.

Morgan, G. (ed.) 1983: *Beyond Method*. Beverly Hills: Sage.

Morris, A.E.J. 1979: *History of Urban Form: Before the Industrial Revolutions*. London: Godwin.

Moser, C. and Levi, C. 1986: 'A theory and methodology of gender planning: meeting practical and strategic gender needs'. *World Development*, 17(1): 1799–825.

Mougeot, J.A. (ed.) 2000: *Agropolis: The Social, Political and Environmental Dimensions of Urban Agriculture*. London: Earthscan.

Mougeot, J.A. 2006: *Growing Better Cities*. Ottawa: The International Development Centre.

Moughtin, J.C. 2004: *Urban Design: Green Dimensions*. Boston: The Architectural Press.

Moughtin, J.C., Oc, T. and Tiesdell, S. 1995: *Urban Design: Ornament and Decoration*. Oxford: The Architectural Press.

Moughtin, J.C., Cuesta, R., Sarris C.A. and Signoretta, P. 2003: *Urban Design, Method and Techniques*. Oxford: The Architectural Press.

Mulvey, L. 1996: *Fetishism and Curiosity*. Bloomington, IN: Indiana University Press.

Mulvey, L. 2006: *Death 24X A Second: Stillness and the Moving Image*. London: Reaktion Books.

Mumford, L. 1938: *The Culture of Cities*. Basingstoke. Macmillan.

Mumford, L. 1952: *Art and Technics*. New York: Columbia University Press.

Mumford, L. 1961: *The City in History*. New York: Harcourt, Brace and Jovanovitch.

Mumford, L. 1962 (orig. 1922): *The Story of Utopias*. New York: Viking Press.

Mumford, L. 1965: 'Utopia, the city and the machine'. In F.E. Manuel (ed.), *Utopias and Utopian Thought*. Boston: Houghton Mifflin, pp. 10–32.

Munro, M. 2005: 'Does it pay to maintain New Urbanist infrastructure? A fiscal comparison of alternative community forms'. *Plan Canada*, 44(1): 25–8.

Nairn, I. (ed.) 1955: 'Outrage'. *The Architectural Review* (Special Issue).

Nairn, I. (ed.) 1956: 'Counter Attack'. *The Architectural Review* (Special Issue).

Nash, C. 1993: 'Renaming and remapping'. *Feminist Review*, 44(1): 39–57.

Negri, A. 1989: *The Politics of Subversion: A Manifesto for the Twenty-First Century*. Cambridge: Polity Press.

Negt, O. and Kluge, A. 1993: *Public Sphere and Experience: Toward an Analysis of the Bourgeois and Proletarian Public Spheres*. Minneapolis, MN: University of Minnesota Press.

Neuman, W.L. 2003: *Social Science Methods: Qualitative and Quantitative Approaches*. Boston: Allyn and Bacon.

Newman, P. 2006: 'The environmental impact of cities'. *Environment and Urbanization*, 18: 275–95.

Newman, P. and Kenworthy, J. 1989: *Cities and Automobile Dependence*. Aldershot: Gower.

Newman, P. and Kenworthy, J. 1999: *Sustainability and Cities: Overcoming Automobile Dependence*. Washington, DC: Island Press.

Newman, P. and Kenworthy, J. 2006: 'Urban design to reduce automobile dependence in centres'. *Opolis*, 2(3): 35–52

Nightingale, A. 2006: 'The nature of gender: work, gender and environment'. *Environment and Planning D: Society and Space*, 24: 165–85.

Noble, T. 2000: *Social Theory and Social Change*. Basingstoke: Palgrave.

Norberg-Schulz, C. 1965: *Intentions in Architecture*. Cambridge, MA: MIT Press.

Norberg-Schulz, C. 1971: *Existence Space and Architecture*. London: Studio Vista.

Norberg-Schulz, C. 1979: *Genius Loci*. New York: Rizzoli.

Norberg-Schulz, C. 1985: *The Concept of Dwelling*. New York: Rizolli.

Norberg-Schulz, C. 1988: *Architecture, Meaning and Place*. New York: Rizzoli.

O'Connor, J. 1971: *The Fiscal Crisis of the State*. New York: St Martin's Press.

O'Neill, P. 2002: 'Taking the flâneur for a spin to the suburbs: the auto-flâneur and a way of looking at the subject in suburban culture'. Available online at: www.slashseconds.org/issues/002/002/articles/poneill/index.php.

Olds, K. 2001: *Globalisation and Urban Change: Capital, Culture and Pacific Rim Mega-Projects*. Oxford University Press: Oxford.

Olofsson, J. 2008: 'Negotiating figurations for feminist methodologies – a manifest for the fl@neur'. Available online at: www.gjss.nl/vol05/nr01/a05.

Olsen, D.J. 1986: *The City as a Work of Art: London, Paris, Vienna*. New Haven, CT: Yale University Press.

Onfray, M. 2005: *The Atheist Manifesto*. Melbourne, Victoria: University of Melbourne Press.

Orr, D. 2002: *The Nature of Design: Ecology, Culture, and Human Intention*. Oxford: Oxford University Press.

Orueta, F.D. and Fainstein, S. 2008: 'The new mega-projects: genesis and impacts'. *International Journal of Urban and Regional Research*, 32(4): 759–67.

Orwell, G. 1992 (orig. 1933): *Nineteen Eighty-Four*. New York: Knopf.

Oxman, R. 1987: *Urban Design Theories and Methods*. Sydney: University of Sydney, Department of Architecture.

Parfect, M. and Power, G. (eds) 1997: *Planning for Urban Quality: Urban Design in Towns and Cities*. London: Routledge.

Parker, S. 1997: *Reflective Teaching in the Postmodern World: A Manifesto for Education in Postmodernity*. Buckingham: The Open University Press.

Parkhurst, P. 1994: 'The *flâneur* on and off the streets of Paris'. In K. Tester (ed.), *The Flâneur*. London: Routledge, pp. 16–38.

Parsons, D. 2000: *Streetwalking the Metropolis: Women, the City and Modernity*. Oxford: Oxford University Press.

Pearsall, J. (ed.) 2001: *The New Oxford Dictionary of English*. Oxford: Oxford University Press.

Pêcheux, M. 1982: *Language Semantics and Ideology*. London: Macmillan.

Perez-Gomez, A. 2000: 'Introduction to architecture and the crisis of modern science'. In M.K. Hays, *Architecture Theory since 1968*. Boston, MA: MIT Press.

Perlman, J. 1976: *The Myth of Marginality*. Berkeley, CA: University of California Press.

Perry, B. and Harding, A. 2002: 'The future of urban sociology: report of joint sessions of the British and American Sociological Associations'. *International Journal of Urban and Regional Research*, 26(4): 844–53.

Phillips, D.L. 1973: *Abandoning Method*. San Francisco: Jossey-Bass.

Pickford, R.W. 1972: *Psychology and Visual Aesthetics*. London: Hutchinson.

Pickvance, C. (ed.) 1976: *Urban Sociology: Critical Essays*. London: Methuen.

Platt, R. (ed.) 1994: *The Ecological City*. Amherst, MA: University of Massachusetts Press.

Plaza, B. 1999: 'The Guggenheim-Bilbao museum effect: a reply to Maria V. Gomez' "Reflective images: the case of urban regeneration in Glasgow and Bilbao"'. *International Journal of Urban and Regional Research*, 23(3): 1999.

Plaza, B. 2006: 'Return on investment of the Guggenheim museum Bilbao'. *International Journal of Urban and Regional Research*, 30(2): 452–67.

Plaza, B. 2008: 'On some challenges and conditions for the Guggenheim museum Bilbao to be an effective economic re-activator'. *International Journal of Urban and Regional Research*, 32(2): 506–17.

Popper, K.R. 1957: *The Poverty of Historicism*. London: Routledge and Kegan Paul.

Popper, K.R. 1959: *The Logic of Scientific Discovery*. London: Hutchison.

Porteous, D.J. 1996: *Environmental Aesthetics: Ideas, Politics and Planning*. London: Taylor and Francis.

Portes, A. and Stepick, A. 1993: *City on the Edge: The Transformation of Miami*. Berkeley, CA: University of California Press.

Poster, M. 1986: *Foucault, Marxism and History*. Cambridge: Polity Press.

Poulantzas, N. 1973 'The problem of the capitalist state'. In J. Urry and J. Wakeford (eds), *Power in Britain*. London: Heinemann, pp. 291–305.

Pouler, P.J. 1994: 'Disciplinary society and the myth of aesthetic justice'. In B. Scheer and W.F.E. Preiser (eds), *Design Review: Challenging Urban Aesthetic Control*. New York: Chapman and Hall, pp. 175–87.

Powell, R. 1994: *Rethinking the Skyscraper: The Complete Architecture of Ken Yeang*. London: Thames and Hudson.

Preson, J.M. 1998: 'Science as supermarket: "post-modern" themes in Paul Feyerabend's later philosophy of science'. *Studies in the History and Philosophy of Science*, 29(1): 34–52.

Preziosi, D. 1979a: *The Semiotics of the Built Environment*. Indiana: Indiana University Press.

Preziosi, D. 1979b: *Architecture, Language and Meaning: The Origins of the Built World and Its Semiotic Organization*. The Hague: Mouton.

Quon, S. 1999: 'Planning for urban agriculture: a review of the tools and strategies for urban planning – cities feeding people'. Report 28. Ottawa: The International Development Research Centre.

Rao, V. 2006: 'Slum as theory. The South/Asian city and globalization'. *International Journal of Urban and Regional Research*, 30(1): 225–32.

Raphael, M. 1981: *Proudhon, Marx, Picasso: Three Essays in Marxist Aesthetics*. London: Lawrence and Wishart.

Rappoport, A. 1977: *Human Aspects of Urban Form*. Oxford: Pergamon.

Reeves, D. (ed.) 2003: *Gender Mainstreaming Toolkit*. London: The Royal Town Planning Institute. Available online at: www.rtpi.org.uk.

Register, R. 2002: *Building Cities in Balance with Nature*. Berkeley, CA: Berkeley Hills Books.

Relph, E. 1976: *Place and Placelessness*. London: Pion.

Rendell, J., Penner, B. and Borden, I. 2000: *Gender, Space, Architecture*. London: Routledge.

Reps, J.W. 1965: *The Making of Urban America*. Princeton: Princeton University Press.

Ricoeur, P. 1981: *Hermeneutics and the Human Sciences*. Cambridge: Cambridge University Press.

Riegl, A. 1982 (orig. 1903): 'The modern cult of monuments: its character and its origin'. *Oppositions*, 25(1): 21–51.

Rifkind, J. 1995: *The End of Work: The Decline of the Global Work-Force and the Dawn of the Post-Market Era*. New York: G.P. Putnam's Sons.

Ritchie, B.W. 2008: 'Contribution of urban precincts to the economy'. In B. Hayllar, T. Griffin and D. Edwards (eds), *City Spaces, Tourist Places: Urban Tourism Precincts*. Oxford: Butterworth-Heinemann, pp. 151–82.

Roberts, M. 1997: 'Future cities, past lives: gender and nostalgia in three contemporary planning visions'. *Planning Practice and Research*, 12(2): 109–18.

Roberts, M. 1998: 'Urban design, gender and the future of cities'. *The Journal of Urban Design*, 3(2): 133–5.

Roberts, M. and Greed, C. 2001: *Approaching Urban Design: The Design Process*. Harlow: Longman.

Robinson, J. 2002: 'Global and world cities: a view from off the map'. *International Journal of Urban and Regional Research*, 26(3): 531–54.

Roderick, R. 1986: *Habermas and the Foundations of Critical Theory*. New York: St Martin's Press.

Rome, A. 2001: *The Bulldozer in the Countryside: Suburban Sprawl and the Rise of American Environmentalism*. New York: Cambridge University Press.

Roseneau, H. 1983: *The Ideal City*. London: Methuen.

Rothman, H. 2002: *Neon Metropolis: How Las Vegas Started the Twenty-First Century*. New York: Routledge.

Rothschid, J. (ed.) 1999: *Design and Feminism: Re-Visioning Spaces, Places and Everyday Things*. New Jersey: Rutgers University Press.

Rowe, C. and Koetter, F. 1978: *Collage City*. Cambridge, MA: MIT Press.

Roweis, S.T. 1983: 'The professional mediation of territorial politics'. *Environment and Planning D, Society and Space*, 1(3): 139–62.

RTPI Working Party 1985: *Women and Planning in Scotland*. London: Royal Town Planning Institute.

Ruchelman, L.I. 2000: *Cities in the Third Wave: The Technological Transformation of Urban America*. Chicago, IL: Burnham.

Ruddock, S. 1996: 'Constructing difference in public spaces: race, class and gender as interlocking systems'. *Urban Geography*, 17(2): 132–51.

Rudofsky, B. 1969: *Streets for People*. Garden City, NY: Doubleday.

Rutheiser, C. 1997: 'Beyond the radiant garden city beautiful: notes on the New Urbanism'. *City and Society*, 91(1): 117–33.

Rykwert, J. 1976: *The Idea of a Town: The Anthropology of Urban Form in Rome, Italy and the Ancient World*. London: Faber and Faber

Saab, J.A. 2007: 'Historical amnesia: New Urbanism and the city of tomorrow'. *Journal of Planning History*, 6(3): 191–213.

Saarikoski, H. 2002: 'Naturalized epistemology and dilemmas of planning practice'. *Journal of Planning Education and Research*, 22(1): 3–14.

Said, E. 1978: *Orientalism*. London: Routledge and Kegan Paul.

Sander, C. 2003: *Migrant Remittances to Developing Countries: A Scoping Study*. London: Bannock Consulting.

Sandercock, L. and Forsyth, A. 1992: 'A gender agenda: new directions for planning theory'. *Journal of the American Planning Association*, 58(1): 49–60.

Saraswati, T. 2000: *Modernisation, Issues of Gender and Space*. Jogyakarta: Jurusan Teknik Arsitektur, Facultas Teknik Sipil dan Perencanaan, Universitas Kristen Petra, pp. 17–23.

Sartre, J.P. 1949: *Nausea*. Norfolk, CN: New Directions.

Sartre, J.P. 1992: *Being and Nothingness: A Phenomenological Essay on Ontology*. New York: Washington Square Press.

Sassen, S. 1991: *The Global City*. New York, London, Tokyo, Princeton, NJ: Princeton University Press.

Sassen, S. 2000: *Cities in the World Economy*. Thousand Oaks, CA: New York Press.

Satterthwaite, D. (ed.) 1999: *Sustainable Cities*. London: Earthscan.

Saunders, P. 1976: *Urban Sociology: Critical Essays*. London: Methuen.

Saunders, P. 1986: *Social Theory and the Urban Question*. London: Hutchinson.

Sayer, A. 1976: 'A critique of urban modelling'. *Progress in Planning*, 6(3): 187–254.

Sayer, A. 1984: *Method in Social Science*. London: Hutchinson.

Scheer, B.C. and Preiser, W.F.E. 1994: *Design Review: Challenging Aesthetic Control*. New York: Chapman and Hall.

Schorske, C.E. 1981: *Fin de Siècle Vienna*. New York: Vintage.

Schottler, P. 1989: 'Historians and discourse analysis'. *History Workshop Journal*, 27: 37–65.

Scott, A.J. 1980: *The Urban Land Nexus and the State*. London: Pion.

Scott, A.J. 1993: *Technopolis: High Technology Industry and Regional Development in Southern California*. Berkeley, CA: University of California Press.

Scott, A.J. 2000: *The Cultural Economy of Cities*. London: Sage.

Scott, A.J. and Roweis, S.T. 1977: 'Urban planning in theory and practice: a reappraisal'. *Environment and Planning D: Society and Space*, 9(4): 1097–119.

Scott, A.J. and Soja, E.W. 1986: 'Los Angeles: capital of the late 20th century'. *Environment and Planning D: Society and Space*, 4(3): 249–54.

Scott, J. 1999: *Gender and the Politics of History*. New York: Columbia University Press.

Scruton, R. 1974: *Art and Imagination*. London: Methuen.

Scruton, R. 1979: *The Aesthetics of Architecture*. Princeton: Princeton University Press.

Seabrook, J. 1996: *Cities of the South*. London: Verso.

Searle, G.H. 2007: 'Sydney's urban consolidation experience: power, politics and community'. Research Paper 12, Urban Research Program, Griffith University, Urban Research Program, Griffith University, Brisbane.

Sebald, W.G. 1995: *The Rings of Saturn*. London: The Harvell Press.

Sendich, E. 2006: *Planning and Urban Design Standards*. New York: Wiley.

Sennet, R. 1986: *The Fall of Public Man*. London: Faber and Faber.

Serres, M. and Latour, B. 1995: *Conversations on Science, Culture and Time*. Ann Arbor, MI: University of Michigan Press.

Sharpe, W. and Wallock, L. 1994: 'Bold new city or build up "burb": redefining contemporary suburbia'. *American Quarterly*, 46(1): 1–30.

Short, C.R. 1982: *Housing in Britain*. London: Methuen.

Silverman, D. 2001: *Interpreting Qualitative Data: Theory and Method in Qualitative Research*. Thousand Oaks, CA: Sage.

Simkin, C.G.F. 1993: *Popper's Views on Natural and Social Science*. New York: Leiden.

Simmel, G. 2000 (orig. 1903): 'The metropolis and mental life'. In M. Miles, T. Hall and I. Borden (eds), *The City Cultures Reader*. London: Routledge, pp. 12–19.

Simon, H. 1969: *The Sciences of the Artificial*. Cambridge, MA: MIT Press.

Sitte, C. 1945 (orig. 1889): *The Art of Building Cities: City Building According to its Artistic Fundamentals*. New York: Reinhold.

Sklair, L. 2002: *Globalisation: Capitalism and its Alternatives*. Oxford: Oxford University Press.

Sklair, L. 2005: 'The transnationalist capitalist class and contemporary architecture in globalising cities'. *International Journal of Urban and Regional Research*, 29(3): 485–500.

Sklair, L. 2006: 'Do cities need icons – iconic architecture and capitalist globalisation'. *City*, 10(1): 21–47.

Slater, D.C. and Morris, M. 1990: 'A critical look at neo-traditional town planning'. PAS Memo.

Slater, P. 1977: *The Origins and Significance of the Frankfurt School: A Marxist Approach*. London: Routledge.

Smith, D. 2001: *Transnational Urbanism*. Oxford: Blackwell.

Smith, N. 1996: *New Urban Frontier: Gentrification and the Revanchist City*. London: Routledge.

Smith, N. 2002: 'New globalism, New Urbanism: gentrification as global urban strategy'. *Antipode*, 34(3): 434–57.

Smith, P. 1974: *The Dynamics of Urbanism*. London: Hutchinson.

Smith, P. 1976: *The Syntax of Cities*. London: Hutchinson.

Soja, E.W. 1986: 'Taking Los Angeles apart: some fragments of a critical human geography'. *Environment and Planning D: Society and Space*, 4(3): 255–72.

Soja, E.W. 1996: *Thirdspace: Journeys to Los Angeles and Other Real-and-Imagined Places*. Oxford: Blackwell.

Soja, E.W. 2000: *Postmetropolis*. Oxford: Blackwell.

Sorensen, A., Marcotullio, P. and Grant J. (eds) 2004: *Perspectives on Managing Urban Regions*. Aldershot: Ashgate.

Sorkin, M. (ed.) 1992: *Variations on a Theme Park: The New American City and the End of Public Space*. New York: Harper Collins.

Spain, D. 1992: *Gendered Spaces*. Chapel Hill, NC: University of North Carolina Press.

Sprieregen, P. 1965: *Urban Design: The Architecture of Towns and Cities*. New York: McGraw-Hill.

Stanley, B. 2005: 'Middle-East city networks and the New Urbanism'. *Cities*, 223: 189–99.

Steadman, P. 2001: 'Binary encoding of a class of rectangular built-forms. Proceedings'. Paper presented at the 3rd International Space Syntax Symposium, Atlanta, GA: 1–15 September.

Steadman-Jones, G. 1981: 'Utopian socialism reconsidered'. In R. Samuel (ed.), *People's History and Socialist Theory*. London: Routledge and Kegan Paul.

Stein, S.M. and Harper, T.L. 2003: 'Power, trust, and planning'. *Journal of Planning Education and Research*, 23(2): 125–39.

Stephenson, B. 2002: 'The roots of the New Urbanism: John Nolen's Garden City ethic'. *The Journal of Planning History*, 1(2): 99–123.

Stephenson, N. 1992: *Snow Crash*. London: Penguin.

Stevens, Q. and Dovey, K. 2004: 'Appropriating the spectacle: play and politics in a leisure landscape'. *Journal of Urban Design*, 9(3): 351–65.

Stillwell, F. 2002: *Political Economy: The Contest of Economic Ideas*. Melbourne: Oxford University Press.

Stretton, H. 1970: *Ideas for Australian Cities*. Melbourne: Georgian House.

Stretton, H. 1996: 'Density, efficiency and equality in Australian cities'. In M. Jenks, E. Burton and K. Williams (eds), *The Compact City: A Sustainable Urban Form?* London: Spon, pp. 45–52.

Sudjic, D. 1991: *The Hundred Mile City*. New York: Andre Deutsch.

Sulaiman, A.B. 2002: 'The role of streets in creating the sense of place of Malaysian cities'. Paper presented at the Great Asian Streets symposium on Public Space, 25–26 July 2002. NUS Singapore.

Sutton, S. 1996: 'Resisting the patriarchal norms of professional education'. In D. Agrest, P. Conway and L. Weisman (eds), *The Sex of Architecture*. New York: Abrams, pp. 287–94.

Swyngedouw, E. 1996: 'The city as hybrid: on nature, society and cyborg urbanisation'. *Capitalism, Nature, Socialism*, 7(2): 65–80.

Swyngedouw, E., Moulaert, F. and Rodriguez, A. 2002: 'Neoliberal urbanisation in Europe: large scale urban redevelopment projects and the New Urban policy'. In N. Brenner and N. Theodore (eds), *Spaces of Neoliberalism: Urban Restructuring in North America and Europe*. Oxford: Blackwell.

Szelenyi, I. 1983: *Urban Inequalities under State Socialism*. Oxford: Oxford University Press.

Szemanski, R. 2008: *Fans of the World Unite: A (Capitalist) Manifesto for Sports Consumers*. Stanford, CA: Stanford Economics and Finance.

Tafuri, M. 1976: *Architecture and Utopia: Design and Capitalist Development*. Cambridge, MA: MIT Press.

Tafuri, M. 1980: *Theories and History of Architecture*. New York: Harper and Rowe.

Talen, E. 2000: 'New Urbanism and the culture of criticism'. *Urban Geography*, 21(4): 318–41.

Talen, E. 2002a: 'Help for urban planning: the transect strategy'. *Journal of Urban Design*, 7(3): 293–312.

Talen, E. 2002b: 'The social goals of New Urbanism'. *Housing Policy Debate*, 13(1): 165–88.

Talen, E. 2006: *New Urbanism and American Planning: The Conflict of Cultures*. London: Routledge.

Talen, E. 2008: 'New Urbanism, social equity, and the challenge of post-Katrina rebuilding in Mississippi'. *Journal of Planning Education and Research*, 27(3): 277–93.

Tarkovsky, A. 1986: *Sculpting in Time*. London: Bodley Head.

Taylor, B. 1981: 'Socialist feminism, utopian or scientific'. In R. Samuel, *People's History and Socialist Theory*. London: Routledge and Kegan Paul, pp. 158–73.

Taylor, N. 1999: 'The elements of townscape and the art of urban design'. *Journal of Urban Design*, 4(2): 195–209.

Taylor, P.J., Derudder, B., Saey, P. and Witlox, F. (eds) 2007: *Cities in Globalisation. Practices, Policies and Theories*. London: Routledge.

Tester, K. (ed.) 1994: *The Flâneur*. London: Routledge.

Therborn, G. 1980: *The Ideology of Power and the Power of Ideology*. London: Verso.

Thomas, R. (ed.) 2003: *Sustainable Urban Design: An Environmental Approach*. London: Spon

Thompson, J.B. 1981: *Critical Hermeneutics: A Study in the Thought of Paul Ricoeur and Jürgen Habermas*. New York: Cambridge University Press.

Thompson, E.P. 1963: *The Making of the English Working Class*. London: Gollancz.

Thompson, H. 2000: 'The female impressionist as *flâneuse*'. Available online at: http://prized writing.ucdavis.edu/past/1999–2000/pdfs/thompson.pdf.

Tiesdell, S. 2002: 'The New Urbanism and English residential design guidance: a review'. *Journal of Urban Design*, 7(3): 353–76.

Tisdell, C. 2010: 'World Heritage Listing of Australian natural sites: effects on tourism, economic value and conservation'. In *Working Papers on Economics, Ecology and the Environment*. Paper No. 72. Australia: The University of Queensland.

Tisdell, C. and Wilson, C. 2011 (forthcoming): *The Economics of Nature Based Tourism and Conservation*. Cheltenham, UK: Edward Elgar.

Tolba, M.K., Abdel-Hadi, A. and Soliman, S. 2006: 'Space and memory in contemporary gated communities: the New Urbanist approach'. Environment Health and Sustainable Development. 11–16. IAPS 19 Conference Proceedings. Vienna Agreement on Monuments 1973.

Troy, P. 1996: *The Perils of Urban Consolidation*. Sydney: The Federation Press.

Troy, P. 2004: 'The structure and form of the Australian city: prospects for improved urban planning'. Griffith University, Urban Policy Program. Issues Paper No. 1.

Tugnutt, A. and Robertson, M. 1987: *Making Townscape*. London: Mitchell.

Tunnard, C. 1953: *The City of Man*. New York: Charles Scribners.

Tunnard, C. 1963: *Man-Made America: Chaos or Control?* New Haven, CT: Yale University Press.

Turner, B.S. 1996: *The Blackwell Companion to Social Theory*. Cambridge, MA: Blackwell.

Turner, B.S. 2000: *The Blackwell Companion to Social Theory*. Oxford: Blackwell.

United Nations–Habitat 2003a: *The Challenge of Slums: Global Report on Human Settlements*. Nairobi: UN.

United Nations–Habitat 2003b: *Slums of the World: The Face of Urban Poverty in the New Millennium*. Nairobi: UN.

Valentine, G. 1990: 'Women's fear and the design of public space'. *Built Environment*, 16(2): 288–303.

Valentine, G. 1995: 'Out and about: geographies of lesbian landscapes'. *International Journal of Urban and Regional Research*, 19(1): 96–111.

Van Melik, R., Van Aalst, I. and Van Weesp, J. 2007: 'Fear and fantasy in the public domain: the development of secured and themed urban space'. *Journal of Urban Design*, 12(1): 25–42.

Vazquez, A.S. 1973: *Essays in Marxist Aesthetics*. London: Monthly Review Press.

Venturi, R., Brown, D.S. and Izenour, S. 1972: *Learning from Las Vegas*. Cambridge, MA: MIT Press.

Vicino, T.V., Hanlon, B. and Short, J.R. 2007: 'Megalopolis 50 years on: the transformation of a city region'. *International Journal of Urban and Regional Research*, 31(2): 344–67.

Vijoen, A. *et al.* 2005: *Continuous Productive Urban Landscapes*. Burlington, MA: The Architectural Press.

Volk, L. and Zimmerman, K. 2002: 'American households on (and off) the urban to rural transect'. *Journal of Urban Design*, 7(3): 341–52.

Von Ankum, K. 1997: *Women in the Metropolis: Gender and Modernity in Western Culture*. Berkeley, CA: University of California Press.

Walkowitz, D.J. and Knauer, L.M. (eds) 2004: *Memory and the Impact of Political Transformation in Public Space*. London: Duke University Press.

Wallerstein, I. 1974, 1980, 1988: *The Modern World System* (3 Vols). New York: Academic Press.

Walton, J. 1993: 'Urban sociology: the contribution and limits of political economy'. *The Annual Review of Sociology*, 19(2): 301–20.

Ward, J. 1979: *The Street is Their Home: The Hobo's Manifesto*. Melbourne: Quartet Australia.

Warner, M. 1985: *Monuments and Maidens: The Allegory of the Female Form*. London: Picador.

Warner, M. 2002: *Publics and Counterpublics*. London: Zone.

Watson, B.G. and Bentley, I. 2007: *Identity by Design*. Oxford: Elsevier.

Watson, S. 1988: *Accommodating Inequality: Gender and Housing*. Sydney: Allen and Unwin.

Webb, M. 1990: *The City Square*. London: Thames and Hudson.

Weber, R. 1995: *On the Aesthetics of Architecture: A Psychological Approach to the Structure and the Order of Perceived Architectural Space*. Brookfield Aldershot: Avebury.

Weddle, S. (ed.) 2001: 'Gender and architecture'. *Journal of Architectural Education* (Themed Issue).

Weinberg, D. 2002: *Qualitative Research Methods*. Malden, MA: Blackwell.

Weisman, L. 1992: *Discrimination by Design: A Feminist Critique of the Man-Made Environment*. Urbana, IL: University of Illinois Press.

Welter, V.M. 2006: *Biopolis: Patrick Geddes and the City of Life*. Cambridge, MA: MIT Press.

White, E. 2001: *The Flâneur*. London: Bloomsbury.

Williams, M., Burton, E. and Jenks, M. (eds) 2000: *Achieving Sustainable Urban Form*. London: Spon.

Wilson, E. 1995: 'The invisible *flâneur*'. In S. Watson and K. Gibson (eds), *Postmodern Cities and Spaces*. Oxford: Blackwell, pp. 59–79.

Wirth, L. 1938a: 'Urbanism as a way of life'. In R.L. LeGates and F. Stout (1996), *The City Reader*, pp. 97–106.

Wirth, L. 1938b: 'Urbanism as a way of life'. *The American Journal of Sociology*, 44(1): 1–24.

Wittgenstein, L. 1970: *Zettel*. Berkeley, CA: University of California Press.

Wittgenstein, L. 1974: *Philosophical Grammar*. Oxford: Blackwell.

Wolch, J. 1996: 'Zoopolis'. *Capital, Nature, Socialism*, 7(2): 21–47.

Wolch, J. 2002: 'Anima urbis'. *Progress in Human Geography*, 26(6): 721–42.

Wolff, J. 1985: 'The invisible *flâneuse*: women and the literature of modernity'. *Theory, Culture, Society*, 2(1): 37–46.

Wolff, J. 1981: *The Social Production of Art*. London: Macmillan.

World Bank/UNCHS (Habitat) 2000: *Cities Alliance for Cities without Slums*. Available online at: www.citiesalliance.org.

Yakhlef, A. 2004: 'Global brands as embodied "generic spaces": the example of branded chain hotels'. *Space and Culture*, 7(2): 237–48.

Yanarella, E.J. and Levine, R.S. 1992: 'The sustainable cities manifesto: pretext, text and post-text'. *Built Environment*, 18(4): 301–37.

Yang, M.M. (ed.) 1999: *Women's Public Sphere in Transnational China*. Minneapolis, MN: University of Minnesota Press.

Yeang, K. 1987: *Tropical Urban Regionalism: Building in a South-East Asian City*. Singapore: Concept Media.

Yeang, K. 1994: *Bioclimatic Skyscrapers*. London: Ellipsis.

Yeang, K. 1995: *Designing with Nature: The Ecological Basis for Design*. New York: McGraw-Hill.

Yeang, K. 1996: *The Skyscraper Bioclimatically Reconsidered. A Design Primer*. London: Wiley.

Yeang, K. 2002: *Reinventing the Skyscraper: A Vertical Theory of Urban Design*. Chichester: Wiley-Academy.

Yeung, Y.M. and Li, X. 1999: 'Bargaining with transnational corporations: the case of Shanghai'. *International Journal of Urban and Regional Research*, 23(3): 513–33.

Zetter, R. and Watson G. 2006: *Designing Sustainable Cities in the Developing World*. Aldershot: Gower House.

Zis, A. 1977: *Foundations of Marxist Aesthetics*. Moscow: Progress.

Zukin, S. 1995: *The Culture of Cities*. Oxford: Blackwell.

Index

Page references in *italic* type indicate relevant figures and tables.